Fostering Pedagogy Through Micro and Adaptive Learning in Higher Education:

Trends, Tools, and Applications

Ricardo Queirós
School of Media Arts and Design, Polytechnic of Porto, Portugal & CRACS INESC TEC, Portugal

Mario Cruz
School of Education, Polytechnic of Porto, Portugal & inED, Portugal

Carla Pinto
School of Engineering, Polytechnic of Porto, Portugal & CMUP, Portugal

Daniela Mascarenhas
School of Education, Polytechnic of Porto, Portugal & inED, Portugal

A volume in the Advances in
Higher Education and Professional
Development (AHEPD) Book Series

Published in the United States of America by
IGI Global
Information Science Reference (an imprint of IGI Global)
701 E. Chocolate Avenue
Hershey PA, USA 17033
Tel: 717-533-8845
Fax: 717-533-8661
E-mail: cust@igi-global.com
Web site: http://www.igi-global.com

Library of Congress Cataloging-in-Publication Data

Names: Queiros, Ricardo, 1975- editor.
Title: Fostering pedagogy through micro and adaptive learning in higher
  education : trends, tools, and applications / edited by Ricardo
  Queirós, Mário Cruz, Carla Pinto, Daniela Mascarenhas.
Description: Hershey, PA : Information Science Reference, [2023] | Includes
  bibliographical references and index. | Summary: "This book is about
  innovation in higher education after the Covid pandemic fostering novel
  approaches to engage disparate students (with different motivations,
  styles and paces) to learn in a consistent, interoperable and amusing
  journey, by using micro and adaptative learning approaches"-- Provided
  by publisher.
Identifiers: LCCN 2023019789 (print) | LCCN 2023019790 (ebook) | ISBN
  9781668486566 (h/c) | ISBN 9781668486603 (s/c) | ISBN 9781668486573
  (ebook)
Subjects: LCSH: Educational innovations. | Internet in higher
  education--Research. | Virtual reality in higher education--Research. |
  COVID-19 Pandemic, 2020---Influence.
Classification: LCC LB1027 .F67 2023 (print) | LCC LB1027 (ebook) | DDC
  378.1/7--dc23/eng/20230523
LC record available at https://lccn.loc.gov/2023019789
LC ebook record available at https://lccn.loc.gov/2023019790

This book is published in the IGI Global book series Advances in Higher Education and Professional Development (AHEPD) (ISSN: 2327-6983; eISSN: 2327-6991)

British Cataloguing in Publication Data
A Cataloguing in Publication record for this book is available from the British Library.

All work contributed to this book is new, previously-unpublished material.
The views expressed in this book are those of the authors, but not necessarily of the publisher.

For electronic access to this publication, please contact: eresources@igi-global.com.

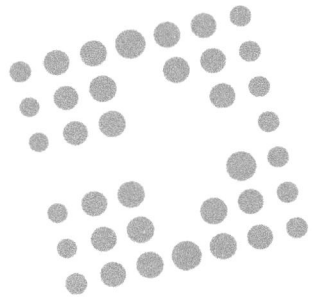

Advances in Higher Education and Professional Development (AHEPD) Book Series

ISSN:2327-6983
EISSN:2327-6991

Editor-in-Chief: Jared Keengwe, University of North Dakota, USA

MISSION

As world economies continue to shift and change in response to global financial situations, job markets have begun to demand a more highly-skilled workforce. In many industries a college degree is the minimum requirement and further educational development is expected to advance. With these current trends in mind, the **Advances in Higher Education & Professional Development (AHEPD) Book Series** provides an outlet for researchers and academics to publish their research in these areas and to distribute these works to practitioners and other researchers.

AHEPD encompasses all research dealing with higher education pedagogy, development, and curriculum design, as well as all areas of professional development, regardless of focus.

COVERAGE

- Adult Education
- Assessment in Higher Education
- Career Training
- Coaching and Mentoring
- Continuing Professional Development
- Governance in Higher Education
- Higher Education Policy
- Pedagogy of Teaching Higher Education
- Vocational Education

IGI Global is currently accepting manuscripts for publication within this series. To submit a proposal for a volume in this series, please contact our Acquisition Editors at Acquisitions@igi-global.com or visit: http://www.igi-global.com/publish/.

Titles in this Series

For a list of additional titles in this series, please visit:
http://www.igi-global.com/book-series/advances-higher-education-professional-development/73681

Cases on Teacher Preparation in Deaf Education
Nena Raschelle Neild (Gallaudet University, USA) and Patrick Joseph Graham (Rochester Institute of Technology, USA)
Information Science Reference • © 2023 • 352pp • H/C (ISBN: 9781668458341) • US $215.00

Sustaining Higher Education Through Resource Allocation, Learning Design Models, and Academic Development
Manyane Makua (Mangosuthu University of Technology, South Africa) and Mariam Akinlolu (London Metropolitan University, UK)
Information Science Reference • © 2023 • 322pp • H/C (ISBN: 9781668470596) • US $215.00

Addressing the Queen Bee Syndrome in Academia
Karis L. Clarke (Touro University California, USA) and Noran L. Moffett (Independent Researcher, USA)
Information Science Reference • © 2023 • 250pp • H/C (ISBN: 9781668477175) • US $215.00

Promoting the Socio-Economic Wellbeing of Marginalized Individuals Through Adult Education
Sampson Tawiah (Durban University of Technology, South Africa) and Itumeleng Innocentia Setlhodi (University of South Africa, South Africa)
Information Science Reference • © 2023 • 255pp • H/C (ISBN: 9781668466254) • US $215.00

Transformation of Higher Education Through Institutional Online Spaces
Rotimi Taiwo (Obafemi Awolowo University, Nigeria) Bimbola Idowu-Faith (Bowen University, Nigeria) and Simeon Ajiboye (Bowen University, Nigeria & University of Augsburg, Germany)
Information Science Reference • © 2023 • 332pp • H/C (ISBN: 9781668481226) • US $215.00

IGI Global
PUBLISHER of TIMELY KNOWLEDGE

701 East Chocolate Avenue, Hershey, PA 17033, USA
Tel: 717-533-8845 x100 • Fax: 717-533-8661
E-Mail: cust@igi-global.com • www.igi-global.com

Table of Contents

Section 1
Innovation in Pedagogy and Educational Tools

Section 2
Experiential Learning and Learning Tools

Section 3
Technology and Learning Environments

Section 4
Creative Learning Strategies and Assessment

Detailed Table of Contents

Section 1
Innovation in Pedagogy and Educational Tools

To cater to the need for a technically qualified workforce, Indian policy-making organizations in the domain of technical education; focused on the quantitative growth of the Technical Education System (TES). The change, in turn, helped increase the availability of the technical workforce but soon became un-controlled; when the supply of the technical force increased continuously, the demand rate reduced. This demand-supply equilibrium shift resulted in unemployment and thus deterred students from persuading technical education. Therefore, almost 50% of the seats in technical institutes are vacant. Therefore, the growth story of Indian TES lacked sustainability and needed qualitative focus. Here, the authors have conducted a systematic literature review to understand the various attributes of sustainability of Indian TES and highlight the future agendas. Stakeholders' perception, Quality Management philosophy, Employability, Management leadership, and Role of accreditation were the key findings of this study having an impact of TES

Chapter 2

Emine Şendurur, Ondokuz Mayıs University, Turkey
Polat Şendurur, Ondokuz Mayis University, Turkey

This chapter aims to review and summarize the principles of instructional material preparation for face-to-face, online, and hybrid environments. The design of mixed instructional materials was first discussed in light of instructional design and technology literature. Multimedia learning, cognitive load theory, and universal design principles were considered the fundamentals of instructional material design. The framework has three dimensions: content type, fidelity, and course phase. In this framework, a hybrid form was offered instead of different forms of materials, but face-to-face and online modalities were also compared. The design and development categorizations were built upon the hybrid nature of the materials. This way, the framework can guide practitioners in designing efficient ways to create instructional materials.

Chapter 3

Dr Sandra Vieira Vasconcelos, School of Hospitality and Tourism,
Polytechnic of Porto, Portugal
Carla Melo, School of Hospitality and Tourism, Polytechnic of Porto,
Portugal
António Melo, School of Hospitality and Tourism, Polytechnic of Porto,
Portugal

Due to its service-oriented nature, Tourism and Hospitality Education relies heavily on experimental learning (EL) approaches, that focus on real-word challenges and can replicate future professional settings. In addition to simulation, project-based learning, fieldtrips and role-play, educators are looking for alternative and innovative strategies to enhance students' learning experiences and support the development of technical and high-level skills. Recognizing the importance of EL, and aiming to contribute towards its development, and support practitioners working in Tourism Higher Education, this chapter focuses on the development of a toolkit that supports activities within this scope. Drawing from a literature and best practice review and their experience, the authors expand on Kolb's experiential learning cycle's model to frame the toolkit's principles and key concepts and describe its creation process, the target audience, and overall sections, that will include different tourism and hospitality subsectors, offering a provisional glimpse of the artefact being created.

Chapter 4

Ricardo Alexandre Peixoto de Queiros, ESMAD, Polytechnic of Porto,
Portugal
Mário Cruz, ESE, Polytechnic of Porto, Portugal
Carla Pinto, ISEP, Polytechnic of Porto, Portugal
Daniela Mascarenhas, ISEP, Polytechnic of Porto, Portugal

In this chapter, we describe the design and implementation of a Pedagogical Innovation Center (PIC) at the Polytechnic of Porto. The COVID-19 pandemic disrupted our day to day lives, our businesses, the world trade and movements. Education was not spared. In fact, it was one of the sectors most heavily affected by COVID-19 pandemic. Teachers were forced, from night to day, to adjust a purely face-to-face teaching style, to a 100\% online set. This is known as emergency remote teaching. Several difficulties have arisen both for teachers and students. The first had to structure all their teaching materials from scratch, had to design and apply new assessment methods, and struggled to get their students' motivation. On their side, the students lacked engagement, social interaction with peers and teachers, the ability to have a more autonomous learning style.

Section 2
Experiential Learning and Learning Tools

Chapter 5

Sandra Vieira Vasconcelos, School of Hospitality and Tourism,
Polytechnic of Porto, Portugal

Focussing on a project carried out within the scope of an English Applied to Tourism course, this chapter describes a teaching and learning strategy, putting forward the underlying rationale and outlining its design, implementation, and assessment phases. The project, whose aims included fostering students' language and critical thinking skills, challenged Hotel Management students to collaborate to produce online training modules for their peers. Relying on the use of digital technologies, most particularly LMS, and cloud-based student engagement and graphic design tools (including Nearpod and Canva), these modules were peer-reviewed and implemented, with students acting as both facilitators and reviewers. Building on existing research on the affordances of peer learning within the scope of foreign language teaching, the author frames the different activities, reflecting on how peer learning strategies can enhance students' engagement and agency, offering insights that can support English for Specific Purposes (ESP) teachers, as well as other practitioners.

Some students prefer a concrete approach to learning whereas others prefer an abstract
one. Algorithms perform transformations of information, thus they have an abstract
nature. Consequently, many students have difficulties in their study. We present two
computer-supported approaches to experiential learning of algorithms. On the one
hand, program visualization automatically generates graphical representations of
the behavior of algorithms, making visible the virtual. On the other hand, algorithm
benchmarking gathers and compares data of the performance of several algorithms,
making visible their properties with respect to given criteria. The chapter includes
a brief motivation and introduction to these issues, followed by a treatment of
each educational approach. For each approach, we present an introduction to its
foundations, relevant features of educational systems intended to support them,
and ways of using them in algorithm courses. We also deal with the successful
instructional integration of program visualization and algorithm benchmarking
systems into algorithm courses.

This chapter investigates the potential of educational escape rooms in higher education
exploring the theoretical frameworks surrounding their design, outcomes, and future
directions. The primary purpose is to provide educators with an understanding of
how these immersive experiences can enhance learning and engagement. The chapter
delves into relevant theoretical frameworks, including constructivism, experiential
learning, game-based learning, and social learning which underpin the effectiveness
of educational escape rooms. The chapter also offers practical recommendations
and discusses emerging opportunities for incorporating escape rooms into various
educational contexts. By examining the multifaceted aspects of educational escape
rooms, this chapter aims to support educators in leveraging these innovative tools
to create engaging learning experiences and foster positive student outcomes.

Section 3
Technology and Learning Environments

Chapter 8

Enhancing Learning Experiences Through Artificial Intelligence: Classroom
Luis Coelho, Instituto Superior de Engenharia do Porto, Portugal
Sara Reis, Instituto Superior de Engenharia do Porto, Portugal

Artificial Intelligence (AI) has evolved rapidly since its inception in the 1950s, from simple rule-based systems to today's advanced deep learning models. AI has impacted society in many ways, ranging from revolutionizing the way we live, work, and interact with technology, to creating new job opportunities, improving decision-making and automating tasks, and solving complex problems in fields like healthcare, finance, and transportation. However, it has also raised concerns about job displacement, privacy and security, and ethical considerations. The evolution of AI is ongoing, and it is expected to continue to shape and transform society in new and profound ways. The impact of AI in education has also been substantial, offering new and innovative ways to personalize learning, enhance educational resources, and improve educational outcomes. In this chapter we will cover the most important aspects related with the teaching-learning process, from a physiological perspective to the different strategies.

Chapter 9

Robertas Damaševičius, Vytautas Magnus University, Lithuania
Tatjana Sidekerskienė, Kaunas University of Technology, Lithuania

The use of immersive and interactive learning environments is gaining traction in science, technology, engineering and mathematics (STEM) education, as educators seek to engage students and enhance learning outcomes. We explore the potential of Metaverse for designing immersive and interactive escape rooms that leverage microlearning to teach STEM concepts and skills. We overview Metaverse and its potential as a learning environment, before delving into the use of escape rooms as a strategy for fostering critical thinking, collaboration, and problem-solving in STEM education. We examine the benefits of incorporating microlearning strategies into escape rooms, including the use of bite-sized content and personalized learning paths. Through a case study of a Metaverse escape rooms implemented in Studio Gometa as a smartphone app and aimed at mathematics education, we highlight the learning outcomes achieved and the challenges faced in the design and implementation process.

Chapter 10

Marjo Joshi, Turku University of Applied Sciences, Finland
Timo Haavisto, Turku University of Applied Sciences, Finland
Vesa Taatila, Turku University of Applied Sciences, Finland
Werner Ravyse, Turku University of Applied Sciences, Finland
Mika Luimula, Turku University of Applied Sciences, Finland

The recent COVID-19 pandemic forced organizations to find new solutions for remote collaboration and refine hybrid education in the context of applied, praxis-based learning. Various tech giants have started investing in more immersive remote communication technologies, such as metaverse. This paper discusses hybrid environments and metaverse in education at Turku University of Applied Sciences (Turku UAS) as the site of the study. The new strategy of the university aims to support people and organizations in a hybrid world where physical and virtual worlds are merged. At Turku UAS, VR environment is seen as a platform that uses social communication for real-life integration through both hands-on skill development and theoretical knowledge transfer. The metaverse technology and collaborative learning environments can be seen as testbeds for future pedagogy and work life. Examples of implementations of interactive technologies in different fields of education are presented. In addition, a revised hybrid education model with future possibilities is introduced.

Section 4
Creative Learning Strategies and Assessment

Chapter 11

Paulo Veloso Gomes, LabRP, CIR, School of Health, Polytechnic of
Porto, Portugal
João Donga, LabRP, CIR, School of Media Arts and Design, Polytechnic
of Porto, Portugal
Sandra Ferreira, Group of Schools of Perafita, Matosinhos, Portugal
Renato Magalhães, LabRP, CIR, School of Health, Polytechnic of Porto,
Portugal
Vítor J. Sá, FFCS, Universidade Católica Portuguesa, Portugal &
ALGORITMI/LASI, University of Minho, Portugal

As digital native learners, Z and Alpha generation students upcoming new challenges for Higher Education Institutions. Their early contact with technological devices does not in itself confer the necessary digital skills to correctly apply technology in academic or professional contexts. Digital skills are fundamental to the future health professionals, improving their academic performance and prepares them for their integration into the labor market. The integration of information and communication technologies in the curricula of higher education courses in the health area is a differentiating factor for academic and professional enhancement. The Autonomous Creative Learning Strategy directed to higher education students in the health area is based on project-oriented approaches, combined with interactive and immersive based-gaming learning activities that appeal to creativity, autonomy and encourage proactivity, self-learning, and the constant search for continuous improvement.

Chapter 12
Fatma Alkan, Hacettepe University, Turkey
Fatma Merve Mustafaoğlu, Hacettepe University, Turkey

New technologies have been widely used in educational environments, as in every field. Web tools attract attention to make learning processes more efficient and to make students active. The microteaching method offers pre-service teachers the opportunity to apply new teaching. The purpose of this research is to determine the pre-service teachers' perception of web tools in micro-teaching and to analyze them according to various variables. The research was designed in a quasi-experimental design model. 75 pre-service teachers studying at the faculty of education participated in the research. Teachers' perceptions towards using web 2.0 tools in lectures scale was used as a data collection tool. As a result of the research, it was determined that micro teaching applications had a significant effect on the pre-service teachers' perception of web tools competence. Pre-service teachers stated that the use of web tools while teaching is beneficial in terms of drawing attention to the lesson and attracting the attention of the students.

Chapter 13
Antonios S. Andreatos, Hellenic Air Force Academy, Greece

Teaching should have a pluralism, containing a variety of alternative educational activities and supporting various learning styles. If so, then assessment should also have a pluralism, testing not only knowledge but also skills and attitudes (where applicable). This is mandatory in practical courses which are common in engineering and science disciplines. In this chapter we draw from our experience and research, and propose ways for designing authentic educational activities and adaptive learning scenarios to cover various learning styles in Higher Education in order to revitalize the learning process. The idea is to put students in action by assigning them authentic and meaningful tasks, individually and in groups, leaving the teams to self-organize by undertaking or assigning specific roles and tasks. Case studies from Computer Networking and Cyber Security are presented. We shall also present alternative assessment for these activities and scenarios. This is a fieldwork, hence, quantitative data from real classes, as well as interviews will be presented.

The chapter discusses the introduction of adaptive learning in art education to provide students with personalized educational content. The methodology of project work is important for fostering creative thinking and addressing pedagogical and artistic challenges. The Visual Arts and Artistic Technologies Course has a diverse curriculum that emphasizes the practical dimension of knowledge to stimulate observation and learning by doing. The curricular units adapt to meet the needs, expectations, and preferences of the students. The chapter proposes an analysis of the curriculum organization of the course using adaptive microlearning.

Preface

In this constantly changing landscape of education, the pursuit of effective pedagogical practices remains a crucial endeavor. As educators, researchers, and learners, we find ourselves at the forefront of a transformative journey, driven by technological advancements and a growing understanding of diferente learning needs.

This book brings together a diverse collection of chapters that delve into the realms of innovation, experiential learning, technology integration, and creative assessment strategies within higher education. Our aim is to explore how micro and adaptive learning approaches can reshape pedagogy, empower educators, and enhance the learning experiences of students in the context of higher education institutions.

In the first section, "Innovation in Pedagogy and Educational Tools," we embark on a journey of innovation, beginning with a systematic literature review evaluating the future of technical education in Indian higher education institutions. We delve into the design and development of hybrid instructional materials, laying the theoretical groundwork for creative learning approaches. The chapter on fostering pedagogical innovation in tourism education introduces an interdisciplinary toolkit that opens up new possibilities for engaging and immersive learning experiences. Lastly, we explore a captivating case study detailing the creation of a culture of innovation within the Pedagogical Innovation Center at the Polytechnic of Porto.

In the second section, "Experiential Learning and Learning Tools," we dive into the realm of learning while teaching, embracing the potential of peer-to-peer interactions to enrich language learning. We explore various approaches and tools for experiential learning, focusing on abstract concepts such as algorithms. Additionally, we unlock the potential of educational escape rooms, providing theoretical frameworks and pathways to ignite excitement in the learning process.

In the next section, "Technology and Learning Environments," we highlight how technology can enhance learning experiences. We delve into the integration of artificial intelligence in the classroom, paving the way for Classroom 5.0. Our exploration of metaverse escape rooms showcases how these virtual environments can revolutionize microlearning in STEM education. Additionally, we explore how the metaverse can be harnessed to support active learning in the transition towards hybrid learning environments.

In the last section, "Creative Learning Strategies and Assessment," we embrace the art of creative learning strategies and assessment. We uncover an autonomous creative learning strategy, directed towards higher education students in the health area, empowering them to take charge of their education. We witness the potential of web tools in lectures, exemplifying micro-teaching in action. The chapter on designing alternative assessment activities and adaptive learning scenarios seeks to accommodate diverse learning styles in higher education, ensuring inclusivity and engagement. Lastly, we venture into the realm of experimentation and creation, emphasizing critical and creative thinking as the driving force behind the reinvention of solutions and the creation of unique works.

This book offers a unique perspective on using micro and adaptive learning approaches to create immersive and personalized environments that cater to the learning styles and paces of diverse students. We hope that it serves as a source of inspiration and knowledge, encouraging educators and learners alike to use the transformative potential of micro and adaptive learning in higher education.

Ricardo Queirós
School of Media Arts and Design, Polytechnic of Porto, Portugal & CRACS INESC TEC, Portugal

Mario Cruz
School of Education, Polytechnic of Porto, Portugal & inED, Portugal

Carla Pinto
School of Engineering, Polytechnic of Porto, Portugal & CMUP, Portugal

Daniela Mascarenhas
School of Education, Polytechnic of Porto, Portugal & inED, Portugal

Section 1
Innovation in Pedagogy and Educational Tools

Chapter 1
Evaluating the Future of Technical Education in Indian Higher Education Institutions:
A Systematic Literature Review

Anugamini Priya Srivastava

ⓘD https://orcid.org/0000-0003-0617-2711
Symbiosis International University (Deemed), India

Prasanna Pradeep Chavare
Symbiosis International University (Deemed), India

ABSTRACT

To cater to the need for a technically qualified workforce, Indian policy-making organizations in the domain of technical education; focused on the quantitative growth of the Technical Education System (TES). The change, in turn, helped increase the availability of the technical workforce but soon became un-controlled; when the supply of the technical force increased continuously, the demand rate reduced. This demand-supply equilibrium shift resulted in unemployment and thus deterred students from persuading technical education. Therefore, almost 50% of the seats in technical institutes are vacant. Therefore, the growth story of Indian TES lacked sustainability and needed qualitative focus. Here, the authors have conducted a systematic literature review to understand the various attributes of sustainability of Indian TES and highlight the future agendas. Stakeholders' perception, Quality Management philosophy, Employability, Management leadership, and Role of accreditation were the key findings of this study having an impact of TES

DOI: 10.4018/978-1-6684-8656-6.ch001

INTRODUCTION

In the 1980s, the need was realised to address the growing demand from industry for a technically qualified workforce. Thus the main focus of the Technical Education System (TES) was to address the gap between the demand and supply of personnel. This recognition of increased demand prompted the Ministry of Human Resource Development (MHRD) to allow private Technical Education Institutes (TEI) entry. This move of allowing self-financed institutes in TES was also in response to the anticipated increase in demand for the technical workforce in the 1990s, fuelled by liberalisation. Until the beginning of the new millennium, there was fear that a shortage of high-quality, technically qualified personnel could prove detrimental to the globalisation of the Indian economy and eventually will lead to a loss of competitiveness of Indian industries in the global scenario.

In the past 35 years, the availability of undergraduate engineering seats has been on a continuous rise, with the latest number being 2.95 million per the All India Council for Technical Education (AICTE) report 2019 ("AICTE Report 2018-19," 2019). These data are pretty assuring in terms of quantitative growth. The research has also shown that this growth has been helpful to the Indian industry to survive and succeed in liberalisation.

But, post-2000, it was observed that the continued addition of institutes soon resulted in the supply of technical workforce exceeding the demand. This excess supply resulted in large pools of unemployed technical graduates. These difficulties in getting jobs deterred students from joining technical education, thus, leaving almost 50% of seats unoccupied in technical education institutes across India ("AICTE Report 2018-19," 2019). Researchers have termed this phenomenon the 'Boomerang Effect' (Upadhayay & Vrat, 2017). Combined with the deteriorating quality of education, this highlighted quantitative growth being unnatural and lacking sustainability (Payal Sharma & Pandher, 2018). Researchers said the declining quality was mainly due to privatisation (Viswanadhan, Rao, & Mukhopadhyay, 2005).

From the beginning of the 1990s, exponential growth was witnessed in the TES. However, the fall side of this growth story was evident towards the end of that decade. Researchers started addressing this concern post-millennium. Overseas, researchers like Kanji, Tambi, & Wallace (1999) studied the methods adopted to ensure the quality of higher education in the US and Malaysia, which further formed the backbone of studying quality issues in technical education institutes well. This paper is divided into eight significant subheads: introduction, objective, background, most discussed parameters affecting the quality sustainability of TES, findings from Systematic Literature Review (SLR), gaps identified and scope of future research, and conclusion.

Objective

This literature review will help the readers by exhaustively surveying the peer-reviewed journal articles studying the quality of TES. The authors believe there is no such comprehensive review covering literature until 2019. Also, the readers are educated about the stepwise process of literature review, starting from the selection criteria for literature. Further, the typology of critical terms and their definitions are explained before discussing the themes identified in the study. Each article is described in-depth and supported by contextual references to the literature. This paper also puts forward the gaps noticed in this survey and the limitations of this work, followed by a brief conclusion. Thus, this study attempts to comprehensively report contextual literature for researchers, academicians, policymakers, and institutions.

In the past three decades, the growth story of Indian TES has been instrumental in propelling the Indian industry and economic growth. But the neglect towards the quality sustainability of TES is lately showing its adverse effects such as lack of required skill set in fresh graduates, thus unemployment and vacant seats in institutes. In this literature survey, an attempt is made to understand the attributes of the quality of the Indian TES. These attributes identified as themes are shortlisted through the conventional and SLR. MS-Excel and VOSviewer were the tools used for SLR. These tools helped me understand the repetition, co-occurrence and connection strength between keywords used by various researchers in this domain. These themes were repeated in the literature, and SLR tools reaffirmed the importance of themes articles; there have been set quality attributes of TES such as 'Curriculum Effectiveness', 'Personal Attributes' and 'Career Adaptability', which are not well-researchedched in the literature reviewed. This clear distinction between the attributes that have been studied in detail and that have not been helped understand the scope of further research to address the issues faced by Indian TES.

Background

Indian higher education sector is the second-largest globally, with 903 universities and 42338 colleges as of April 2018. In 2017-18, the All India Survey of Higher Education (AISHE); showed that out of 903 total universities, there are 114 technical universities. Further, out of 36.6 million students registered for higher education, 14.1% are studying 'Engineering and Technology,' the highest share after 'Arts/Humanities/Social Sciences and 'Science' (MHRD, 2018).

As per the data from statistics published by AICTE for 2017-18, there are 10400 institutes approved by AICTE with a total intake capacity of 2.95 million engineering students. However, the enrolment and placement percentage are around

50 concerning the full intatotalapacity and enrolment, which is respect to technical education institutes across India ("AICTE Report 2018-19," 2019). This declined ratio depicts the lack of sustainability in the growth story of Indian technical education; and indicates the need for research in this area.

The statistics confirm that the state policies adopted for the Technical Education System (TES) growth have successfully achieved quantitative growth. But the qualitative growth remains under question. Now the focus needs to be changed to achieve qualitative growth to ensure the employability of fresh graduates and the sustainability of the growth story of the Indian economy.

Kanji, Tambi, & Wallace (1999) mentioned that, while defining quality, one must consider the final product's input, process, and quality. This focus is of the utmost importance to ensure the quality of TES in India. Researchers also mentioned that the emergence of knowledge and technology-driven economies of the twenty-first Century would call for a large number of a highly skilled and technically qualified competent workforce. And such demand may reach as high as 100 million technocrats by 2025. Thus, there is still much to be done regarding both the quantitative and qualitative growth of TES in India.

In this literature survey, however, the primary focus is on the qualitative growth aspects of the Indian TES. Through this, a pathway for further studies can be laid to develop policies for arresting quality issues in Indian TES and further ensure the sustainable growth of the same, thus, ensuring the improved supply of a well-qualified technical workforce helping the nation's overall development.

RESEARCH METHODOLOGY

Literature Search

Research papers discussing the quality of technical education were screened from the Scopus database. Only research articles from peer-reviewed journals were considered for this literature survey, thus, avoiding grey literature. Other forms of literature, such as books and book chapters, are not evaluated solely because books extensively explore the topic; research papers have more focused content. Here the publication date is not restricted to ensure no meaningful article is excluded.

Selection Process

The keywords used were 'quality of technical education, 'TQM concepts in technical education, 'employability of technical graduates', 'role of management in TES', 'sustainability of TES', 'accreditation', 'quality parameters for TES', and 'India'.

Based on the pre-defined selection criteria for literature, the following filters were applied; (a) field - Article title, Abstract and Keywords; (b) document type – Article; (c) source type – Journals; (d) language – English.

A total of 839 articles were found as a combined total for all the keyword searches. These were added in an MS-excel sheet to identify the duplicate articles found through more than one keyword, which were deleted to leave 554 documents. Authors further read the titles of all these articles to sort them out into relevant and non-relevant. This helped identify 515 relevant documents. Then 456 papers exclusively discussing Indian TES were shortlisted.

As the next step, the authors read the relevant documents' abstracts to segregate them according to broader themes. These more general themes were beyond the quality sustainability and included other aspects of technical education such as demography and geography, women's education, vocational courses, etc. These themes were further narrowed down to the core focus of this study to give 123 articles. Fifty-four research papers were identified based on the maximum unity with the identified themes from the documents included in this study to discuss the identified themes and the relevant analysis. Along with these research papers, the authors have also cited some key reports sourced from the policymakers and governing authorities of Indian TES, such as MHRD, AICTE, NAAC, NBA, etc., wherever required.

Before the paper moves ahead with the most discussed themes concerning the Indian TES, the introduction to the typology and its definitions is given in Table 1.

Most Discussed Parameters Affecting the Sustainability of Indian TES

Here the author has identified five themes core to the sustainability studies of TES in India. These are summarised as follows; Stakeholders' perception of factors affecting the quality of TES, Total Quality Management (TQM) philosophy in quality of TES, Employability, Management leadership, and Role of accreditation in quality of TES.

Stakeholders' Perception About Factors Affecting Quality of TES

Once regarded as a service, it becomes easier to identify the factors affecting the quality of technical education. And education indeed is a service composed of tangible and intangible components. Like all services, the quality of education also depends on all the stakeholders' performance. The stakeholders include service provider (management), service buyer or customer (parents), service recipient (student), service giver (faculty, staff, etc.), end-user of services (employer), others such as

Table 1. Typology and definitions

Typology	Definition
Career inclination	It is a term similar to career anchor, defined by Schein (1996) as; one's inclination toward a career mainly evolved out of self-realized knowledge and competence, core values, motivation and need to pursue the career.
Personal attributes	Attributes are desirable qualities of an engineer, including technical skills such as fundamental engineering knowledge, ability to control quality, audit and personal skills such as loyalty, honesty, good communication skills, and logical thinking (Nguyen, 1998).
Student perception	The way student looks at, understand and imbibe things is perception. Students' perception is essential as it is a catalyst for continuing coursework and other learning opportunities (Picciano, 2002).
Selection rigour	The entry barriers established by the education institutes ensure the admission of suitable candidates by judging educational, personal, analytical and financial capabilities and the motivation level to continue with the curriculum (Gudo & Olel, 2011).
Comprehensive Curriculum	A well-organised and structured curriculum with apt attention to the objectives of the curriculum, content of curriculum, teaching process, educational strategies and subsequent assessment can be regarded as a comprehensive curriculum (Harden & Stamper, 1999).
Career adaptability	Rudolph, Lavigne, & Zacher (2017) have found that career adaptability is an amalgamation of adaptivity measures such as proactive personality, self-esteem, big five personality traits, adapting response measures such as career planning, career decision making, and other relevant constructs of adaptation such as career identity, employability, job stress and finally age as well as education.
Leadership	Integrity, courage, passion, consideration, trustworthiness, responsiveness, adaptability, ability to envision changes in future, skills to develop and manage people, skills to establish collaborations, being supportive, and ability to positively influence others; are the set of qualities ensuring efficient leadership (PalaniNathaRaja, Deshmukh, & Wadhwa, 2006).
Sustainable higher education	Sustainable higher education is a quality of the relationships between stakeholders and institutes reflected in the ability to meet appropriately; educational expectations and scientific advancement, guarantee employment and contribute to a country's economic and social wellbeing (Salvioni, Franzoni, & Cassano, 2017).
Employee life cycle	An employee in an organisation will be made of 5 distinct stages: Onboarding, Orientation, Career Planning, Career Development, Termination (Nagendra, 2014).

alumni, policymakers, and society at large etc. (Gambhir & Wadhwa, 2013; Puthal et al., 2018; Puthal, et al., 2018; Sayeda et al., 2010).

The stakeholders of TES range from parents to employers and policymakers, with varying levels of interaction with the system and perceptions and expectations from the system. TES must be able to fulfil the expectations of such a wide range of stakeholders. This poses problems for policy planning to implement quality control and quality improvement programs. Thus, it is suggested to identify the quality factors or parameters that accommodate the expectations of all the stakeholders before implementing any quality control and improvement program. Mahapatra & Khan (2007) suggested EduQUAL, a survey-based model specially developed to cater to the needs of TES.

In the present times, where the poor quality of technical education is a significant concern, available literature reports several factors which perhaps are responsible for the same. Lack of up-gradation of curriculum, scarcity of quality faculty, old-fashioned teaching pedagogy, non-existent management commitment and vision, unreasonable state policies, poor entry barriers, lack of academic collaborations and industry-academia co-operation, insufficient level of research and development, lack of connecting with alums, poor, undermined extra-curricular activities, underdeveloped and out of date infrastructural facilities such as buildings, labs, libraries, etc. are responsible for dreadful quality of TES in India (Mahapatra & Khan, 2007; Mittal, Garg, & Yadav, 2018; PalaniNathaRaja et al., 2006)

As highlighted in the introduction, MHRD allowed for private institutes in TES as a need of the hour. Within a couple of decades of this decision, the downfall of the quality of TES started in India. In the contextual literature review, it is found that researchers have studied nine parameters in context with the privatisation of TES, which had a deep level of impact on the quality of TES. These nine parameters are leadership pledged to quality, customer-centric behaviour, course rendition, communication, infrastructure, nurturing environment for learning and ongoing improvement and assessment (Viswanadhan et al., 2005).

Many researchers have used Interpretive Structural Modelling (ISM) to understand critical barriers and enablers of quality in TES (Debnath & Shankar, 2012; Gambhir & Wadhwa, 2013; Gambhir, Wadhwa, & Grover Sandeep. 2016a; Pal Pandi et al., 2016; Pandi et al., 2016; Prasad & Suri, 2011). The factors affecting quality in any system are classified as enablers, facilitating the quality enhancement and the barriers which obstruct. Thus, quality enhancement in TES is achieved by removing the barriers and supporting enablers (Debnath & Shankar, 2012). Superfluous enablers and interactive enablers are the basic categories of enablers of TES. Infrastructure, institution ranking, placements, alum feedback, etc., are some of the enablers of TES that define a system's quality standards without getting involved in the design and thus classified under superfluous enablers. At the same time, faculty and staff, pedagogy, governing rules and policies, instruments, equipment and other facilities, etc., are some of the enablers representing the service quality standards of an institute by directly interacting with the system and thus classified under interactive enablers.

Gambhir & Wadhwa (2013) identified ten enablers viz., students themselves, supportive involvement of other stakeholders, the financial condition of an institute, interaction with industry, pedagogy, the commitment of senior management, governing norms and policies, faculty and staff, research and development initiatives, and infrastructure.

Further research done in 2016 revealed a worrying gap between the quality and the quantity of TES in India. The factors attributed to this gap are; poor industry-academia interaction, the dearth of quality faculty, outdated infrastructure, and poor-quality implementation of policy and governing policies (Gambhir, Wadhwa, & Grover, 2016).

The role of self-financed engineering institutes in the growth story of Indian TES cannot be ignored. Also, the needs and issues of self-financed institutes must be addressed differently. The study revealed that financial resources, primary physical resources, supporting staff adequacy, student intake, and industry initiatives do not seem different for aided and self-financing engineering programmes. In contrast, significantly lower components for the self-financing programmes are supplementary physical resources, faculty and staff components, student components, industry-institute interaction components, and R&D activities (Viswanadhan et al., 2005). The most critical factors that need to be attended to on priority are faculty adequacy both in quantity and quality, focus on research and development activities, inclusive and visionary policies, resource allocation and planning (Viswanadhan, 2009).

Also, over the years, it has been noticed that the self-financing engineering institutes are failing to provide quality education and thus not fulfilling the expectations of their stakeholders. According to the researchers, this is a lack of adherence to the best practices of best-in-class institutes. The benchmarking of good practices, novel ideas, and efficient processes can be helpful for self-financing engineering institutes to match the quality of best-in-class institutes (P. S. Rao, Viswanadhan, & Raghunandana, 2015).

Total Quality Management (TQM) Philosophy in Quality of TES

TQM is a holistic management process based on 'Management by Process' and 'Management by Continuous Improvement. Many researchers have tried to study the implementation of the TQM approach in the quality of TES. Researchers have studied applying TQM principles from the management's perspective, as the decision-maker for institutional policy management is of utmost importance (Sayeda et al., 2010). Researchers -Sahu, Shrivastava, & Shrivastava (2012, 2013) have identified critical success factors of TQM to address several conflicting aspects to ensure quality sustainability of technical education through organisational performance. The approach of TQM is also envisioned as incorporated into the accreditation system for TES (Mahadeven, Shivaprakash, & Bose, 2013).

For higher education, a quality excellence model encompassing four principles; (a) management by fact, (b) stakeholder-oriented management, (c) continuous improvement, and (d) customer satisfaction, is studied and put forth by researchers (Kanji et al., 1999). Education can be regarded as a service that leaves the longest-lasting impact on the customer. Thus, the quality of this service should be paramount to ensure the maximum benefit to the customer. The quality of this service can be evaluated using the yardsticks of multi-item SERVQUAL (Parasuraman, Zeithaml, & Berry, 1985). This multi-item approach considers human resource management, social responsibility, service culture, customer focus and employee satisfaction which predict the customer quality perception or service quality. On the same grounds as SERVQUAL, EduQUAL was developed by Mahapatra & Khan (2007) to evaluate the quality of technical education.

To help assess the quality of TES using neural networks, EduQUAL is an integrative approach; this instrument has the following dimensions: academics, learning outcomes, responsiveness/acceptance, physical facilities, and personality development.

Some researchers also prompt active involvement of industry as the end-user of TES; in developing the quality of TES. As the industry is proactively involved in improving the quality of its raw material suppliers, the same is expected out of the industry for one of its most crucial input resources, human resources Recent studies have shown that expenses incurred by industries across various sectors to train fresh graduates hired from technical education institutes before putting them on the actual job have increased. But still, the industry working hard on quality improvement at the input stage; has overlooked academia which is the supplier of the essential resource to any industry, i.e. human capital (Upadhayay & Vrat, 2016b).

Many dimensions of TQM are successfully implemented in the manufacturing and service sectors. Still, they are tried for the first time in TES by Sayeda et al. (2010) to present a holistic TQM model for achieving institutional excellence. Dimensions suggested by this model are Industry Interface, Management Information and Analysis, Knowledge Management, etc. The additional dimensions suggested by this study are; (a) healthy and Innovative Practices (HIP) which are enumerated to connect with the culture of the institutional processes and thus strengthen the image of the institute, and (b) feeder Institution Partnership (FIP) which suggests partnering with higher secondary and even secondary schools to ensure the supply of correct quality of students at the entry-level of TES (Sayeda et al., 2010).

Honnutagi & Sonar (2016) suggested that the implementation of TQM in TES has been construed as an approach that positively impacted the activities and processes of TES. This implementation focused on improving a TES's core activities, pedagogy, learning techniques, curriculum comprehensiveness and resource optimisation and the overall quality enhancement of its processes, continuous improvement, pupil's academic advancement, the betterment of the institution's status. This will overall lead to sustainable institutional outcomes and stakeholders' satisfaction. The literature revealed that properly administered TQM helps organizations be dynamic to ensure sustainability in a rapidly changing environment (Honnutagi, Abdul Razak Rajendra & Subash, 2016).

Sakthivel, Rajendran & Raju (2005) incorporated five TQM variables to give a 5-C TQM model to help achieve academic excellence across technical institutions in India. These variables are; top management assurance, stakeholder feedback mechanism for improvement curriculum comprehensiveness, courtesy, and infrastructure.

Researchers have also studied the implementation of TQM in isolation and other converging aspects of quality such as ISO 9000 Quality Management System, Knowledge Management (KM) (i.e. a process of identifying, organising and managing knowledge resources), lean thinking, and Six Sigma. This has resulted in the concept of Integrated Total Quality Management (ITQM) (Pal Pandi, Jeyathilagar, & Kubendran, 2013; U. S. Rao & Pandi, 2007). The critical factors of ITQM were identified as Top Management Commitment, System Approach to Management, Customer Satisfaction, Employee Involvement, Training, Team Work and Continuous Improvement. These factors are evaluated further through the perception of faculty, students and other stakeholders such as parents, policymakers, and the public (Pal Pandi et al., 2013).

Employability

One of the primary reasons India is progressing slowly on the ranks of the Human Development Index is unemployment (Sharma, Uppal, & Mahendru, 2016). Thinking and learning can make fresh engineering graduates either employable or unemployable. Employability includes core and soft skills and formal and actual competence, interpersonal skills, and personal attributes (Nilsson, 2010).

The steep quantitative growth of Indian TES has a flip side as a deteriorating quality evident from the increasing number of graduates lacking employability (Shukla & Garg, 2017). Unemployment of technical graduates is a serious concern. The problem is unresolved due to the economy's global recession and the institutions' lack of focus on the quality of education and capability development of graduates (Shukla & Garg, 2017). One of the reasons for the unemployment of technical graduates in India is the dependency on first-world MNCs for employment (G. D. Sharma et al., 2016). The low employability of technical graduates has had a significant adverse effect on the perception of technical education in Indian society. To achieve better placements, researchers have suggested implementing the principle of selective assembly. In this process, the compatibility between the recruiter and prospective candidate will be pre-checked to ensure employment to a more significant number of candidates, lesser attrition, and better on-job performance in future (Upadhayay & Vrat, 2016a).

Research has revealed that the placement of technical graduates is the function of students' skills and related competencies during their time spent at the technical education institute (Sahu et al., 2013). Some of the parameters which make a fresh graduate engineer unemployable are a lack of; (a) technical skills, (b) basics needed to work in a professional environment, (c) awareness of current technical trends, (d) guidance, (e) motivation (Kulkarni, Khan, Mishra, Raikwar, & Prajapat, 2014).

One of the critical reasons for the reduced employability of students is the poor efficiency and quality of knowledge and skills transferred to students from faculty. This poor knowledge transfer is attributed to the dearth of attention to the inclusive career growth of faculty and insufficient training opportunities (Gambhir, Wadhwa, & Grover, 2016).

Another important stakeholder in the industry which can play a pivotal role in improving employability is This role is in terms of providing the right inputs to upgrade the syllabi and curriculum and offering an opportunity to hone technical skills through hands-on projects and industry training (Pandi, Sethupathi, Jeyathilagar, & Rajesh, 2016; Upadhayay & Vrat, 2016b). Recently the industry has been forced to spend heavily on 'before the job' training of fresh recruits. A recent study has attributed the unemployment of 80% of technical graduates to the high degree of mismatch between demand and supply of technical skills in the employment industry (Mittal et al., 2018).

From the perspective of institutes and the management as well, the employability of their graduates has a significant meaning. This importance is because the higher employability score of the institute as compared to the standard indices is an essential measure of the excellence of technical education institutes (Sahu et al., 2008, 2013). While researching in Tamil Nadu, a state of India; it was observed that lack of adaption and adherence to the international quality standards has resulted in the institutes producing graduates lacking industry-relevant skills; thus, causing unemployment (Pal Pandi et al., 2013). In the contemporary literature, the issue of employability skill is well addressed directing the educators, institutes and AICTE to ensure imbibing' employability skills' as the paramount focus. This may need a paradigm shift in the thorough process from teaching to training, corrective actions to proactive actions and voluntary to mandatory measures. This includes soft skills training, industry interactions, on-job training or mandatory apprenticeships (Mahajan & Golahit, 2017).

Management Leadership

Contemplation, veracity, desire and valor, responsiveness, change acceptance, ability to envision changes in future, skills to develop and manage people, skills to establish collaborations with other academic and industrial institutions, being supportive, reliability, compliance, ability to positively influence others, being supportive; are the various qualities always associated with the efficient leadership as discussed in the contextual literature (PalaniNathaRaja, Deshmukh and Wadhwa, 2006; Sayeda, Rajendran and Lokachari, 2010; Abdul Razak Honnutagi, Rajendra Sonar, 2016; Mittal, Garg and Yadav, 2018).

Researchers have identified the leadership and people management to have a significant role in improving the service quality by way of developing a vision for quality and institutional effectiveness (PalaniNathaRaja et al., 2006; Sayeda et al., 2010). This role of leadership at TEIs is further elaborated in; (a) defining vision, mission and goals of institute; (b) developing policies and designing programmes for implementing the same; (c) setting up an incessant development mechanism through responses; (d) monitoring all the above functions (Sahu et al., 2008, 2013). The result of a study highlighted that, 'Management Leadership' was the only attribute covered by all 20 Excellence Model / National Quality Awards including Malcolm Baldrige National Quality Awards (Honnutagi, Abdul Razak Rajendra & Subash, 2016). When the attributes emerged from this study were subjected to the Analytical Hierarchy Process (AHP),' Leadership' emerged as the attribute with the highest importance and 'Strategic Planning' as one with relatively higher importance. And further after applying ISM, 'Leadership' was found to have the highest driving power with 'Strategic Planning' in close vicinity (Honnutagi, Abdul Razak Rajendra & Subash, 2016).

While studying the key factors affecting the quality of TES due to privatization, Viswanadhan et al., (2005) found leadership is one of these 9 identified factors. In the case of self-funded engineering institutes, the 'management leadership' does have a direct impact on the attributes like strategic planning and resources allocation; and thus, have a major impact on the quality of institutional performance. Another researcher studying about the faculty members commitment in public and private technical schools; highlighted the role of management leadership, stating, the leadership of the private technical schools is more proactive in identifying faculty welfare strategies to create a long-term win-win for both organization as well as its members (Pooja Sharma, 2015).

Kanji in 1996, proposed a modified pyramid model for business excellence; where 'Leadership' was assumed as a prime foundation. This model further enunciated four principles: customer satisfaction, management by fact, stakeholder centric management and incessant improvement (Kanji et al., 1999).

According to the faculty's perception, top management fails to recognize human resource as an asset to the organization and many at times it adopts ad hoc measures to address customer concerns about quality (Pal Pandi et al., 2013). Rao et al., (2015) concluded in their research that, the adaption and implementation of the best practices of top-ranked institutes by the management of the self-financed TEIs can surely help improve their service quality.

Role of Accreditation Agencies in Quality of TES

In India, to voluntarily assess and accredit institutions of higher education; the University Grants Commission (UGC) established an autonomous body; the National Assessment and Accreditation Council (NAAC) in 1994, with its headquarters at Bangalore.

Whereas for TES, to ensure quantitative growth, "approval" is a mandatory tool used by AICTE to allow starting or continuing operations for any TEI. To ensure the qualitative growth initiatives in TES, AICTE established the National Board of Accreditation (NBA) as an autonomous body in 1994 which eventually separated from AICTE in 2010. The NBA conducts the periodical evaluation of the technical programmes of the institutions following the specified norms and standards as recommended by AICTE. Various diplomas, degrees and postgraduate technical programs, and institutes offering such programmes come under the purview of the NBA. The NBA recognition guarantees the minimum quality of education in technical institutions in the country at par with the industry requirements (NAAC, 2017; NBA, 2012)

This quality assurance comes by confirming that the graduates of the TEIs have gained the necessary knowledge, expertise and attitude to meet expectations of various stakeholders. This is based on the comparison of a programme's performance with the established benchmarks (G. Prasad & Bhar, 2010).

The accreditation is meant to serve two prime functions; ensure quality control and quality assurance; referring to a certification or grading system in the domain of education and training. In some countries, accreditation is performed by an agency of the Ministry of Education, while in several developed countries it is undertaken by voluntary agencies or professional societies (Natarajan, 2000).

Accreditation is utilized as a primary quality control mechanism for technical education in several countries for several years now. Various service quality dimensions are used by different accreditation bodies (PalaniNathaRaja et al., 2006). Accreditation agencies being similar to quality assessment agencies; have many criteria in common. Accreditation Board for Engineering and Technology (ABET) has 76% of sub-clauses common with ISO 9001:2000 (Pandi, Sethupathi, & Jeyathilagar, 2016). Such accreditation is essential for TEI to stay in the business; but at the same time, higher grading awarded by an independent accreditation agency is helpful for the institute to prove its performance excellence. This performance excellence will help in building a brand and fetch better students (Sahu et al., 2013).

A failure of strict adherence to the norms is evident through the void. In this situation Integrated Educational Quality Management System (IEQMS) can prove helpful. A well-structured IEQMS can help in continuous monitoring of the performance of TEI as a self-administered tool. Effective implementation of IEQMS, thus helps TEIs in the accreditation process by enhancing their performance (Pandi, Sethupathi, Jeyathilagar, et al., 2016). In India, the quality of TEI depends on various factors ranging from financial to sociological. Thus, to help the institutes and accreditation agencies, a 'quantifiable quality model' has been developed (Gambhir, Wadhwa, & Grover Sandeep, 2016b). Despite the concerns that the success of a quality assurance accreditation framework depends on the extent to which its standards and procedures are valued and used; accreditation mechanisms can ensure better institutional performance because of; (a) external pressure from a quality assurance i.e. accreditation agency; (b) self-motivation to achieve higher grades in accreditation to attract better students, projects, research contracts, etc.; (c) the competitive spirit amongst the institutes (Senthil Kumar & Sivakumar, 2014).

As of 10th April 2019, only 1584 institutes approved by AICTE were having NBA accredited programs ("AICTE Report 2018-19," 2019; "AICTE Approved Institutions having NBA Accredited Courses," 2019; "National Board of Accreditation," n.d.). This strikingly a low number is attributed to primary reasons being, accreditation is voluntary and does not yield either any immediate benefits or pose any threats. Secondary reasons are related to the accreditation process is rigid, difficult, time-consuming and labour intensive. To increase acceptance of accreditation, researchers have suggested NBA follow following measures; (a) enhance superiority and consistency of assessment, (b) adopt a more quantitative assessment process, (c) lessen subjectivity in assessment, (d) simplify and fast track assessment process, (e) transparent process (G. Prasad & Bhar, 2010).

Findings from SLR of the Surveyed Literature

The CSV file created from this final set of literature shortlisted as explained in the research methodology; was subjected to further analysis using tools such as MS-Excel and VOSViewer to obtain results as below.

Citation Strength of Authors

The below diagram generated using the VOSviewer analysis, demonstrates the co-citation strength of the key authors whose literature is a part of the literature reviewed. This helps understand and justify the synergy in the works of researchers working on the same domain. The maximum citation strength with the seminal work can also help identify other important researches in the said domain (see *Figure 1*).

Figure 1. Citation strength of authors

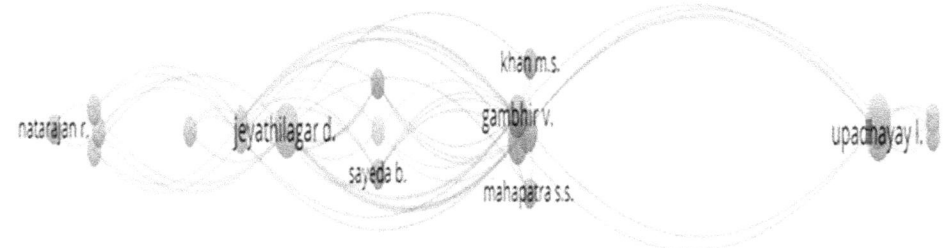

Multiple Documents by Author

Below is the graphical representation of authors who have more than one research papers in the same domain. This shows the in-depth work done by the said researcher in exploring the subject from various perspectives and by applying different theories. The works by these authors has also earned a greater number of citations (see figure 2).

Co- occurrence of Themes

Below representation using VOSviewer highlights the co-occurrence of the themes as identified by authors in the same research paper. This demonstrates the importance

Figure 2. Multiple documents by author

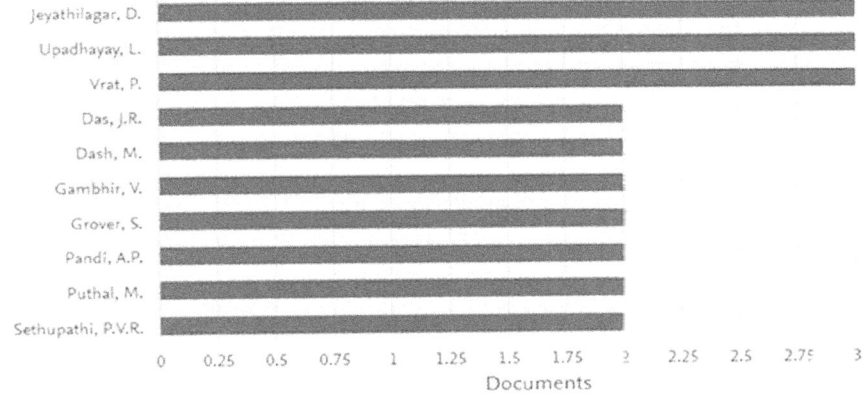

given by earlier researchers to themes identified in this literature survey such as Critical factors affecting quality in TES, TQM application in quality of TES, the role of management leadership, the role of accreditation or quality assurance agencies (see figure 3).

Figure 3. Co-occurrence of themes

Co-occurrence of Author Keywords

The co-occurrence of the keywords as listed by different researchers in their research papers across the literature reviewed is represented in Figure 4.

This helps identify the terms which are considered by various authors as important in their literature.

No. of Citations for Key Authors

Out of the authors whose literature is reviewed in this work, below is the graphical representation of the number of citations earned by 27 authors (see Figure 5).

Relationship Between Terms from Title and Abstracts

The relationship strength between various keywords from the title and abstracts of the reviewed literature is shown below. This has helped identify themes such as factors

Figure 4. Co-occurrence of author keywords

Figure 5. No. of citations for key authors

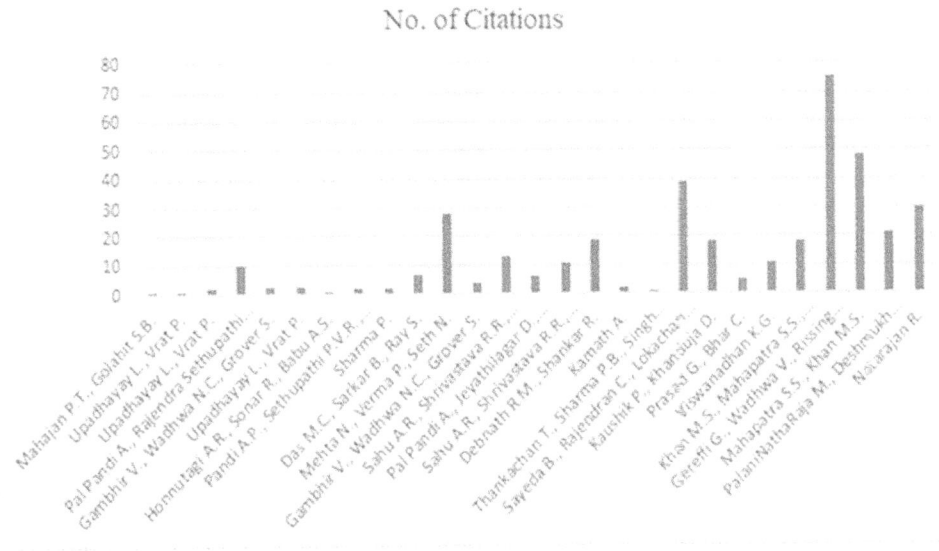

affecting the quality of TES, employability, TQM application in quality of TES, the role of management leadership, the role of accreditation or quality assurance agencies. (see Figure 6).

Figure 6. Relationship between terms from title and abstract

Segregation of Research Papers

Below table shows the list of journals and the total number of papers published, which are part of this review (see Table 2).

Table 3 provides segregation of reviewed papers based on the identified themes. It can be noticed that, as some of the research papers are working on more than one of the mentioned themes of this study; they appear more than once and thence the total count here is more than 48.

Gaps Identified from Literature Survey and Scope of Future Research

In case of quality of Indian TES researchers have worked on various attributes as mentioned in the themes above. But the authors are of the opinion that there are yet some important attributes that need a focused study to understand and address the issues such as declining quality of education, unemployment of technical graduates, increased expenses by recruiters in pre-job training, etc. Also, there is a plethora of

Table 2. TES Articles published in journals

Journal	Articles = 48
International Journal of Productivity and Quality Management	3
Quality Assurance in Education	3
International Journal of Business Excellence	2
Journal of Vocational Behavior	2
International Journal of Applied Engineering Research	2
International Journal of Mechanical Engineering and Technology	2
The TQM Journal	2
Universal Journal of Management	1
Total Quality Management,	1
Journal of Entrepreneurship Education	1
On the Horizon	1
International Journal of Engineering Education	1
Education and Training	1
International Journal of Management Science and Engineering Management	1
Total Quality Management and Business Excellence	1
International Journal of Services and Operations Management	1
International Journal of Enterprise Network Management	1
Journal of Marketing	1
European Journal of Engineering Education	1
Global Journal of Flexible Systems Management	1
International Education Studies	1
Journal of Engineering Education Transformations	1
The Career Development Quarterly	1
Benchmarking: An International Journal	1
Global business and organizational excellence	1
Higher Education, Skills and Work-based Learning	1
International Journal of Services, Economics and Management	1
Maritime Policy and Management	1
Computers and Industrial Engineering	1
Journal of Advances in Management Research	1
International Journal of Industrial and Systems Engineering	1
Journal of Services Research	1
Academy of Management Perspectives	1
Procedia Economics and Finance	1
Global Journal of Engineering Education	1
International Journal of Business and Social Science	1
Journal of Asynchronous Learning Networks	1
Medical Teacher	1
Sustainability (Switzerland)	1

Table 3. Theme wise distribution of surveyed research papers

Theme	Articles
Stakeholders Perception About Factors Affecting Quality of TES	19
Total Quality Management (TQM) Philosophy in Quality of TES	13
Employability	13
Management Leadership	12
Role of Accreditation Agencies in Quality of TES	7

literature about linking unemployment with the quality of TES; however, there is a dearth of literature linking attrition with the quality of TES. Authors suggest that there is a scope of research to establish any link between the poor transfer of knowledge in undergraduate years leading to the poor knowledge level of the graduates; which further results in poor performance at the job and thus job dissatisfaction ultimately causing attrition.

Thus, the major gap noticed is, the holistic link between student perception, sustainability of TES and employee life cycle is unexplored yet.

Other gaps are,

- Student perception about the service quality of TES is studied (Puthal, Das, et al., 2018) but the way Student's perception is shaped is not.
- Employment generation is linked with quality of TES (Nilsson, 2010; Upadhyay & Vrat, 2016a, 2017); but the employee life cycle or attrition is not linked with the quality of TES.
- The relation between career adaptability and sustainable higher education is unexplored (Savickas, 1997; Creed, Fallon & Hood, 2009).
- Following attributes of sustainability of TES lack the required amount of literature and the same is evident from the network diagrams from VOSviewer analysis of the shortlisted literature from Scopus data base after applying filters as explained in the section titles' Findings from SLR of the Surveyed Literature'; (a) curriculum effectiveness, (b) personal inclination / attributes of Student, (c) career inclination, (d) selection rigour.

"Career Inclination", "Personal Attributes" and "Student Perception" are nowhere to be seen and nor is "Employee Life Cycle" (see Figure 7 & Figure 8).

"Career Inclination", "Personal Attributes" and "Student Perception" are nowhere to be seen nor is "Employee Life Cycle".

"Quality of Education" or "Sustainable Higher Education" are nowhere to be seen.

"Quality of Education" or "Sustainable Higher Education" are nowhere to be seen.

Figure 7. Keywords extracted from the literature searched using "sustainable higher education"

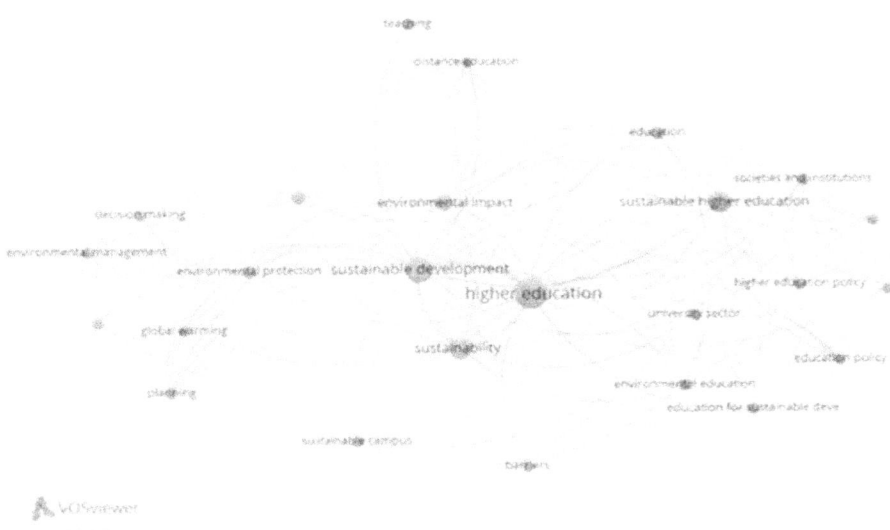

Figure 8. Keywords extracted from the literature searched using "quality higher education"

Figure 9. Keywords extracted from the literature searched using "employee" and "life cycle"

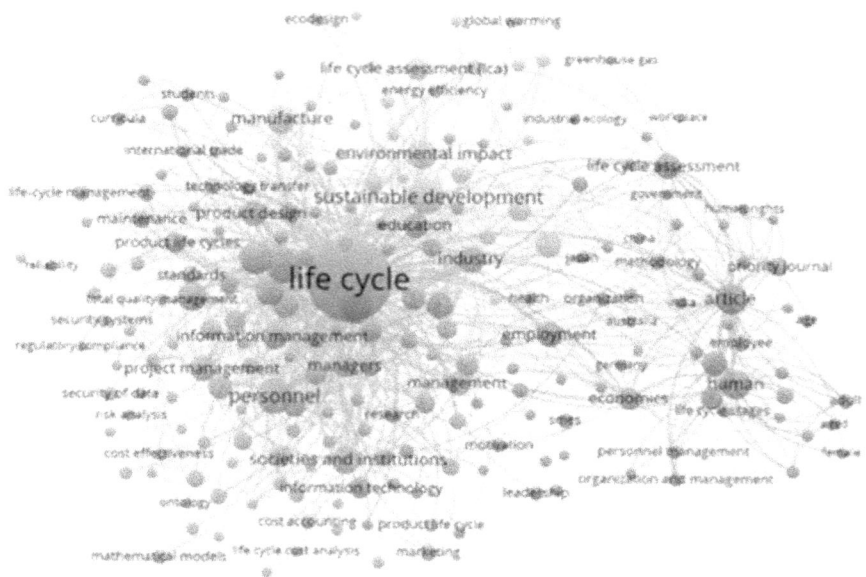

Figure 10. Keywords extracted from the literature searched using "employee life cycle"

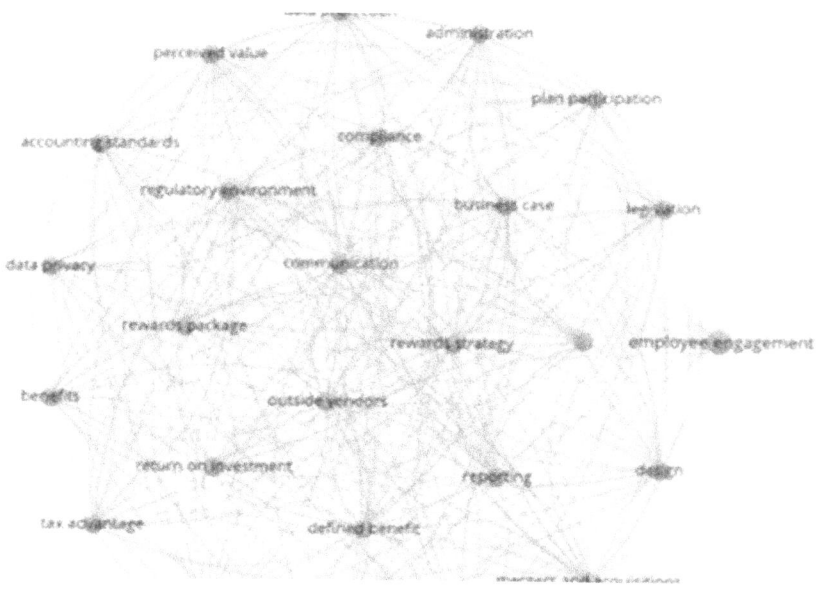

Scope of Future Research

Through survey of the literature, it is evident that the available literature has studied the various attributes of quality of technical education using quantitative as well as qualitative tools; however certain unique streams of technical education such as aeronautical, marine, ocean engineering remains less researched. Though these are branches of technical education; they need separate attention due to the uniqueness of the professional aspects of these fields. Here the authors suggest the need for in-depth research towards the sustainability of Marine Engineering Education in India as issues such as unoccupied undergraduate seats, unemployment of fresh graduates are plaguing the marine engineering institutes in India (DGS, 2017); whereas the shipping industry is struggling with excessive spending on before the job training for freshers and attrition at junior positions (BIMCO & ICS, 2015; Caesar, 2013; Thai, Balasubramanyam, Yeoh, & Norsofiana, 2013).

Here the authors have focused only on the research papers from peer-reviewed journals. Other forms of literature such as books and book chapters can be surveyed further to support the findings of this survey. Also, the scope of this work is restricted to India; and thus, can be extended to any other nations facing the sustainability issues about its TES.

CONCLUSION

Through a review of the literature, the authors have identified the various attributes of the sustainability of Indian TES. Some of these attributes are well researched as evident from this work. But there are some attributes of TES that need further research. These attributes are listed under the 'Gaps Identified from Literature Survey and Scope of Future Research'. The combined research on these attributes will help address the sustainability crisis faced today by the TES.

Indian TES is facing a sustainability crisis due to vacant seats at undergraduate study programmes thus adversely affecting revenue and forcing institutes to lower entry barriers. This further affects the quality of graduates and results in un-employability. On the other side, recruiters are facing issues such as higher spending on before the job training and attrition amongst the junior level engineers. This scenario is dreadful to the overall future growth of the Indian economy.

These issues can be addressed through research of various attributes owing to poor quality of TES such as; 'Curriculum Effectiveness', 'Career Inclination', 'Personal Attributes' and 'Career Adaptability' of students. This is the right time to undertake such a study before it is too late and ends up affecting the Indian economy.

REFERENCES

AICTE Approved Institutions having NBA Accredited Cources. (2019). https://doi. org/ doi:2019-04-10

BIMCO, & ICS. (2015). *Manpower Report Executive Summary 2015*, 6.

Caesar, L. (2013). Sustaining the Supply of Ship Officers:Making a Case for Succession Planning in Seafarer Recruitment. *Universal Journal of Management*, *1*(1), 6–12. doi:10.13189/ujm.2013.010102

Creed, P. A., Fallon, T., & Hood, M. (2009). The relationship between career adaptability, person and situation variables, and career concerns in young adults. *Journal of Vocational Behavior*, *74*(2), 219–229. doi:10.1016/j.jvb.2008.12.004

Debnath, R. M., & Shankar, R. (2012). Improving service quality in technical education: Use of interpretive structural modeling. *Quality Assurance in Education*, *20*(4), 387–407. doi:10.1108/09684881211264019

DGS. (2017). Intake Utilization Matrix. Retrieved July 1, 2019, from https://www. dgshipping.gov.in/WriteReadData/CMS/Documents/201805040624390335728Ca pacityUtilizationReport.pdf

Gambhir, V., & Wadhwa, N. C., & Grover Sandeep. (. (2016a). Quality Assurance in Education Article information. *Quality Assurance in Education*, *24*(1), 2–25. doi:10.1108/QAE-07-2011-0040

Gambhir, V., Wadhwa, N. C., & Grover, S. (2013). Interpretive structural modelling of enablers of quality technical education : An Indian perspective. *International Journal of Productivity and Quality Management*, *12*(4), 393–409. doi:10.1504/ IJPQM.2013.056734

Gambhir, V., Wadhwa, N. C., & Grover, S. (2016b). Quality Concerns in Technical Education in India - A Quantifiable Quality Enabled Model. *Quality Assurance in Education*, *24*(1), 2–25. doi:10.1108/QAE-07-2011-0040

Gudo, C. O., & Olel, M. A. (2011). Students' Admission Policies For Quality Assurance: Towards Quality Education In Kenyan Universities. *International Journal of Business and Social Science*, *2*(8), 177–183.

Harden, R. M., & Stamper, N. (1999). What is a spiral curriculum? *Medical Teacher*, *21*(2), 141–143. doi:10.1080/01421599979752 PMID:21275727

Honnutagi, A. R. R., Sonar, R., & Babu, A. S. (2016). Achieving quality excellence in Indian engineering education : Modelling and analysis using system dynamics. *Internal Journal of Business Excellence*, *10*(1), 90–119. doi:10.1504/IJBEX.2016.077622

Kanji, G. K., Tambi, A., & Wallace, W. (1999). A Comparative Study of Quality Practices in Higher Education Institutions in the US and Malaysia. *Total Quality Management*, *10*(3), 357–371. doi:10.1080/0954412997884

Kulkarni, A., Khan, A., Mishra, N., Raikwar, S., & Prajapat, S. (2014). DC-Model for Quality Improvement in Technical Education, 308–312.

Mahadeven, R., Shivaprakash, N. C., & Bose, S. K. (2013). Quality assessment of technical education in Indian Engineering Institutions. *IEEE Global Engineering Education Conference, EDUCON*, (1), 973–977.

Mahajan, P. T., & Golahit, S. B. (2017). Incorporating 11 P's of Service Marketing Mix and Its Impact on the Development of Technical Education. *Journal of Entrepreneurship Education*, *20*(2), 1–14.

Mahapatra, S. S., & Khan, M. S. (2007). A neural network approach for assessing quality in technical education: An empirical study. *International Journal of Productivity and Quality Management*, *2*(3), 287–306. doi:10.1504/IJPQM.2007.012451

MHRD. (2018). *AISHE Report 2017-18*. https://doi.org/ doi:29-Sept-2018

Mittal, R. K., Garg, N., & Yadav, S. K. (2018). Quality assessment framework for educational institutions in technical education: A literature survey. *On the Horizon*, *26*(3), 270–280. doi:10.1108/OTH-08-2017-0066

N.A.A.C. (2017). *NAAC Manual for Self-study Report Affiliated / Constituent Colleges*.

Nagendra, A. (2014). Paradigm Shift in HR Practices on Employee Life Cycle Due to Influence of Social Media. *Procedia Economics and Finance*, *11*(14), 197–207. doi:10.1016/S2212-5671(14)00188-9

Natarajan, R. (2000). The Role of Accreditation in Promoting Quality Assurance of Technical Education. *International Journal of Engineering Education*, *16*(2), 85–96.

National Board of Accreditation. (n.d.). Retrieved May 19, 2019, from https://www.nbaind.org/wa_program.aspx

NBA (2012). *Manual for Accreditation of Undergraduate Engineering Programs*.

Nguyen, D. Q. (1998). The Essential Skills and Attributes of an Engineer: A Comparative Study of Academics, Industry Personnel and Engineering Students. *Global Journal of Engineering Education*, 2(1), 65–75.

Nilsson, S. (2010). Enhancing individual employability: The perspective of engineering graduates. *Education + Training*, 52(6), 540–551. doi:10.1108/00400911011068487

Pal Pandi, A., Jeyathilagar, D., & Kubendran, V. (2013). A study of integrated total quality management practice in engineering educational institutions. *International Journal of Management Science and Engineering Management*, 8(2), 117–125. doi:10.1080/17509653.2013.798949

Pal Pandi, A., Rajendra Sethupathi, P. V., & Jeyathilagar, D. (2016). The IEQMS model for augmenting quality in engineering institutions – an interpretive structural modelling approach. *Total Quality Management & Business Excellence*, 27(3–4), 292–308. doi:10.1080/14783363.2014.978647

PalaniNathaRaja, M., Deshmukh, S. G., & Wadhwa, S.PalaniNathaRaja. (2006). Measuring service quality in technical education and healthcare services. *International Journal of Services and Operations Management*, 2(3), 222–236. doi:10.1504/IJSOM.2006.009858

Pandi, A. P., Sethupathi, P. V. R., & Jeyathilagar, D. (2016). Quality sustainability in engineering educational institutions - a theoretical model. *International Journal of Productivity and Quality Management*, 18(2/3), 364–384. doi:10.1504/IJPQM.2016.076715

Pandi, A. P., Sethupathi, P. V. R., Jeyathilagar, D., & Rajesh, R. (2016). Structural equation modelling for analyzing relationship between IEQMS criteria and performance of engineering institutions. *International Journal of Enterprise Network Management*, 7(2), 87–97. doi:10.1504/IJENM.2016.077525

Parasuraman, A., Zeithaml, V. A., & Berry, L. L. (1985). A Conceptual Model of Service Quality and Its Implications for Future Research. *Journal of Marketing*, 49(4), 41–50. doi:10.1177/002224298504900403

Picciano, A. G. (2002). Beyond Student Perceptions: Issues of Interaction, Presence, and Performance in an Online Course. *Journal of Asynchronous Learning Networks*, 6(1), 21–40.

Prasad, G., & Bhar, C. (2010). Accreditation system for technical education programmes in India: A critical review. *European Journal of Engineering Education*, 35(2), 187–213. doi:10.1080/03043790903497294

Prasad, U. C., & Suri, R. K. (2011). Modeling of Continuity and Change Forces in Private Higher Technical Education Using Total Interpretive Structural Modeling (TISM). *Global Journal of Flexible Systems Managment, 12*(3 & 4), 31–40. doi:10.1007/BF03396605

Puthal, M., Das, J. R., & Dash, M. (2018). An Exploratory Study on Effects of Service Quality on Technical Education in the Indian Context. *International Journal of Mechanical Engineering and Technology, 9*(8), 1255–1265.

Puthal, M., Rout, P. K., Das, J. R., & Dash, M. (2018). A Model for Service Quality in Indian Technical Education. *International Journal of Mechanical Engineering and Technology, 9*(6), 1081–1092.

Rao, P. S., Viswanadhan, K. G., & Raghunandana, K. (2015). Best Practices for Quality Improvement—Lessons from Top Ranked Engineering Institutions. *International Education Studies, 8*(11), 169–183. doi:10.5539/ies.v8n11p169

Rao, U. S., & Pandi, A. P. (2007). Quality Enhancement In Engineering Institutions Through Knowledge Management And Total Quality Management. *The Journal of Engineering Education Transformation, 20*(3), 10–15.

Report, A. I. C. T. E. 2018-19. (2019). Retrieved May 19, 2019, from http://www.facilities.aicte-india.org/dashboard/pages/dashboardaicte.php

Rudolph, C. W., Lavigne, K. N., & Zacher, H. (2017). Career adaptability: A meta-analysis of relationships with measures of adaptivity, adapting responses, and adaptation results. *Journal of Vocational Behavior, 98*, 17–34. doi:10.1016/j.jvb.2016.09.002

Sahu, A. R., Shrivastava, R. L., & Shrivastava, R. R. (2008). Key Factors Affecting The Effectiveness of Technical Education–An Indian Perspective. *Proceedings of the World Congress On Engineering, II*, 2–6.

Sahu, A. R., Shrivastava, R. R., & Shrivastava, R. L. (2012). Development and validation of an instrument for measuring critical success factors (CSFs) of technical education - a TQM approach. *International Journal of Productivity and Quality Management, 11*(1), 29–56. doi:10.1504/IJPQM.2013.050567

Sahu, A. R., Shrivastava, R. R., & Shrivastava, R. L. (2013). Critical success factors for sustainable improvement in technical education excellence - A literature review. *The TQM Journal, 25*(1), 62–74. doi:10.1108/17542731311286432

Salvioni, D. M., Franzoni, S., & Cassano, R. (2017). Sustainability in the higher education system: An opportunity to improve quality and image. *Sustainability (Basel)*, *9*(6), 914–941. doi:10.3390u9060914

Savickas, M. L. (1997). Career Adaptability - An Integrative Construct for Life-Span, Life-Space Theory. *The Career Development Quarterly*, *45*(3), 247–259. doi:10.1002/j.2161-0045.1997.tb00469.x

Sayeda, B., Rajendran, C., & Lokachari, P. S. (2010). An empirical study of total quality management in engineering educational institutions of India: Perspective of management. *Benchmarking*, *17*(5), 728–767. doi:10.1108/14635771011076461

Schein, E. H. (1996). Career Anchors Revisited: Implications for Career Development in the 21st Century. *The Academy of Management Perspectives*, *10*(4), 80–88. doi:10.5465/ame.1996.3145321

Senthil Kumar, M., & Sivakumar, P. (2014). Enhancing the quality of technical education accreditation system using current communication system. *International Journal of Applied Engineering Research: IJAER*, *9*(23), 20421–20432.

Sharma, G. D., Uppal, R. S., & Mahendru, M. (2016). Technical education as a tool for ensuring sustainable development: A case of India. *International Conference on Sustainability, Technology and Education 2016*, (December), 229–236.

Sharma, P. (2015). Organizational Commitment Among Faculty Members in India : A Study of Public and Private Technical Schools. *Global Business and Organizational Excellence*, *34*(5), 30–38. doi:10.1002/joe.21624

Sharma, P., & Pandher, J. S. (2018). Quality of teachers in technical higher education institutions in India. *Higher Education. Skills and Work-Based Learning*, *8*(4), 511–526. doi:10.1108/HESWBL-10-2017-0080

Shukla, O. P., & Garg, S. K. (2017). Perception of faculty members on factors affecting quality education and employability skills in technical education sector: An empirical analysis. *International Journal of Services. Economics and Management*, *8*(1/2), 109–131.

State vs No of Institutes, 2018-19. (2019). Retrieved May 20, 2019, from https://www.facilities.aicte-india.org/dashboard/pages/angulardashboard.php#!/graphs

Thai, V. V., Balasubramanyam, L., Yeoh, K. K. L., & Norsofiana, S. (2013). Revisiting the seafarer shortage problem: The case of Singapore. *Maritime Policy & Management*, *40*(1), 1–25. doi:10.1080/03088839.2012.744480

Upadhayay, L., & Vrat, P. (2016a). An ANP Based Selective Assembly Approach Incorporating Taguchi's Quality Loss Function to Improve Quality of Placements in Technical Institutions Introduction. *The TQM Journal, 28*(1), 112–131. doi:10.1108/TQM-06-2014-0054

Upadhayay, L., & Vrat, P. (2016b). Analysis of impact of industry-academia interaction on quality of technical education: A system dynamics approach. *Computers & Industrial Engineering, 101*, 313–324. doi:10.1016/j.cie.2016.09.022

Upadhayay, L., & Vrat, P. (2017). Policy boomerang in technical education: A system dynamics perspective. *Journal of Advances in Management Research, 14*(2), 143–161. doi:10.1108/JAMR-08-2016-0065

Viswanadhan, K. G. (2009). Quality indicators of engineering education programmes: A multi-criteria analysis from India. *International Journal of Industrial and Systems Engineering, 4*(3), 270–282. doi:10.1504/IJISE.2009.023542

Viswanadhan, K. G., Rao, N. J., & Mukhopadhyay, C. (2005). Impact of privatization on engineering education. *Journal of Services Research*, (special), 109–129.

Chapter 2
Design and Development of Hybrid Instructional Materials:
A Theoretical Framework

Emine Şendurur
https://orcid.org/0000-0002-0340-6378
Ondokuz Mayıs University, Turkey

Polat Şendurur
Ondokuz Mayis University, Turkey

ABSTRACT

This chapter aims to review and summarize the principles of instructional material preparation for face-to-face, online, and hybrid environments. The design of mixed instructional materials was first discussed in light of instructional design and technology literature. Multimedia learning, cognitive load theory, and universal design principles were considered the fundamentals of instructional material design. The framework has three dimensions: content type, fidelity, and course phase. In this framework, a hybrid form was offered instead of different forms of materials, but face-to-face and online modalities were also compared. The design and development categorizations were built upon the hybrid nature of the materials. This way, the framework can guide practitioners in designing efficient ways to create instructional materials.

INTRODUCTION

The history of instructional design and technologies (IDT) consists of several milestones. World War II, Sputnik, the programmed instruction movement, and the introduction of the world wide web are some examples of these milestones. Although each milestone seems irrelevant to the field of education at first sight, its impacts of

DOI: 10.4018/978-1-6684-8656-6.ch002

them are evident in the literature on IDT (Cuban, 1986; Reiser, 2012; Saettler, 2004). One example of IDT's history is an instructional methodology called programmed instruction, introduced by Skinner (Saettler, 1990). Based on behavioral tradition, the programmed instruction movement significantly impacted the educational practice of its age. Moreover, its impact can be observed in today's educational practice, including mobile learning applications, online learning materials, digital educational games, etc. Learning at their own pace, receiving immediate feedback, and many other characteristics of this movement still exist in current self-learning materials. Those examples demonstrate that the paradigm shift is not an instant process having exact starting and ending points. The emergence of a paradigm shift does not guarantee the total acceptance of its requirements. Another example is that the first instructional design process was shaped into its modern form during World War II because the soldiers should have been trained as quickly as possible using available resources (Reiser, 2012). This was not the first time that people dealt with how to teach something, but the modeled approaches inspired the world of education. Since then, the field of instructional design has been evolving into various forms. The area sought efficient and effective ways to improve instruction conditions in the post-pandemic era. One of the sophisticated forms is the blended (hybrid) ones.

The development and increasing accessibility of digital technologies has dramatically expanded the reach of microlearning opportunities. Thanks to portable technologies and the internet, the learning experience has become almost independent of space and environment. Therefore, it is necessary to consider different learning environments (face-to-face, hybrid, and online) with microlearning experiences. Controlling the cognitive load in microlearning is one of the primary issues. This is reflected in the design and development of the necessary learning materials. Therefore, it would be appropriate to consider microlearning, different learning environments, and material design processes together.

This chapter aims to review and summarize the principles of instructional material preparation for face-to-face, online, and hybrid environments. Based on the state of the art, a new framework was proposed. In this framework, a hybrid form was offered instead of different forms of materials. The design and development categorizations were built upon the hybrid nature of the materials. This way, the framework can guide practitioners in designing efficient ways to create instructional materials.

Post-Pandemic Era

There should be situations pointing to radical changes to claim that a paradigm shift is in progress. The difference in learning environments that came with the Covid-19 pandemic today is a paradigm shift. However, it is an undeniable fact that there are powerful signals. The use of instruments and technologies specific to distance education has become a necessity for all stakeholders of education during the transition that we are all facing at all levels, from primary to tertiary education. The proper use of these technologies and instruments, which generally require a longer acceptance process, has begun to be used whether or not individuals accept them. It is possible that relatively novel technologies and instruments accelerated acceptance. For example, educators with limited digital literacy skills started to conduct synchronous lectures in virtual classrooms with teleconferencing applications like Zoom, Google Meet, or Microsoft Teams. They have tried to assign homework or manage group works through LMSs. However, it may not be wise to claim that the extensive use of digital technologies brings about a technology acceptance with the same broad scope because this rapid change has revealed several novel technology integration problems. Creating digital materials for virtual online learning environments, developing appropriate measurement and evaluation methods for learning outcomes, and providing informal learning environments outside the classroom can be given as examples of causing integration problems. The fact that third-generation artificial intelligence tools are much more accessible has led to the diversification of the related problem areas. The possible unforeseen effects of natural language processing tools such as Chat GPT, which have recently gained popularity in educational environments, have emerged as an essential topic of discussion. All these situations provide strong evidence that a paradigm shift is taking place and even that we are in a paradigm shift. In the literature, the terminology emerged as evidence of this change because the words "pre-pandemic" (Zheng et al., 2021) and "post-pandemic" (Rapanta et al., 2021) exist in many studies in a broad range of fields.

The industrial paradigm was in demand of people working individually, but the post-industrial paradigm appreciates and supports collaborative work (Reigeluth, 2016). Despite this apparent demand, the current educational practice may only sometimes reach this output. Resistance always serves as a barrier to paradigm changes. The history of instructional technology conveys many examples of teachers' resistance. The introduction of each new instructional technology had premises to solve the problems of teaching and learning, but they still needed to achieve it. In its earlier times, the radio was expected to boost educational practice, the motion pictures were perceived as the panacea of all academic problems, and the television was perceived as revolutionary for learning something. However, specific issues had yet to be embraced as practical (Reiser, 2012). One of the main problems was teachers' resistance besides infrastructural issues because it was the teacher who integrated these technologies into classrooms (Cuban, 1986). Today, this may be valid even for hybrid forms of instruction.

For the current paradigm shift triggered by Covid 19 pandemic, the problems may remain the same. Like teachers resisting not using televisions in their classrooms, teachers insist on traditional materials, tools, methods, and environments. During the pandemic, many institutions, from kindergarten to higher education, preferred synchronous communication tools such as live videoconferencing. The teachers needed choices about what to use, so the resistance was low-quality practice. Changing the approaches, methods, techniques, and materials for remote teaching can be considered as a way of resistance. Indeed, the problem is a reflection of poor technology integration practices. Unlike its predecessors, computer-based technologies require the literacy of software, hardware, network, etc. This means teachers are expected to be the troubleshooters of this technology, which may cause them to feel overwhelmed. If the teacher has no technical barriers, s/he can design and develop instructional materials based on their needs. However, this does not mean that s/he can integrate them meaningfully. During the pandemic, many teachers had access to technology and were literate enough to design and develop their materials, but still, students complained about the overall instruction structure. Indeed, this is a genuine problem of integration. Although there are no barriers, such as administrative support, teachers need help integrating the available tools into digital environments. The same hesitation might be observed during the transition from the pandemic to the new standard. At that point, the general practice might need new adaptive and generic principles for technology integration.

Hybrid Learning

Since we started talking about distance learning and face-to-face education, the idea of using these two learning environments has come up. For example, educational radios in classrooms, educational TV broadcasts prepared by educational programs, and the accessibility of course content via the Internet can be blended learning applications. The definitions of blended learning in the literature also address similar points. For example, Graham (2006) defines integrated learning environments as "... systems combine face-to-face instruction with computer-mediated instruction" (p.41). In this definition, Graham also states that face-to-face and computer-mediated learning environments are getting closer to each other and becoming more intertwined. It is observed that the convergence process defined by this idea takes place much faster in the post-pandemic era. Therefore, time and individual perceptions will reveal different definitions of blended learning environments.

Similarly, Garrison and Kanuka (2004) based their purpose of blended learning on integrating face-to-face and online activities. In a more recent definition, Cronje (2022) defines blended learning as "the appropriate use of a mix of theories, methods, and technologies to optimize learning in a given context" (p. 121). Driscoll (2002, p.1) emphasized that the definition of blended learning will vary from person to person and stated that there are four essential conceptual counterparts:

1. To accomplish an educational goal, combine or mix modes of web-based technology (e.g., live virtual classroom, self-paced instruction, collaborative learning, streaming video, audio, and text).
2. Combine various pedagogical approaches (e.g., constructivism, behaviorism, cognitivism) to produce an optimal learning outcome with or without instructional technology.
3. Combine any form of instructional technology (e.g., videotape, CD-ROM, web-based training, film) with face-to-face instructor-led training.
4. Mix or combine instructional technology with actual job tasks to create a harmonious effect of learning and working.

Driscoll emphasized that the media, pedagogical approaches, and environment (face-to-face and online) are the main variables used in blending instruction. With a similar approach, Graham (2006) stated that this process can be realized at the "activity," "course," "program," and "institutional" levels while blending the learning environment. Based on these approaches, many factors come to the fore for a course to be conducted as integrated. Due to the urgent need for online education during the pandemic, many institutions have invested in their infrastructure for instructional technologies and distance education. This situation causes blended environments to appear, with many more examples in the post-pandemic era.

Offering online content for a course to be blended is not enough. Moreover, Helms (2014) states that using web-based materials such as videos or webpages in face-to-face classes cannot be considered hybrid. Blended learning is not a simple layering or random gathering of face-to-face and online learning experiences but a meaningful integration of both (Garrison & Kanuka, 2004). According to Allen and Sherman (2010), for a course to be blended, at least 30% of its content must be delivered online. When this rate exceeds 80%, the study should be defined as online. Watson (2008) described blended learning as a continuum between face-to-face and online and explained with various examples that a designed system can be positioned between face-to-face and online. He defined this continuum in seven steps. These steps are given below respectively (p.6);

1. Fully online curriculum with all learning done online and at a distance and no face-to-face component
2. Fully online curriculum with options for face-to-face instruction, but not required.
3. Mostly or entirely online curriculum with select days required in the classroom or computer lab
4. Mostly or entirely online curriculum in a computer lab or classroom where students meet every day

5. Classroom instruction with significant, required online components that extend learning beyond the classroom and the school day
6. Classroom instruction integrates online resources but limited or no requirements for students to be online.
7. Traditional face-to-face settings with few or no online resources or communication

Gumennykova et al. (2020) categorized blended learning into four models: rotational, self-mixed, virtual enriched, and flex. The rotational model is the most flexible of all models. Its basic approach is to increase access to content by integrating current educational technologies into the face-to-face course. Students alternate between traditional and online activities. Another model, the self-mixed model, is a blend of techniques within a program rather than a single system. Students attend specific courses online and others face-to-face. In the virtual enriched model, students divide their time between online and face-to-face activities. Students do not have to be in school for all course sessions. In the Flex model, almost all content and interaction take place online. Students can receive face-to-face support from the instructor when they request it. This model is the closest to being entirely online in Watson (2008)'s continuum.

There are many other approaches to categorizing blended learning environments. However, in general, these categorizations do not differ from each other. Instead, the variables they refer to create diversified categories. These variables include students' time in the online environment, the pedagogical approach, and the blended teaching methods. For this reason, different names can be given to integrated learning environments in practical applications. Graham's (2006) definition and other definitions emphasize the integration of digital technologies in blended learning environments. Today, a "hybrid learning environment" can be used for different blended learning environments. Hybrid learning is a term primarily used in higher education. According to Linder (2017), in a hybrid learning environment, a particular portion of the student's time in the classroom is transferred to the online environment. There are many obstacles to implementing the application within the scope of this definition in primary and secondary education. The education systems of most countries mandate primary and secondary education. In addition, the efficiency of hybrid learning environments will decrease in case of poor self-regulation skills in young age groups. For this reason, hybrid courses are primarily used in higher education and are considered synonymous with blended learning.

The developments of the technologies used in the transition from face-to-face to online learning environments have been observed in different ways in other elements of learning environments. Even if studies focus on student and instructor behavior, it can be observed that the instructional methods and materials utilized may not go beyond traditional use. More than concentrating on technological developments, increasing access to these technologies will be required to develop learning environments. As the environments differentiate, the characteristics of the necessary instructional materials should be able to keep up with this differentiation. In this context, there is a need for studies on the design, development, and implementation of hybrid instructional materials.

DESIGN OF INSTRUCTIONAL MATERIALS

In any instructional design model, the design and development of instructional materials are linked to other phases. In other words, they are separate from the rest of the process because all instruments of design services achieve intended outcomes. The instructional plan aims to solve instructional problems. Considering a hybrid learning environment, the problems can range from communicational to technical issues. Whatever the case is, providing the solutions requires a starting point, which can be identified throughout the analysis phase. Course objectives and learning outcomes can lead to the rest. The instructional material design is built upon instructional objectives and goals but is also contingent upon the analysis results. However, more than sticking to those is needed to guarantee excellent design. There are many factors affecting the quality and success of instructional materials. The analysis phase of instructional design models generally provides base information to consider during the design. Some of the factors to be considered in the design stage are introduced in the following subtitles.

Course Objectives & Learning Outcomes

The aim of the course and the expected outcomes are at the core of any instruction. All initiatives are based on them, and the assessment and evaluation reveal if they were achieved. Instructional materials are the tools designed to achieve them. To specify the learning outcomes, taxonomy selection in the target domain is required. Although the most commonly known taxonomy belongs to Bloom, many others are in different fields. Specifying the target domain is directly related to the content and the material. There are three domains: cognitive, affective, and psychomotor. Suppose the learning outcome is in the cognitive domain. In that case, the percentage of online materials can be higher, whereas if it is in the psychomotor domain, it would be wise to increase the rate of face-to-face tasks and materials due to the need for feedback.

Making Objectives and Progress Visible

Monitoring own progress can contribute to the self-regulation skills of hybrid learners. Completing the course expectations visible and showing how much the learner approached to master them should be made explicit in the course management systems. Learning analytics tools in Moodle-based systems enable monitoring of students' progress. Monitoring is considered a challenge in hybrid learning. Jensen et al. (2022) indicated that on-demand scaffolding is essential but hard to achieve in a virtual format. That's why the contingent design of materials can eliminate this disadvantage of virtual-only materials. In addition, each material, regardless of its modality, should include the aim of this material, which may trigger the previous learning. Moreover, hybrid learning requires well-structured linking among design elements; thus, informing the students about each fabric can enhance this link.

Age & Cognitive Development

Cognitive development stages guide how to appeal to specific age groups. In an instructional material design process, the principles for the selection of visuals, the language used, the sequence of the content, the choice of examples, the utilization of colors, the placement of design elements, etc., are applied depending on the target audience's age. For example, using abstract images might not be appropriate for elementary school students. Moreover, if the target learners are adults, one might need to consider assumptions of andragogy, which is very different from pedagogy. For hybrid learning materials, in addition to the mentioned principles, the allocation of time/effort spent for each face-to-face and online material should be made explicit to all learners. If they are adults, they might seek the reasons for these allocations, and thus the workload can be announced in advance online. Age is also essential in deciding the level of control denoted to the learner. This might be diminished as the age group decreases because online learning readiness is related to age (Rafique et al., 2021). For example, much more guidance or scaffolding can be provided to younger learners for the online materials.

Accessibility Needs

The instructional design should be inclusive to all target learners regardless of the mode of instruction. Nevertheless, being sensitive to the unique needs of students is vital for either online or hybrid learning environments. The instructional materials should meet universal design principles, including accessibility standards. For example, the combination of colors may hinder the readability of the text due to color blindness, or ignoring closed captioning may make the students with hearing disabilities look for alternative tools/software to transcribe the video content. Designing ubiquitous learning environments via universal design principles can reduce the risk of ignorance of various groups of learners with disabilities. The modalities might be listed at the top; the same content can be prepared in alternative modalities so that the user can pick the one that is appropriate to their needs.

Socio-Economical-Status (SES)

In traditional learning environments, SES matters because the affordances may hinder access to certain instructional materials. In hybrid environments, SES can become a barrier, especially for online learning. The digital divide is still a barrier for many people worldwide, and current literature emphasizes that demographics are the main actors of online learning (Rizvi et al., 2019). Accessing digital content requires a budget for the device, data package, electricity, etc. Online learning activities and materials are essential in hybrid learning since face-to-face teaching is linked to online learning. Therefore, allocating resources between online and offline modes should be designed depending on the target learners' SES. If data packages and personally owned devices are available for most learners, then the percentage of online materials can be increased. Otherwise, these materials can be accessed in face-to-face sessions, but in that case, they would not be called hybrid anymore.

Digital Literacy Level

Literacy, in its simplest form, means reading, writing, and doing basic math operations. In the 21st, literacy conveys deeper meanings than its simple definition. Today's technologically rich environment demands more skills to process information than reading or writing. According to some researchers, multiliteracies are necessary to survive in the information age (Selber & Selber, 2004). Specifically having many dimensions of information and communication technologies, digital literacy as an umbrella term is proposed by Gilster (1997). In the literature, competency in computer-related skills is reported as a predictor of success in online learning (Yustika & Iswati, 2020). That's why designing hybrid instructional materials requires special attention to the target learners' digital literacy levels. The online self-study materials should not demand high digital literacy levels as long as the learners are limited in technical handling skills. If the content is procedural and the material is interactive, then a short pre-training would be beneficial for those who have no idea what to do with the material.

Previous Knowledge/Experience/Skills

In both cognitive and constructivist learning approaches, what the learner already knows is essential to make the learning process meaningful. In hybrid learning environments, pre-analysis of learners' knowledge/experience/skill levels is vital. The instructional material having unfamiliar terms, examples, tasks, and so on might hinder the learning process. Although hybrid learning environments can monitor learners' progress in face-to-face sessions, the lack of prior knowledge might not be observed directly in those sessions. That's why it could be wiser if the analysis is completed in advance so that necessary complementary instructional materials can be designed. The flexible nature of hybrid learning environments can enable labeling the materials by difficulty levels. Hence learners can pick the ones that are appropriate to their level. Providing visual progress bars or benefitting from learning analytics can help learners to monitor their accomplishments. In addition, the teacher can monitor the mastery of students. Identifying the beginning skills of learners can guide the teachers during the design of hybrid materials. For example, if the learners are unfamiliar with machines, introducing real photos or actual video footage of engines might not be a good start. Instead, one can benefit from illustrations and simple animations. More realistic simulations or video footage can be introduced as the learners gain expertise.

On the contrary to this audience, if the target learners have prior theoretical knowledge of machines, then the introduction of high-fidelity materials can contribute to learning. Otherwise, they might get bored with simple forms of materials. Tuning the balance of materials to appeal to the target learners might take time. The iterations or "just-in-time analysis" can help shape the materials whenever necessary (Reigeluth & An, 2020). The teacher might realize that the learners have misconceptions. In that case, supplementary materials can be created, even if it was not planned in the beginning.

Language

The native language (mother tongue) is biologically primary knowledge, which means automatic cognitive processing, but domain-specific content or content in another language is biologically secondary knowledge requiring mental effort to deal with (Sweller et al., 2019). In hybrid learning materials, the language of materials should be designed carefully to eliminate misconceptions and prevent extraneous cognitive load. If there are students whose native languages are different from the content delivery language, additional features should be designed. For example, subtitles can be added in other languages, transcriptions of videos can be provided in text-based modalities, or glossaries can be delivered to facilitate the comprehension of terminologies. The discourse should be consistent among all materials, and it should be free of slang words.

On the other hand, the personalization principle of multimedia learning emphasizes that informal conversations in multimedia appeal to learners compared to formal ones (Mayer, 2002). That's why deciding on a style of discourse may be helpful to transfer the instructional messages in hybrid materials. This might also help create a feeling of being a learning community member.

Expectations

Having certificates or diplomas at the end of formal education can affect forming expectations. For some learners, the ultimate goal has a title/license. For others, the point is to learn and to have expertise in specific domains. For the rest, it is just a necessity beyond their personal choices. Analyzing learners' expectations can provide insights into how much they are willing to spend efforts. In the online learning part of hybrid learning, self-regulation is crucial, especially if such blended learning models as flex are at the stage. Students should define their ways of understanding so that their intrinsic goal orientations predict their overall success and level of engagement (Al Fadda, 2019; Goda et al., 2023). The instructional materials matching learners' expectations can increase the possibility of goal achievement; however, if the materials are more arduous than expected or vice versa, the learner can face engagement problems. The flow theory suggests that the difficulty level should be optimized to keep the learner in the flow zone (Nakamura & Csikszentmihalyi, 2009). This is confirmed by the cognitive load theory suggestion of considering the level of expertise to avoid excessive cognitive load (Sweller et al., 2019).

Moreover, materials with high element interactivity (i.e., sophisticated content) can cause cognitive load for novice learners (Sweller et al., 2019). To sum up, to increase the possibility of learner engagement, learners' expectations should be considered before designing the hybrid materials. For groups having professional expectations, higher element interactivity and complex materials can be supplied as alternatives to regular ones.

Attitudes

Attitudes towards the course or mode of the system can hinder achieving goals. Unlike the other domains, the purposes of the affective domain are challenging, and attitude change is one of the toughest ones because it takes time. Gender, prior experiences with hybrid learning, and computer literacy affect attitudes toward hybrid learning (Sanpanich, 2021). In addition to those factors, the student's attitudes towards the subject area, course, material types, mode of instruction, or the instructor can hinder the overall learning experience. The material design should be as flexible as possible to eliminate negative attitudes. If the learner feels overwhelmed by reading something online, alternative modalities should be presented. If the learner finds watching instructional videos a time loss, a video script can be given as an alternative. In this way, they can feel having control of their learning instead of direct imposing.

Available Technologies

Rapid developments in information and communication technologies make it harder to keep up with the changes. Providing up-to-date information prepared via recent technologies is quite challenging for today's educators. Artificial intelligence tools, Web 2.0 tools, and many others have been assisting in designing and developing appealing materials. On the other hand, not all hybrid environments are eligible to use them. For example, an interactive material published in Actionbound, which creates bounds to be accessed anytime, anywhere, can be used online and encourages mobility. However, this material may fail if the learner has no alternative devices other than a desktop to connect to the Internet. That's why one needs to analyze available technologies to design textiles, even for face-to-face sessions. The percentages of synchronous and asynchronous materials and tasks should be aligned with the available technologies.

Allocation of Time and Resources

In the iron triangle of instructional design, effectiveness, efficiency, and appeal are the main characteristics of a successful strategy (Honebein & Honebein, 2015). In user experience studies, the ISO usability standards, namely effectiveness, efficiency, and satisfaction (ISO 9241-11), are similar to the iron triangle. Design for hybrid learning environments consists of a group of decision-making. Allocation of time means defining the percentages of activity, task, and material engagement durations to be devoted to complete online and face-to-face modes, respectively. Such credit systems as European Credit Transfer and Accumulation System (ECTS) can help to make decisions on the percentages based on the workload. The level of engagement with the material, complexity level, content length, and similar factors can guide balanced choices. In hybrid format, the materials can be divided into phases to be experienced entirely online, face-to-face, and as an extension of both. The structure of the content is also essential to decide how much time to be spent to master the content. If it is a skill, then the amount could be enhanced for face-to-face materials due to the scaffolding needs of students. Allocation of resources means defining the percentages of online and face-to-face materials. These do not only consist of numbers but also modalities. The same content can be designed in textual and visual modalities if it is vital.

On the other hand, if the materials are supplementary rather than fundamental, then the alternative modalities can be optional. To allocate resources into meaningful percentages depends on the content itself. One might need to extend the number and modalities if it is too complex to be mastered with a few resources. In addition, the quality of resources matters. Even if the quality does not directly influence the learning outcomes, it might impact the learner's satisfaction with the learning experience in the hybrid modality (Muller et al., 2023).

Bias-Free Approaches

"Generation Z knows how to stay connected," "Digital natives have advanced digital skills," "Young learners can easily access valid and accurate online information," and "Adults fail to approach critically online resources" are Some biased assumptions to be avoided. For some instances, the listed assumptions might be correct, but approaching the design issues with those in mind might lead to emotional content. Instead, one should be practical and work iteratively for hybrid materials. Not all materials can appeal to all populations. That's why analyzing learners' prior knowledge and beginning skills can be necessary before the material design. Unlike traditional pre-analysis, the analysis for blended modes requires two dimensions: domain and technology. The learners' theoretical and practical knowledge can be tested in the domain dimension. To a technical extent, students' previous technology-based courses or experiences can be investigated. In a STEM course, students' previous technology skills should be considered before designing the laboratory sheets (online or face-to-face). The materials can be built upon coding-related tasks if they are familiar with the algorithm terminology. Biased approaches are not limited to knowledge and skills. Gender, nationality, culture, previous success, and so on can trigger small designs. To prevent such narrow approaches, the preliminary analysis can be utilized properly.

Pacing/Segmentation

In radical behaviorism, each individual learns at their speed, so the material should allow pacing. In cognitive load theory, it is called as segmentation principle. Based on the assumption of individual differences, designing the materials in small pieces can reduce cognitive load (Sweller et al., 2019). There are better approaches than presenting exclusive content under one title. Instead, typographical tools such as title leveling can make this segmentation. These issues have been discussed in the field of message design. Recently, the length of instructional videos has been a hot topic owing to the boosted usage during the pandemic. Manasrah et al. (2021) reported that the optimum size of an instructional video should be between 6-10 minutes. If the content is lengthy, it can be divided into sub-videos, or interactions can be added to create segments.

Transfer of Knowledge and Skills

Transfer of knowledge and skills is the ultimate goal of any instruction. It can be near (transfer to the familiar context) or far (transfer to the unfamiliar context). Designing materials triggering near and far transfer is quite challenging for any field. Hybrid fabrics can enrich the opportunity to create a transfer context, but it might be planned with a systemic approach. Increasing the number and variety of examples with various modalities can facilitate near transfer. For far transfer creating opportunities is a bit complex. The teacher might look for interdisciplinary collaboration to make the far transfer possible.

Sequencing the Content, Modality, & Interaction Nodes

Considering the hybrid learning experience, designing sequences of certain features is vital to eliminate cognitive load and misunderstanding. Creating smooth learning experiences is possible unless the structure of sequencing appeals to the learners. The content can be sequenced from simple to complex or vice versa. Other ways to sequence the range are from general to specific (or vice versa); from theory to practice (or vice versa); chronological; or hierarchical. The sequencing style might depend on the target learners' prior knowledge or skills. Sequencing the modality is another vital step for hybrid learning. The modalities for each sequence can be defined based on the content sequencing style. If the content is sequenced hierarchically, visual materials such as infographics can help impose the relations first, and then textual modality can be presented.

Providing the textual modality might not be a good start for such sequencing. Finally, the sequencing of the interaction nodes is required to answer when and how these materials are introduced, what kind of engagement is expected, and what kind of facilitation/feedback/guidance is available. Interaction in a hybrid learning environment means learner-learner, learner-teacher, and learner-content (Moore, 2011). To prevent the feelings of social isolation frequently occurring in online modality (Palmer et al., 2022), the materials can be designed to encourage group work. It is reported that connection to the course material in online modality is quite limited (Pollock, 2022), but hybrid is reported as causing fewer feelings of isolation (McCleary-Gaddy et al., 2022). While planning interaction nodes, it would be wise to create spaces for learner feedback, which might enable to revision of the materials. When switching between tasks, materials, and modalities, the user should not think of why; instead, the transitions should be transparent and harmonious. The last but not the least important point in sequencing is the model of the sequencing. The learner cannot switch between the materials if it is a rigid sequencing. If it is flexible sequencing, the learner can control their way. Both approaches have advantages and disadvantages. Specific disciplines, such as clinical ones, might require a hierarchical rigid content sequencing with strictly defined interaction nodes.

DEVELOPMENT OF INSTRUCTIONAL MATERIALS

Reusable Learning Objects

Reusable learning objects (RLOs) can fill a significant gap considering the teaching materials needed in hybrid learning environments. The effectiveness of RLOs has been demonstrated in many different learning environments. For example, it is observed that the integration of RLOs in computer programming education (Topali & Mikropoulos, 2019), engineering education (Onofrei & Ferry, 2020), high school physics education (Papastergiou & Mastrogiannis, 2021), language education (Burazer et al., 2020), and many other similar fields have produced positive results.

By definition, RLOs can be characterized as hybrid materials. For example, Wiley (2000) described learning objects as reusable digital materials that support learning. Similarly, learning objects are defined by IEEE (2023) standards as all digital or non-digital entries used for learning purposes. Since instructional material has a higher potential to be used in distance education when it is digital, on the other hand, face-to-face education environments also have the infrastructure that allows the use of digital materials in many aspects. In this respect, there is no obstacle to using materials those materials in face-to-face learning environments with an appropriate integration process. The pedagogical approach, material compatibility, technological infrastructure, and learner characteristics should be considered at this point. In other words, there is a need for a standard that will enable the use of RLO in both online and face-to-face environments. This standard should also cover Hyflex education environments.

At this point, it would be appropriate to emphasize the critical considerations presented by Norman and Porter. Norman and Porter (2007) list these key considerations to be taken into account in the learning design process as follows:

1. What is the learning objective? Are learner characteristics suitable for RLO?
2. Is RLO better than other options?
3. What are the target audience's age, technological competence, and motivation?
4. How will RLO be integrated into the learning environment?
5. Is there a need for different media with RLO?

6.   Are there any copyright issues?
7.   How will learners evaluate the process?

These key considerations apply not only to the use of RLO but also to all teaching materials. However, it is necessary to add some additional reviews when the aim is to make the materials usable regardless of the medium. The first of these points is whether or not the RLO is to be used media-independent. A digital RLO should be simultaneously applicable and usable with media in both face-to-face and online environments. For example, it is straightforward to implement an online survey application in a distance education environment. Because learners need to have basic infrastructure such as a computer and internet to participate in an online learning environment; for example, thanks to the structure of the online learning environment, they can easily participate in an online questionnaire application and get quick feedback. However, to realize the same application in a face-to-face setting, in-class media, such as mobile devices for each student, a classroom computer, etc., will be needed. In other words, a hybrid RLO should be created by considering both face-to-face and online environments.

Another consideration is whether the RLO contributes similarly to the learning outcomes in two different learning environments. For example, an RLO, which has an interactive structure and offers different levels of interaction in online and face-to-face environments, will be a sign that its hybrid feature will be open to discussion. Another issue is whether the teacher's competence in creating and using RLO is at a level to manage two different learning environments. An RLO may require other instructor competencies in online and face-to-face environments. If the differences between the skills needed in online and face-to-face environments are too high, adapting the RLO to hybrid environments will be uneven. Therefore, teacher competencies must be reviewed by considering online and face-to-face environments to create the object.

Web 2.0 Tools

Designing digital or non-digital RLOs requires both a pedagogical approach and literacy skills toward the use of technology. Although RLOs are described as small-sized and relatively easy-to-prepare materials, RLOs are not the only materials in learning environments. Apart from RLOs, there may be many different teaching materials that teachers and students need. For this reason, the level of digital literacy skills required of students and instructors may be higher than that needed by RLOs.

When the historical process of instructional technologies is analyzed, it is observed that the area covered by computer technologies has increased rapidly in the last few decades. However, this is not only due to the advancement of computer technologies but also to the increase in instructors' and students' digital literacy levels. Today, several tools can be used to design digital instructional materials for instructors and students with limited digital literacy. Web 2.0 tools offer the opportunity to produce and implement several types of content thanks to primary computer and internet literacy skills. Sendurur (2022) emphasized that even individuals with basic computer literacy have become content producers with the help of Web 2.0 tools. However, she also drew attention to the information and content pollution caused by this situation.

Web 2.0 tools that can be integrated into learning environments are categorized by Orehovački et al. (2012) from three different dimensions. The first dimension is the type of Web 2.0 tool, the second dimension is its function, and the last is cognitive processes. Considering the second dimension, Orehovački et al. (2012) stated that Web 2.0 tools could have tasks like collaboration, sharing, communication, knowledge organization, learning support, and artifact merging. When the features of Web 2.0 tools mentioned in the function dimension are considered from a general point of view, they point to attributes that will enable the development of hybrid teaching materials.

For example, student collaboration tools can be easily integrated into face-to-face and online environments. Korhonen et al. (2019) stated that social media tools such as Whatsapp and Facebook increase student collaboration, improve the social atmosphere, develop the dialogue between students and teachers, and ultimately contribute to student satisfaction. Alkoudmani et al. (2021) also conducted a study on using Web 2.0 with a learning support function to support students in developing pharmaceutical knowledge and reported positive results. In addition to supporting collaboration and learning, it is also possible to access studies that contribute to knowledge organization (Kompen et al., 2019) to help merge artifacts into design processes (Alsuwaida, 2022).

It is clear from the literature that Web 2.0 tools are widely accepted in face-to-face, online, and blended learning environments. In other words, there is considerable evidence for the potential of these tools to provide hybrid instructional materials. However, at this point, it is necessary to mention specific considerations that should be considered in instructional material design processes. Ünal and Çakır (2021) tested Web 2.0 tools to support collaborative learning and found that these tools did not contribute to students' level of participation in collaboration. Even if it is not possible to conclude that Web 2.0 tools do not contribute to the level of involvement in collaborative activities in each situation, from the perspective of hybrid instructional material, it is concluded that integration processes should be examined multi-dimensionally. Although the importance of Web 2.0 in the context of all the dimensions mentioned by Orehovački et al. (2012) offers the space for designing, developing, and implementing teaching materials, it is vital to be aware of its limitations in terms of teaching as a medium (Larsen et al., 2020).

Artificial Intelligence

Current learning theories and approaches claim that learning is a process of individual construction and that meaning is constructed by the individual in line with social interactions. The purpose-built by each person will be unique. Therefore, the structure of individualized learning environments is very crucial from the perspective of the learning approach to creating meaning. Technological advancements have started to increase their popularity to meet individual learning needs. Recently, we have witnessed everyone with a certain level of familiarity with the internet and computers interact directly with Chat GPT, a language model constructed on artificial intelligence. The curiosity and interest created by Chat GPT have led to questions that fundamentally challenge the education paradigm. Because with this technology, it can produce personalized answers to many questions comparable to the solutions of an expert. Therefore, people question many issues in terms of educational practices. Will there be a need for a teacher after this technology? How can it be understood that artificial intelligence does not complete homework and answer exam questions? While it is possible to increase these questions, it will take more work to produce answers. However, when this situation is approached from a different perspective, it will be seen that artificial intelligence and accompanying technologies have a high potential in designing, developing, and implementing hybrid teaching materials and environments.

Adaptive learning environments and intelligent tutoring systems are the superior technologies in this context. Adaptive learning environments can be defined as the transfer of new materials based on the learner's interaction with previous content and the learner's behavior during this interaction (Kerr, 2016). The system continuously tries to collect information about the learner and organizes the content it presents in light of the data it collects. In other words, it tries to get to know the learner and understand individual learning behavior with an artificial intelligence algorithm. Liu et al. (2017) argue that adaptive learning systems can form the basis of a significant transformation in education. Many studies shed light on the positive effects of adaptive learning systems (Liu et al., 2017; Vanbecelaere et al., 2020; Yang et al., 2014).

Intelligent tutoring systems are structures built on similar dynamics to adaptive learning systems. They are intelligent systems that model and combine instructor and student behavior (Nagao & Nagao, 2019; Nkambou et al., 2010). Although the primary purpose of intelligent tutoring systems is to transfer the content to the student, it is possible to make the content sensitive to student characteristics by modeling teacher behavior. As a result, adaptive learning environments and intelligent instructional systems need large amounts of data, i.e., learning analytics, to run their algorithms.

From the perspective of hybrid instructional materials, the type and amount of analytics that can be obtained from the learner in online and face-to-face environments will differ. Although there are many more clues about the learner's learning process in the face-to-face environment, recording these clues will pose a significant problem. Recording the student's non-verbal behaviors, behaviors in informal learning environments, and similar issues and processing them by an algorithm must be performed promptly with the existing technologies. In the online environment, almost all behavior patterns can be recorded, and the data obtained can form the data set required by the algorithms. Although analyzing non-verbal behaviors has difficulties online, new technologies have also produced solutions. Therefore, we are witnessing attempts to integrate artificial intelligence-based applications into online learning environments (Cao et al., 2020; Cope et al., 2021; Ouyang et al., 2023; Seo et al., 2021; Sun et al., 2021).

The difference in the analytics that can be obtained in online and face-to-face learning environments is a factor that makes it challenging to prepare AI-based hybrid teaching materials. However, it is necessary to mention that there is a high potential in the long term. Learning and content management systems (LMSs) are frequently used today, not only in online learning environments (Govender, 2010; Mozahem, 2020; Saito & Ulbricht, 2012). The combination of artificial intelligence and LMSs will offer a new perspective in the coming years for designing, developing, and implementing teaching materials in both face-to-face and online environments.

THE FRAMEWORK: DD-HIM

The offered framework is called DD-HIM, standing for Design and Development of Hybrid Instructional Materials. The instructional materials used in hybrid format can be listed under six categories: printed, visual, audio, audio-visual, interactive, objects, and models.

- *Published*: Textbooks, lecture notes, encyclopedias, journals, worksheets/cheatsheets, magazines, booklets, maps, flashcards, brochures, leaflets, letters, documents, reports, etc., can be considered as the primarily printed materials.
- *Visual*: Pictures, illustrations, photos, cartoons, drawings, diagrams, posters, charts, infographics, graphs, puzzles, maps, schema, concept maps, and animated gifs are the primary visual materials used in hybrid learning environments.

- *Audio*: Sound recordings, podcasts, voice books, files in mp3 format, sound clips, conversation recordings, etc., are the primary learning materials in audio format.
- *Audio-Visual*: Video, animation, digital stories, documentaries, movies, cartoon series, video clips, screen recordings, lecture recordings, etc., can fall into the audio-visual instructional materials category.
- *Interactive*: Z-book, interactive videos, virtual museums, simulations, games, online tests, pools, metaverse, etc., are the interactive instructional materials.
- *Objects and Models*: This category consists of the virtual objects and models experienced via VR/AR tools and the actual objects and models.

Microlearning environments and DD-HIM have many common points. The integrated microlearning proposed by Gassler, Hug and Glahn (2004) is based on the ability to pause and pick up where you left off while working with digital tools. In this way, the learner can take a break and have a microlearning experience while using the digital agency for its primary purpose. Microlearning requires a focused learning process in a short period and may require the use of multiple devices (Shail, 2019). Therefore, materials developed in this direction will be essential. The materials to be developed with DD-HIM have the potential to be integrated into micro-learning environments. The hybrid learning materials mentioned above can be used in such short and focused learning environments. For example, podcasts, videos, and small printed materials are among the materials that can be used for microlearning (De Gagne et al., 2019; Kossen; & Ooi, 2021, Lin et al., 2020). It is important that the cognitive load is low in the microlearning process. Therefore, the materials are small in size and allow the learner's self-regulation. DD-HIM can guide material development in this regard.

DD-HIM considers these materials and combines them with three utilization categories: content type, fidelity, and course phase. The materials mentioned above can fall into one or more cells depending on the aim of the course. That's why the authors do not place them strictly in one of the cells. The following framework aims to facilitate the design and development stages for instructional materials of hybrid learning environments. Table 1 demonstrates the details of the framework. The overall categorization has its basis in different fields of study. Content type, fidelity, and course phase are the main classification of the framework. The categorization of the content type is based on Morrison et al.'s (2019) structure. It ranges from facts to attitudes. While defining the cells, their relation to cognitive domain taxonomies was also considered. The classification for fidelity is borrowed from human-computer interaction literature (Rudd et al., 1996). In usability studies, the user can interact with various types of prototypes. A drawing from on a piece of paper represents the low fidelity interface but the functionally working interface is a high fidelity one.

Table 1. DD-HIM framework for face-to-face, online, and blended/hybrid educational environments

		Face-to-face	Online	Blended/Hybrid
By Content Type	Facts	Theory and topic focused Teach topic and provide guidance face-to-face	Balances focus between topic and technology Teach topic with technology Provide guidance online	Balanced modality Teach topic with technology Provide guidance face-to-face
	Concept	Theory and topic focused Teach topic and provide guidance face-to-face	Provide cognitive tools Tools for shared meaning making Provide guidance online	Balanced modality Tools for shared meaning making Provide guidance face-to-face
	Rules/ Principles	Theory and practice together Face-to-face modeling	Technology supported practice	Face-to-face modeling Technology supported practice
	Procedures	Demonstration and practice balanced Monitor and provide timely feedback	Synchronous sessions for monitoring Provide frequent feedback on video-based or portfolio assignments	Technology-supported demonstration Face-to-face modelling Monitor and provide timely feedback On-demand scaffolding
	Interpersonal Skills	Modelling Face-to-face opportunities for communication and collaboration Corrective feedback	Technology enhanced modelling Virtual spaces for communication and collaboration Informative feedback	Modelling (live and technology enhanced Opportunities for communication and collaboration Informative and corrective feedback
	Attitudes	Modelling Monitoring Get feedback (focus group, interview)	Technology enhanced modelling Get feedback (online questionnaires, rating, comments, etc.)	Modelling (live and technology enhanced) Monitoring Get feedback (focus group, interview, online questionnaires, rating, comments, etc.)
		Face-to-face	Online	Blended/Hybrid
By Fidelity	Low	Printed or digitally printed materials Textbooks Hard copy materials	Digitally printed materials	Both Printed and digitally printed materials
	Medium	Face-to-face sessions Technology enhanced materials Software Multimedia materials	Interactive videos Live course sessions	Face-to-face and live course sessions technology embedded activities
	High	Case studies Applications	Simulations Digital games role playing software	Augmented reality Interactive applications and software
		Face-to-face	Online	Blended/Hybrid
By Course Phase	Pre-class	Plan for face-to-face class sessions Plan for face-to-face assessment	Manage and control LMS virtual classroom software Plan for asynchronous, and synchronous course sessions Plan for online assessment	Plan for face-to-face class sessions Manage and control LMS virtual classroom software Decide among face-to-face and online assessment options Plan for assessment
	Class	Face-to-face course sessions	Asynchronous, and synchronous course sessions	Face-to-face, asynchronous, and synchronous course sessions
	Post-class	Face-to-face feedback	Asynchronous, and synchronous feedback	Face-to-face, asynchronous, and synchronous feedback

Having the same perspective, the fidelity considered in this framework is classified into three: low, medium, and high. The course phase classification is inspired from instructional design theories and models (Reigeluth & An, 2020). The instructional design process generally includes the before, during, and follow-up activities. In this framework, the classification is entitled: pre-class, class, and post-class.

In both formal and informal learning environments, it can be advocated that creating an effective learning environment is the goal. With the framework we have proposed, we have tried to provide suggestions for the learner to have a practical experience in every environment. Some principles should be considered for DD-HIM to be more effective. These principles are based on reduced cognitive load and effective use of memory. Since a high focus is required in micro-learning environments in a limited time, it is essential to eliminate the elements that may cause cognitive load. In this way, resources can be used more efficiently. From this point of view, the following principles should be considered during the utilization of the DD-HIM framework for instructional material design and development:

- Decide on the best practical categorization for the delivery of content (face-to-face, online, blended/hybrid). Define the smooth transition whenever necessary (one material can be used for pre-class and post-class, so one should decide on the procedures).
- Decide on the most applicable categorization of DD-HIM (content type, fidelity, course phase), then select the second-order categorization such as fidelity>low, and then focus on the characteristics such as fidelity>low>blended (both printed and digitally printed materials).
- Define the scaffolding structure of the materials. If applicable, provide self-regulation mechanisms such as skipping options with a preliminary quiz.
- Create materials that are adaptable to other categories in the framework. For example, a low fidelity material can be converted into an interactive instructional video or a pre-class material can be converted into a face-to-face interpersonal skills material.
- Always prepare plan-B or provide alternatives for the materials (subtitles, closed caption or scripts, various modalities, skipping features, etc.)
- The set of materials should be complementary to each other in terms of style and content.
- The preparation of materials should be sustainable and budget-friendly.
- Consider prevalent standards such as SCORM.
- Prepare metadata to make the materials accessible to others. Provide information about the difficulty of the material, label the related keywords, etc.
- Mind the intellectual properties, cite whenever necessary, try to include license free design elements.

- Value learner feedback because satisfaction in user experience is important, then revise the material if necessary.
- Provide edited content free from misinformation.
- Mind visual design principles.
- Mind multimedia learning principles.
- Mind the cognitive load theory.
- Mind the social interaction (student-student and student-teacher).
- Mind the user experience (student-content interaction).
- Promote motivation via gamification.
- Benefit from artificial intelligence tools whenever necessary.

CONCLUSION

The message design as a field of study is quite challenging because any new technology brings about its own affordances besides its emergence of side effects. The offered framework can offer a flexible way to integrate available technologies into class regardless of the delivery content. In practice, DD-HIM might require attention to certain case-specific features such as the primary language, available tools, digital literacy levels, equipment, and so on. On the other hand, the utilization of DD-HIM can contribute to the flexible instructional material design. The overall practice might depend on the practitioners, content, and technological background, however, as this is a theoretical framework, it needs to be studied further by researchers.

REFERENCES

Al Fadda, H. (2019). The Relationship between Self-Regulations and Online Learning in an ESL Blended Learning Context. *English Language Teaching*, *12*(6), 87–93. doi:10.5539/elt.v12n6p87

Alkoudmani, R. M., Elkalmi, R. M., Hassali, M. A., & Apolinário-Hagen, J. (2021). The effect of generic medicines e-learning course via Web 2.0 tools on knowledge of pharmacists and pharmacy students. *Pharmacy Education*, *21*, 679–689. doi:10.46542/pe.2021.211.679689

Allen, I. E., & Seaman, J. (2010). Class differences: Online education in the United States, 2010. *Sloan Consortium (NJ1)*.

Alsuwaida, N. (2022). Designing and Evaluating the Impact of Using a Blended Art Course and Web 2.0 Tools in Saudi Arabia. *Journal of Information Technology Education*, *21*, 25. doi:10.28945/4923

Burazer, M., Ebner, M., & Ebner, M. (2020). Implementation of interactive learning objects for German language acquisition in primary school based on learning analytics measurements. EdMedia+ Innovate Learning, Cao, W., Wang, Q., Sbeih, A., & Shibly, F. (2020). Artificial intelligence based efficient smart learning framework for an education platform. *Inteligencia Artificial*, *23*(66), 112–123.

Cope, B., Kalantzis, M., & Searsmith, D. (2021). Artificial intelligence for education: Knowledge and its assessment in AI-enabled learning ecologies. *Educational Philosophy and Theory*, *53*(12), 1229–1245. doi:10.1080/00131857.2020.1728732

Cronje, J. (2020). Towards a new definition of blended learning. *Electronic journal of e-Learning, 18*(2), pp114-121-pp114-121.

Cuban, L. (1986). *Teachers and machines: The classroom use of technology since 1920*. Teachers College Press.

De Gagne, J. C., Park, H. K., Hall, K., Woodward, A., Yamane, S., & Kim, S. S. (2019). Microlearning in health professions education: Scoping review. *JMIR Medical Education*, *5*(2), e13997. doi:10.2196/13997 PMID:31339105

Driscoll, M. (2002). Blended learning: Let's get beyond the hype. *E-learning*, *1*(4), 1–4.

Garrison, D. R., & Kanuka, H. (2004). Blended learning: Uncovering its transformative potential in higher education. *The Internet and Higher Education*, *7*(2), 95–105. doi:10.1016/j.iheduc.2004.02.001

Gassler, G., Hug, T., & Glahn, C. (2004). Integrated Micro Learning–An outline of the basic method and first results. *Interactive computer aided learning, 4*, 1-7.

Gilster, P. (1997). *Digital literacy*. Wiley Computer Pub.

Goda, Y., Yamada, M., Matsuda, T., Kato, H., Saito, Y., & Miyagawa, H. (2023). From adaptive learning support to fading out support for effective self-regulated online learning. In *Research Anthology on Remote Teaching and Learning and the Future of Online Education* (pp. 254–274). IGI Global.

Govender, D. W. (2010). Attitudes of students towards the use of a Learning Management System (LMS) in a face-to-face learning mode of instruction. *Africa Education Review*, *7*(2), 244–262. doi:10.1080/18146627.2010.515394

Graham, C. R. (2006). Blended learning systems. The handbook of blended learning: Global perspectives, local designs, 1, 3-21.

Gumennykova, T., Pankovets, V., Liapa, M., Miziuk, V., Gramatyk, N., & Drahiieva, L. (2020). Applying instructional design methods to improve the effectiveness of blended-learning. *International Journal of Management*, *11*(5).

Helms, S. A. (2014). Blended/hybrid courses: A review of the literature and recommendations for instructional designers and educators. *Interactive Learning Environments*, *22*(6), 804–810. doi:10.1080/10494820.2012.745420

Honebein, P. C., & Honebein, C. H. (2015). Effectiveness, efficiency, and appeal: Pick any two? The influence of learning domains and learning outcomes on designer judgments of useful instructional methods. *Educational Technology Research and Development*, *63*(6), 937–955. doi:10.100711423-015-9396-3

Jensen, J., Smith, C. M., Bowers, R., Kaloi, M., Ogden, T. H., Parry, K. A., Payne, J. S., Fife, P., & Holt, E. (2022). Asynchronous Online Instruction Leads to Learning Gaps When Compared to a Flipped Classroom. *Journal of Science Education and Technology*, *31*(6), 718–729. doi:10.100710956-022-09988-7 PMID:35971508

Kerr, P. (2016). Adaptive learning. *ELT Journal*, *70*(1), 88–93. doi:10.1093/elt/ccv055

Kompen, R. T., Edirisingha, P., Canaleta, X., Alsina, M., & Monguet, J. M. (2019). Personal learning Environments based on Web 2.0 services in higher education. *Telematics and Informatics*, *38*, 194–206. doi:10.1016/j.tele.2018.10.003

Korhonen, A.-M., Ruhalahti, S., & Veermans, M. (2019). The online learning process and scaffolding in student teachers' personal learning environments. *Education and Information Technologies*, *24*(1), 755–779. doi:10.100710639-018-9793-4

Kossen, C., & Ooi, C. Y. (2021). Trialling micro-learning design to increase engagement in online courses. *Asian Association of Open Universities Journal*, *16*(3), 299–310. doi:10.1108/AAOUJ-09-2021-0107

Larsen, T., Tabor, L., & Smith, P. (2020). End of the field? Hacking online and hybrid environments for field-based learning in geography education. *The Journal of Geography*, *120*(1), 3–11. doi:10.1080/00221341.2020.1858325

Lin, J., Sun, G., Cui, T., Shen, J., Xu, D., Beydoun, G., Yu, P., Pritchard, D., Li, L., & Chen, S. (2020). From ideal to reality: Segmentation, annotation, and recommendation, the vital trajectory of intelligent micro learning. *World Wide Web (Bussum)*, *23*(3), 1747–1767. doi:10.100711280-019-00730-9

Linder, K. E. (2017). Fundamentals of hybrid teaching and learning. *New Directions for Teaching and Learning*, *2017*(149), 11–18. doi:10.1002/tl.20222

Liu, M., McKelroy, E., Corliss, S. B., & Carrigan, J. (2017). Investigating the effect of an adaptive learning intervention on students' learning. *Educational Technology Research and Development*, *65*(6), 1605–1625. doi:10.100711423-017-9542-1

Manasrah, A., Masoud, M., & Jaradat, Y. (2021). Short videos, or long videos? A study on the ideal video length in online learning. 2021 international conference on information technology (ICIT), Mayer, R. E. (2002). Multimedia learning. [). Elsevier.]. *Psychology of Learning and Motivation*, *41*, 85–139.

McCleary-Gaddy, A., Yu, E. T., & Spears, R. D. (2022). In-Person, Remote, or Hybrid Instruction? A Quality Improvement Assessment of a Six Week Interprofessional Education Pathway Program for Undergraduate Pre-Health Students. *Health Care*, *10*(12), 2399. Advance online publication. doi:10.3390/healthcare10122399 PMID:36553922

Moore, M. G., & Kearsley, G. (2011). *Distance education: A systems view of online learning*. Cengage Learning.

Morrison, G. R., Ross, S. J., Morrison, J. R., & Kalman, H. K. (2019). *Designing effective instruction*. John Wiley & Sons.

Mozahem, N. A. (2020). Using learning management system activity data to predict student performance in face-to-face courses. [IJMBL]. *International Journal of Mobile and Blended Learning*, *12*(3), 20–31. doi:10.4018/IJMBL.2020070102

Nagao, K., & Nagao, K. (2019). Artificial intelligence in education. *Artificial Intelligence Accelerates Human Learning: Discussion Data Analytics*, 1-17.

Nakamura, J., & Csikszentmihalyi, M. (2009). Flow theory and research. Handbook of positive psychology, 195, 206.

Nkambou, R., Mizoguchi, R., & Bourdeau, J. (2010). *Advances in intelligent tutoring systems* (Vol. 308). Springer Science & Business Media. doi:10.1007/978-3-642-14363-2

Norman, S., & Porter, D. (2007). Designing Learning Objects for online learning.

Onofrei, G., & Ferry, P. (2020). Reusable learning objects: A blended learning tool in teaching computer-aided design to engineering undergraduates. *International Journal of Educational Management*, *34*(10), 1559–1575. doi:10.1108/IJEM-12-2019-0418

Orehovački, T., Bubaš, G., & Kovačić, A. (2012). Taxonomy of Web 2.0 applications with educational potential. *Transformation in teaching: Social media strategies in higher education*, 43-72.

Ouyang, F., Wu, M., Zheng, L., Zhang, L., & Jiao, P. (2023). Integration of artificial intelligence performance prediction and learning analytics to improve student learning in online engineering course. *International Journal of Educational Technology in Higher Education*, *20*(1), 1–23. doi:10.118641239-022-00372-4 PMID:36683653

Papastergiou, M., & Mastrogiannis, I. (2021). Design, development and evaluation of open interactive learning objects for secondary school physical education. *Education and Information Technologies*, *26*(3), 2981–3007. doi:10.100710639-020-10390-2

Pollock, N. B. (2022). Student performance and perceptions of anatomy and physiology across face-to-face, hybrid, and online teaching lab styles. *Advances in Physiology Education*, *46*(3), 453–460. doi:10.1152/advan.00074.2022 PMID:35759525

Rafique, G. M., Mahmood, K., Warraich, N. F., & Rehman, S. U. (2021). Readiness for Online Learning during COVID-19 pandemic: A survey of Pakistani LIS students. *Journal of Academic Librarianship*, *47*(3), 102346. doi:10.1016/j.acalib.2021.102346 PMID:36536686

Rapanta, C., Botturi, L., Goodyear, P., Guàrdia, L., & Koole, M. (2021). Balancing technology, pedagogy and the new normal: Post-pandemic challenges for higher education. *Postdigital Science and Education*, *3*(3), 715–742. doi:10.100742438-021-00249-1

Reigeluth, C. M. (2016). Instructional theory and technology for the new paradigm of education. *Revista de Educación a Distancia (RED)*(50).

Reigeluth, C. M., & An, Y. (2020). *Merging the instructional design process with learner-centered theory: The holistic 4D model*. Routledge. doi:10.4324/9781351117548

Reiser, R. (2012). *A history of instructional desgin and technology In?" from Trends and Issues in Instructional Design and Technology, Saddle River*. Pearson.

Reiser, R. A. (2012). A history of instructional design and technology. In J. V. D. R. A. Reiser (Ed.), *Trends and issues in instructional design and technology* (Vol. 3). Pearson Education.

Rizvi, S., Rienties, B., & Khoja, S. A. (2019). The role of demographics in online learning; A decision tree based approach. *Computers & Education*, *137*, 32–47. doi:10.1016/j.compedu.2019.04.001

Rudd, J., Stern, K., & Isensee, S. (1996). Low vs. high-fidelity prototyping debate. *interactions*, *3*(1), 76-85.

Saettler, P. (1990). The evolution of American educational technology. *Englewood, Col.: Libraries unlim.*

Saettler, P. (2004). *The evolution of American educational technology.* IAP.

Saito, D. S., & Ulbricht, V. R. (2012). Learning Managent Systems and Face-to-Face Teaching in Bilingual Modality (Libras/Portuguese). *Revista IEEE América Latina, 10*(5), 2168–2174. doi:10.1109/TLA.2012.6362362

Sanpanich, N. (2021). Investigating Factors Affecting Students' Attitudes toward Hybrid Learning. *Reflections: The SoL Journal, 28*(2), 208–227.

Selber, S., & Selber, S. A. (2004). *Multiliteracies for a digital age.* SIU Press.

Sendurur, E. (2022). Öğretme ve Öğrenme Aracı Olarak Teknolojik Araçlar-Programlar-Projeler. In S. D. K. N. Demirci Saygı (Ed.), *Dijitalleşme ve Eğitim* (Vol. 1). Eğiten Kitap.

Seo, K., Tang, J., Roll, I., Fels, S., & Yoon, D. (2021). The impact of artificial intelligence on learner–instructor interaction in online learning. *International Journal of Educational Technology in Higher Education, 18*(1), 1–23. doi:10.118641239-021-00292-9 PMID:34778540

Shail, M. S. (2019). Using micro-learning on mobile applications to increase knowledge retention and work performance: A review of literature. *Cureus, 11*(8). Advance online publication. doi:10.7759/cureus.5307 PMID:31511813

Sun, Z., Anbarasan, M., & Praveen Kumar, D. (2021). Design of online intelligent English teaching platform based on artificial intelligence techniques. *Computational Intelligence, 37*(3), 1166–1180. doi:10.1111/coin.12351

Sweller, J., van Merriënboer, J. J., & Paas, F. (2019). Cognitive architecture and instructional design: 20 years later. *Educational Psychology Review, 31*(2), 261–292. doi:10.100710648-019-09465-5

Topali, P., & Mikropoulos, T. A. (2019). Digital learning objects for teaching computer programming in primary students. Technology and Innovation in Learning, Teaching and Education: First International Conference, TECH-EDU 2018, Thessaloniki, Greece, June 20–22, 2018, Revised Selected Papers 1, Unal, E., & Cakir, H. (2021). The effect of technology-supported collaborative problem solving method on students' achievement and engagement. *Education and Information Technologies, 26*(4), 4127–4150.

Vanbecelaere, S., Van den Berghe, K., Cornillie, F., Sasanguie, D., Reynvoet, B., & Depaepe, F. (2020). The effectiveness of adaptive versus non-adaptive learning with digital educational games. *Journal of Computer Assisted Learning, 36*(4), 502–513. doi:10.1111/jcal.12416

Watson, J. (2008). *Blended Learning: The Convergence of Online and Face-to-Face Education. Promising Practices in Online Learning*. North American Council for Online Learning.

Wiley, D. A. (2000). Connecting learning objects to instructional design theory: A definition, a metaphor, and a taxonomy. *The instructional use of learning objects, 2830*(435), 1-35.

Yang, Y. T. C., Gamble, J. H., Hung, Y. W., & Lin, T. Y. (2014). An online adaptive learning environment for critical-thinking-infused E nglish literacy instruction. *British Journal of Educational Technology, 45*(4), 723–747. doi:10.1111/bjet.12080

Yustika, G. P., & Iswati, S. (2020). Digital literacy in formal online education: A short review. *Dinamika Pendidikan, 15*(1), 66–76. doi:10.15294/dp.v15i1.23779

Zheng, M., Bender, D., & Lyon, C. (2021). Online learning during COVID-19 produced equivalent or better student course performance as compared with pre-pandemic: Empirical evidence from a school-wide comparative study. *BMC Medical Education, 21*(1), 1–11. doi:10.118612909-021-02909-z PMID:34530828

Chapter 3
Fostering Pedagogical Innovation in Tourism Education Through Experiential Learning:
An Interdisciplinary Toolkit

Dr Sandra Vieira Vasconcelos
iD https://orcid.org/0000-0003-4062-331X
School of Hospitality and Tourism,
Polytechnic of Porto, Portugal

António Melo
School of Hospitality and Tourism,
Polytechnic of Porto, Portugal

Carla Melo
iD https://orcid.org/0000-0003-3097-4108
School of Hospitality and Tourism,
Polytechnic of Porto, Portugal

ABSTRACT

Due to its service-oriented nature, Tourism and Hospitality Education relies heavily on experimental learning (EL) approaches, that focus on real-word challenges and can replicate future professional settings. In addition to simulation, project-based learning, fieldtrips and role-play, educators are looking for alternative and innovative strategies to enhance students' learning experiences and support the development of technical and high-level skills. Recognizing the importance of EL, and aiming to contribute towards its development, and support practitioners working in Tourism Higher Education, this chapter focuses on the development of a toolkit that supports activities within this scope. Drawing from a literature and best practice review and their experience, the authors expand on Kolb's experiential learning cycle's model to frame the toolkit's principles and key concepts and describe its creation process, the target audience, and overall sections, that will include different tourism and hospitality subsectors, offering a provisional glimpse of the artefact being created.

DOI: 10.4018/978-1-6684-8656-6.ch003

INTRODUCTION

The development of technical and transversal skills is a fundamental component of Tourism and Hospitality Higher Education (THE), not only because the industry is contingent on service and personal interaction, but also because most programs assume some kind of practical training, which might take place in classes (theoretical and/or practical) seminars and workshops, or on-the-job, e.g., through work placements. Nevertheless, despite this assumption and the perceived importance of practical skills within this scope, there is an ongoing debate on what some scholars consider to be the "vocational nature of tourism" programs, as opposed to more "credible" academic subjects (Roberts, 2022, p. 1), which has led to several discussions within THE institutions as to achieve balanced solutions that can somehow address these questions, but also meet students and the industry's needs.

Considering the key role of teachers and THE providers, these challenges are also prompting the development of initiatives that can foster innovation and pedagogical capacity building, as well as interdisciplinary collaboration and experiential learning. Drawing from this premise and aiming to support other practitioners, in this chapter authors outline the "IN_SPIRE – Sharing Best Practices in Tourism Education" project, an interdisciplinary toolkit whose key goals are to: 1) promote pedagogical innovation, through the dissemination of good practices in the scope of THE and training; 2) contribute to teacher training in the area of HE pedagogy and experiential teaching/learning within the scope of THE; 3) create a dynamic repository of resources that allows teachers of tourism, hospitality and catering to access and share methodologies, strategies, materials and tools that can further support their teaching practices; 4) reflect on the current state of THE and training, thus contributing towards the development of this scientific area and its assertion in the academic and social contexts.

Recognizing the importance of EL, interdisciplinarity and collaboration, this chapter will focus on the development of the toolkit, outlining the underlying theoretical framework and describing its main components, which will include general guidelines for educators/ practitioners, expected outcomes, topics and activities (featuring projects, strategies, plans, materials and tools) and other resources, while providing the authors' insights on the project and its different implementation stages. Considering the project is currently on an ideation stage, the chapter will also include a future work section.

BACKGROUND

Defined as "the process whereby knowledge is created through the transformation of experience" (Kolb, 2014), experiential learning (EL) is an widely used educational approach that, despite its limitations, is considered to promote active learning through direct experience and contact with specific subjects and settings. It involves learning by doing, reflection on the experience and applying that knowledge in other situations, going beyond traditional classroom-based instruction.

Considered to be the father of experiential learning (concomitantly with John Dewey) (Luthuli et al., 2019), in 1984 David Kolb, following in the footsteps of Lewin, Dewey and Piaget, published his Experiential Learning Theory, laying the grounds for future researchers and educational theories. Based on the link "between theory and practice" (Hyasat, 2022, p. 293) and the concept of concrete experience, this theory emphasizes the importance of involving individuals in learning processes, following an iterative and "holistic integrative" four-stage cycle (Figure 1).

Figure 1. Kolb's EL cycle
(Kolb, 2104, p.90)

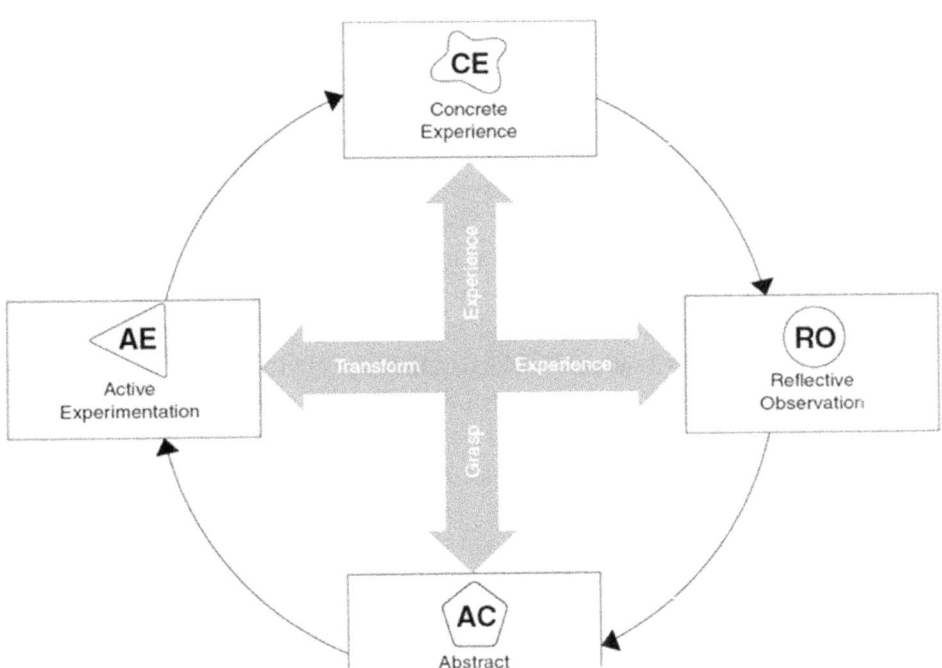

According to this theory, when placed within specific settings having to interact with a concrete experience or challenge (i.e., a first-hand experience involving a real-life situation, event or activity), students are required to observe and reflect on what they learnt, conceptualizing and making sense of that experience. This process of 'abstract conceptualization' (stage 3) in which students "reflect, describe, communicate, and learn from their experiences", allows them to link concepts and theories as to "draw conclusions from past and present experiences", leading up to new ideas, which can then be applied in new situations, adding to previous experiences ('active experimentation'), (Wong & Wong, 2009, p. 25), with the cycle repeating itself "adding direct experience content in knowledge acquisition" (Huertas-Valdivia, 2021, p. 2).

Despite its importance and widespread adoption in education, since its development, Kolb's experiential learning theory has been the subject of discussion, resulting in multiple revisions intending to further refine it. In addition to Kolb, who has revisited his theory overtime as to include additional dimensions and elements (Gencel et al., 2021; A. Y. Kolb & Kolb, 2005; D. A. Kolb, 2014), and developing a rubric for EL highlighting the role of Learning Spaces and Educator Role Profiles (Gencel et al., 2021), authors such as Roger Greenway, also expended Kolb's work by further refining the experiential learning cycle and exploring the role of reflection within this setting.

Referring to the concept of "dynamic debriefing" as learners "expressing, examining, and exploring their experiences in ways that enable them to learn, grow, develop and make changes in their lives (Greenaway, 2007, p. 61) developed additional frameworks as to support the role of educators and facilitate experiential learning. Also subject of discussion was the concept of concrete experience within the framework. Considered to be the "basis for observations and reflections" (Kolb, 2014, p. 64), this concept was recently reviewed by Morris, who, based on a systematic review, further elaborates on the concept describing it as a "highly contextualised, primary, experience that involves hands on learner experience in uncontrived real-world situations" (Morris, 2020, p. 1070). Referring to the need to interact with people, the author points out the fact by working in these contexts, students must not only engage in different levels, but also collaborate, thus reinforcing the social and interactive nature of the learning cycles, something that had also been previously highlighted by Jarvis (2012). These revisions on the theory reflect its dynamic nature, also extending to its application in a wide variety of fields and its adaptation to contemporary educational practices and challenges.

Experiential Learning in THE

EL's scope and focus on real-life, practical settings had led to its "widespread application [...] in tourism and hospitality education" (Kee & Zhang, 2022, p. 8). Considering its potential to "explore the integration of theory and practice into curriculum design to develop positive educational outcomes", Kee and Zhang (2022), drawing on the work of Dredge et al (2011) and Tribe, considers that EL approaches can empower and engage students, ultimately leading to behavioural changes. A "a core research topic in many studies on hospitality and tourism education", EL can promote "a greater level of real-life business contexts, compared to "traditional, lecture-based learning" (Kim & Jeong, 2018, p. 120), bridging the gap between theory and practice. In addition to internships (Lyu et al., 2016; Yiu & Law, 2012), a staple of tourism education, other EL activities such as field trips (Arcodia et al., 2021; Bidder et al., 2019; González-Herrera & Giralt-Escobar, 2021; Sanders & Armstrong, 2008; Sotomayor, 2021; Wong & Wong, 2009), role-plays and simulations (Armstrong, 2003; Dicen et al., 2019; Guachalla & Gledhill, 2019; Huertas-Valdivia, 2021; Ruhanen, 2005), job fairs (Beam, 2016; Hertzman et al., 2015; Lee et al., 2020) have been widely discussed in the literature having been found to hold great potential when it comes to preparing students' for the "the changing requirements of the job" (van Laar et al., 2017, p. 577), which now require them to develop a wider range of skills (both technical and transversal) (OECD, 2019; Skills, 2009) . As a result, "experiential, practical, and participative experience [have] become a mandatory requirement for the educational models and curricula for different university studies" (González-Herrera & Giralt-Escobar, 2021, p. 471).

Nevertheless, despite this "recent increase in research on experiential learning for the field of tourism studies" (Xie, 2004, p. 101) (Xie), and its widespread application by THE institutions (Askren & James, 2021), questions remain on how experiential learning best contribute to tourism courses making it necessary to carry out further research within this scope.

METHODOLOGY

In this chapter, authors aim to document the ongoing development of an interdisciplinary toolkit for THE.

With the goal of supporting practitioners working in this field, they adopted a holistic approach, based on interdisciplinarity, as to collect and present contributions from a team of teachers working within different HE programs specializing in different tourism subsectors, that would, at the same time, encompass experiential learning principles, and support practitioners within this scope.

Drawing from a literature and best practice review and their experience as teachers and educational researchers, the authors expand on Kolb's experiential learning cycle's model, as to outline the conceptual framework underpinning the development of the toolkit. Thus, the methodology is practiced-based, reflecting the toolkit's iterative nature, being aligned with action research (Cohen et al., 2018), best practice research (Vesely & others, 2011) and design-based approaches, involving "processes of development, improvement and continuous learning" (Dewar & Sharp, 2006, p. 221). Data collection was carried out using documentary research, observation and checklists, with future work being expected to include focus-groups and interviews, particularly in the project's piloting stage.

"IN_SPIRE – SHARING BEST PRACTICES IN TOURISM EDUCATION"

Defined as "a set of tools [...] used for a particular purpose" (Oxford English Dictionary), an educational toolkit can be considered a collection of resources, materials and strategies whose goal is to support teaching and learning in a specific field/subject. Aimed at educators, educational toolkits can have different goals, taking on different forms, ranging from curriculum guides, reference materials and lesson plans, to activities and assessment tools, that can be available either online or in a physical format (i.e., as a textbook or practical handbook, for example).

Considering the previously established need to carry out further research regarding EL and its application in THE, the growing need to foster pedagogical innovation, and stimulate the development of students' essential skills, encouraging their active involvement in active/experimental activities that mirror real settings, the authors set out to develop a toolkit that could help disseminate what they consider to be best practices in THE, and support other educators, ultimately aiming to scaffold the creation of communities of practice that can help advance THE. The development of this toolkit stemmed from a wide variety of conditions, that made it possible to identify existing gaps and areas for development in THE and training. In the last three academic years the authors have been involved in a wide range of projects which have set the tone and helped to identify this growing need, which they propose to meet with the IN_SPIRE toolkit.

These initiatives, which included the feedback from students (namely, in debriefing session and end of semester questionnaires), contacts with stakeholders and participation in specialized discussion forums, as well as previous research work developed by the authors, followed different methodological approaches and can be considered good practices within the scope of THE. From these, the authors have highlighted four projects which are relevant to the analysis at hand: 1) Tourism and Sustainability: From Theory to Practice (3 editions); 2) Interdisciplinary Project (IP@...) (2 editions); 3) Soft Skills and Tourism; and 4) "Rota dos Sabores: a gastronomic and cultural event" (5 editions).

The project 'Sustainability and Tourism: From theory to practice' is a project framed in the Education for Sustainability approach (EfS), in which students are challenged to research, reflect and develop content of different nature (texts, posters, podcasts, videos, etc.) on the topic of sustainability in tourism, both from the perspective of demand and supply. The development of the project is supported by a set of activities, such as webinars, discussion and feedback sessions and interviews with companies, among others, with the content created by the students being published on a blog created for this purpose.

The project 'IP@...' was developed in 2021-2022 and 2022-2023, with the collaboration of two different partners. In the first edition, the students collaborated with ATA (Village Tourism Association – IP@ATA) in the development of an innovative tourism experience and its marketing strategy. In the second year, the project partner was the CIPVV (Wine Interpretation and Promotion Centre – IP@ CIPVV), that challenged the groups to develop a wine tourism route, oriented to specific market segments, as well as its marketing strategy. Following an initial presentation by the partner, in which it presented challenges to the students, several feedback sessions were held throughout the semester, with both teachers and experts. The students were required to make two project pitches, the first to discuss the 'product' idea, and the final one to present their project. Field trips and thematic seminars were also organized, to provide an immersive experience of the destination/ local community.

The project 'Soft Skills and Tourism', which was carried out in 2020 (2nd semester), aimed at providing a snapshot of the relevance of soft skills for tourism professionals, and the perceived differences stemming from specific activities, such as accommodation, events, travel agents, restaurants, and so on. The theme was selected due to its relevance for students and because it was perceived as cross-cutting. It combined contents of 5 different courses. Besides a literature review, students had to conduct a set of interviews with professionals from different fields as to identify the most relevant soft skills within each tourism subsector. They were then challenged to develop a short paper, in which they presented the findings of their research.

Lastly, the project 'Rota dos Sabores: A Gastronomic and Cultural Event'. Having been initiated in 2018/2019 this project involves students attending a Hotel Operations Management curricular unit, who are challenged to organize a gastronomic event focussing on different countries/cuisines. Working in groups of 4-5, students must develop, participate, organize, plan, and evaluate the various tasks inherent to the management and operation of the event (concept, logistics, resource allocation, resource management, budgeting costs and revenue, communication, and promotion of the event for 60-80 persons). The event will then be held and assessed considering the different stages, as well as the final outcome. By resorting to a role-play methodology and simulated practices that require an active participation, this project requires students to be deeply implicated and engaged in their own learning and assessment, at the same time it fosters their creativity and autonomy.

Table 1 summarizes some of the most relevant aspects of the projects listed as well as the lessons learnt, i.e., reflections that have led to development of the

Table 1. Aspects of projects

	Methodology/ Approach	Outcomes/ Skills	Lessons Learnt	Potential Inputs for the IN_SPIRE toolkit	Published Research
Sustainability and Tourism: From theory to practice	Interdisciplinarity Project-based Learning Multimodality	Holistic overview of Sustainable Development Teamwork Communication Creativity Critical Thinking Time management Decision-making	Importance of (formative) feedback and of multicriteria assessment	Templates Guidelines	Vasconcelos, S., Melo, C., (2023). Vasconcelos, S., & Melo, C. (2022). Vasconcelos, S., Melo, A., Melo, C., & Mouta, C. (2022).
IP@...	Interdisciplinarity Project-based Learning Experiential learning University-Industry Collaboration Co-creation	Complementarity of CU contents Networking Creativity Decision-making	Importance of partner involvement, field trips, immersive experiences and U-I collaboration (rhythm, expectations, involvement)	Step-by-step guidelines Collaboration Agreements	Melo, C., Mouta, C., Pereira, P. (2023). Melo, C., Mouta, C., Pereira, P. (2023a). Melo, C., Mouta, C., Pereira, P. (2022).
Soft Skills and Tourism	Interdisciplinarity Stakeholder involvement Collaboration	Soft Skills Awareness and development Networking Employability Academic Writing	Time management Articulation between CU	Templates Support materials Replicability potential	Vasconcelos, S., Melo, A., Melo, C., Liberato, D., & Lopes, M.C. (2022a). Vasconcelos, S., Melo, C., Melo, A., & Liberato, D. (2022b). Vasconcelos, S., Melo, C., Melo, A., & Liberato, D. (2022c). Melo, A., Melo, C., Vasconcelos, S., Liberato, D. & Lopes, M.C. (2021).
Rota dos Sabores	Role-play Simulation	Internal Communication, Commitment, Research, Involvement, Task completion Teamwork, Focus on Goals	Improved the creativity, professional abilities, and skills of the students	Event planning checklist, Assessment tools for guest satisfaction	Melo, A., Melo, C., Vasconcelos, S. (2023).

toolkit and potential inputs for the project. The publications/communications on these initiatives are also listed, thus demonstrating the existence of research that can scaffold the design and implement the toolkit.

All the projects reinforced the importance of a careful and timely planning, the provision of guidelines, templates, plannings and checklist, timelines and step-by-step guidance from the teachers involved.

Based on the forementioned premises, as well as on the described experiences, the toolkit (whose acronym – IN_Spire – stands for "Sharing Best Practices in Tourism Education") was designed as to act as potential catalyst for learning and sharing to be implemented in different stages, each of which adding on to previous work. Based on the concepts of interdisciplinarity (integrating contributions from different areas of knowledge and a wide range of technical and transversal skills), multimodality (referring to the diversity of experiences and strategies presented, and its hybrid format) adaptability (with the resources/materials presented being adaptable and customizable, hence making them applicable to different teaching levels and settings), this toolkit, currently on its ideation stage, is expected to be developed in 3 Phases, depicted in Figure 2.

Figure 2. IN_Spire: toolkit's iterative implementation phases
(Source: authors)

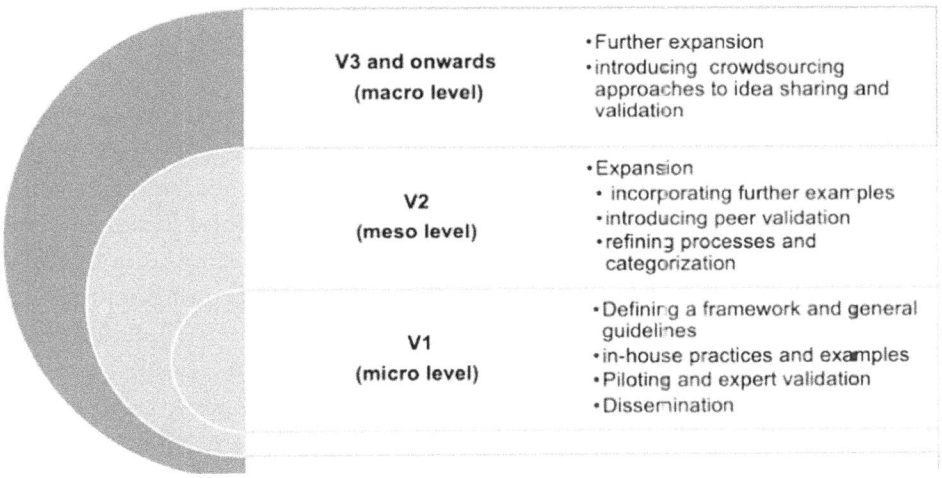

Arising from the need to foster innovation, research and share best practices in THE, as well as from the growing importance of the sector and the emergence of technologies that promote and facilitate interactive and simulation practices, this toolkit intends to be dynamic and flexible, as mirrored by its implementation stages (corresponding to the 2023-2024; 2024-2025 and 2025-2026 academic years). It is, therefore, an iterative project that aims at the continuous improvement, being open to different themes/activities and contributions.

Stage 1 – Framework, guidelines and platform development

The first stage will focus on activities developed at ESHT (School of Hospitality and Tourism – Polytechnic of Porto, Portugal) (micro-level) as to disseminate best practices and set an example/model for future work, as well as promote reflection on EL in THE. In addition to collecting and selecting content to be integrated into the toolkit, in this stage authors will also create the first version of the digital platform (website) supporting the project, and of the first physical artefact (comprising a textbook and activity cards).

The idea originated at ESHT (see Table 1) following a set of initiatives that made it possible for the authors to identify a set of activities considered to be innovative and effective in what concerns the engagement of students, collaboration (of students and teachers), interdisciplinarity, and the use of active learning methodologies (including, but not limited to, simulation, project-based learning, co-creation and role-play). Having carried out research on THE and their own teaching practices, authors believed that their experience and reflections could inspire other practitioners, having decided to join forces as to create a dynamic repository that could facilitate strategy and material sharing and discussion with a broader community.

Drawing from their experience and based on observation and documentary evidence (stemming from previous research and data collected though questionnaires and interviews to stakeholders), they designed a project which involved creating a platform that could provide a rationale for this initiative and act as a dynamic space for sharing and discussion. Having agreed on a timeline, they then established key theoretical concepts, having agreed on adopting EL-based methods and principles, as to support the creation of the toolkit. Following this initial ideation stage (currently being concluded), they proceeded to define the goals and structure of the toolkit (described in the following sections, that are to embody its underlying concepts: interdisciplinarity, multimodality and adaptability. As a result, the creation process was collaborative and practice-based, being consistent with design-based approaches.

Key Sections

Considering the previous sections and underlying rationale, the toolkit is to include the following sections: General guidelines for Educators and Practitioners (section 1); Expected Outcomes (section 2); Topics and Activities (section 3) and Other Resources (section 4).

Section 1: General guidelines for Educators/ Practitioners

Reflecting the principles and rubrics of EL, this section will include the outline of the toolkit, detailing and explaining the different sections and offering insights on how to navigate them, as well as put forward key concepts. In addition, based on current tourism and hospitality professionals' profiles and skills frameworks (OECD, 2019; Skills, 2009), this section will also include a skill an activity matrix, supporting its future use in different settings and levels.

Section 2: Expected Outcomes

According to the previously defined objectives (see introduction), this toolkit is expected to achieve significant impacts. This section will expand on those impacts both from the teachers' and the students' perspectives. Regarding the impacts on teachers, it is expected that the toolkit will raise awareness towards innovative and student-centered methodologies, motivating a change in paradigms and fostering the adoption of innovative pedagogical approaches which are aligned with current trends and recommendations. Simultaneously, by acting as a repository, it is expected that the toolkit facilitates access to systematized and annotated information about methodologies within EL, enhancing its application on a larger scale, by a greater number of teachers, which can potentially have an impact on future research.

From the students' point of view, the toolkit is expected to positively impact their engagement, also developing their grasp on content.

These impacts will be measured and assessed throughout the project's different implementation stages, based on feedback, number of visits to the website, learning analytics, questionnaires, and focus-groups.

Section 3: Topics and Activities

Presenting the teachers/trainers' contributions, this section will feature different projects, strategies, lesson plans, materials and tools, being organized into 3 key areas: Tourism, Hospitality and Catering. Based on the authors' contributions (each author is expected to submit 1-2 activities/items, stemming from their own practices), these activities will then be grouped and classified according to different categories: subsector; targeted skill; and type of activity/approach (i.e., simulation, role-play, laboratory, field project, and so on). In addition, using a template, authors proposing these activities must also describe them, detailing the expected learning outcomes, step-by-step implementation, assessment strategies used and their insights on the activity. When applicable, upon discussion, each item can also include a list of additional suggestions/alternatives, that can support its application in other settings.

Section 4: Other Resources

To be included in the *meso* and *macro* implementation stages (see Figure 2), these sections will feature additional resources found in the literature. This section is expected to act as an annotated list of activities, reflecting the insights of the authors and other practitioners. The activities will be grouped according to their application (area and subsector) targeted skills and intended outcomes.

Phase 2 – Material Selection and Categorization

As mentioned in the previous sections, all the items submitted to the toolkit, must comply with previously defined standard and guidelines and will undergo peer review. In Phase 1, considering the items will be put forward by the authors, this process will be conducted in-house, i.e, by the team working on the toolkit, which will discuss their validity and the ensuing categorization process. This discussion will be instrumental and defining procedures for phases 1 and 2, acting as a benchmark for future work. In addition to the afore-mentioned template, each item must also be in line with the Principles of EL: Intention, Preparedness and Planning, Authenticity, Reflection, Orientation and Training, Monitoring and Continuous Improvement, Assessment and Evaluation and Acknowledgment (Experiential, 1998).

Phases 3 and 4 – Validation and Implementation

In addition to internal peer review and discussion, the materials included in the *beta* and subsequent versions of the toolkit will also be validated by experts. With the first version of the toolkit (both in physical and digital, online format) being expected to be completed in June 2024, this validation is expected to take place in conferences and special sessions, as well as meeting with stakeholders, both prior and after this date. Moreover, the validation process is part of a wider dissemination strategy that will include publications in academic papers discussing different component and practices included in the toolkit, publications and presentation on professional/ sectorial magazines and newsletters, a project kick-off events with practitioners and industry representatives, as well as other events aiming to showcase the beta version, upon its release. Some of these sessions/meetings are also expected to act as piloting sections, giving other educators the opportunity to test and discuss the activities proposed, with their feedback and recommendations being collected using questionnaires and checklists. This feedback will then be taken into account when working on future versions of the toolkit, that ae to be developed in 2024-2025 and 2025-2026 schoolyears (versions 2 and 3, respectively).

FUTURE RESEARCH DIRECTIONS

Considering the different development phases, future work will include working on its creation and the expected snowball effect on practitioners and other educators. Considering the proposed timeline, current priorities include concluding stage 1, regarding guidelines and setting up the website (platform). At the moment, in addition to weekly project meetings, authors are also working on their proposals for the toolkit, making it necessary to work on the final design (deciding what to include and whether there will be limits). All those decisions will be contingent on the proposals. Future research should reflect this collaborative process and ensuing categorization and design stages, putting forward examples that can inspire others and be validated by experts. Overall, the project is expected to produce a snowball effect, growing organically with the support of the community.

CONCLUSION

Currently in an early stage of development, the IN_SPIRE toolkit will consist of a theoretical framework and wide range of annotated resources and materials that not only reflect the researchers' experience and teaching practices but can also inform similar initiatives within the scope of THE. Bearing in mind recent trends and market needs, in addition to guidance and practical suggestions, this toolkit will also provide an interdisciplinary outlook on the different resources and their potential application and impact on skill development.

Meeting the need of adopting active learning strategies and bridging the gap between theory and practice, the toolkit has the potential to support tourism educators and practitioners in developing and implementing activities that are aligned with current trends, as well as with key principles of EL. Moreover, it is also expected to have an impact on students' technical and transferable skills, thus meeting both the industry and academia's demands and challenges, being aligned with current expectations from both areas. Dynamic, hands-on and committed to continuous improvement, it will augment the potential of THE, reflecting positively on faculty, institutions and ultimately students, as all can benefit from the activities and discussion resulting from the project.

REFERENCES

Arcodia, C., Abreu Novais, M., Cavlek, N., & Humpe, A. (2021). Educational tourism and experiential learning: Students' perceptions of field trips. *Tourism Review*, *76*(1), 241–254. doi:10.1108/TR-05-2019-0155

Armstrong, E. K. (2003). Applications of role-playing in tourism management teaching: An evaluation of a learning method. *Journal of Hospitality, Leisure, Sport and Tourism Education*, *2*(1), 5–16. doi:10.3794/johlste.21.24

Askren, J., & James, W. (2021). Experiential Learning Methods in Culinary Course Can Bridge the Gap: Student Perceptions on How Hands-On Curriculum Prepares Them for Industry. *Journal of Hospitality \& Tourism Education, 33*(2), 111–125. doi:10.1080/10963758.2020.1791134

Beam, E. A. (2016). Do job fairs matter? Experimental evidence on the impact of job-fair attendance. *Journal of Development Economics*, *120*, 32–40. https://doi.org/ https://doi.org/10.1016/j.jdeveco.2015.11.004. doi:10.1016/j.jdeveco.2015.11.004 PMID:34712002

Bidder, C., Kibat, S. A., & Johnny, C. (2019). Tourism Education: Students' Perceived Values of Field Trips. In A. N. Mat Noor, Z. Z. Mohd Zakuan, & S. Muhamad Noor (Eds.), *Proceedings of the Second International Conference on the Future of ASEAN (ICoFA) 2017 - Volume 1* (pp. 135–143). Springer Singapore.

Cohen, L., Manion, L., & Morrison, K. (2018). *Research Methods in Education* (8th ed.). Routledge.

Dewar, B., & Sharp, C. (2006). Using evidence: How action learning can support individual and organisational learning through action research. *Educational Action Research*, *14*(2), 219–237. doi:10.1080/09650790600718092

Dicen, K. B., Yodsuwan, C., Butcher, K., & Mingkwan, N. (2019). The institutional context for experiential learning investment in hospitality education: A case study from Thailand. *Tourism Education and Asia*, 143–160.

Experiential, E. S. for. (1998). *Eight Principles of Good Practice for All Experiential Learning Activities*. Eight Principles of Good Practice for All Experiential Learning Activities - Society for Experiential Education.

Gencel, I. E., Erdogan, M., Kolb, A. Y., & Kolb, D. A. (2021). Rubric for Experiential Training. *International Journal of Progressive Education*, *17*(4), 188–211. doi:10.29329/ijpe.2021.366.13

González-Herrera, M.-R., & Giralt-Escobar, S. (2021). Tourism Experiential Learning Through Academic Field Trips in Higher Education: A Case Study of Copper Canyon (Mexico). *Tourism: An International Interdisciplinary Journal*, *69*(4), 471–493. doi:10.37741/t.69.4.1

Greenaway, R. (2007). Dynamic debriefing. In M. L. Silberman (Ed.), *The Handbook of Experiential Learning* (pp. 59–80). John Wiley & Sons.

Guachalla, A., & Gledhill, M. (2019). Co-creating learning experiences to support student employability in travel and tourism. *Journal of Hospitality, Leisure, Sport and Tourism Education*, *25*, 100210. https://doi.org/https://doi.org/10.1016/j.jhlste.2019.100210. doi:10.1016/j.jhlste.2019.100210

Hertzman, J. L., Moreo, A. P., & Wiener, P. J. (2015). Career Planning Strategies and Skills of Hospitality Management Students. *Journal of Human Resources in Hospitality \& Tourism, 14*(4), 423–443. doi:10.1080/15332845.2015.1002071

Huertas-Valdivia, I. (2021). Role-Playing a staffing process: Experiential learning with undergraduate tourism students. *Journal of Hospitality, Leisure, Sport and Tourism Education*, *29*, 100334. https://doi.org/https://doi.org/10.1016/j.jhlste.2021.100334. doi:10.1016/j.jhlste.2021.100334

Hyasat, A. S. (2022). The Experiential Learning Theory as Base for Tourism and Hospitality Courses and Internship Programs. *Indian Journal of Economics and Business*, *21*(1), 291–303.

Jamal, T., Taillon, J., & Dredge, D. (2011). Sustainable tourism pedagogy and academic-community collaboration: A progressive service-learning approach. *Tourism and Hospitality Research*, *11*(2), 133–147. doi:10.1057/thr.2011.3

Jarvis, P. (2012). *Adult learning in the social context* (Vol. 78). Routledge. doi:10.4324/9780203802724

Kee, T., & Zhang, H. (2022). Digital Experiential Learning for Sustainable Horticulture and Landscape Management Education. *Sustainability (Basel)*, *14*(15), 9116. Advance online publication. doi:10.3390u14159116

Kim, H. J., & Jeong, M. (2018). Research on hospitality and tourism education: Now and future. *Tourism Management Perspectives*, *25*, 119–122. doi:10.1016/j.tmp.2017.11.025

Kolb, A. Y., & Kolb, D. A. (2005). Learning styles and learning spaces: Enhancing experiential learning in higher education. *Academy of Management Learning \& Education, 4*(2), 193–212.

Kolb, D. A. (2014). Experiential learning: Experience as the source of learning and development (N. Jersey (ed.); 2nd ed.). Pearson Education.

Lee, M. J., Lee, P. C., Dopson, L. R., & Yoon, S. (2020). What dimensions of career expos have the most impact on student satisfaction? *Journal of Hospitality, Leisure, Sport & Tourism Education, 27*, 100263. https://doi.org/https://doi.org/10.1016/j.jhlste.2020.100263

Luthuli, S., Nyawo, J. C., & Mashau, P. (2019). Effectiveness of training and development on employees' performance in South African municipalities with special reference to Umzumbe Local Municipality. *African Journal of Development Studies, 9*(Special 1), 117.

Lyu, J., Li, M., & Wang, D. (2016). Experiential learning and its effectiveness from the perceptions of hospitality students. *Journal of Teaching in Travel \& Tourism, 16*(4), 296–315. doi:10.1080/15313220.2016.1213149

Melo, A., Melo, C., & Vasconcelos, S. (2023). 'Rota dos Sabores' – Simulation-Based Learning In Tourism, Hospitality and Catering Education and Training. In L. G. Chova, A. L. Martînez & J. Lees (Eds.) *INTED2023 Proceedings*, (pp. 3384-3390). 10.21125/inted.2023.0920

Melo, A., Melo, C., Vasconcelos, S., Liberato, D., & Lopes, M. C. (2021). Soft skills & turismo: do mercado à academia. In *Fórum Interno 21 Livro de Resumos Desafios do "Novo Normal"*, (p.20). Edições Politema. https://recipp.ipp.pt/bitstream/10400.22/20439/1/livroResumos21.pdf

Melo, C., Mouta, C., & Pereira, P. (2022). Innovation in Tourism Higher Education: A project-based approach to Village Tourism. L. G. Chova, A. L. Martînez & J. Lees (Eds.), EDULEARN 2022 Proceedings, pp. 6283-6288. IATED Academy. doi:10.21125/edulearn.2022.1478

Melo, C., Mouta, C., & Pereira, P. (2023). How do tourim students' feel about interdisciplinarity? In L. G. Chova, A. L. Martînez, & J. Lees (Eds.), *INTED 2023 Proceedings* (pp. 6344–6348). IATED Academy., doi:10.21125/inted.2023.1676

Melo, C., Mouta, C., & Pereira, P. (2023). How cool is collaboration? Students' perceptions on partnering with the tourism industry. In L. G. Chova, A. L. Martînez, & J. Lees (Eds.), *INTED 2023 Proceedings* (pp. 3596–3604). IATED Academy., doi:10.21125/inted.2023.0970

Morris, T. H. (2020). Experiential learning – a systematic review and revision of Kolb's model. *Interactive Learning Environments, 28*(8), 1064–1077. doi:10.1080/10494820.2019.1570279

OECD. (2019). *OECD Future of Education and Skills 2030 - OECD Learning Compass 2030.* https://www.oecd.org/education/2030-project/contact/OECD_Learning_Compass_2030_Concept_Note_Series.pdf

Roberts, M. D. (2022). Secondary School Students' Views of Tourism Education and Tourism Careers. *Journal of Hospitality \& Tourism Education*, 1–12.

Ruhanen, L. (2005). Bridging the Divide Between Theory and Practice. *Journal of Teaching in Travel \& Tourism, 5*(4), 33–51. https://doi.org/ doi:10.1300/J172v05n04_03

Sanders, D., & Armstrong, E. K. (2008). Understanding students' perceptions and experience of a tourism management field trip: The need for a graduated approach. *Journal of Hospitality \& Tourism Education, 20*(4), 29–37.

Skills, T. P. for 21st C. (2009). *Framework for 21st Century Learning.*

Sotomayor, S. (2021). Long-term benefits of field trip participation: Young tourism management professionals share their stories. *Journal of Hospitality, Leisure, Sport and Tourism Education, 29*, 100285. https://doi.org/https://doi.org/10.1016/j.jhlste.2020.100285. doi:10.1016/j.jhlste.2020.100285

van Laar, E., van Deursen, A. J. A. M., van Dijk, J. A. G. M., & de Haan, J. (2017). The relation between 21st-century skills and digital skills: A systematic literature review. *Computers in Human Behavior, 72*, 577–588. https://doi.org/https://doi.org/10.1016/j.chb.2017.03.010. doi:10.1016/j.chb.2017.03.010

Vasconcelos, S., Melo, A., Melo, C., Liberato, D., & Lopes, M. C. (2022). Soft Skills in Action: Developing Tourism Students Skills Through Interdisciplinarity. In J. V. Carvalho, P, Liberato & A. Peña (Eds), Advances in Tourism, Technology and Systems. Smart Innovation, Systems and Technologies, 284 (2), (pp. 203-213). Springer. doi:10.1007/978-981-16-9701-2_17

Vasconcelos, S., Melo, A., Melo, C., & Mouta, C. (2022). Fostering Student Agency in Tourism Education: Examples from the Tourism and Hospitality Field. In L. G. Chova, A. L. Martînez, & J. Lees (Eds.), *Edulearn22 Proceedings* (pp. 6457–6461). IATED Academy., doi:10.21125/edulearn.2022.1526

Vasconcelos, S., & Melo, C. (2022). Transforming Tourism Education: An Interdisciplinary Approach to Sustainable Tourism Management. In L. C. Carvalho, N. Teixeira, & P. Pardal (Eds.), *Interdisciplinary and Practical Approaches to Managerial Education and Training* (pp. 100–119). IGI Global., doi:10.4018/978-1-7998-8239-8.ch006

Vasconcelos, S., & Melo, C. (2023). A Learning Journey Towards Sustainable Tourism Education – Mapping an Interdisciplinary Project. In L. G. Chova, A. L. Martînez & J. Lees (Eds.) *INTED2023 Proceedings*, (pp. 3582-3586). 10.21125/inted.2023.0967

Vasconcelos, S., Melo, C., Melo, A., & Liberato, D. (2022). Interdisciplinarity in Action: Developing Students' Soft Skills Through Project-Based Learning and Field Work. In L. G. Chova, A. L. Martínez & I. C. Torres (Eds.), *INTED2022 Proceedings* (pp.4852–4859). IATED Academy. 10.21125/inted.2022.1267

Vesely, A., & ... (2011). Theory and methodology of best practice research: A critical review of the current state. *Central European Journal of Public Policy*, 5(02), 98–117.

Wong, A., & Wong, C.-K. S. (2009). Factors Affecting Students' Learning and Satisfaction on Tourism and Hospitality Course-Related Field Trips. Journal of Hospitality \& Tourism Education, 21(1), 25–35. doi:10.1080/10963758.2009.10 696934

Xie, P. F. (2004). Tourism field trip: Students' view of Experiential Learning. *Tourism Review International*, 8(2), 101–111. doi:10.3727/1544272042782219

Yiu, M., & Law, R. (2012). A Review of Hospitality Internship: Different Perspectives of Students, Employers, and Educators. Journal of Teaching in Travel \& Tourism, 12(4), 377–402. doi:10.1080/15313220.2012.729459

ADDITIONAL READING

Agarwal, P. (2021). Shattered but smiling: Human resource management and the wellbeing of hotel employees during COVID-19. *International Journal of Hospitality Management*, 93, 102765. https://doi.org/https://doi.org/10.1016/j.ijhm.2020.102765. doi:10.1016/j.ijhm.2020.102765 PMID:36919177

Chandra, S., Ranjan, A., & Chowdhary, N. (2022). Online Hospitality and Tourism Education-Issues and Challenges. *Tourism (Zagreb)*, 70(2), 298–316. doi:10.37741/t.70.2.10

Chen, M., Pei, T., Jeronen, E., Wang, Z., & Xu, L. (2022). Teaching and Learning Methods for Promoting Sustainability in Tourism Education. *Sustainability (Basel)*, 14(21), 14592. Advance online publication. doi:10.3390u142114592

Fidgeon, P. R. (2010). Tourism education and curriculum design: A time for consolidation and review? *Tourism Management, 31*(6), 699–723. doi:10.1016/j.tourman.2010.05.019

Goh, E. (2020). Educating the Future Hospitality and Tourism Workforce: Trends, Issues, and Directions in Australia and New Zealand. *Journal of Hospitality \& Tourism Education, 32*(4), 193. doi:10.1080/10963758.2019.1688162

Huang, A., de la Mora Velasco, E., & Haney, A. (2022). Examining Instructional Technologies in Hospitality and Tourism Education: A Systematic Review of Literature. *Journal of Hospitality & Tourism Education*, 1–19. doi:10.1080/1096 3758.2022.2109480

Vasconcelos, S., Melo, A., Melo, C., Liberato, D., & Lopes, M. C. (2022). Soft Skills in Action: Developing Tourism Students Skills Through Interdisciplinarity. In J. V. de Carvalho, P. Liberato, & A. Peña (Eds.), *Advances in Tourism, Technology and Systems* (pp. 203–213). Springer Nature Singapore. doi:10.1007/978-981-16-9701-2_17

Vasconcelos, S. V., & Melo, C. (2022). Transforming Tourism Education: An Interdisciplinary Approach to Sustainable Tourism Management. In Interdisciplinary and Practical Approaches to Managerial Education and Training (pp. 100–119). IGI Global.

Wakelin-Theron, N., Ukpere, W. I., & Spowart, J. (2018). Perception of tourism graduates and the tourism industry on the important knowledge and skills required in the tourism industry. *African Journal of Hospitality, Tourism and Leisure, 7*(4), 1–18.

KEY TERMS AND DEFINITIONS

Collaboration: the action of working with someone to produce something, collaboration is perceived as a key skill. It implies that there is a shared goal, that everyone in the same group/team is working to achieve.

Design-based research: aligned with different research methods, this methodological approach is based on the identification of a problem/issue and the design of potential solutions that must be tested and further improved on based on evidence. In education, it ultimately aims to positively contribute to improve student learning.

Role-play: Within the scope of experiential learning, role plays are activities in which learners take on different roles, assuming a character, personality or function within a group. Participants engaging in these activities are challenged to interact and participate in diverse and complex settings.

Simulation: Also within the scope of experiential learning, simulations provide learners with real world-like situations, thus allowing them to practice their knowledge and skills and experiment with different solution in a safe environment.

Toolkit: Set of tools and resources that can be used for a variety of purposes. In education the word often refers to a collection of guidelines, materials and/or resources that can support educators/practitioners.

Tourism Higher Education: Specific area within higher education, consisting of specialized subjects and curricula focusing on specific industry-related and academic skills.

Chapter 4
Creating a Culture of Innovation:
The Case of the Pedagogical Innovation Center at the Polytechnic of Porto

Ricardo Alexandre Peixoto de Queiros
iD https://orcid.org/0000-0002-1985-6285
ESMAD, Polytechnic of Porto, Portugal

Mário Cruz
iD https://orcid.org/0000-0001-8894-8821
ESE, Polytechnic of Porto, Portugal

Carla Pinto
iD https://orcid.org/0000-0002-0729-1133
ISEP, Polytechnic of Porto, Portugal

Daniela Mascarenhas
ISEP, Polytechnic of Porto, Portugal

ABSTRACT

In this chapter, we describe the design and implementation of a Pedagogical Innovation Center (PIC) at the Polytechnic of Porto. The COVID-19 pandemic disrupted our day to day lives, our businesses, the world trade and movements. Education was not spared. In fact, it was one of the sectors most heavily affected by COVID-19 pandemic. Teachers were forced, from night to day, to adjust a purely face-to-face teaching style, to a 100\% online set. This is known as emergency remote teaching. Several difficulties have arisen both for teachers and students. The first had to structure all their teaching materials from scratch, had to design and apply new assessment methods, and struggled to get their students' motivation. On their side, the students lacked engagement, social interaction with peers and teachers, the ability to have a more autonomous learning style.

DOI: 10.4018/978-1-6684-8656-6.ch004

INTRODUCTION

In this chapter, we describe the design and implementation of a Pedagogical Innovation Center (PIC) in Polytechnic of Porto. The COVID-19 pandemic disrupted our day to day lives, our businesses, the world trade and movements. Education was not spared. In fact, it was one of the sectors most heavily affected by COVID-19 pandemic. Teachers were forced, from night to day, to adjust a purely face-to-face teaching style, to a 100\% online set. This is known as emergency remote teaching. Several difficulties have arisen both for teachers and students. The first had to structure all their teaching materials from scratch, had to design and apply new assessment methods, and struggled to get their students' motivation. On their side, the students lacked engagement, social interaction with peers and teachers, the ability to have a more autonomous learning style.

The new "normal" prompted the Higher Education Institutions to transform their campuses into hybrid teaching structures. In these are applied innovative teaching and learning practices and is promoted necessary training to form new teachers' profiles.

PIC was designed to respond to this new reality.

The teaching and learning process requires the (re)building of a teaching professionality in a dynamic, continuous, and complex way which depends on the critical reflection process (Loughran, Keast, & Cooper, 2016). In this context, the literature on teaching and learning and the building of teaching professionality accounts for a professional knowledge that is multifaceted, including: a) content knowledge, b) didactic and pedagogical knowledge of the content, c) sociology, the philosophy, and history underlying the curriculum (Nóvoa, 2017). On the one hand, this knowledge results from higher-level and specialized training, but it should also derive from an investigative, cultural, and contextual update (Loughran, Keast, & Cooper, 2016). The quality of the teaching and learning process, as well as the pedagogical training of higher education teachers, are topics that have been on the agenda. The literature itself reveals a need to encourage practices that focus on the hybridization of learning (Marques & Pinto, 2012), (Xavier & Leite, 2019). The COVID-19 pandemic forced teachers to rethink the teaching and learning processes, having exposed several issues which raised the questioning of practices and strategies, namely: a) lack of student interest, b) the inability to study autonomously, c) limited social interactions and, still, d) little immersion in learning content. In this context, teachers were forced to update themselves in terms of their digital skills, to be able to keep up with the current generation of learners. They started to integrate computers or mobile devices in the context of teaching and learning, elements that are part of students' daily lives, and hence also may act as springboards to develop their soft skills, namely: collaboration, creativity, critical thinking, among others (Cruz, 2021). These transitions, induced by the pandemic and emergency context we are experiencing, have resulted in a questioning of the campus where we operate, students and teachers, in the sense of transforming it into a hybric campus, which implies an effective transformation of teaching and learning practices and strategies and reconfiguration of the professionality of the teachers of the Polytechnic of Porto. In this context, PIC emerges, as a structure that will seek in the coming academic years:

- to map pedagogical practices developed in the different organic units of the Polytechnic of Porto.
- to encourage the reconfiguration of the teaching professionalism of the Polytechnic of Porto.
- In teachers, by investing in pedagogical (re)training for hybrid contexts;
- to develop public discussion practices on the experimentation of innovative teaching-learning approaches and strategies;
- to promote the creation of pedagogical innovation projects, supporting their incubation and achievement.

PEDAGOGICAL INNOVATION CENTER

PIC aims to promote pedagogical enhancement as a differentiating element of the teaching-learning process adjusted to best practices, creating a growing dynamic of knowledge development. This is achieved through the enhancement of the pedagogical component of the teachers, the improvement in the educational models of the cycles of study and curricular units, the pedagogical or scientific transversality or the growing centrality of the student in the development process.

With the main objective of permanently improving the teaching and learning processes developed in the organic units of the Polytechnic of Porto. PIC will include the following spaces for interaction and intervention, from/with the community:

A. Distance Learning Office;
B. Training and Pedagogical Development Office;
C. Innovation Lab.

PIC will be the interface for two types of users: teachers and students. Teachers will need all areas supported by the center, namely in training, in the transition from their traditional (in person) courses to hybrid or totally distance courses and in the creation of educational resources that adapt to the new teaching formats. With all these valences, teachers will be able to deploy their courses in an innovative and sustained way to a learning platform on the cloud. On the other hand, students will

Figure 1. Composition of the PIC and interconnection between the aforementioned spaces

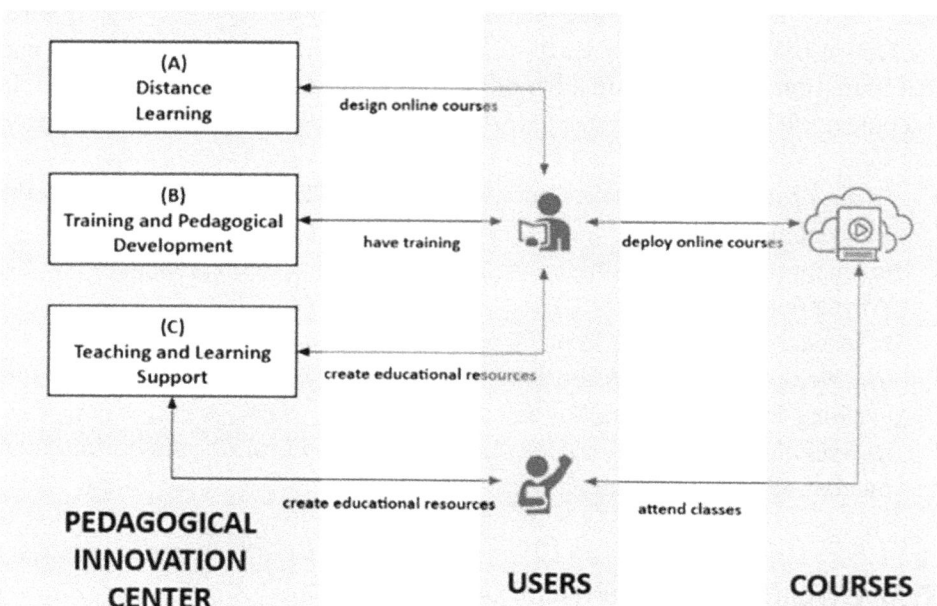

also be able to create their educational resources and interacting with their teachers in online courses.

In the next subsection all the three areas supported by PIC are presented in more detail.

Distance Learning Office

This office will focus on the fields of development and implementation of new methodologies and pedagogies in order to boost innovation in the forms of teaching/learning/training in the Polytechnic of Porto community and in its area of influence. As such, pedagogical and scientific support will be provided to teachers regarding their training both for working with students at a distance, as well as for the development of knowledge and practices on the migration of courses in face-to-face format to distance, either partially (b-learning) or fully (e-learning).

The main tasks of this office will be:

a)   to feed e-learning systems and applications;

b)   to contribute to increasing the amount of pedagogical content made available by the Institute, in a blended-learning and distance education perspective;

c) to develop multimedia resources in the context of pedagogical processes;

d) to support teachers who wish to provide e-learning and b-learning pedagogical content;

e) to collect and disseminate indicators on the use of educational technologies;

f) to support initiatives to encourage e-learning and evaluate emerging teaching and learning methodologies, with a view to their implementation;

g) to support the creation of Massive Open Online Courses (MOOC);

h) to support specific training in their fields of intervention, especially concerning the pedagogical training of teachers, including online training and the elaboration of answers to frequently asked questions;

i) to provide specialized training in the areas of pedagogical innovation and educational technologies.

The office will prioritize learning platforms that promote interoperability so that both teachers and students have the same entry point for the teaching-learning process and that, from there, new applications can be launched without the need for multiple authentications (Leal et al., 2022). This novel vision will be based on new IMS specifications, namely the Learning Tools Interoperability (LTI) specification[1]. With LTI teachers can use their favorite applications, which will be orbiting in the school's LMS, and, in real-time, monitor their student's progress from the LMS (Queirós, 2022).

Training and Pedagogical Development Office

This office exercises its competencies in the fields of development of the training process (teaching-learning), as well as in the introduction of innovative pedagogical methodologies, namely:

a) to promote actions for the reception and integration of teachers, in new methodologies and the promotion of an active formative process, centered on the student, with articulation with the research domains and connection with the market;

b) to survey training needs, developing and managing training programs and plans aimed at improving skills for the performance of professional duties, particularly with regard to teaching;

c) to survey training needs, developing and managing training programs and plans aimed at improving skills for the performance of professional duties, particularly about teaching;

d) to ensure the Office's own expedient, information filing and data protection.

Innovation Lab (IL)

An IL is defined as a suitable physical environment that offers the necessary resources to stimulate the creativity of users in innovation projects, working in a dynamic environment (Lewis & Moultrie, 2005) and (Moultrie et al., 2007). IL favors collaborative and multidisciplinary work, promoting a physical manifestation of dynamic capability and double-loop learning concepts (Lewis & Moultrie, 2005). Higher Education Institutions (HEIs) social responsibility towards society has been firmly rooted and any new solution to environmental, and/or social, and/or economic problems will be supported by new teaching, research and transference methodologies, technology, and strong interaction with local and regional communities (Masseck, 2017).

It is necessary to create conditions for collaborative dialogue between HEIs and Small and Medium Entreprises (SMEs), to promote a culture of open innovation within SMEs (Van Goolen et al., 2014), concerning: (i) stimulating business model innovation in companies; SMEs; (ii) develop a systematic approach to innovation processes, adjusted to its limited financial and market resources.

PIC's IL will have as its main focus the provision of an educational environment, specially designed to test innovative teaching-learning methods, concepts, and technologies for its target groups. For this, the IL will:

- cluster innovation activities in the education sector involving all stakeholders;
- increase the innovation competence of teachers and students, involved in testing new teaching-learning methods, concepts, and technologies;
- support the creation of interactive educational resources by the entire academic community;
- create interactive test and development environments to generate new questions and innovation projects;
- promote lifelong education and the development of transversal skills;
- promote sustainable education, within the scope of SDG 4 objectives: `Ensure inclusive and equitable quality education and promote lifelong learning opportunities for all[2].

The IL will have to anticipate and adapt to the very likely and demanding future challenges of Society.

CORRELATION BETWEEN DISTANCE LEARNING AND MICRO-LEARNING

In recent years, the field of education has witnessed a rapid growth in the adoption of distance learning as a means to deliver educational content remotely. This shift has been primarily driven by advancements in technology, making it possible to bridge geographical barriers and provide learning opportunities to students who may not have access to traditional classroom settings. However, while distance learning offers numerous advantages, it also presents unique challenges in terms of maintaining student engagement and facilitating effective pedagogical practices.

One technique that has gained prominence in both traditional and distance learning environments is micro teaching/learning. Micro teaching/learning involves breaking down complex concepts into smaller, manageable units or "micro" lessons, enabling learners to grasp and assimilate information more effectively. This technique often utilizes interactive and experiential learning strategies, encouraging active student participation and enhancing comprehension.

The correlation between distance learning and the micro teaching/learning technique is multi-faceted and can be viewed from different angles. Let us explore some of the key aspects of this correlation.

Chunking and Modular Design

Distance learning courses are often structured in a modular format, dividing the curriculum into smaller units or modules. This modular design aligns well with the principles of micro teaching/learning, where the content is chunked into manageable portions. By organizing the material into smaller modules, instructors can present information in a structured manner, ensuring that learners can engage with the material at a pace suitable to their individual learning needs. This facilitates better comprehension and retention, enhancing the overall learning experience.

Interactive and Engaging Learning Activities

Distance learning environments can sometimes be perceived as isolating, lacking the face-to-face interactions found in traditional classrooms. To address this limitation, incorporating micro teaching/learning techniques can introduce interactive and engaging activities into the online learning experience. For example, instructors can design short quizzes, discussions, or problem-solving exercises that encourage active participation from learners. By integrating such activities, learners are actively involved in the learning process, promoting a deeper understanding of the subject matter.

Personalized Learning Opportunities

Distance learning often caters to a diverse student population with varying backgrounds, learning styles, and preferences. Micro teaching/learning can accommodate this diversity by allowing learners to engage with the content at their own pace and in a manner that suits their individual learning needs. By offering bite-sized lessons, learners can navigate through the material, focusing on areas where they require more practice or spending additional time on challenging concepts. This personalized learning approach enhances student autonomy and fosters a sense of ownership over the learning process, ultimately leading to better learning outcomes.

Formative Assessment and Feedback

Formative assessment plays a crucial role in the micro teaching/learning approach, providing learners with timely feedback and opportunities for improvement. In distance learning, formative assessment can be integrated through various digital tools and platforms, allowing instructors to gauge student progress and understanding. By leveraging these assessment mechanisms, instructors can provide targeted feedback to learners, addressing misconceptions, reinforcing key concepts, and guiding them towards mastery. This feedback loop enhances the effectiveness of distance learning by bridging the gap between instructor and student, promoting a supportive and collaborative clearing environment.

In conclusion, the correlation between distance learning and the micro teaching/learning technique demonstrates the potential for enhancing the efficacy of remote education. By leveraging the principles of micro teaching/learning, instructors can design modular, interactive, and personalized learning experiences that address the challenges associated with distance learning. This correlation enables instructors to provide engaging and effective instruction while fostering student autonomy and promoting continuous improvement through formative assessment. By embracing the synergies between distance learning and micro teaching/learning, educators can unlock the full potential of remote education and empower learners to succeed in their educational endeavors.

LEARNING TOOLS AND APPLICATIONS

There are several tools and learning applications available that support and facilitate micro-learning. Here are some examples:

1. Learning Management Systems (LMS):
    ◦ Moodle: Moodle is a popular open-source LMS that allows instructors to create and deliver micro-learning modules, track learner progress, and provide assessments and feedback.

- ○ Canvas: Canvas is a cloud-based LMS that offers features for creating and organizing micro-learning content, including multimedia resources, quizzes, and discussions.
- ○ Blackboard: Blackboard is an LMS that supports the creation and delivery of micro-learning content, providing features like multimedia integration, assessments, and collaboration tools.

2. Mobile Learning Apps:
   - ○ Duolingo: Duolingo is a language learning app that utilizes micro-learning techniques with short, gamified lessons to teach languages in bite-sized chunks.
   - ○ Memrise: Memrise is a language learning app that uses spaced repetition and micro-learning principles to help learners memorize vocabulary and language concepts.
   - ○ Khan Academy: Khan Academy's mobile app offers micro-learning lessons across various subjects, providing short instructional videos, practice exercises, and quizzes.

3. Micro-Learning Platforms:
   - ○ Axonify: Axonify is a micro-learning platform that delivers personalized, bite-sized content to learners, focusing on employee training and development.
   - ○ Grovo: Grovo is a micro-learning platform that offers a library of short, targeted video lessons on various topics, designed for employee training and professional development.

4. Flashcard Apps:
   - ○ Anki: Anki is a popular flashcard app that uses spaced repetition algorithms to help learners review and retain information effectively. It supports micro-learning by providing small, focused flashcard decks.
   - ○ Quizlet: Quizlet is a flashcard app that allows learners to create and access flashcards on various subjects. It offers different study modes, including micro-learning options like matching games and short quizzes.

5. Content Creation Tools:
   - ○ Articulate Rise: Articulate Rise is an authoring tool that enables the creation of responsive e-learning content, including micro-learning modules with interactive components and assessments.
   - ○ Adobe Captivate: Adobe Captivate is an e-learning authoring tool that supports the development of micro-learning content, including multimedia elements, quizzes, and simulations.

Each tool offers different features and functionalities, catering to diverse learning needs and contexts. When selecting a tool or application for micro-learning, it is important to consider factors such as ease of use, scalability, interactivity, and compatibility with your learning goals and technology infrastructure.

CONCLUSION

In this work, we unfold the design and implementation of PIC, in Polytechnic of Porto. The difficulties felt by teachers and students during the emergency remote teaching, due to the COVID-19 pandemic, prompted the appearance of such a center. In 2020, HEIs were faced with a dramatic situation and no time to think and/or act. They could only react. But then something beautiful came from this chaotic scenario, from this catastrophe, which led HEIs to think forward, to adapt their teaching and learning styles, and structures, to our present and beyond. Ultimately, this is the goal of PIC, to promote the very best of Education experience to students and teachers now and beyond.

The appearance of micro-learning brings a new fresh approach to learning by providing accessible, engaging, and personalized learning experiences. Its efficiency, effectiveness, and adaptability to the needs of modern learners make it a valuable tool in today's learning landscape, catering to the demands of a fast-paced, technology-driven world.

REFERENCES

Cochran-Smith, M. (2004). The problem of teacher education. *Journal of Teacher Education, 55*(4), 295–299. doi:10.1177/0022487104268057

Cruz, M. (2019). Escaping from the traditional classroom-The 'Escape Room Methodology' in the Foreign Languages Classroom. Babylonia-Rivista svizzera per l'insegnamento delle lingue, 3, 26-29.

Cruz, M. (2021). CLIL Approach and the Fostering of "Creactical Skills" towards a Global Sustainable Awareness. *MEXTESOL Journal, 45*(2), n2.

Delgado, L., Galvez, D., Hassan, A., Palominos, P., & Morel, L. (2020). Innovation spaces in universities: Support for collaborative learning. *Journal of Innovation Economics Management, 31*(1), 123–153. doi:10.3917/jie.pr1.0064

Ferreira, J. (2022, April). Um terço dos docentes que ensinam futuros professores não tem formação no ramo educacional. Pessoas by ECO. Retrieved from [URL]

Leal, J. P., Queirós, R., Ferreirinha, P., & Swacha, J. (2022). A Roadmap to Convert Educational Web Applications into LTI Tools. In A. Simões & J. C. Silva (Eds.), Third International Computer Programming Education Conference (ICPEC 2022), Open Access Series in Informatics (OASIcs) (Vol. 102, pp. 12:1-12:12). Schloss Dagstuhl -- Leibniz-Zentrum für Informatik.

Lewis, M., & Moultrie, J. (2005). The Organizational Innovation Laboratory. *Creativity and Innovation Management, 14*(1), 73–83. doi:10.1111/j.1467-8691.2005.00327.x

Loughran, J., Keast, S., & Cooper, R. (2016). Pedagogical reasoning in teacher education. In *International handbook of teacher education* (pp. 387–421). Springer. doi:10.1007/978-981-10-0366-0_10

Loughran, J., Keast, S., & Cooper, R. (2016). Pedagogical reasoning in teacher education. In *International handbook of teacher education* (pp. 387–421). Springer. doi:10.1007/978-981-10-0366-0_10

Loughran, J., & Menter, I. (2019). The essence of being a teacher educator and why it matters. *Asia-Pacific Journal of Teacher Education*, *47*(3), 216–229. doi:10.108 0/1359866X.2019.1575946

Marques, J., & Pinto, P. R. (2012). Formação pedagógica de professores do ensino superior--a experiência na universidade nova de Lisboa. Revista Portuguesa de Pedagogia, 129-149.

Masseck, T. (2017). Living Labs in Architecture as Innovation Arenas within Higher Education Institutions. *Energy Procedia*, *115*, 383–389. doi:10.1016/j. egypro.2017.05.035

Mendonça, J., Pinto, C., & Babo, L. (2020). Industry 5.0 expectations of engineering critical thinking. In EDULEARN20 Proceedings (pp. 8518-8529).

Moultrie, J., Nilsson, M., Dissel, M., Haner, U.-E., Janssen, S., & Van der Lugt, R. (2007). Innovation Spaces: Towards a Framework for Understanding the Role of the Physical Environment in Innovation. *Creativity and Innovation Management*, *16*(1), 53–65. doi:10.1111/j.1467-8691.2007.00419.x

Nicola, S., Mendonça, J., Pinto, C., & Pereira, A. (2019). Education by challenge: innovation-driven spirit. In INTED2019 Proceedings (pp. 5182-5190). IATED. MATH-DIGGER. (2022). MATH-DIGGER - MAThematics DiGital Escape Rooms. ERASMUS+ Partnerships for cooperation and exchanges of practices. Project Reference 2021-1-PT01-KA220-HED-000032234. Retrieved from [URL] DrIVE-MATH. (2017). DrIVE-MATH - Development of Innovative Mathematical Teaching Strategies in European Engineering Degrees. ERASMUS+ Cooperation for innovation and the exchange of good practices. Project Reference 2017-1-PT01-KA203-035866. Cruz, M. (2018). Chicos, sacad el móvil de vuestras mochilas porque lo vamos a usar: Empowering Spanish As Foreign Language Students Through Mobile Devices. The Turkish Online Journal of Educational Technology, 1(Special Issue for INTE-ITICAM-IDEC), 282-298. 10.21125/inted.2019.1292

Nóvoa, A. (2017). Firmar a posição como professor, afirmar a profissão docente. *Cadernos de Pesquisa*, *47*(166), 1106–1133. doi:10.1590/198053144843

Nóvoa, A. (2017). Firmar a posição como professor, afirmar a profissão docente. *Cadernos de Pesquisa*, *47*(166), 1106–1133. doi:10.1590/198053144843

Pinto, C., Babo, L., & Mendonça, J. (2020). Engineering students' awareness of their present and future professional expertises. In EDULEARN20 Proceedings (pp. 8360-8369). IATED.

Pinto, C. M. A., Mendonça, J., & Nicola, S. (2022). DrIVE-MATH Project: Case Study from the Polytechnic of Porto, PT. *Open Education Studies*, *4*(1), 1–20. doi:10.1515/edu-2022-0001

Queirós, R. A. P. (2022). Integration of a Learning Playground into an LMS. In *Proceedings of the 27th ACM Conference on on Innovation and Technology in Computer Science Education* Vol. 2 (pp. 626). ACM. 10.1145/3502717.3532175

Van Goolen, R., Evers, H., & Lammens, C. (2014). International Innovation Labs: An Innovation Meeting Ground between SMEs and Business Schools. *Procedia Economics and Finance*, *12*, 184–190. doi:10.1016/S2212-5671(14)00334-7

Xavier, A. R. C., & Leite, C. (2019). Mapeamento da Formação Pedagógica de docentes universitários nas Universidades Públicas Portuguesas. *Revista Lusófona de Educação*, *45*(45), 109–123. doi:10.24140/issn.1645-7250.rle45.08

Zannin, M., Lima, N., & Pinto, C. (2021). Use of Hands-on and Remote Lab with an Inquiry-Based Approach to Learn Statistics in Engineering. In *Ninth International Conference on Technological Ecosystems for Enhancing Multiculturality (TEEM'21)* (pp. 565-569). 10.1145/3486011.3486513

KEY TERMS AND DEFINITIONS

Distance Learning: Distance learning refers to a form of education where students and instructors are physically separated, and instruction is delivered remotely through various technologies such as online platforms, video conferencing, or correspondence.

Synchronous Learning: Synchronous learning is a type of distance learning where students and instructors participate in real-time, interactive activities at the same time. This can include live lectures, discussions, or collaborative activities facilitated through video conferencing or virtual classrooms.

Asynchronous Learning: Asynchronous learning is a type of distance learning where students access and engage with learning materials and activities at their own pace and time. This can involve pre-recorded lectures, discussion boards, or self-paced modules that allow flexibility in learning.

Learning Management System (LMS): A learning management system is a software platform that facilitates the administration, delivery, and tracking of online courses or training programs. It provides tools for content creation, communication, assessment, and learner management.

Blended Learning: Blended learning, also known as hybrid learning, combines online and face-to-face instruction. It involves a mix of traditional classroom-based learning and online learning activities, allowing for flexibility and personalized learning experiences.

Micro-Learning: Micro-learning is an approach to learning that focuses on delivering small, bite-sized units of content or learning activities. It involves short learning modules or resources designed to address specific learning objectives, often delivered in a time-efficient manner.

Spaced Repetition: Spaced repetition is a learning technique that involves reviewing information at increasingly spaced intervals over time. It aims to enhance long-term retention and memory recall by reinforcing learning at optimal intervals.

Just-in-Time Learning: Just-in-time learning refers to accessing learning resources or information when it is needed, typically to address an immediate challenge or problem. It allows learners to acquire knowledge or skills relevant to a specific context or task at the moment of need.

Gamification: Gamification is the integration of game elements and mechanics into non-game contexts, such as learning experiences. It incorporates elements like points, badges, leaderboards, and rewards to enhance engagement, motivation, and learning outcomes.

Personalized Learning: Personalized learning involves tailoring educational experiences to meet individual learner needs, preferences, and goals. It emphasizes learner-centric approaches that provide customized content, pacing, and assessments based on learner characteristics and progress.

Learning Analytics: Learning analytics involves the collection, analysis, and interpretation of data generated from learning activities to inform instructional decisions and improve learning outcomes. It enables educators to gain insights into learner progress, engagement, and performance.

Mobile Learning: Mobile learning, also known as m-learning, refers to learning experiences delivered through mobile devices such as smartphones or tablets. It allows learners to access learning resources anytime, anywhere, promoting flexibility and on-the-go learning.

ENDNOTES

1   URL: https://www.imsglobal.org/activity/learning-tools-interoperability
2   URL: https://sdgs.un.org/goals/goal4

Section 2
Experiential Learning and Learning Tools

Chapter 5
Learning While Teaching:
Harnessing the Potential of Peer-to-Peer Learning to Enhance Language Learning

Sandra Vieira Vasconcelos

iD https://orcid.org/0000-0003-4062-331X

School of Hospitality and Tourism, Polytechnic of Porto, Portugal

ABSTRACT

Focussing on a project carried out within the scope of an English Applied to Tourism course, this chapter describes a teaching and learning strategy, putting forward the underlying rationale and outlining its design, implementation, and assessment phases. The project, whose aims included fostering students' language and critical thinking skills, challenged Hotel Management students to collaborate to produce online training modules for their peers. Relying on the use of digital technologies, most particularly LMS, and cloud-based student engagement and graphic design tools (including Nearpod and Canva), these modules were peer-reviewed and implemented, with students acting as both facilitators and reviewers. Building on existing research on the affordances of peer learning within the scope of foreign language teaching, the author frames the different activities, reflecting on how peer learning strategies can enhance students' engagement and agency, offering insights that can support English for Specific Purposes (ESP) teachers, as well as other practitioners.

INTRODUCTION

Considered to be active, student-centred learning methods, collaborative and peer teaching and learning activities are perceived as being effective in promoting (meta) cognitive skills such as reflection, knowledge transfer and creativity (Bezanilla et al.,

DOI: 10.4018/978-1-6684-8656-6.ch005

2019; Tang et al., 2022; Ting & Shukor, 2022; Vani, 2016), as well as in motivating students and involving them in dialectic processes that imply communication, negotiation, affective and social skills (Havnes et al., 2016).

Even though the concept of peer learning is far from new, recent technological and societal developments stemming from: 1) the prominence and growing versatility of online collaborative platforms (Chandra & Palvia, 2021; Jeong et al., 2020); and 2) changes in the workplace and the skills required by prospective employers and the labour market (Hutchinson et al., 2022; Willey & Gardner, 2010), have rehashed and added depth to the ongoing need to further discuss its potential. On the other hand, events such as the recent COVID-19 pandemic and the emergence of Artificial Intelligence (AI), have also given rise to other discussions involving the social component of learning and the importance of critical thinking and inquiry (Lin et al., 2016), which are in line with the use of peer-based activities in learning.

Based on these premises and aiming to describe a recently implemented project, as well as to reflect on the potential affordances of peer-learning, this chapter outlines a collaborative assignment designed within the scope of an English for Specific Purposes (ESP) course. In addition to mapping out previous research on the topic, the author sets out to describe the teaching and learning activities carried out, reflecting on the underlying rationale and revisiting the project's planning, implementation, and assessment phases. Following this description, drawing on documentary evidence and observation, the author offers insights on its strengths and weaknesses, making a case for peer review and peer-learning as ways of enhancing students' engagement and agency.

Even though it primarily targets other ESP teachers and practitioners, this chapter reflects the author's hands-on experience in addressing everyday classroom challenges. As a result, its inputs can inform teaching and learning initiatives in a wide range of areas, contributing to the ongoing discussion on the role of active and student-centred approaches within the scope of Higher Education (HE).

BACKGROUND

Defined as "students learning from and with each other in both formal and informal ways" (Boud, 2001, p. 4), peer learning can be described as "the acquisition of knowledge and skills through active helping and support among peers who are equals in standing or matched companion" (Gogus, 2012). Rooted in Vygotsky's sociocultural theory (Vygotsky, 1962) and the construct of learning as social and cultural process that "occurs through meaningful negotiation and interaction between learners" (Rahimi, 2013, p. 67), peer learning is an "active and constructive process" (Keerthirathne, 2020, p. 1) that can be used in a wide range of settings, with different objectives, using different strategies and tools. That being so, even though it has been an extensively used educational practice, the way it is perceived and applied has evolved, as a result of multiple challenges and changes, most particularly, the development and widespread use of learning technologies and platforms (Jeong et al., 2020; Lin et al., 2016).

Considered to reinforce "the new roles assigned to educational actors", in that teachers are increasingly perceived as facilitators, whereas students become "a worker, self-directed learner, and teacher" (Carvalho & Santos, 2022, p. 3), within the scope of peer learning, digital technologies have come to play both a functional and paradigm-shifting role (Carvalho & Santos, 2022; Chen, 2021; Tang et al., 2022).

Considering the former, from a practical point of view, digital platforms are considered to be accessible (Crouse-Machcinski, 2019), easy to use (Beaumont et al., 2012), and offer multiple functionalities and tools that can support peer strategies (Burhan-Horasanlı, 2022; Crouse-Machcinski, 2019). In addition, these platforms can be used to collect and keep extensive records, which can ultimately inform faculty and assist them in tailoring activities and outcomes (Carvalho & Santos, 2022). On the other hand, the use of digital platforms is also considered to leverage socialization and the creation of communities (Beaumont et al., 2012; Burhan-Horasanlı, 2022; Carvalho & Santos, 2022), as well as fostering skills such as creativity and critical thinking (Bezanilla et al., 2019; Tang et al., 2022; Ting & Shukor, 2022; Vani, 2016). By relying on digitally interaction and on student centred approaches, digitally supported peer-learning is reshaping how we relate and build on existing knowledge, having become a key issue for educators.

In the literature there are different studies documenting the use of peer learning strategies within this setting, with several authors highlighting its perceived advantages when it comes to not only promoting students' engagement (Gyamfi et al., 2022) and their creative, communication and metacognitive skills, but also more specific skills such as writing (Huisman et al., 2018) and what Latifi and Noroozi (2021, p. 768) describe as "domain-specific learning". Other studies highlight the potential of student-created learning resources (Blake, 2021; Moiseenko, 2015) and experiential learning (Sutherland & Marchand, 2021), as an effective way of creating engagement, developing a repository of revision items and receiving feedback (Gyamfi et al., 2022).

Often linked to the concept of agency, peer feddback, i.e., situations in which feedback is given from one student to a fellow student (Boud, 2001), is another key element within the scope of peer teaching and learning. Relying on a structured process based on mutual feedback, peer assessment (or peer review) activities support the development of reflective skills, as students are expected to provide feedback (thus reflecting on their peers' work), also having the possibility of receiving feedback on their own work and improving on it. As a result, besices being empowering, as students can exchange ideas and build on their knowledge, sharing their insights and taking responsibility for their own learning, peer feedback allows them to become more familiarized with assessment criteria and develop feedback literacy skills, developing higher-order learning and critical thinking and collaboration competences. Traditionally carried out in onsite, face-to-face settings (in activities involving group discussions and presentations), currently, peer assessment is currently supported and facilitated by most VLE, as these platforms can facilitate feedback provision, save time and make the overall process more dynamic (Canham, 2017; Ching, 2014; Irwin, 2019).

Despite these benefits, the literature also points out possible hindrances regarding peer learning, such as the fact that feedback might be superficial, specially if students are inexperienced (Latifi & Noroozi, 2021). In addition, it is often difficult for students to understand the benefits of peer feedback (Price et al., 2010). On the other hand, in order for feedback to be effective, it must also be timely, personalized, and constructive, which can be challenging and time-consuming (Hattie & Clarke, 2018).

Other drawbacks include potential bias (Carvalho & Santos, 2022; Latifi & Noroozi, 2021; Topping, 2005), an initial resistance from students (Bell & Lygo-Baker, 2019), and communication and technological issues (Raymond et al., 2016; Topping, 2005). Authors such as Hutchinson et al. (2022) also highlight the need to train facilitators as to ensure better outcomes for all those involved, a need also stressed by Latifi and Noroozi (2021), who call for more support in implementing peer strategies in Higher Education.

Peer Learning and Language Learning

In 1985, referring to learners as a "largely underused educational resource", Stephen Gaies (1985, p. 8) makes an early case for peer involvement in language learning, as a way of promoting proficiency and complement classroom instruction. Since then, many researchers have studied the potential of peer learning strategies (including peer tutoring and mentoring, peer teaching, peer feedback and peer assessment) within the scope of language learning, documenting its perceived benefits and drawbacks. In addition to what Gaies described as "by-products of participation in a peer involvement program" (1985, p. 10) (i.e., increased motivation and cross-cultural understanding, a stronger sense of self and reduced inhibitions), peer learning is considered to be an effective way of enhancing speaking, listening and writing skills (Burkšaitienė, 2022; Latifi & Noroozi, 2021) and promoting a more authentic language use, making for an enjoyable way of learning languages. Moreover, over the last decade, several studies have also shown the potential of peer learning in developing problem-solving and critical-thinking skills (Latifi & Noroozi, 2021; Lin et al., 2016) and as "a powerful tool for promoting learner autonomy" (Moiseenko,

2015, p. 14), particularly when scaffolded by digital platforms and collaborative tools (Bunts-Anderson, 2016; Hsu, 2021).

Focussing on ESP, other studies also highlight the potential of peer learning strategies when it comes to the use of technical terminology (Rodis & Locsin, 2019; Zhang et al., 2016), arguing that "students not only study the terms but use and explain them to their classmates during their presentation as student-teachers" (Rodis & Locsin, 2019). Using a foreign language to mediate communication, can also result in a "non-threatening, but pleasant, and supportive environment" (Rodis & Locsin, 2019, p. 4), as students feel more comfortable interacting with each other, which can be instrumental in promoting empathy and motivation. Moreover, peer learning strategies can be combined with other approaches, such as flipped learning, leading to "deeper understanding of the content" (Zou & Xie, 2019, p. 1129).

Describing a flipped strategy combined with technology-enhanced peer instruction activities, used within the scope of an English for Academic Purposes writing course, Zou and Xie (2019), reflect on the affordances of peer instructions, arguing it can lead to higher learning performances, making it easier for students to focus on specific knowledge points and manage their own learning, making reference to "peer pressure", in that students feel the need to keep up the group (Zou & Xie, 2019, p. 1138).

Also perceived as an effective peer learning strategy in foreign language teaching settings, the creation of learning materials by students is also documented within this scope. In addition to a "repository of revision items" (Gyamfi et al., 2022, p. 1129), these materials can also promote active engagement and autonomy (Blake, 2021; Moiseenko, 2015) and the development of communication skills, particularly when that language is a medium of interaction (Mohamed et al., 2019; Moiseenko, 2015). However, despite these advantages, the fact that these materials can vary when it comes to quality and accurateness, requires them to be monitored, with researchers often resorting to rubrics and co-creative approaches as to assure they are relevant and error-free (Dollinger et al., 2018; Gyamfi et al., 2022).

PROJECT OUTLINE

Methodology

Considering educational research must "speak directly to problems of practice" (Plomp et al., 2013, p. 11), this exploratory study followed a design-based methodology to explore the potential of peer-learning as a way of complementing classroom learning and support the development of communicative activities and strategies (Creswell, 2003). Perceived as a series of complimentary "approaches, with the intent of producing new theories, artefacts, and practices that account for and potentially impact learning and teaching in naturalistic settings" (Barab & Squire, 2004, p. 2), the phases of the project are aligned with Reeves's model, as presented in Pool (2016): 1) Analysis/Investigation; 2) Design; and 3) Evaluation; leading up to reflection and ensuing intervention and theoretical understanding. Cyclical in nature, this practice-oriented approach should be flexible and iterative, as to generate inputs that can clarify existing issues and problems and support the development of solutions. The results clarify these problems and ideally put forward and adopt solutions, with a "dual focus on theory and practice"(Pool & Laubscher, 2016, p. 43).

Drawing from these premises and focusing on the first iteration of the project, the description and provisional results described within this chapter are based on observation and documentary analysis, drawing from portfolios and checklists analysis.

Context and Participants

The study took place at the School of Hospitality and Tourism (ESHT) of the Polytechnic Institute of Porto (Portugal). Participants consisted of 39 second year undergraduate students enrolled in an English III course as part of their degree in Hotel Management. As part of their degree, students are required to take part in an interdisciplinary project involving all courses. In the first year, students are asked to draw plans for a new hotel/accommodation unit. In addition to a business plan and a brand, they should consider the different departments and services to be provided (e.g., Marketing, Human Resources, Health & Safety and Events), all of which will be discussed and worked on in different courses throughout their degree. Within the scope of English courses, students mostly address issues regarding marketing and staff training, taking into consideration the need to work with international offices and teams.

In the project described in this chapter, working in groups of 3-5, students were challenged to design and implement asynchronous training modules on a topic related to Health and Safety (1 per group). Aimed at hotel staff, these modules must focus on specific procedures and technical vocabulary, and be interactive, including multimedia elements and supplementary material (e.g., infographics, quizzes, etc..), as to be implemented in an online environment. Each module should take from 20 to 30 minutes to complete and be made available to other students. In addition to the module itself, each group was also expected to prepare a 10-minute presentation on the overall session (providing a summary and presenting key findings) to take place at the end of the semester.

Project Design and Implementation

As outlined in Table 1, in line with the methodology described in the previous section, the project followed different stages, specifically Planning (based on previous work developed by and with the students), Design (including Piloting and Upgrade), and Implementation (which included a final presentation and evaluation).

Table 1. Outline: Project stages and activities

Stages	**1.** Planning
	• Group formation • Topic selection • Structure definition (based on pre-defined guidelines)
	2. Design

	• Material design
	   o Introduction
	   o Main Activities/ Demonstration (simulation, presentation, instructional video, and additional materials)
	   o Final summary/checkpoint
	   o Assessment (quiz, assignment, challenge, …)
	   o Feedback collection
	   o Conclusion

	3. Piloting
	• Peer-review (beta version) o Piloting checklist
	4. Upgrade
	• Feedback-based material revision
	5. Implementation
	• Online Training o Random group allocation (each group must complete 2 training modules)
	6. Final presentation
	• 10-minute oral presentation on the module developed and key results (based on the participants' assessment and overall feedback).

The project was designed taking its interdisciplinary nature into consideration, as well as the feedback from previous editions. Having been previously established that the main topic must involve staff training and Health & Safety topics, students were expected to develop a training plan and materials targeting hotel staff. In previous years, these materials were either not put into use (but only designed and presented) or implemented during onsite sessions. Though perceived as more successful, the latter (having students implement the actual training sessions for their peers) was not only extremely time-consuming, but also lacking when it came to interaction and the expected integration with the syllabus, as there were several timeline issues to be addressed. As a result, drawing on students' feedback (by means of questionnaires applied in the previous year) referring to the lack of interactivity within the scope of the project, it was decided to redesign it by shifting the training modules online, minimizing timing issues and encouraging interaction and participation.

Hence, based on these premises, as well as on the need to reinforce the role of specific terminology within the scope of Health & Safety, and to improve engagement levels, new guidelines were created as to facilitate implementation. Believed to have the potential to foster students' involvement in the project as a whole, namely by taking part in the different modules, this new approach also required participants to take on a more active role, by reviewing each other's outputs, thus engaging in peer activities (peer learning and peer review).

Peer Review

Following group formation and topic selection (in which they were given a choice between a wide range of Health & Safety Topics, based on their interest and on previous assignments), students were asked to define a target audience, set learning outcomes, and develop an overall work plan, based on the guidelines outlined in Table 2. This plan was developed over a two-week period and was then discussed with the teacher in 10-minute tutorial sessions with each group.

In the Design stage, students were given four weeks to work on content, after which they had to submit the materials so they could be reviewed by other students (Piloting stage). As to facilitate the review process, each group was randomly

Table 2. Session planning overview: Student guidelines

General Plan	
Introduction (2/3 minutes)	Introduce the topic and explain how the session will unfold. Outline the key content and outcomes
Main Activities/ Demonstration (8-15 minutes)	Explain/demonstrate the procedures you wish the participants to follow. This might include a live simulation, a video or other materials.
Review (2/3 minutes)	Sum up key content.
Assessment (3/5 minutes)	Prepare an assessment activity (quiz, assignment, etc…) aimed at the participants.
Feedback (2-3 minutes)	Ask for feedback from the participants.
Conclusion	Close the session (e.g., share a final message, issue a certificate, etc...)

assigned 3 modules to review using a pre-defined checklist. In addition to testing the modules in terms of timing and overall functionality, this stage also aimed to foster metacognitive and critical thinking skills, in that it required students to provide feedback on their peers' work and make suggestions on possible improvements. On the other hand, this also allowed the different groups to rethink some of the strategies used in designing their own modules, by comparing their work to that of other groups.

In order to assist students with the task, the teacher provided the groups with a checklist featuring closed and open-ended items regarding the perceived quality and relevance of the materials, as well as of the different elements that made up the module (see Table 2). In addition to checking whether the module under review complied with the guidelines, reviewers had the opportunity to make observations, as well as comments on potential improvements and corrections. This task was not considered in the project's assessment, even though the teacher registered all the annotations and comments for future analysis. After receiving their peers' feedback, groups had two weeks to resubmit their modules so that they could be made available in the course's Moodle area, thus initiating the implementation stage.

Overall, students produced 11 asynchronous modules, having used different formats and assessment strategies (featured in Table 3). Even though several groups

Table 3. Student-produced modules: topics, tools, and assessment strategies

Topics	Learning materials (tools/format)	Assessment strategies

• Kitchen Hygiene
  o Knive washing and storing
	• PowerPoint
	  o Slides (text/image)
	  o Student-produced videos
		Kahoot (quiz)

• Cross contamination	• Nearpod (presentation)	Nearpod (game and quiz)

• Food Storage	• PowerPoint
	  o Slides (text/image)
	  o Student-produced videos
		Quizur (online platform)

Personal and Kitchen Hygiene	• Nearpod (presentation) • Slides • Infographics • Youtube videos	Nearpod (quiz)

Personal and Kitchen Hygiene	• PowerPoint
	  o Slides (text/image)
	  o YouTube videos
		Kahoot

Personal and Kitchen Hygiene	• Nearpod (presentation)	Kahoot
Personal Hygiene	• Nearpod (presentation) • Youtube video	Nearpod (quiz)
Personal and kitchen Hygiene	• Nearpod • Youtuve video	Nearpod quiz
Mental Health	• PowerPoint	Kahoot
Hand Hygiene	• Nearpod • Student-produced video	Nearpod quiz
Health and Safety in the Kitchen	• Nearpod	Nearpod quiz

focused on personal and kitchen hygiene, there were different approaches to the topic, with some groups focusing on apparel and others on utensils and sanitation practices, with the content of the modules having previously been validated by the teacher.

To avoid potential bias and work overload, it was decided that each group of students was to be assigned a minimum of 3 modules, which they should complete over a period of two weeks. In addition to these, students could also enrol in other modules, based on their interest and availability. As part of each module, participants were required to complete some type of assessment and provide feedback on the training. The data would then be analysed by the group in charge of each module, with the ensuing conclusions being presented to the class (Stage 6 – Final Presentation).

Key Findings

Overall, students designed 11 online modules with topics ranging from personal hygiene, cross-contamination and knife storage and handling to mental health. In addition to Nearpod, students used PowerPoint and Kahoot to develop their modules (see Table 3), which were then imported into Moodle.

Considering the learning materials, most groups favoured multimodal approaches, having combined the use of text and images (11/11 groups) with video (9/11 – of which 7 were produced by the students) and audio (8/11).

Regarding assessment, most groups (10/11) resorted to quizzes (using Kahoot and Nearpod) or other gamified strategies (interactive online exercises). Only 1 group suggested a practical activity (photo-upload: spotting hazards in the workplace).

Of the 39 students taking part in the class, all of them completed the assigned modules. In addition, 37 (94.8% voluntarily took part in a least 2 additional learning modules) with 28 (71.8%) having successfully completed 8 of the 11 modules.

Based on the students' presentations and the peer-review checklists, most modules were upgraded taking into consideration the suggestions made in the piloting stage. These pertained mostly to design (the use of appealing images and the reduction of the amount of text per slide), minor corrections (spelling mistakes and typos), timing issues (as some of the beta versions did not comply with the 20-minute workload estimate) and interactivity and focus (with comments referring to the fact that the presentations were monotonous and that the materials were too wide-ranging).

Regarding participation and overall feedback on the modules, all groups highlighted the fact that the materials were well made and appealing, as well as content/time balance, considering the timing was appropriate for the content being presented. In addition to content pertaining to the topics of the lesson, 8 groups also considered that taking the online modules helped them apply and revise technical vocabulary, giving them the opportunity to complete different assignments, without being too repetitive. In general, students favoured the use of gamified approaches and the fact they could manage their own time, which ultimately resulted in them completing more modules than those required.

As for students' results, all participants were able to successfully complete the project and get a passing grade. Considering specific learning outcomes, it is also possible to state that the strategy facilitated the use of technical vocabulary pertaining to students' field of activity, especially as far as organisation and execution are concerned. Future analyses will focus on comparing these outcomes with that of previous years.

SOLUTIONS AND RECOMMENDATIONS

Considering the key findings and based on observation, the project and the different stages of development are aligned with the literature and current trends, particularly when it comes to the affordances of student-generated content, the development of creativity and critical-thinking skills and the application of technical language.

As possible recommendations for future iterations, it should be noted that students' work within the project was counted for 25% of their final grade, taking into consideration the module they developed, the completion of the assigned modules and their final presentation. Reflecting on the amount of time required to develop and take part in the modules, this percentage could be increased as to reflect and further encourage student participation in the modules. Another recommendation would be to provide other examples of materials, as students tended to use the same tools and approaches presented in class (e.g., the use of the cloud-based platform Nearpod, which was used as an example by the teacher). Considering the hindrances outlined in the literature, particularly when it comes to students understanding the benefits of peer feedback and their need for more support, future iterations of the project could also include tutorials and the provision of feedback training sessions.

Regarding the methodology, it would have been interesting to complement the existing data with that of questionnaires applied to the students. A final questionnaire would help validate the findings and allow the author to crosscut students' individual perceptions, to those presented by the group at the end of the project.

FUTURE RESEARCH DIRECTIONS

As the first iteration of the project has only now been completed, the findings are preliminary and incipient. As a result, future work will include a more in-depth analysis of the materials produced and, more specifically, the language exponents and terminology used. Moreover, drawing from Moodle's reports, a more detailed analysis of the modules and students' participation will also ensue.

As the project is expected to be continue in coming years, with future editions incorporating some of the recommendations outlined in the previous section, it might also be possible to further expand the project's scope by including other students/courses. This would make it possible to collect further data and, in the long run, carry out a longitudinal and cross-sectorial analysis, whose findings could be applied in a wider range of settings.

CONCLUSION

Leveraged by technology, collaborative learning is considered to be a catalyst for building communities of inquiry, bringing together peers, teachers and technology. Encompassing the ideas of collaboration and cooperation, peer-to-peer educational strategies are increasingly being used in Higher Education being considered active and student-centered methodologies. Aiming to reflect on the potential affordances of peer-learning, this chapter described a collaborative project that challenged higher education students to produce online training modules targeting their peers. In addition to working together to design the materials, participants were also challenged to act as reviewers, having had an active role in analyzing and commenting on their peers' assignments.

The data indicates that students taking part in the project were overall satisfied with the learning experience. As a result, there seems to be positive indicators as to students' participation and engagement, with future analysis on the results being expected to further support this argument, as well as determine whether the strategy was successful in supporting skill development and language learning.

Having established the affordances of collaborative and peer learning, this project and the ensuing analysis can be perceived as a positive indicator to the applicability and potential of peer learning strategies to other ESP courses.

Moreover, the strategy described has also contributed towards promoting students' language and critical thinking skills, having challenged them take on an active role by developing materials and reviewing other students' work. Having relied heavily on the use of digital technologies, most particularly LMS, and cloud-based student engagement and graphic design tools (including Nearpod and Canva), it was able to foster students' engagement and agency, with being expected to provide more significant insights that can support other educators and practitioners, as well as future research and initiatives within this scope.

REFERENCES

Barab, S., & Squire, K. (2004). Design-based research: Putting a stake in the ground. *Journal of the Learning Sciences*, *13*(1), 1–14. doi:10.120715327809jls1301_1

Beaumont, T. J., Mannion, A. P., & Shen, B. O. (2012). From the Campus to the Cloud: The Online Peer Assisted Learning Scheme. *Journal of Peer Learning*, *5*(6), 20–31.

Bell, L., & Lygo-Baker, S. (2019). Student-centred learning: A small-scale study of a peer-learning experience in undergraduate translation classes. *Language Learning Journal*, *47*(3), 299–312. doi:10.1080/09571736.2016.1278030

Bezanilla, M. J., Fernández-Nogueira, D., Poblete, M., & Galindo-Domínguez, H. (2019). Methodologies for teaching-learning critical thinking in higher education: The teacher's view. *Thinking Skills and Creativity*, *33*, 100584. https://doi.org/https://doi.org/10.1016/j.tsc.2019.100584. doi:10.1016/j.tsc.2019.100584

Blake, J. (2021). Asynchronous peer teaching using student-created multimodal materials. *International Journal of Information and Education Technology (IJIET)*, *11*(6), 286–291. doi:10.18178/ijiet.2021.11.6.1524

Boud, D. (2001). Making the move to peer learning. *Peer Learning in Higher Education: Learning from and with Each Other*, *1*, 20.

Bunts-Anderson, K. (2016). Successful online learning collaboration: Peer feedback and technology integration in English composition courses. *Arab World English Journal (AWEJ) Special Issue on CALL, 3*.

Burhan-Horasanlı, E. (2022). Digital social reading: Exploring multilingual graduate students' academic discourse socialization in online platforms. *Linguistics and Education*, *71*, 101099. https://doi.org/https://doi.org/10.1016/j.linged.2022.101099. doi:10.1016/j.linged.2022.101099

Burkšaitienė, N. (2022). Translation students' peer feedback for learning English for Specific Purposes (ESP). Findings from a case study in Lithuania. *The Journal of Education, Culture, and Society*, *13*(1), 173–187. doi:10.15503/jecs2022.1.173.187

Canham, N. (2017). Comparing Web 2.0 applications for peer feedback in language teaching: Google Docs, the Sakai VLE, and the Sakai Wiki. *Writing \& Pedagogy, 9*(3).

Carvalho, A. R., & Santos, C. (2022). Developing peer mentors' collaborative and metacognitive skills with a technology-enhanced peer learning program. *Computers and Education Open, 3*, 100070. https://doi.org/https://doi.org/10.1016/j.caeo.2021.100070

Chandra, S., & Palvia, S. (2021). Online education next wave: Peer to peer learning. *Journal of Information Technology Case and Application Research*, *23*(3), 157–172. doi:10.1080/15228053.2021.1980848

Chen, J. H. (2021). Augmenting Student and Professional Training with Peer Learning Groups: Results from Focus Group Interviews. Rutgers The State University of New Jersey, Graduate School of Applied and~....

Ching, Y.-H. (2014). Exploring the impact of role-playing on peer feedback in an online case-based learning activity. *International Review of Research in Open and Distance Learning*, *15*(3), 292–311. doi:10.19173/irrodl.v15i3.1765

Creswell, J. W. (2003). Research design: qualitative, quantitative, and mixed method approaches. In V. Knight (Ed.), Thousand Oaks Calif (Vol. 2nd). Sage Publications. doi:10.2307/3152153

Crouse-Machcinski, K. (2019). The Benefits of Utilizing Learning Management Systems in Peer Tutor Training. *Learning Assistance Review*, *24*(2), 73–84.

Dollinger, M., Lodge, J., & Coates, H. (2018). Co-creation in higher education: Towards a conceptual model. *Journal of Marketing for Higher Education*, *28*(2), 210–231. doi:10.1080/08841241.2018.1466756

Gaies, S. J. (1985). *Peer Involvement in Language Learning. Language in Education: Theory and Practice No. 60* (1st ed.). National Institute of Education.

Gogus, A. (2012). Peer Learning and Assessment. In N. M. Seel (Ed.), *Encyclopedia of the Sciences of Learning* (pp. 2572–2576). Springer US., doi:10.1007/978-1-4419-1428-6_146

Gyamfi, G., Hanna, B., & Khosravi, H. (2022). Supporting peer evaluation of student-generated content: A study of three approaches. *Assessment & Evaluation in Higher Education*, *47*(7), 1129–1147. doi:10.1080/02602938.2021.2006140

Hattie, J., & Clarke, S. (2018). *Visible learning: feedback*. Routledge. doi:10.4324/9780429485480

Havnes, A., Christiansen, B., Bjørk, I. T., & Hessevaagbakke, E. (2016). Peer learning in higher education: Patterns of talk and interaction in skills centre simulation. *Learning, Culture and Social Interaction*, *8*, 75–87. https://doi.org/https://doi.org/10.1016/j.lcsi.2015.12.004. doi:10.1016/j.lcsi.2015.12.004

Hsu, P.-Y. (2021). Academic use of Social Networking Technology for English Learning: Implementing Videotaped Peer Evaluation into English Speech Class. *2021 12th International Conference on E-Education, E-Business, E-Management, and E-Learning*, 248–253.

Huisman, B., Saab, N., Van Driel, J., & Van Den Broek, P. (2018). Peer feedback on academic writing: undergraduate students' peer feedback role, peer feedback perceptions and essay performance. *Assessment\& Evaluation in Higher Education, 43*(6), 955–968.

Hutchinson, S., Woodford, K., Ellis, A., Hamilton-Hinch, B., Stilwell, C., & Manuel, C. (2022). Exploring the role of peer-assisted learning for professional preparation in recreation. *Leisure/Loisir, 46*(1), 23–48. doi:10.1080/14927713.2021.1922092

Irwin, B. (2019). Enhancing peer feedback practices through screencasts in blended academic writing courses. *The JALT CALL Journal, 15*(1), 43–59. doi:10.29140/jaltcall.v15n1.158

Jeong, L., Smith, Z., Longino, A., Merel, S. E., & McDonough, K. (2020). Virtual Peer Teaching During the COVID-19 Pandemic. *Medical Science Educator, 30*(4), 1361–1362. doi:10.100740670-020-01065-1 PMID:32929390

Keerthirathne, W. K. D. (2020). Peer learning: An overview. *International Journal of Scientific Engineering and Science, 4*(11), 1–6.

Latifi, S., & Noroozi, O. (2021). Supporting argumentative essay writing through an online supported peer-review script. *Innovations in Education and Teaching International, 58*(5), 501–511. doi:10.1080/14703297.2021.1961097

Lin, M., Preston, A., Kharrufa, A., & Kong, Z. (2016). Making L2 learners' reasoning skills visible: The potential of Computer Supported Collaborative Learning Environments. *Thinking Skills and Creativity, 22*, 303–322. https://doi.org/https://doi.org/10.1016/j.tsc.2016.06.004. doi:10.1016/j.tsc.2016.06.004

Mohamed, M. N., Nurizah, N., Nurzarina, A. S., & Powzi, N. F. A. (2019). E-collaboration among students of two regions: Impacts on English language learning through peer learning. *International Journal of Learning. Teaching and Educational Research, 18*(9), 201–215.

Moiseenko, V. (2015). Encouraging Learners to Create Language-Learning Materials. *English Teaching Forum, 53*(4), 14–23.

Plomp, T., van den Akker, J., Bannan, B., Kelly, A. E., & Nieveen, N. (2013). *Educational design research: An introduction* (T. Plomp & N. Nieveen, Eds.). SLO.

Pool, J., & Laubscher, D. (2016). Design-based research: Is this a suitable methodology for short-term projects? *Educational Media International, 53*(1), 42–52. doi:10.1080/09523987.2016.1189246

Price, M., Handley, K., Millar, J., & O'donovan, B. (2010). Feedback: all that effort, but what is the effect? *Assessment\& Evaluation in Higher Education, 35*(3), 277–289.

Rahimi, M. (2013). Is training student reviewers worth its while? A study of how training influences the quality of students' feedback and writing. *Language Teaching Research, 17*(1), 67–89. doi:10.1177/1362168812459151

Raymond, A., Jacob, E., Jacob, D., & Lyons, J. (2016). Peer learning a pedagogical approach to enhance online learning: A qualitative exploration. *Nurse Education Today, 44*, 165–169. https://doi.org/https://doi.org/10.1016/j.nedt.2016.05.016. doi:10.1016/j.nedt.2016.05.016 PMID:27429347

Rodis, O. M. M., & Locsin, R. C. (2019). The implementation of the Japanese Dental English core curriculum: Active learning based on peer-teaching and learning activities. *BMC Medical Education, 19*(1), 256. doi:10.118612909-019-1675-y PMID:31291939

Sutherland, L.-A., & Marchand, F. (2021). On-farm demonstration: Enabling peer-to-peer learning. []. Taylor \& Francis.]. *Journal of Agricultural Education and Extension, 27*(5), 573–590. doi:10.1080/1389224X.2021.1959716

Tang, Y. M., Lau, Y., & Chau, K. Y. (2022). Towards a sustainable online peer learning model based on student's perspectives. *Education and Information Technologies, 27*(9), 12449–12468. doi:10.100710639-022-11136-y PMID:35668899

Ting, C., & Shukor, N. A. (2022). Effects of Peer Learning on Pupils' Learning Performance and Creativity in English Writing Skills using Digital Storytelling. *Sains Humanika, 14*(3–2), 105–115.

Topping, K. J. (2005). Trends in Peer Learning. *Educational Psychology, 25*(6), 631–645. doi:10.1080/01443410500345172

Vani, V. V. (2016). Enhancing Students' Speaking Skills through Peer Team Teaching: A Student Centered Approach. *Journal on English Language Teaching, 6*(4), 19–26.

Vygotsky, L. (1962). *Thought and Language* (E. Hanfmann & G. Vakar, Eds.). MIT Press. doi:10.1037/11193-000

Willey, K., & Gardner, A. P. (2010). Collaborative peer learning to change learning culture and develop the skills for lifelong professional practice. *Annual Conference of Australasian Association for Engineering Education.*

Zhang, Z., Hansen, C. T., & Andersen, M. A. E. (2016). Teaching Power Electronics With a Design-Oriented, Project-Based Learning Method at the Technical University of Denmark. *IEEE Transactions on Education, 59*(1), 32–38. doi:10.1109/TE.2015.2426674

Zou, D., & Xie, H. (2019). Flipping an English writing class with technology-enhanced just-in-time teaching and peer instruction. *Interactive Learning Environments, 27*(8), 1127–1142. doi:10.1080/10494820.2018.1495654

ADDITIONAL READING

Bailey, D., & Cassidy, R. (2019). Online peer feedback tasks: Training for improved L2 writing proficiency, anxiety reduction, and language learning strategies. *Call-Ej, 20*(2), 70–88.

Batardière, M.-T., & Jeanneau, C. (2020). Towards Developing Tandem Learning in Formal Language Education. *Recherche et Pratiques Pédagogiques En Langues de Spécialité. Cahiers de l'Apliut, 39*(1).

Carvalho, A. R., & Santos, C. (2020). Teachers and peer teacher students' perceptions on ICT tools usage in peer learning projects : Findings from a multiple case study. *2020 15th Iberian Conference on Information Systems and Technologies (CISTI)*, 1–6. https://doi.org/10.23919/CISTI49556.2020.9140912

Gonglewski, M., & Baker, L. (2021). Curricular peer mentoring in first-semester German: Novice learners' perceptions of a "Language Learning Assistant" program. *Foreign Language Annals, 54*(4), 952–973. doi:10.1111/flan.12564

Kaendler, C., Wiedmann, M., Rummel, N., & Spada, H. (2015). Teacher competencies for the implementation of collaborative learning in the classroom: A framework and research review. *Educational Psychology Review, 27*(3), 505–536. doi:10.100710648-014-9288-9

Keerthirathne, W. K. D. (2020). Peer learning: An overview. *International Journal of Scientific Engineering and Science, 4*(11), 1–6.

Masterson, M. (2020). An exploration of the potential role of digital technologies for promoting learning in foreign language classrooms: Lessons for a pandemic. [IJET]. *International Journal of Emerging Technologies in Learning, 15*(14), 83–96. doi:10.3991/ijet.v15i14.13297

Molapo, M., Moodley, C. S., Akhalwaya, I. Y., Kurien, T., Kloppenberg, J., & Young, R. (2019). Designing digital peer assessment for second language learning in low resource learning settings. *Proceedings of the Sixth (2019) ACM Conference on Learning@ Scale*, 1–13. 10.1145/3330430.3333626

KEY TERMS AND DEFINITIONS

Constructive feedback: the provision of prompt and timely reviews or learning suggestions, based on specific tasks or assignments. It involves the identification of problem areas, encouraging questioning, and possible suggestions and/or solutions. This feedback can be measured and facilitated by the use of digital tools.

English for Specific Purposes (ESP): A division of English as a Foreign Language, refering to the teaching of English that focuses on terminology and developing communicative skills in a particular field or occupation. ESP courses are designed to meet specific needs of the learners, with reference to the particular vocabulary and register required in their field of studies.

Nearpod: online learning and presentation platform that combines interactive activities (such as quizzes and interactive videos) with content delivery, both synchronously and asynchronously. The platform can be used to implement assessment activities and is compatible with multiple applications.

Project-based Learning (PBL): A student-centred approach that implies the development of a project oriented towards the solution of a real-world problem/ challenge, with the teachers acting as facilitators, responsible for engaging students in building their own learning.

Rubrics: Set of instructions and quality descriptors used as means of communicating assessment standards and criteria between students and instructors, paticularly when structuring peer-evaluation. Despite the wide acceptance of rubrics, their impact is considered to be under-explored.

Student Agency: Student agency refers to students' active and responsive involvement in both learning and assessment practices, as opposed to more traditional, lecture driven approaches. The concept implies that students are engaged in a process of looking for (rather than just receiving) feedback from different sources and at different times, crosscutting it with their own experience and context, and using it to make informed and independent choices regarding their learning.

Chapter 6
Approaches and Tools for Experiential Learning of Abstract Concepts:
The Case of Algorithms

J. Ángel Velázquez-Iturbide
🆔 https://orcid.org/0000-0002-9486-8526
Universidad Rey Juan Carlos, Spain

ABSTRACT

Some students prefer a concrete approach to learning whereas others prefer an abstract one. Algorithms perform transformations of information, thus they have an abstract nature. Consequently, many students have difficulties in their study. We present two computer-supported approaches to experiential learning of algorithms. On the one hand, program visualization automatically generates graphical representations of the behavior of algorithms, making visible the virtual. On the other hand, algorithm benchmarking gathers and compares data of the performance of several algorithms, making visible their properties with respect to given criteria. The chapter includes a brief motivation and introduction to these issues, followed by a treatment of each educational approach. For each approach, we present an introduction to its foundations, relevant features of educational systems intended to support them, and ways of using them in algorithm courses. We also deal with the successful instructional integration of program visualization and algorithm benchmarking systems into algorithm courses.

DOI: 10.4018/978-1-6684-8656-6.ch006

INTRODUCTION

Several disciplines have an abstract nature, but their abstraction has different features. Thus, it is different the abstraction present in physics, poetry, or philosophy. Although some students feel comfortable with abstraction, other students prefer an experiential approach to learning (Felder & Silverman, 1988). Consequently, the former students may have difficulties studying these matters.

Some education theoreticians (e.g., John Dewey or Jerome Bruner) emphasized experience as a means to develop students' capabilities to solve problems and live in society. Bruner's constructivist theory (Bruner, 1960) suggests that learning new material is effective when a progression is followed from inactive (action-based) to iconic (image-based) to symbolic (language-based) modes of representation. His conception laid a foundation for a spectrum of instructional practices for abstract matters, being the Concrete-Representation-Abstract (CRA) sequence (Hoong, Kin & Pien, 2015) particularly well-known as it has proved to be effective for learning mathematics and it is used to teach mathematics to primary school students in Singapore.

Some fields of informatics also are abstract, given that informatics deals with the virtual world, which is invisible. In particular, algorithmics is a field with a strong mathematical basis, where problems that consist in information transformation are solved. Thus, an algorithm is a procedure consisting of precise steps, which transforms given input data into output data. Different students' difficulties and misconceptions on algorithms have been reported in the informatics literature (e.g., Farghally *et al.*, 2017). In this chapter, we present two ways of providing an experiential approach to learning algorithms, namely visualization and experimentation. We describe both approaches, also addressing their instrumental and instructional aspects.

Both approaches provide an opportunity to integrate students with different learning styles into algorithm courses. Using the terminology of Felder's model of learning styles (Felder & Silverman, 1988), students who feel comfortable with a mathematical approach, use a "reflective" (i.e., based on introspection) approach to processing information, an "intuitive" (i.e., abstract) approach to knowledge, and a "verbal" (i.e., written) approach to information. However, the two alternatives for algorithm instruction named above support an "active" (i.e., based on action) approach to processing information, a "sensing" (i.e., concrete) approach to knowledge, and a "visual" approach to information. In terms of the CRA sequence, visualization supports algorithm learning at the concrete and representation models, while experimentation supports concrete learning.

Our proposal also is compatible with Kolb's experiential learning cycle (Kolb, 1984), frequently advocated in engineering education (e.g., Abdulwahed & Nagy, 2009). According to Kolb, there are two modes of grasping experience (namely, concrete experience and abstract conceptualization), and two modes of transforming experience (namely, reflective observation and active experimentation). He suggests that for a complete learning experience, students must go through all modes, which can be modeled as a learning cycle composed of four stages. The two approaches here presented mainly contribute to concrete experience and active experimentation, but they also provide additional elements to support abstract conceptualization and reflective observation.

The structure of the chapter follows. The following section provides a brief introduction to the visualization and experimentation approaches as well as some algorithmic preliminaries. The two following sections describe visualization and benchmarking in algorithmics, respectively. Both sections start with an introduction to the approach and then present features of their accompanying educational software and their instructional aspects. We conclude with some final, common instructional remarks on both approaches, as well as future research directions.

BACKGROUND

In this section, we briefly introduce several issues aimed at explaining smoother our proposal regarding visualization and experimentation.

Recursion

Shortly, recursion is the definition of something by means of itself. It may be a surprising rhetoric resource, but it is used in several fields. For instance, the recursive definition of the factorial of a natural number n, denoted $n!$, follows:

$$n! = \begin{cases} 1 & if\ n = 0 \\ n(n-1)! & otherwise \end{cases}$$

This recursive definition can be used as an algorithm to constructively compute the factorial of any natural number (see Figure 1).

Note that the recursive process has two parts: a "forward" part where all the recursive calls are "unfolded", leaving pending operations (here, multiplications), and a "backwards" part where pending operations are solved (in reverse order of their creation).

There are more complex formats of recursion than the lineal recursion shown in the example. In programming, understanding recursion is even more difficult than in mathematics, because the execution of programming languages involves

Figure 1. Recursive computation of the factorial of 4

$$
\begin{aligned}
4! & \\
&= 4 \cdot 3! \\
&= 4 \cdot (3 \cdot 2!) \\
&= 4 \cdot (3 \cdot (2 \cdot 1!)) \\
&= 4 \cdot (3 \cdot (2 \cdot (1 \cdot 0!))) \\
&= 4 \cdot (3 \cdot (2 \cdot (1 \cdot 1))) \\
&= 4 \cdot (3 \cdot (2 \cdot 1)) \\
&= 4 \cdot (3 \cdot 2) \\
&= 4 \cdot 6 \\
&= 24
\end{aligned}
$$

Forward

Backwards

non-trivial bookkeeping mechanisms of control flow and memory allocation (Velázquez-Iturbide, 2000). Consequently, recursion is one of the most difficult programming concepts to learn (Lahtinen, Ala-Mutka & Järvinen, 2005), being its education an active area of research (Rinderknecht, 2014). Students' difficulties have been studied, and common unviable mental models have been identified in students (Götschi, Sanders & Galpin, 2003).

Software Visualization

Broadly speaking, information visualization (Card, Mackinley & Shneiderman, 1999) provides a way of making visible the invisible (e.g., the hierarchy in an organization) or of providing a more effective representation (i.e., the evolution of certain data over time). In particular, software visualization (Stasko *et al.*, 1998) allows making visible the information transformation processes performed by programs and algorithms. Traditionally, two trends have been distinguished within software visualization, namely program and algorithm visualization (Price, Baecker & Small, 1998). Program visualization automatically generates visualizations of the code and data structures present in programs. It exhibits the advantages of automation and generality (within the domain supported by the system), but also the disadvantage of low level of abstraction. On the other hand, algorithm visualization displays more abstract views of computing processes, at the cost of needing to develop manually each specific visualization. Despite the existence of some intermediate approaches (e.g., Sirkiä, 2017), this basic dichotomy continues to be valid.

The automation and universality properties of program visualization are a key feature for a visualization system to be adopted by instructors and students. In effect, both kinds of users may use the system in educational activities to visualize any algorithm developed by themselves. In our experience, additional requirements are necessary for its educational adoption. The most important feature of the system is high interactivity, as the user typically does not know the features or the contents of the visualizations generated, and he/she must interact until a meaningful visualization is obtained. Hence, the popular mantra of information visualization also is applicable to program visualization (Shneiderman, 1996): "overview first, zoom and filter, then details-on-demand".

Despite the different features of program and algorithm visualization, their visualizations are similar for certain classes of algorithms, provided they display the same computational elements. For instance, recursion is always displayed for divide-and-conquer algorithms, or tables for dynamic programming algorithms. In the chapter, we focus on program visualization because it guarantees automation and generality while also providing high-level expressiveness by supporting the visualization of selected essential elements. In particular, we illustrate this approach with the visualization of recursion.

Another common dichotomy in software visualization lies between static versus dynamic visualizations (Price, Baecker & Small, 1998). Thus, the term algorithm animation refers to visualizations whose contents are at the algorithm level of abstraction and have a dynamic nature. Dynamic visualizations are usually played by using VCR-like controls.

Analysis of Algorithms

Algorithms can be analyzed with respect to several criteria. Obviously, the most relevant is correctness, since an incorrect algorithm is useless. However, the dichotomy between correct/incorrect algorithms gives way to a range of quality values for some types of algorithms. Thus, we may refer to the quality of numeric or optimization algorithms by analyzing the error they produce with respect to exact or optimal solutions, respectively. In this case, the criterion is solution quality; in the case of optimization algorithms, the criterion can be called solution optimality, or optimality for short.

The second most important analysis criterion is time efficiency, since it determines whether a given problem can be solved by al algorithm in an acceptable lapse of time. Computer science theory has determined that some problems cannot be solved in an "acceptable" length of time, assigning this attribute to algorithms whose execution time can be stated as a polynomial of input data size. Otherwise, their run-time will take longer than minutes or hours (even billions of years). A related criterion is space-efficiency, which measures the memory space allocated in the computer to conduct the algorithmic process.

Finally, redundancy is a criterion related to time efficiency. A redundant algorithm repeatedly computes the same subtasks, thus resulting in unnecessarily long run-times and therefore in poor time efficiency. Identification of redundancy in a recursive algorithm is the first step for its removal.

It must also be noticed that analysis of algorithms can be conducted by both formal and experimental means. Formal methods of analysis are the only ones capable of proving certain properties, such as algorithm correctness or time complexity. Despite their limitations, experimental means provide evidence in cases where formal methods are difficult to use or cannot even be applied. In addition, experimentation provides students with hands-on experience with algorithm behavior.

Algorithm Experimentation and Benchmarking

Traditionally, the time efficiency of algorithms (i.e., their time complexity) is analyzed in algorithm courses by mathematical means. Space complexity can also be formally analyzed, but this analysis is less frequent. However, some students have difficulties in understanding the implications of the complexity function of an algorithm for the evolution of its running time for increasing data sizes. Conducting experiments aimed at measuring running times provides a more vivid, experiential observation of this phenomenon (McCracken, 1989).

Conducting a reliable experiment with algorithms requires careful scheduling (Sanders, 2002). A research field exists devoted to this goal, which deals with many experimental difficulties (McGeoch, 2012). However, for educational purposes, there is no need to obtain as complete or elaborated results as in research, but they must be reasonably approximate. In particular, the careful scheduling needed makes algorithm experimentation similar to scientific experimentation (Matocha, 1992).

An educationally valuable instance of experimentation consists in comparing the performance of alternative algorithms that solve a given problem, i.e., algorithm benchmarking. By comparing alternative algorithms for a given problem, the student may better appreciate the pros and cons of each individual algorithm. For the time efficiency criterion, benchmarking typically shows the difference in time growth of algorithms with different complexity functions. For the optimality criterion, benchmarking allows showing that inexact algorithms may yield suboptimal (but valid) solutions, whereas an exact algorithm always yields optimal solutions. Making explicit variations in a phenomenon is a key of learning according to variation theory (Marton & Tsui, 2004).

VISUALIZING ALGORITHMS

In this section, we present the program visualization approach to learning algorithms, using recursion as the programming construct visualized. Firstly, we present different representations of recursion. Secondly, we present the features that a program visualization system must have to be educationally appealing and useful. Finally, we elaborate on the integration of visualizations into the algorithm course.

Visualizations of Recursion

There are multiple graphical representations of recursion (Haynes, 1996), which are introduced here and illustrated with the SRec system (Velázquez-Iturbide, Pérez-Carrasco & Urquiza-Fuentes, 2008). A review of other visualization systems can be found in (Velázquez-Iturbide *et al.*, 2008).

Consider a more complex recursive algorithm than the factorial presented above. It is the well-known, multiple recursive definition of the series of Fibonacci, coded as a Java method:

```java
public static int fib (int n) {
    if (n==0 || n==1)
        return 1;
    else
        return fib(n-1) + fib(n-2);
}
```

A common graphical representation is the recursion tree. A recursion tree is a tree-shaped display where each node represents a method call. A call is displayed as a node split into two areas, with input data in the upper area and output in the lower area. Figure 2 shows a partial recursion tree that corresponds to the sixth Fibonacci number, computed with the recursive method included above. Note at the right of the figure that a call to *fib*(0) is the active call and there are three pending calls, *fib*(2), *fib*(4) and *fib*(6); the final outcome of the whole process will be 13 (not shown in this visualization).

Another representation of recursion is the trace. A trace shows the pre-order traversal of a recursion tree, making explicit the order of computation of the recursive process as a sequence of events. Figure 3 shows a trace corresponding to the recursive computation of *fib*(6). The trace in the figure has a textual format, but a graphical

Figure 2. Four alternative visualizations of the recursive computation of fib(6): (a)
recursion tree

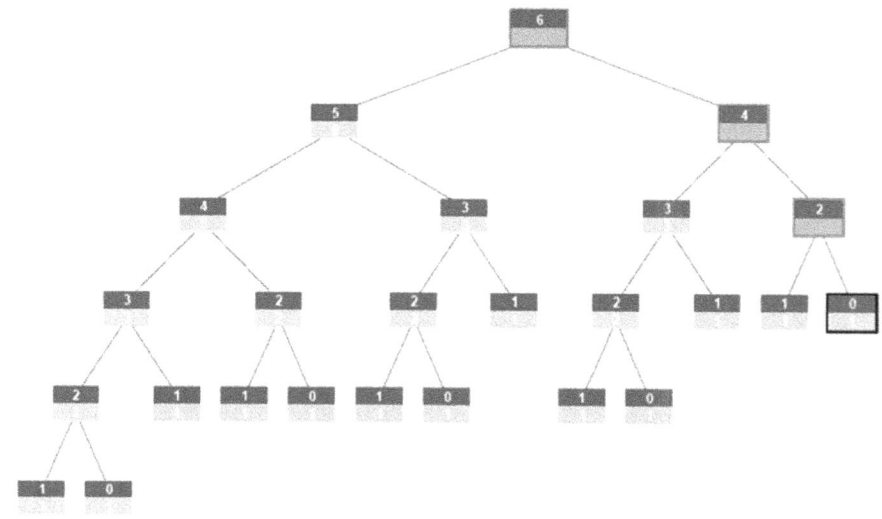

format can also be generated in some cases (Velázquez-Iturbide, Pérez-Carrasco &
Urquiza-Fuentes, 2009).

An implementation-based representation of recursion is the control stack. The
stack stores pending method calls as well as the active call. A control stack is
isomorphic to the branch of the recursion tree that hosts the active and pending
calls, as shown in Figure 4. Actually, the other calls displayed in a recursion tree
correspond to completed calls, therefore the memory allocated in the control stack
for them was released on exit.

Finally, a dependency graph (Cormen *et al.*, 2009) is a directed acyclic graph.
It is a representation that can be derived from a recursion tree by joining equal
nodes while preserving their linking edges. Figure 5 shows the dependency graph
corresponding to the recursion tree of *fib*(6).

Additional representations of recursion can be found, but they are either less
common or specific of certain classes of algorithms (Stern & Naish, 2002; Velázquez-
Iturbide *et al.*, 2009).

Educational visualization systems

Adoption of a visualization system by teachers and students does not only depend
on its technical features, but also on its adequacy to their needs. In our experience,
the following features are necessary.

Figure 3. (b) trace

```
in  : n==6
  in  : n==5
    in  : n==4
      in  : n==3
        in  : n==2
          in  : n==1
          return : return 1
          in  : n==0
          return : return 1
        return : return 2
        in  : n==1
        return : return 1
      return : return 3
      in  : n==2
        in  : n==1
        return : return 1
        in  : n==0
        return : return 1
      return : return 2
    return : return 5
    in  : n==3
      in  : n==2
        in  : n==1
        return : return 1
        in  : n==0
        return : return 1
      return : return 2
      in  : n==1
      return : return 1
    return : return 3
  return : return 8
  in  : n==4
    in  : n==3
      in  : n==2
        in  : n==1
        return : return 1
        in  : n==0
        return : return 1
      return : return 2
      in  : n==1
      return : return 1
    return : return 3
    in  : n==2
      in  : n==1
      return : return 1
      in  : n==0
      return : return 1
    return : return 2
  return : return 5
return : return 13
```

Figure 4. (c) stack

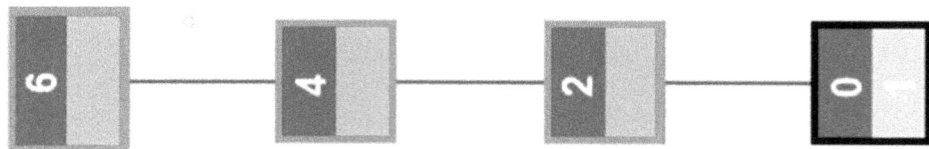

Figure 5.(d) dependency graph

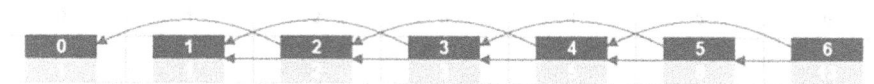

Usability. It is a feature necessary for the adoption of any software system, but in education it is even more critical. Usability comprises many different features, but we highlight the ease of generating visualizations, often called effortlessness.

Effortlessness is a complex construct with several factors (Ihantola *et al.*, 2005). An important factor is how easy and fast is the process of visualization generation, which is necessary for the use of the system by students and instructors. As an example of effortlessness, SRec allows generating a visualization by following a few simple steps:

1. Load a Java class that contains the methods to visualize. The system processes the file without user's awareness.
2. Select the method to visualize.
3. Enter input data for the target visualization.
4. Interact with the views automatically generated by the system to obtain a meaningful display.

Engagement. The term student engagement has been used to refer to the learner involvement with the teaching system that includes the interaction with the system, instructor, or other students within the system (Al-Sakkaf, Omar & Ahmad, 2019). Although there are no definite recommendations to achieve engagement, there is an agreement on several basic features (Naps *et al.*, 2003), such as allowing student to control animation, to be able to backtrack in animations and to introduce his/her own input data.

Interactivity. It is a necessary feature for any visualization system. In general, a visualization generated automatically does not satisfy the user needs, who must interact to customize the visualization until it fits his/her needs. There are many types of interaction with visualizations (Velázquez-Iturbide & Pérez-Carrasco, 2010). In our experience, the most useful interactions are:

– Navigate in time (i.e., animate the visualizations).
– Navigate in space, if the visualization displays a large recursive process.
– Zoom in/out.
– Filter methods and parameters.
– Re-order the elements in a visualization while keeping their relationship.
– Switch between the different graphical representations.

Other educational support. SRec provides direct educational support by making the installation and execution of the system easy. In addition, it allows instructors and students to export the different visualizations and animations in a range of graphical file formats. As a consequence, any document (e.g., instructional materials or assignment reports) may easily import those files as figures. Finally, the user may select the natural language used in the system interface, currently either English or Spanish.

Visualization of Recursion in an Algorithms Course

Given the automatic generation of program visualizations, systems such as SRec can be used easily and profitably by both instructors and students. We focus here on the educational goals that systems such as SRec may support; integration of visualization into the course instruction is addressed in another section.

In a programming course, SRec can be used to support novices in learning recursion, as it supports different views of recursion as well as their animation. In particular, animation makes visible the tracing of recursion, facilitating its understanding and making more difficult to develop misunderstandings of recursion behavior.

In an algorithms course, it is assumed that students already understand and have basic mastery of the design of recursive algorithms. Therefore, SRec can be integrated into an algorithms course by supporting different aspects of algorithms.

Firstly, SRec can be used to understand algorithm behavior (Velázquez-Iturbide *et al.*, 2008). It is the most common use of program and algorithm visualizations. Such an understanding can be achieved by means of either static visualizations that preserve the algorithm history or animations. In the latter case, the user should be able to control flexibly the animation at least in the forward and backwards directions. In addition, SRec allows both automatic and manual play. Manual play can proceed step-by-step, going back home, going to the end and executing the active call in one step. Moreover, the user may select any previous recursive call and make it the active call.

Recursion trees generated by SRec also can be used to analyze algorithms with respect to three criteria, namely time efficiency, space efficiency, and computational redundancy. Time efficiency is proportional to the number of nodes of the recursion tree. SRec provides several statistics about the size of the recursion tree. The asymptotic complexity of run time can be appreciated by comparing the rate of growth of the tree size with respect to the growth of input data size. SRec even allows generating in one step several visualizations, each one corresponding to different input data, thus making easier their comparison (Velázquez Iturbide, Hernán-Losada & Pérez-Carrasco, 2016). Figure 2 shows that the recursion tree for *fib*(6) has 25 nodes; if we increased the parameter *n* by one (to 7), the number of nodes would be increased to 41. Actually, the time complexity of the recursive definition of the Fibonacci series is $O(\Phi^n)$, where $\Phi \approx 1.618$ is the golden ratio.

Time and space must be measured differently because space is reused (by the operating system), while time cannot be reused. Thus, the maximum amount of memory space used by a recursive algorithm is not proportional to the size of the recursion tree but to the maximum allocation of memory along the algorithm execution. That memory corresponds to the length of the longest branch of the recursion tree. For the Fibonacci series, its space complexity is $O(n)$ (see Figure 2).

Redundancy is analyzed by looking for repeated occurrences of any recursive method calls in a recursion tree (excluding base cases). SRec provides two ways of conducting this analysis. On the one hand, the user may watch the recursion tree, trying to find two identical recursive calls. Then, he/she may query identical calls by means of either a dialog or direct interaction with the tree. Figure 2 shows the result of searching for *fib*(3) calls, with 5 identical nodes. On the other hand, the user may directly ask for redundancy statistics. As a consequence, the system provides global information on redundancy, as well as several parameter values with redundant calls. The top part of Figure 3 shows that there are only 2 non-redundant recursive nodes in the computation of *fib*(6) and 18 redundant nodes; the bottom part breaks down those 18 nodes into four cases, including the 5 nodes of *fib*(3). Either way of obtaining visual evidence of redundancy illustrates the need of system interactivity to obtain information not displayed in the first visualization generated by the system for specific input data.

A final, uncommon use of program visualization is as an aid for algorithm development (Velázquez Iturbide & Pérez-Carrasco, 2016). SRec provides assistance to transform inefficient, redundant recursive algorithms into efficient, non-redundant algorithms. SRec may transform, on demand, a recursion tree into its corresponding dependency graph. This way, dependencies between calls are made explicit. Furthermore, SRec allows mapping the nodes of any dependency graph

Figure 6. Redundancy in a recursive the computation of fib(6): (a) recursion tree with some redundant nodes highlighted

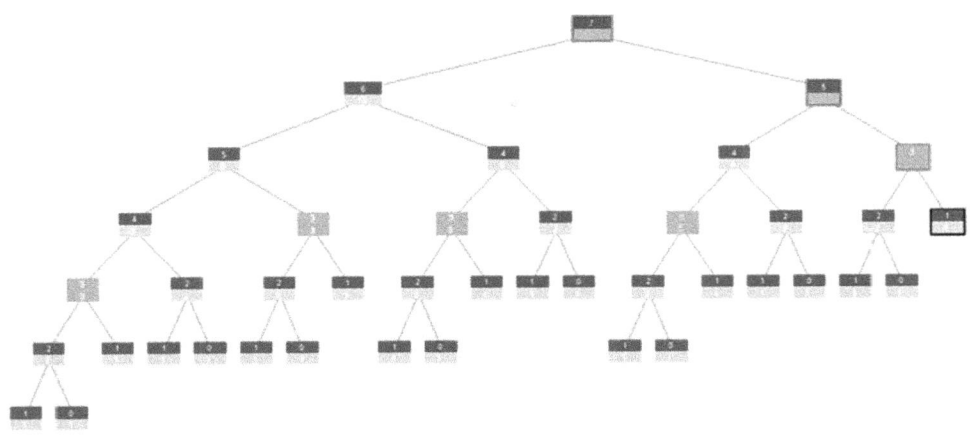

Figure 7. (b) dependency statistics

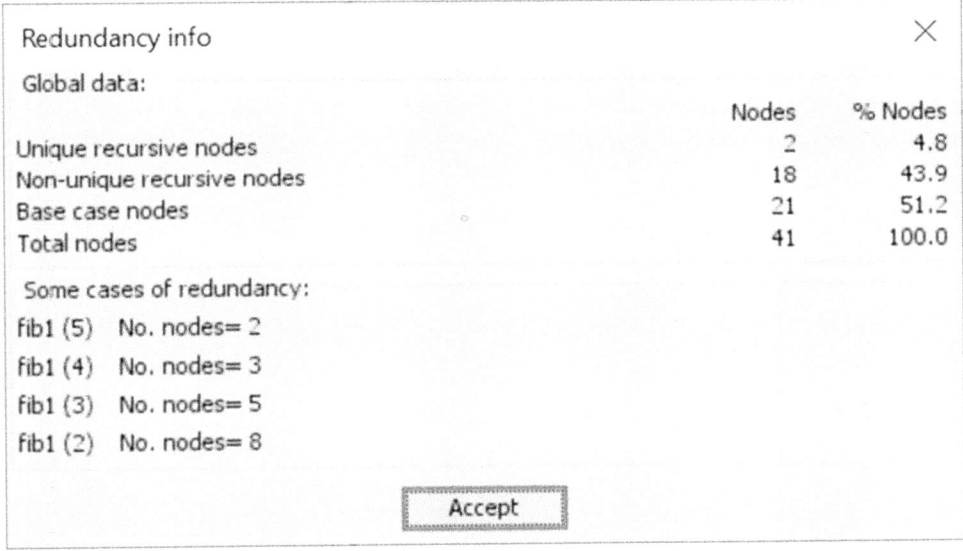

into cells of a uni- or bi-dimensional table (see Figure 5). This can be made either manually or automatically. In the former case, the user may declare the shape and size of the table, and place the distinct graph nodes on the table cells. In the latter case, the user may declare how the graph nodes will be distributed on the table by means of expressions that relate algorithm parameters with rows and columns. SRec automatically uses those expressions to compute the size of the table and lay out the different nodes, also warning in case any nodes collide in the same cell.

For instance, consider the bioinformatics problem of global alignment (D'Antonio, 2003). It can be solved with the following recursive algorithm:

$$A(0,0) = 0$$
$$A(0,j) = -2j \qquad se\ inserta\ y_1,...,y_j$$
$$A(i,0) = -2i \qquad se\ borran\ x_1,...,x_i$$

$$A(i,j) = \max \begin{cases} A(i,j-1) - 2 & se\ inserta\ y_j \\ A(i-1,j) - 2 & se\ borra\ x_i \\ A(i-1,j-1) + \begin{cases} +1 & si\ x_i = y_j \\ -1 & si\ x_i \neq y_j \end{cases} \end{cases}$$

If we use this algorithm to determine an alignment with maximal similarity score between DNA sequences GGGCAT and GGACA, we obtain the recursion tree displayed in Figure 8. Its conversion into a dependency graph provides a basis for the polynomial-time Neddleman-Wunsch algorithm. In Figure 9, we show a mapping produced with SRec from the dependency graph into the bi-dimensional table used by this iterative algorithm.

Figure 8. Two visualizations of the computation of A("GGGCAT","GGACA"): (a) recursion tree

The user will have noticed that the recursion tree displayed in Figure 8 is so large (it has 5,480 nodes) that we hardly can watch anything but its wide shape and low height. SRec provides interaction facilities to handle the vision of such large trees, including an overview+detail interface, filtering, zooming and scrolling. Actually, Figure 8 shows a small portion of the tree in detail on the top area and an overview of the complete tree in the bottom area. However, Figure 9 shows that the tree only contains 42 different nodes. The recursive algorithm is therefore highly redundant.

Figure 9. (b) dependency graph layout on a bi-dimensional table

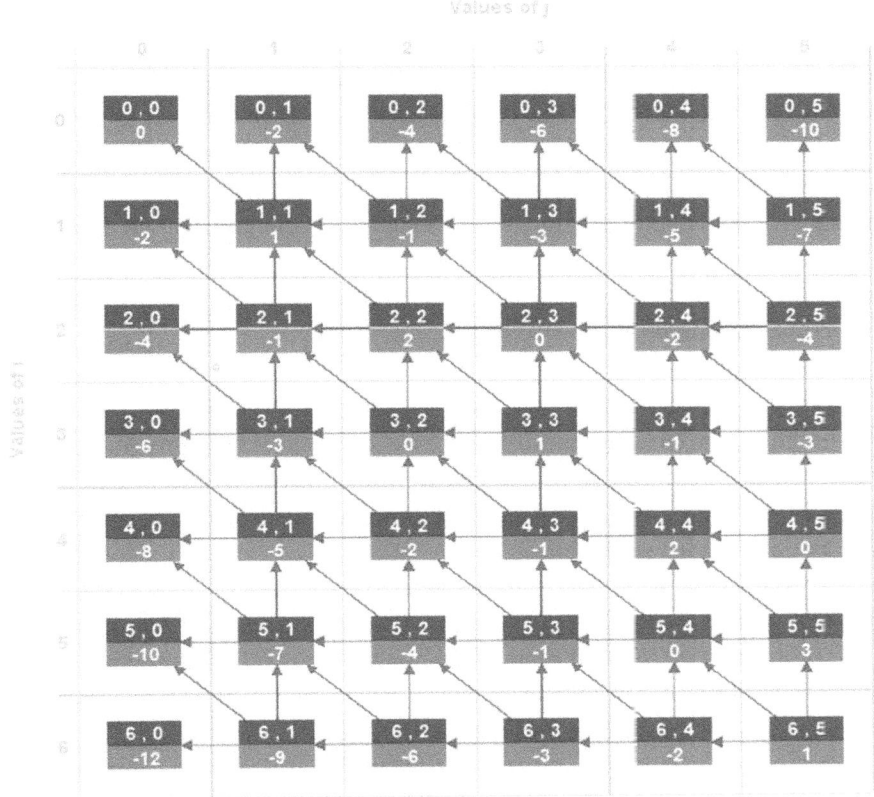

BENCHMARKING ALGORITHMS

In this section, we present the benchmarking approach to understanding algorithms performance, focusing on optimization algorithms. Firstly, we introduce the benchmarking of algorithms for two different criteria, namely time efficiency and optimality. Secondly, we present the features that a benchmarking system must have to be educationally appealing and useful. Finally, we elaborate on the integration of benchmarking into the algorithm course.

Benchmarking Optimization Algorithms

Optimization problems are a specific class of computational problems, characterized by a specification that not only describes what a valid solution is but also what an optimal solution is. Algorithms that solve this important class of problems can either always yield an optimal solution (i.e. an exact algorithm) or just yield a valid, but probably suboptimal solution (i.e., an inexact algorithm). Heuristic and approximation algorithms are inexact algorithms while algorithms designed according to other design techniques (e.g., dynamic programming or branch-and-bound algorithms) are exact.

For instance, consider the bin packing problem (Baase & van Gelder, 2000). The problem has two versions, a maximization and a minimization one. In the minimization version, we are given n objects, where object i has weight w_i, and a number of identical storage bins with capacity w, where every bin can hold any number of objects provided their total weight does not exceed the bin capacity. Objects may not be split between bins. The problem goal consists in storing the n objects in the minimum number of bins.

There are a number of heuristic algorithms for this problem (Baase & van Gelder, 2000), some of them computing solutions within a bounded deviation from optimal solutions (i.e., approximate algorithms). This bound can be formally proved, but their proofs usually are intricate. A complementary, more vivid educational approach consists in benchmarking alternative algorithms for the problem, ideally including both exact and inexact algorithms.

Furthermore, benchmarking allows inquiring on measures that cannot be obtained analytically. For example, it can be shown the percentage of cases for which an inexact algorithm yields an optimal solution, as well as other dispersion measures with respect to optimal solutions (e.g., mean deviation). Results often are surprising and unexpected (Velázquez-Iturbide & Debdi, 2011).

To illustrate this concern, we present the result of randomly generating 500 instances of the problem, with 10 objects of weight ranging between 1 and 7, and storage bins of capacity ranging between 7 and 20. We have run four algorithms against these 500 problem instances: two approximation algorithms (the "next-fit" and the "first-fit decreasing" heuristics), a backtracking algorithm and a branch-and-bound algorithm.

Figures 10 and 11 illustrates the results of conducting this experiment with the benchmarking AlgorEx system (Velázquez-Iturbide, 2021). Figure 10 shows several indicators which cannot be deduced analytically. In addition to checking that the backtracking and the branch-and-bound algorithms are exact, we note that the next-fit heuristic delivers about one half of optimal outcomes whereas the first-fit heuristic is near to exact for this set of instances. However, the former heuristic has produced suboptimal outcomes with less deviation from optimal outcomes than the latter. The seventh row shows a mean deviation of 25.45% above optimal outcomes for instances where the former heuristic was not optimal vs. 34.72% for the latter heuristic. Figure 11 shows the percentages of suboptimal outcomes and mean and maximal deviation in two charts.

Figure 10. Results of benchmarking optimality for four algorithms that solve the minimization version: (a) tabular format

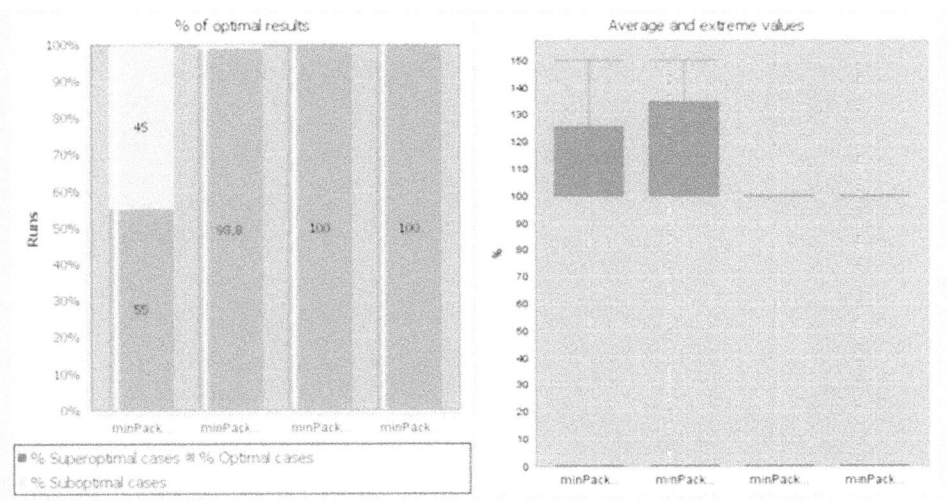

Figure 11. (b) graphical format

Measures	minPackingApprox1	minPackingApprox2	minPackingBaB	minPackingBack
Num. runs	500	500	500	500
Num. runs correct by Method	500	500	500	500
Num. correct total runs	500	500	500	500
% Suboptimal outcomes	45,00 %	1,20 %	0,00 %	0,00 %
% Optimal solutions	55,00 %	98,80 %	100,00 %	100,00 %
% Superoptimal solutions	0,00 %	0,00 %	0,00 %	0,00 %
% Suboptimal average difference	125,45 %	134,72 %	0,00 %	0,00 %
% Suboptimal maximum difference	150,00 %	150,00 %	0,00 %	0,00 %
% Superoptimal average difference	0,00 %	0,00 %	0,00 %	0,00 %
% Superoptimal maximum difference	0,00 %	0,00 %	0,00 %	0,00 %

Benchmarking optimization algorithms with respect to their optimality does not exclude benchmarking them with respect to their time-efficiency. On the contrary, both criteria enrich the understanding of pros and cons of these algorithms. Furthermore, supporting the benchmarking of time-efficiency allows extending the benefits of benchmarking to any computable problem.

Figure 12 presents both a tabular and a graphical summary of the run-times of the same algorithms and for the same test cases as in Figure 10. Figure 12 illustrates that approximate algorithms are the fastest, while the backtracking algorithm is the slowest. The branch-and-bound also exhibits good time performance, without being as efficient as approximate algorithms.

Figure 12. Results of benchmarking running-times for four algorithms that solve the minimization version: (a) tabular format

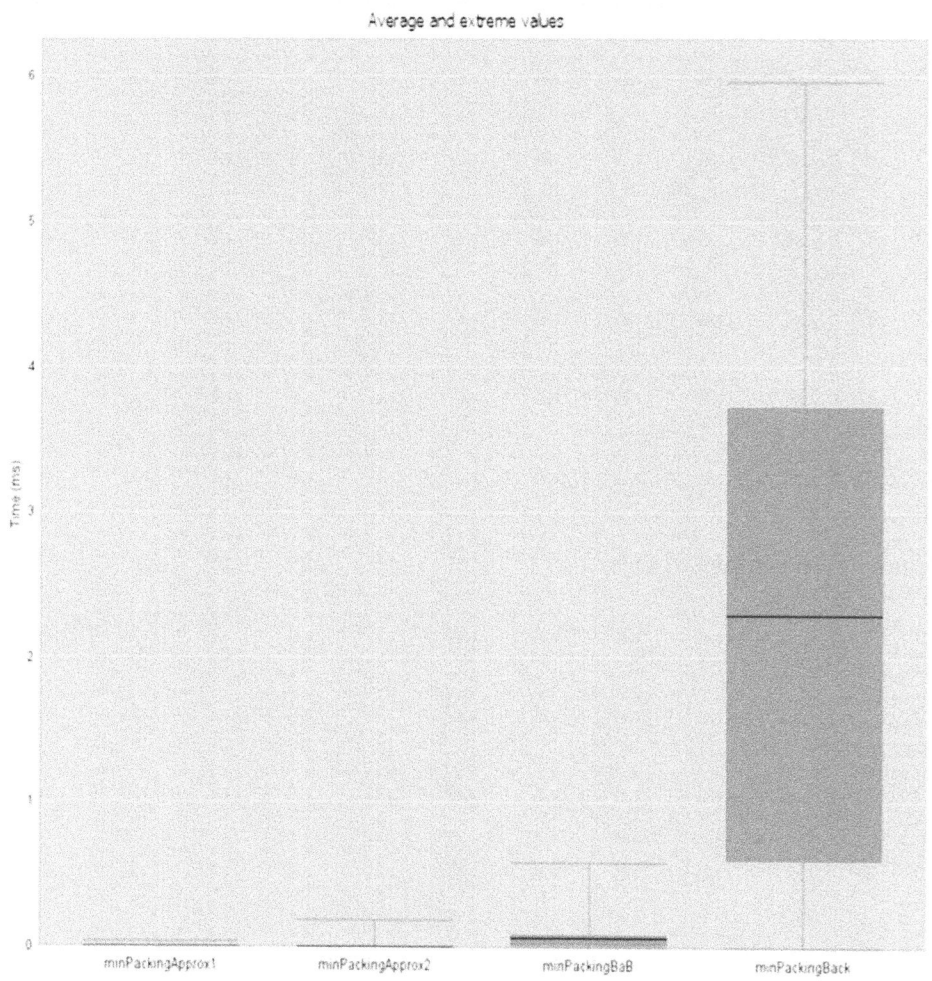

Figure 13. (b) graphical format

Measures	minPackingApprox1	minPackingApprox2	minPackingBaB	minPackingBack
Num. runs	500	500	500	500
Num. runs correct by Method	500	500	500	500
Num. correct total runs	500	500	500	500
Maximum time	0.039 ms	0.183 ms	0.578 ms	5.955 ms
Medium time	0.002 ms	0.003 ms	0.065 ms	2.299 ms
Minimum time	0.001 ms	0.001 ms	0.003 ms	0.003 ms

Educational Benchmarking Systems

Benchmarking demands programming certain mundane functions, which are alien to the educational goals of an algorithm course. Their integration in a benchmarking system (Velázquez-Iturbide, 2021) relieves instructors and students from devoting time to programming these tasks again and again. These functions follow.

Generation of input data. The benchmarking system must provide the user with the capability to obtain flexibly input data from several sources. The most common sources of data are files (either own or obtained from a third part), interactive (usually to introduce specific test cases) and random generation.

If the system is intended to benchmark any kind of algorithm, random generation of input data is not a trivial issue (McGeoch, 2012). Random generation based on intervals for numeric, Boolean and character values is easy to integrate. However, most problems also require randomly generating data structures, such as vectors, matrices or graphs, in some cases with specific properties (e.g., directed graphs).

Gathering and comparing outcomes. A benchmarking system must gather the outcomes of the algorithms and compare them. This is a relatively simple issue, although these functionalities may be elaborated. Thus, outcomes can be compared graphically, as shown in Figure 11, or tables may support user interaction to sort files according to either the values of specific parameters or the outcomes of individual algorithms.

An important issue is how the optimal result for each test case is to be known. We present the policy integrated into AlgorEx, but alternative measures of the solution quality can be envisaged, at least for some problems (McGeoch, 2012; Shindler *et al.*, 2022). In case one or more of the benchmarked algorithms are exact, the values computed by such an algorithm assume this role. In case all the algorithms are inexact, their outcomes are compared. It is highly improbable that one heuristic algorithm always produces better results than the other heuristic algorithms.

Gathering of running times is more complex, as they depend on many factors (McGeoch, 2012; Sahni, 2004). An alternative consists in gathering alternative measures that are directly related to the algorithm running time (Matocha 1992), such as the number of nodes of a search tree expanded by a backtracking algorithm.

Other educational support. AlgorEx provides direct educational support by making installation and execution easy. In addition, it allows instructors and students to export tables and charts of different data and with different degree of detail in a range of file formats (either graphical or spreadsheets). As a consequence, the user may easily import graphical files into any document (e.g., instructional materials or assignment reports) or analyze outcomes with statistics software. Finally, the user may select the natural language used in the system interface, currently either English or Spanish.

Usability and interactivity. Obviously, the usability and interactivity properties identified for visualization systems also are important here. Thus, the system must support a simple but flexible experimentation process, so that the user may quickly conduct his/her experiments, even when he/she made a wrong choice at a previous step. For instance, the system should support successive generation of random data sets, or switching between different criteria to benchmark the same algorithms.

We illustrate this with an ideal, sequential experimentation process (which can be abandoned by performing different actions if necessary):

1. Load a Java class that contains the algorithms to compare. The system processes the file without user's awareness.
2. Set the experiment conditions (Velázquez-Iturbide, 2021), including selecting the algorithms to compare, the benchmarking criterion (either time efficiency, optimality or just running the algorithms) and, in case optimality is the benchmarking criterion, whether the target function intends maximization or minimization and whether results are presented with relative or absolute values.
3. Generate input data.
4. Run the algorithms using these input data.
5. Compare the outcomes in either numeric or graph formats.

Obviously, all the features described above are desirable in generic benchmarking systems. It is also possible to construct more limited, introductory benchmarking systems. It is the case of the GreedEx system (Velázquez-Iturbide *et al.*, 2013), which was an antecessor of AlgorEx, intended to work as an introduction to greedy algorithms by just supporting the activity selection problem (Cormen *et al.*, 2009) and five variations of the knapsack problem (Baase & van Gelder, 2000; Cormen *et al.*, 2009). Knowledge of the specific problems to handle allowed to provide custom visualizations, with a wide range of animation controls.

Benchmarking Algorithms in an Algorithms Course

Benchmarking can be used in algorithms courses in several ways. We focus here on its use in assignments; integration of benchmarking into the course instruction is addressed in the next section. Assignments need not be completely devoted to experimentation, but it can be just a part of an algorithm development assignment. We present some activities for running times and others for algorithm outcomes.

Students may be asked to analyze the time complexity of one or several algorithms, deriving time functions, and check that their running times have an asymptotic growth that is consistent with the predictions of the time functions. This basic scheme may take different forms. Thus, the algorithms may be provided or not to students, and their run-time analysis may be provided or demanded to students. Students could even be asked to conduct a detective activity consisting in relating given algorithms and complexities (Epp, 1992; Fenwick, Norris & Wilkes, 2002).

Inquiry may also be oriented to determine the performance of algorithms whose time complexity cannot be determined by analytical means. It is the case of backtracking, branch-and-bound or memoizing algorithms. This activity is more stimulating to students (and even to instructors) that the previous one, as the results are unknown in advance.

A more interesting form of delivering assignments consists in designing a series of related assignments, all of them dealing with the same optimization problem. Every assignment is devoted to the development and analysis of one or several algorithms designed according to a given design technique. As the same optimization problem is visited again and again, it is an instance of spiral curriculum (Bruner, 1960). We have devoted assignments of this kind to heuristic algorithms, backtracking, branch and bound, dynamic programming and, when it was sensible, probabilistic algorithms. The analysis part of each assignment can be partially or completely addressed by means of experimentation. Each assignment benchmarks the new algorithms developed against algorithms developed in previous assignments, making explicit their performance similarities and differences.

Designing a series of assignments is not a simple task, but it is rewarding. An optimization problem must be selected with a degree of difficulty appropriate for students to be able to solve it with all the design techniques dealt in the course. In particular, for some problems, it is difficult to design a bounding function or to tabulate its recursive solutions.

In our experience, the first of the series of assignments must be devoted to heuristic algorithms. Otherwise, students are used to exact algorithms and become confused with the final presence of inexact algorithms. However, designing one or several heuristic algorithms in a first assignment allows students to become familiarized with suboptimal results from the beginning. Actually, some heuristic algorithms designed in this first assignment might look exact. However, the next assignment intended to construct an exact algorithm will reveal that all the heuristic algorithms are inexact.

Evaluating alternative algorithms with respect to the two criteria (time efficiency and optimality) provides a more comprehensive understanding of the merits and demerits of each algorithm design technique. Thus, students may check that heuristic algorithms and tabulated dynamic programming typically are fast, while backtracking and recursive dynamic programming algorithms are inefficient, with branch-and-bound algorithms in an intermediate behavior. However, from the point of view of optimality, heuristic algorithms are inexact and the remaining algorithms are exact.

INSTRUCTIONAL INTEGRATION

A key concern in the use of educational technology is its tight integration into the course. Using a marvelous software system into a course without careful consideration of its relation to the course contents, educational materials and evaluation tasks will probably lead to poor students' results. Although other actions can be considered, we summarize the actions we addressed to tightly integrate SRec and AlgorEx into an advanced algorithms course:

- Revise the course contents to align it with the concepts embedded into the applications. Some concepts will have to be reinforced. For instance, dependency graphs must be defined.
- Integrate products delivered by the systems, if they exist, into the course lecture notes and slides. For instance, visualizations generated by SRec or benchmarking summaries generated by AlgorEx.
- Allocate, if possible, lab sessions aimed at introducing the educational systems. These introductory sessions may consist in a first explanation of the system objectives and capabilities, illustrated with a demonstration, followed by some tasks that students must perform with the system, in increasing order of difficulty.
- Write user manuals, making them available to students.
- Use the systems in class and suggest their use to solve assignments.

The visualization and experimentation approaches encourage students to play an active learning role. They only are partially adequate for instructional activities that involve cognitive processes placed at lower categories of the revised Bloom's taxonomy (Anderson *et al.*, 2001), such as Remember and Apply. The SRec and AlgorEx systems support familiarization with some terminology (e.g., recursion tree or maximization/ minimization) and the automatic application of some methods (e.g., conversion of a recursion tree into a directed acyclic graph). However, it is more interesting to activate more active cognitive processes, such as Understand, Analyze and Evaluate; SRec even supports partially the Create category. The two previous subsections described several activities involving either SRec or AlgorEx in an algorithms course. Some activities were described by using the verbs Understand or Analyze, therefore they can easily be identified. Benchmarking corresponds to the Evaluate category.

Two central issues for instructional integration are availability and usability of the SRec and AlgorEx systems. Both systems are Java desktop applications which are available both at their websites[1] and at the university LMS. They can be downloaded and executed, the only prerequisite for their use being the availability of a JDK installed in the personal computer. The high usability of SRec and AlgorEx allows using them in several scenarios. Students may use the systems as an aid for self-study or for their assignments. Similarly, instructors may use them to prepare lectures, educational materials and even to use it on-the-fly in the classroom.

The high degree of instructional alignment and usability of both SRec and AlgorEx is the result of a long-term effort of using, evaluating and enhancing both systems in real educational settings. For the interested reader, this enhancement process is documented for the GreedEx system (Velázquez-Iturbide *et al.*, 2013), predecessor of AlgorEx.

FUTURE RESEARCH DIRECTIONS

The two applications used to illustrate approaches to experiential learning of algorithms have been refined and extended along many years of continued usage, evaluation and enhancement. Different versions of SRec can be found in Velázquez-Iturbide *et al.* (2008), Velázquez-Iturbide *et al.* (2009), Velázquez-Iturbide & Pérez-Carrasco (2016) and Velázquez-Iturbide & Ivanov-Andreev (2022). Similarly, the framework presented in Velázquez-Iturbide (2021) was distilled from our experience developing AlgorEx. A full description of the evolution of the more limited system GreedEx can be found in Velázquez-Iturbide *et al.* (2013).

Both AlgorEx and SRec can still be further extended. For instance, AlgorEx has just been extended with several special-purpose data generators, aimed at generating tasks, permutations and different types of graphs (McGeoch, 2012). However, our main effort in the near future will be oriented to provide visual support to block-based programming.

Block-based programs (Weintrop, 2019) provide a more tangible form of programming than textual programming, based on blocks rather than on text. Consequently, editing a program consists in assembling blocks, similarly to Lego toys, instead of typing text. It is a kind of programming accessible to everybody, including young children. The execution of a block-based program usually involves visual and auditory effects on characters in a scenario, thus their programming environments hardly include any debugging facilities. Although this restriction is not a big problem for students, it does is a problem for teacher development. Certainly, teachers should be educated to achieve a precise understanding of block-based languages. Therefore, they should have facilities to trace and inquire the internal state of a program execution. We are currently working in this direction for the language ScratchJr (Flannery *et al.*, 2013). A first version of a tracer has been constructed and we plan to evaluate it with pre- and in-service teachers enrolled in master's studies.

CONCLUSION

The chapter has presented two different ways of experiential learning for an abstract subject matter, namely algorithmics. The two approaches are visualization and experimentation, and make more tangible the behavior and properties of algorithms. We have stressed both the features of the applications for educational use and the need of a tight instructional integration into the course syllabus and assignments. We have proposed two specific approaches to experiential learning of algorithms, but other insights might inspire and lead to alternative experiential approaches. Actually, adoption of these approaches was not scheduled in advance, but they are the result of a gradual process of use, evaluation and enhancement in an advanced algorithms course.

Experiential approaches may also be adopted to learn other disciplines which demand high level of abstraction. Instructors must guess, refine and evaluate their candidate approaches. For instance, some authors have proposed visual proofs for mathematics (Nelsen, 1993), while others use experiments to motivate and reinforce the study of discrete mathematics (Cordova, 2022). However, educational systems to support either approach should be designed according to principles different from those underlying the systems presented in the chapter. A different experiential approach, which is promising for engineering education, is augmented reality. This technology has potential to visualize phenomena which are invisible (e.g., electricity) and it supports spatial display in three dimensions (Álvarez-Marín & Velázquez-Iturbide, 2021).

REFERENCES

Abdulwahed, M., & Nagy, Z. K. (2009). Applying Kolb's experiential learning cycle for laboratory education. *Journal of Engineering Education*, *98*(3), 283–294. doi:10.1002/j.2168-9830.2009.tb01025.x

Al-Sakkaf, A., Omar, M., & Ahmad, M. (2019). A systematic literature review of student engagement in software visualization: A theoretical perspective. *Computer Science Education*, *29*(2-3), 283–309. Advance online publication. doi:10.1080/0 8993408.2018.1564611

Álvarez-Marín, A., & Velázquez-Iturbide, J. Á. (2021). Augmented reality and engineering education: A systematic review. *IEEE Transactions on Learning Technologies*, *14*(6), 817–831. doi:10.1109/TLT.2022.3144356

Anderson, L. W., Krathwohl, D. R., Airasian, P. W., Cruikshank, K. A., Mayer, R. E., Pintrich, P. R., Raths, R., & Wittrock, M. C. (2001). *A taxonomy for learning, teaching and assessing. A revision of Bloom's taxonomy of educational objectives.* Pearson Education.

Baase, S., & van Gelder, A. (2000). *Computer algorithms* (3rd ed.). Addison Wesley Longman.

Bruner, J. S. (1960). *The process of education.* Harvard University Press.

Card, S. K., Mackinley, J. D., & Shneiderman, B. (1999). *Readings in information visualization.* Morgan Kaufmann.

Cordova, J. (2022). Motivating the study of discrete structures with experiments. *Journal of Computing Sciences in Colleges*, *37*(7), 23–30.

Cormen, T. H., Leiserson, C. E., Rivest, R. L., & Stein, C. (2009). *Introduction to algorithms* (3rd ed.). The MIT Press.

D'Antonio, L. (2003). Incorporating bioinformatics in an algorithms course. In *Proceedings of the 10th annual conference on innovation and technology in computer science education, ITiCSE'05*, pp. 211-214. https://doi.org/10.1145/961511.961569

Epp, E. C. (1992). Yet another analysis of algorithms laboratory. *SIGCSE Bulletin*, *24*(4), 11–14. doi:10.1145/141837.141842

Farghally, M. F., Kohy, K. H., Ernstz, J. V., & Shaffer, C. A. (2017). Towards a concept inventory for algorithm analysis topics. In *Proceedings of the 48rd SIGCSE technical symposium on computer science education, SIGCSE'17*, pp. 207-212. http://dx.doi.org/10.1145/3017680.3017756

Felder, R. M., & Silverman, L. K. (1988). Learning and teaching styles in engineering education. *Engineering Education*, *78*(7), 674–681.

Fenwick, J. B., Norris, C., & Wilkes, J. (2002). Scientific experimentation via the matching game. In *Proceedings of the 33rd SIGCSE technical symposium on computer science education, SIGCSE'02*, pp. 326-303. https://doi.org/10.1145/563340.563469

Flannery, L. P., Kazakoff, E. R., Bontá, P., Silverman, B., Bers, M. U., & Resnick, M. (2013). Designing ScratchJr: Support for early childhood learning through computer programming. In *Proceedings of the 12th International Conference on Interaction Design and Children, IDC '13*, pp. 1-10. 10.1145/2485760.2485785

Götschi, T., Sanders, I., & Galpin, V. (2003). Mental models of recursion. In *Proceedings of the 34th SIGCSE technical symposium on computer science education, SIGCSE'03*, pp. 346-350. https://doi.org/10.1145/611892.612004

Haynes, S.M. (1995). Explaining recursion to the unsophisticated. *ACM SIGCSE Bulletin 27*(3), 3-6 and 14. https://doi.org/ doi:10.1145/209849.209850

Hoong, L. Y., Kin, H. W., & Pien, C. L. (2015). Concrete-pictorial-abstract: Surveying its origin and charting its future. *The Mathematics Educator*, *16*(1), 1–18. http://hdl.handle.net/10497/18889

Ihantola, P., Karavirta, V., Korhonen, A., & Nikander, J. (2005). Taxonomy of effortless creation of algorithm visualizations. In *Proceedings of the 1st international computing education research workshop, ICER'05*, pp. 123-133. https://doi.org/10.1145/1089786.1089798

Kolb, D. A. (1984). *Experimental learning: experience as the source of learning and development*. Prentice Hall.

Lahtinen, E., Ala-Mutka, K., & Järvinen, H. M. (2005). A study of the difficulties of novice programmers. In *Proceedings of the 10th annual conference on innovation and technology in computer science education, ITiCSE'05*, pp. 14-18. https://doi.org/10.1145/1067445.1067453

Marton, F., & Tsui, A. B. M. (2004). *Classroom discourse and the space of learning*. Routledge. doi:10.4324/9781410609762

Matocha, J. (1992). Laboratory experiments in an algorithms course: Technical writing and the scientific method. In *Proceedings of the 22nd ASEE/IEEE frontiers in education conference, FIE'92*, pp. T1G 9-13. https://doi.org/10.1109/FIE.2002.1157917

McCracken, D. D. (1989). Three "lab assignments" for an algorithms course. *SIGCSE Bulletin*, *21*(2), 61–64. doi:10.1145/65738.65750

McGeoch, C. C. (2012). *A guide to experimental algorithmics*. Cambridge University Press. doi:10.1017/CBO9780511843747

Naps, T., Roessling, G., Almstrum, V., Dann, W., Fleischer, R., Hundhausen, C., Korhonen, A., Malmi, L., McNally, M., Rodger, S., & Velázquez-Iturbide, J. Á. (2003). Exploring the role of visualization and engagement in computer science education. *SIGCSE Bulletin*, *35*(4), 131–152. doi:10.1145/782941.782998

Nelsen, R. B. (1993). *Proofs without words: Exercises in visual thinking*. The Mathematical Association of America.

Price, B., Baecker, R., & Small, I. (1998). An introduction to software visualization. In J. Stasko, J. Domingue, M. H. Brown, & B. A. Price (Eds.), *Software visualization* (pp. 3–27). The MIT Press.

Rinderknecht, C. (2014). A survey on teaching and learning recursive programming. *Informatics in Education*, *13*(1), 87–119. doi:10.15388/infedu.2014.06

Sahni, S. (2004). *Data structures, algorithms, and applications in Java* (2nd ed.). Silicon Press.

Sanders, I. (2002). Teaching empirical analysis of algorithms. In *Proceedings of the 33rd SIGCSE technical symposium on computer science education, SIGCSE'02*, pp. 321-325. https://doi.org/10.1145/563340.563468

Shindler, M., Goodrich, M. T., Gila, O., & Dillencourt, M. (2022). Beyond big O: Teaching experimental algorithmics. *Journal of Computing Sciences in Colleges*, *37*(10), 23–36.

Shneiderman, B. (1996). The eyes have it: A task by data type taxonomy for information visualizations. In *Proceedings 1996 IEEE symposium on visual languages, VL'96*, pp. 336-343. https://doi.org/10.1109/VL.1996.545307

Sirkiä, T. (2018). Jsvee & Kelmu: Creating and tailoring program animations for computing education. *Software: Evolution and Process, 30*(2), e1924. https://onlinelibrary.wiley.com/doi/10.1002/smr.1924

Stasko, J., Domingue, J., Brown, M. H., & Price, B. A. (Eds.). (1998). *Software visualization*. The MIT Press.

Stern, L., & Naish, L. (2002). Visual representations for recursive algorithms. In *Proceedings of the 33th SIGCSE technical symposium on computer science education, SIGCSE'02*, pp. 196-200. https://doi.org/10.1145/563340.563414

Velázquez-Iturbide, J. Á. (2000). Recursion in gradual steps (is recursion really that difficult?). In *Proceedings of the 31st SIGCSE technical symposium on computer science education, SIGCSE'00*, pp. 310-314. https://doi.org/10.1145/330908.331876

Velázquez-Iturbide, J. Á. (2021). A unified framework to experiment with algorithm optimality and efficiency. *Computer Applications in Engineering Education*, *29*(6), 1793–1810. doi:10.1002/cae.22423

Velázquez-Iturbide, J. Á., & Debdi, O. (2011). Experimentation with optimization problems in algorithm courses. In IEEE international conference on computer as a tool, EUROCON'11, 4 pp. https://doi.org/ doi:10.1109/EUROCON.2011.5929294

Velázquez-Iturbide, J. Á., Debdi, O., Esteban-Sánchez, N., & Pizarro, C. (2013). GreedEx: A visualization tool for experimentation and discovery learning of greedy algorithms. *IEEE Transactions on Learning Technologies*, 6(2), 130–143. doi:10.1109/TLT.2013.8

Velázquez Iturbide, J. Á., Hernán-Losada, I., & Pérez-Carrasco, A. (2016). A «multiple executions» technique of visualization. In *Proceedings of the 21st annual conference on innovation and technology in computer science education, ITiCSE'16*, pp. 59-64. https://doi.org/10.1145/2899415.2899451

Velázquez Iturbide, J. Á., & Ivanov-Andreev, R. (2022) Recursion-based visualizations of search algorithms in state-spaces. In *Proceedings of the 2022 international symposium on computers in education, SIIE'22*. https://doi.org/10.1109/SIIE56031.2022.9982362

Velázquez-Iturbide, J. Á., & Pérez-Carrasco, A. (2010). InfoVis interaction techniques in animation of recursive programs. *Algorithms*, 3(1), 76–91. doi:10.3390/a3010076

Velázquez-Iturbide, J. Á., & Pérez-Carrasco, A. (2016). Systematic development of dynamic programming algorithms assisted by interactive visualization. In *Proceedings of the 21st Annual Conference on Innovation and Technology in Computer Science Education, ITiCSE'16*, pp. 71-76. https://doi.org/10.1145/2899415.2899450

Velázquez-Iturbide, J. Á., Pérez-Carrasco, A., & Urquiza-Fuentes, J. (2008). SRec: An animation system of recursion for algorithm courses. In *Proceedings of the 13th annual conference on innovation and technology in computer science education, ITiCSE'08*, pp. 225-229. https://doi.org/10.1145/1384271.1384332

Velázquez-Iturbide, J. Á., Pérez-Carrasco, A., & Urquiza-Fuentes, J. (2009). A design of automatic visualizations for divide-and-conquer algorithms. *Electronic Notes in Theoretical Computer Science*, 224, 159–167. doi:10.1016/j.entcs.2008.12.060

Weintrop, D. (2019). Block-based programming in computer science education. *Communications of the ACM*, 62(8), 22–25. doi:10.1145/3341221

ADDITIONAL READING

Ben-Ari, M., & Reich, N. (1997). Recursion: From drama to program. *Journal of Computer Science Education*, 11(3), 9–12.

Berque, D., Bogda, J. G., Fisher, B. D., Harrison, T. G., & Rahn, N. (1994). The KLYDE workbench to study experimental algorithm analysis. In *Proceedings of the 25th SIGCSE Technical Symposium on Computer Science Education, SIGCSE'94*, pp. 83–87. https://doi.org/10.1145/191029.191065

Chen, M.-Y., Wei, J.-D., Huang, J.-H., & Lee, D. T. (2006). Design and applications of an algorithm benchmark system in a computational problem solving environment. In *Proceedings of the 11th annual conference on innovation and technology in computer science education, ITiCSE'06*, pp. 123-127. https://doi.org/10.1145/1140124.1140159

Coffey, J. W. (2013). Integrating theoretical and empirical computer science in a data structures course. In *Proceedings of the 44th SIGCSE technical symposium on computer science education, SIGCSE'13*, pp. 23-27. https://doi.org/10.1145/2445196.2445211

Ginat, D., & Blau, Y. (2017). Multiple levels of abstraction in algorithmic problem solving. In *Proceedings of the 48th SIGCSE technical symposium on computer science education, SIGCSE'17*, pp. 237-242. http://dx.doi.org/10.1145/3017680.3017801

Kather, P., & Vahrenhold, J. (2021). Is algorithm comprehension different from program comprehension? In *Proceedings of the IEEE/ACM 29th international conference on program comprehension, ICPC'21*, pp. 455-466. https://doi.org/10.1109/ICPC52881.2021.00053

Luu, M., Ferland, M., Rao, V. N., Arora, A., Huynh, R., Reiber, F., Wong-Ma, J., & Shindler, M. (2023). What is an algorithms course? Survey results of introductory undergraduate algorithms courses in the U.S. In *Proceedings of the 54th SIGCSE Technical Symposium on Computer Science Education, SIGCSE'23*, pp. 284-290. https://doi.org/10.1145/3545945.3569820

Perrenet, J., & Kaasenbrood, E. (2006). Levels of abstraction in students' understanding of the concept of algorithm: The qualitative perspective. In *Proceedings of the 11th annual conference on innovation and technology in computer science education, ITiCSE'06*, pp. 270-274. https://doi.org/10.1145/1140124.1140196

Velázquez-Iturbide, J. Á. (2019). Students' misconceptions of optimization problems. In *Proceedings of the 24th Annual Conference on Innovation and Technology in Computer Science Education, ITiCSE 2019*, pp. 464-470. https://doi.org/10.1145/3304221.3319749

Velázquez-Iturbide, J. Á., & Pérez-Carrasco, A. (2016). How to use the SRec visualization system in programming and algorithm courses. *ACM Inroads*, 7(3), 42–49. doi:10.1145/2948070

KEY TERMS & DEFINITIONS

Algorithm benchmarking: Experimental comparison, with respect to a given criterion, of the outcomes or the performance of several algorithms that solve the same problem.

Experimentation: Practical activity where an entity is studied by gathering and analyzing data of its behavior. Ideally, experimentation should be based on the scientific method.

Instructional alignment: Consistency between the learning goals, instructional activities and assessment tasks of a course.

Optimality: Property of optimization algorithms regarding whether their outcomes are maximal (for maximization problems) or minimal (for minimization problems).

Optimization problem: Combinatorial problem whose solution must optimize a given measure, either as maximization or minimization.

Program visualization: Graphical representation of a piece of software so that the representation has a close relationship to the source code.

Random data generation: Automated process that produces one or multiple sets of data whose values are unpredictable in advance and there is no apparent relation between them. Data generation may involve simple values or aggregations of values into data structures.

Recursion: A linguistic mechanism consisting in defining something in terms of itself. In mathematics and computer programming, recursion is a valuable tool for definitions and for problem solving.

Redundancy removal: Procedure that transforms a given inefficient algorithm into an equivalent efficient one, where repeated computations of the same subproblems have been eliminated.

Time efficiency: Judgment of the running time of an algorithm solves its associated problem in a reasonable lapse of time. It is typically made according to the order of complexity resulting from its formal analysis.

ENDNOTE

[1]   https://blogs.etsii.urjc.es/lite/tools/srec/srec-download/,
https://blogs.etsii.urjc.es/lite/tools/experimental-algorith
mics/algorex-download/

Chapter 7
Unlocking the Potential of Educational Escape Rooms in Higher Education:
Theoretical Frameworks and Pathways Ahead

Iris Lim
https://orcid.org/0000-0001-5866-8968
Bond University, Australia

ABSTRACT

This chapter investigates the potential of educational escape rooms in higher education exploring the theoretical frameworks surrounding their design, outcomes, and future directions. The primary purpose is to provide educators with an understanding of how these immersive experiences can enhance learning and engagement. The chapter delves into relevant theoretical frameworks, including constructivism, experiential learning, game-based learning, and social learning which underpin the effectiveness of educational escape rooms. The chapter also offers practical recommendations and discusses emerging opportunities for incorporating escape rooms into various educational contexts. By examining the multifaceted aspects of educational escape rooms, this chapter aims to support educators in leveraging these innovative tools to create engaging learning experiences and foster positive student outcomes.

DOI: 10.4018/978-1-6684-8656-6.ch007

INTRODUCTION

The variety of active learning strategies continues to expand in the higher education setting with the rising incorporation of game-based learning, gamification, and serious games into the curriculum. Implementing game-based elements offers opportunities for active learning, creativity, problem-solving, fun, and social interaction, and can appeal to a wide range of learning styles (Ritzko, 2011). Some examples of non-digital and digital games that could be used to implement game-based elements in education include crosswords, puzzles, role-playing, and simulations. Recently, the novel use of escape rooms as a didactic game-based learning tool has arisen.

Regardless of their mode of delivery, be it digital or physical, educational escape rooms have demonstrated their potential as versatile, practical, and effective tools that enrich the learning experience. Initial evidence underscores the impact of escape rooms on various aspects of education, transcending disciplinary boundaries. For instance, they have been found to boost knowledge acquisition (Christopoulos et al., 2022), providing learners with a stimulating environment that facilitates deeper understanding and retention of the subject matter. Moreover, escape rooms foster camaraderie and communication skills (Lundholm et al., 2022), as the collaborative nature of these activities encourages participants to work effectively in teams, exchange ideas, and negotiate solutions to complex problems. In addition to enhancing interpersonal skills, educational escape rooms have also been shown to significantly improve student motivation and engagement (Terrasi et al., 2020). By incorporating elements of gamification and challenge, escape rooms capture the interest of learners and provide a sense of accomplishment upon successful completion. Furthermore, they create a learner-centered environment where students are actively involved in their education, promoting a sense of ownership and commitment to their learning process. They also contribute to the development of problem-solving and critical thinking skills (Nelson & Crea, 2021).

This chapter will review the use of educational escape rooms in higher education and the reported outcomes they have achieved, discuss the theoretical frameworks that underpin their design and implementation, and provide practical tips and recommendations on the design and integration of escape rooms into curricula. The differences in physical vs digital education escape rooms will also be highlighted. Challenges and opportunities associated with the use of escape rooms in higher education and future directions for research and practice in this area will be discussed.

BACKGROUND

Escape rooms have become a popular form of entertainment worldwide, offering a unique and engaging experience for players of all ages. The concept of an escape room can be traced back to early computer games and puzzle books, but the first commercially successful escape room, a single room game for teams of five to six players, opened in Japan in 2007 (Nicholson, 2015). Since then, the industry has grown exponentially, with escape rooms emerging in major cities around the world. Approximately 50 000 escape room outlets worldwide were estimated in November 2019 ("International Escape Room Markets Analysis," 2019). This is not surprising as the activity appeals to a wide audience range of all age groups, including adults, youth and children and have become increasingly popular in recent years as an engaging and immersive form of entertainment (Nicholson, 2015). Originally designed as a form of entertainment, escape rooms have since been adapted for a variety of purposes, including team building (Cohen et al., 2021), education (Fotaris & Mastoras, 2019), and even professional development (Gomez, 2020). Today, escape rooms continue to offer a unique and engaging experience for people of all backgrounds and interests.

An escape room is defined as a "live-action team-based game where players discover clues, solve puzzles, and accomplish tasks in one or more rooms in order to accomplish a specific goal (usually escaping from the room) in a limited time" (Nicholson, 2015). Physical escape rooms require participants to be physically present in a designated space and solve puzzles in order to escape. Digital escape rooms, on the other hand, are web-based and can be accessed from anywhere with an internet connection, which is convenient for remote learning (Ang et al., 2020). They often incorporate multimedia elements such as videos and interactive quizzes. While originally designed as a recreational activity, educators within various levels and disciplines have recognized the potential of escape rooms as a tool for teaching and learning in various educational settings (Taraldsen et al., 2022). Over the past six years or so, educational escape rooms and activities and/or games inspired by escape rooms have been designed and implemented to achieve a myriad of learning objectives. They are designed to incorporate educational content and learning objectives within the game structure, creating an engaging and interactive experience for students. They can be used to teach various subjects and skills, such as problem-solving, critical thinking, and teamwork, among others (Clauson et al., 2019). Educational escape rooms also provide an opportunity for learners to apply theoretical concepts in a practical, hands-on setting (Adams et al., 2018).

Educational escape rooms games typically involve a combination of problem-solving, critical thinking, and teamwork skills. The puzzles and tasks within the room can vary in design and difficulty level and may be based on a variety of themes. The key is to choose a theme that is relevant and engaging to students, and to design puzzles that challenge them to think critically and apply what they have learned in a fun and interactive way. In terms of design, several common and overarching features are present in most educational escape games. They typically involve a physical or digital space with puzzles, riddles, and challenges that students must solve to "escape" the room. The puzzles may involve a variety of skills, such as decoding messages (Sundsbø, 2018), manipulating objects (Pérez et al., 2021), or solving math problems (Stohlmann, 2020). The escape room may also include elements such as lighting, sound, and visual effects to enhance the experience (Chen, 2022). Typically, the experience begins with an introduction where a facilitator or instructor (usually known as the 'game master'), written message, or video introduces the participants to the room and explains the rules of the game. During this introduction, the participants are also referred to as "teams" that need to work together to succeed. Another common feature is that participants are given a limited timeframe to solve problems and complete the escape room challenge (Clarke et al., 2017), although the challenges given to teams and the design of the escape room can vary. The 'game master' may also be present to provide guidance or hints throughout the game and facilitate the debriefing process after the experience.

Within higher education, subject-specific educational escape rooms are the most common types reported in the literature. These rooms are designed to incorporate subject-specific content and skills into the puzzles and challenges that participants encounter. These types of escape rooms are popular in higher education because they provide an engaging and immersive way for students to apply their learning in a fun and interactive way. Subject-specific escape rooms can be used as a revision technique to reinforce learning objectives, assess student understanding, and provide a fun and engaging way to review content (Horn, 2023). They can also be used to introduce new material or concepts in a more interactive and memorable way in, particularly in comparison to traditional lectures and/or readings (Cruz, 2019). Overall, subject-specific escape rooms can be a powerful tool for enhancing student engagement, motivation, and learning outcomes in higher education. Some examples that have resulted in positive outcomes reported include:

- Escape rooms designed for chemistry classes that require students to solve puzzles related to chemical reactions and properties (Ang et al., 2020; Avargil et al., 2021; Cai, 2022; Peleg et al., 2019; Vergne et al., 2020)
- Biology-themed escape rooms that might require participants to solve puzzles related to cell biology (Christopoulos et al., 2022), molecular biology (Alonso & Schroeder, 2020), genetics (Brady & Andersen, 2021), cancer (Wilby & Kremer, 2020) or ecology (Heim et al., 2022)
- Linguistics-themed escape rooms that require participants to solve puzzles incorporating essential language skills (Cruz, 2019; da Cruz, 2019; López, 2019)
- Computer science-themed escape rooms that require participants to solve puzzles related to cybersecurity (Löffler et al., 2021; Mello-Stark et al., 2020),

cryptography (Ho, 2018; Seebauer et al., 2020), programming (López-Pernas et al., 2019a, 2019b)
- Mathematics-themed escape rooms that require participants to solve math equations and problems (Fuentes-Cabrera et al., 2020; Glavaš & Stašcik, 2017; Stohlmann, 2020)

This extensive, but not exhaustive list of examples illustrates the versatility of escape rooms in higher education, as they can be tailored to suit various subjects and learning objectives. As the use of educational escape rooms continues to expand, more themes and subject areas will likely emerge in response to the evolving needs of educators and students.

Escape rooms have also been used in other ways within higher education. Career-oriented escape rooms have been designed to help students explore potential career paths, gain practical experience, and develop career readiness skills. These escape rooms are often used in higher education to prepare students for the workforce and to help them identify their interests and strengths. One example of a career-oriented escape room is the 'career exploration' escape room, where students are presented with a series of challenges and puzzles related to different careers (Emmenegger, 2020). Students may need to solve problems related to specific industries, such as healthcare or engineering, or solve tasks related to job search skills, such as networking and interviewing (Connelly et al., 2018; Goodman & Landgren, 2021). Another example is the 'leadership development' escape room, where students are presented with challenges related to developing leadership skills (Egan et al., 2021). These challenges may include problem-solving, communication, decision-making, and conflict resolution. Career-oriented escape rooms can be designed for individual or group participation, and they can be tailored to meet the needs of specific student populations, such as first-generation college students or underrepresented groups. The primary goal of career-oriented escape rooms is to help students gain valuable skills and experiences that will prepare them for the workforce. By participating in these activities, students can develop essential skills such as teamwork, problem-solving, communication, and critical thinking. They can also gain insights into different career paths and industries, which can help them make informed decisions about their future careers.

Team-building escape rooms have also been designed to promote teamwork and collaboration. For example, an escape room designed for a student organization may require members to work together to solve puzzles related to the organization's mission (Zhang et al., 2018). Team-building escape rooms are designed to promote collaboration, communication, and problem-solving among members of a team. These types of escape rooms are often used in corporate and organizational settings but can also be effective in higher education contexts for team-building exercises. In team-building escape rooms, participants are often divided into groups of four to eight people and are presented with a series of challenges or puzzles that must be solved in order to "escape" the room. These challenges may require a combination of skills and knowledge, including critical thinking, problem-solving, and communication. The key to the success of team-building escape rooms is the emphasis on collaboration and teamwork. Participants must work together to solve the puzzles and complete the challenges, relying on each other's strengths and skills to achieve success. The escape room serves as a metaphor for real-life situations where effective teamwork is essential to achieving shared goals. In the higher education context, team-building escape rooms can be used to promote collaboration and communication among students, as well as to help develop essential skills for future careers (Taraldsen et al., 2022). For example, team-building escape rooms can be used in business or engineering courses to teach students about the importance of collaboration and problem-solving in their respective fields (Ross & Bennett, 2020; Warmelink et al., 2017). Similarly, team-building escape rooms can be used in health sciences courses to emphasize the importance of teamwork and effective communication in the delivery of patient care (Brown et al., 2019; Foltz-Ramos et al., 2021). Overall, team-building escape rooms can be an effective tool for promoting collaboration, communication, and problem-solving among students in higher education, and can help prepare them for success in their future careers.

Overall, the literature on educational escape rooms in higher education demonstrates promising results in terms of their effectiveness as a learning tool. However, there are potential disadvantages and challenges to consider. One such concern is accessibility for all learners. For instance, learners with physical disabilities or sensory impairments may encounter difficulties participating in a physical escape room. Inclusivity must be addressed during the design process to ensure that escape rooms cater to diverse learners. Moreover, the cost of designing and implementing an escape room can be high, potentially limiting the feasibility for some institutions or organizations. This challenge can be addressed by leveraging digital escape rooms or exploring cost-effective approaches to design and material sourcing (Tercanli et al., 2021). Another concern is the potential for poorly designed or implemented escape rooms to lead to frustration and disengagement among learners. Like any other learning activity, ensuring that the activity is well-designed and aligns with learning objectives is critical for a positive experience (Reeves, 2006). Furthermore, utilizing escape rooms as a form of assessment may negatively impact learners' grades and learning outcomes if not properly designed (Shepard et al., 2017). Lastly, the content of the escape room may not cater to every learner's individual interest and needs, resulting in limited engagement and learning outcomes (Hartt et al., 2020). Designers should consider incorporating varied themes and activities that appeal to diverse learning styles and preferences. Despite these potential disadvantages and challenges, when designed and implemented effectively, educational escape rooms can provide a unique and engaging learning experience for students. They warrant further exploration as a valuable tool for enhancing learning across various educational contexts.

MAIN FOCUS OF THE CHAPTER

Theoretical Frameworks for Educational Escape Rooms

Theoretical frameworks provide a foundation for understanding and interpreting the design and implementation of any pedagogical tool. In the context of educational escape rooms, theoretical frameworks refer to the overarching theories, concepts, and principles that inform the pedagogical goals, design choices, and assessment of learning outcomes. There are several theoretical frameworks that can be applied to educational escape rooms, each offering unique perspectives and approaches to designing and implementing them effectively. In this section, we will explore some of the most prominent theoretical frameworks for educational escape rooms and discuss how they can be applied to create meaningful learning experiences.

Experiential Learning

Experiential learning theory is a learning model that emphasizes the importance of experience and reflection in the learning process. This theory posits that people learn best through direct experiences, where they can actively engage with the material and relate it to their prior knowledge and experiences (Kolb et al., 2014). The theory suggests that learning is most effective when it is an immersive and interactive process that involves the learner in a cycle of concrete experience, reflective observation, abstract conceptualization, and active experimentation (Kolb et al., 2014). According to this theory, learners construct their knowledge through reflection on their experiences, which allows them to identify patterns and connections between what they already know and what they are learning (McCarthy, 2010). By engaging in active experimentation and applying what they have learned in new situations, learners can refine and deepen their understanding.

Educational escape rooms align well with this theory by providing learners with a hands-on, immersive experience that encourages active engagement and problem-solving. The immersive and interactive nature of an escape room helps to create an environment that facilitates active learning and problem-solving, which are key components of experiential learning. By working collaboratively with their peers, students are able to engage in the social and emotional aspects of learning, including communication, leadership, and teamwork. In this way, the design and implementation of educational escape rooms can be seen as a practical application of experiential learning theory. The following is an outline on how this theory can be applied to a medical-themed escape room (Guckian et al., 2020):

1. **Experience:** In an escape room, learners engage in a hands-on, immersive experience by actively participating in the challenges presented. They encounter real-life situations or scenarios that require them to apply their knowledge and skills. Example: In a medical-themed escape room, students may encounter a simulated patient with specific symptoms. They have to use their clinical knowledge to identify the patient's condition and determine the appropriate treatment plan.
2. **Reflection:** Upon completing the escape room challenges, learners reflect on their experiences, identifying what they learned, what they found challenging, and what they could have done differently. This reflection process helps them to gain a deeper understanding of the experience and their own learning process. After the escape room, medical students can discuss the challenges they faced in diagnosing the patient, including any mistakes or incorrect assumptions they made. This reflection allows them to better understand their thought processes and decision-making during the activity.
3. **Conceptualization:** Learners use their reflections to form new concepts, ideas, or approaches that they can apply to future situations. They integrate their experiences with existing knowledge to develop a more comprehensive understanding of the subject matter. Based on their reflections, students may recognize gaps in their medical knowledge or identify specific areas where they need to improve their clinical skills. They can then seek out additional resources or training to address these needs.
4. **Experimentation:** Learners apply their new concepts and ideas in different contexts, testing their effectiveness and refining their understanding. This iterative process allows learners to continually improve their skills and knowledge. Students who have completed the medical-themed escape room may apply their newfound insights in future clinical practice or simulations, leading to more accurate diagnoses and better patient care.

Constructivism / Social Constructivism

Constructivism is a learning theory that asserts that individuals construct knowledge by actively participating in the learning process rather than simply receiving it from an external source (Bretz, 2001). Learners build their own understanding and knowledge of the world by interacting with it and reflecting on those experiences. According to constructivism, learning is a process of creating meaning from one's experiences and previous knowledge (Bretz, 2001). Constructivism, or social constructivism, also emphasizes the role of social interaction in the learning process, as learners share and construct knowledge with others through communication and collaboration (Adams, 2006). By creating an environment that supports active participation, exploration, and reflection, educators can facilitate the construction of new knowledge and understanding in learners based on their existing beliefs and experiences.

Escape rooms align with constructivism by providing a learner-centered approach to education, where learners actively construct their own knowledge and understanding of a particular topic. Escape rooms require learners to actively engage with the tasks and challenges presented, fostering an environment that promotes active construction of knowledge. Learners must explore, manipulate, and interact with the escape room elements to solve problems and progress through the experience. For example, in a chemistry-themed escape room, students may need to mix chemicals in the correct order and proportions to create a reaction that unlocks the next clue. They actively construct knowledge of chemical reactions by physically engaging with the materials and observing the outcomes of their actions.

Additionally, escape rooms often require teamwork and collaboration among learners, which can facilitate the exchange of ideas, perspectives, and knowledge, leading to a richer understanding of the subject matter. As an example, in a history-themed escape room, students might need to work together to decipher a series of historical documents and artifacts. Each team member could bring their unique perspective and knowledge of historical events, and through discussion and collaboration, the team constructs a shared understanding of the historical context and significance of the artifacts.

Multiple Intelligences

Multiple intelligences theory is a model proposed by Howard Gardner that suggests there are several types of intelligence that people possess. These different types of intelligence include linguistic, logical-mathematical, musical, spatial, bodily-kinesthetic, interpersonal, intrapersonal, and naturalist (Gardner, 1993). Gardner believed that individuals have unique profiles of these intelligences, with some being stronger in certain areas than others. For example, a person who excels in music may have a high level of musical intelligence, while someone who is skilled in interpersonal communication may have a high level of interpersonal intelligence. This theory suggests that traditional measures of intelligence, such as IQ tests, are limited and do not fully capture the breadth of abilities that people possess and that individuals have different strengths and abilities. In the education context, educators are thus encouraged to design activities that cater to these different learning styles and intelligences (Kezar, 2001).

Educational escape rooms can incorporate a variety of activities that cater to different intelligences, such as puzzles for logical-mathematical learners, visual cues for spatial learners, and teamwork for interpersonal learners. In designing escape rooms, educators can incorporate various types of challenges that require the use of different intelligences, such as logical-mathematical, spatial, bodily-kinesthetic, and interpersonal intelligence. For example, a puzzle that requires logical reasoning or mathematical calculations appeals to individuals who are strong in logical-mathematical intelligence. A task that involves physical movements, such as unlocking a padlock, is suitable for individuals who excel in bodily-kinesthetic intelligence. Collaborative challenges or social interactions can engage learners who are high in interpersonal intelligence. Thus, educational escape rooms can cater to the diverse strengths and preferences of students and provide a platform for them to develop and apply their multiple intelligences.

Situated Learning

Situated learning theory proposes that learning occurs best when situated within a specific context or situation. It suggests that knowledge is best acquired through authentic, real-world experiences rather than in abstract or disconnected ways (Patel, 2018). This theory emphasizes the importance of social interaction and collaboration in the learning process, as well as the role of context and culture in shaping our understanding of knowledge. In a situated learning environment, learners are provided with opportunities to participate in authentic activities and to engage in problem-solving tasks that are relevant to their personal interests and goals (Arnseth, 2008). Through these experiences, learners are able to connect theoretical concepts to practical applications, and to develop a deep understanding of the subject matter (Arnseth, 2008).

Escape rooms can align with situated learning theory in several ways:

1. **Authentic Context:** Escape rooms are designed to simulate real-life situations or problems, providing learners with an authentic context for learning. The immersive environment allows learners to apply their knowledge and skills in a realistic setting, which can lead to deeper understanding and better retention of information.

2. **Social Interaction:** Situated learning theory emphasizes the importance of social interaction and collaboration in the learning process. Escape rooms typically

require teamwork, communication, and collaboration among participants, facilitating the exchange of ideas, knowledge, and perspectives.

3. **Learning by Doing:** Escape rooms engage learners in hands-on problem-solving experiences that challenge them to apply their knowledge in practical ways.

4. **Transferable Skills**: Escape rooms often foster the development of critical thinking, problem-solving, teamwork, and communication skills that are valuable across disciplines and professional contexts and can be applied in various real-life situations.

By incorporating these elements, escape rooms can create meaningful and engaging learning experiences that help learners apply and retain knowledge in real-world situations.

Game-based Learning

Game-based learning theory is an approach to education that involves the use of games as a learning tool. The theory is based on the premise that games provide an engaging and immersive environment that can help students learn and retain information more effectively (Bado, 2022). The games used in game-based learning are designed to be interactive, challenging, and enjoyable, and they can cover a wide range of subjects and topics. The theory emphasizes that games can be used to teach a variety of skills, such as critical thinking, problem-solving, collaboration, and decision-making (Plass et al., 2015). Game-based learning theory highlights the importance of using games in education to make learning more engaging and enjoyable for students, and to help them develop important skills that are relevant to real-world situations.

It is not surprising that educational escape rooms align with game-based learning theory. Like games, escape rooms have clear goals and objectives that learners must achieve to succeed, such as solving puzzles, deciphering codes, or completing challenges within a set time limit. These goals provide a sense of purpose and direction, motivating learners to actively engage with the content (Shi & Shih, 2015). Most escape rooms feature a series of increasingly difficult puzzles and challenges that require learners to apply their knowledge and skills in creative ways. This gradual increase in difficulty keeps learners engaged and motivated to overcome challenges, fostering a sense of accomplishment and mastery. In escape rooms, learners receive immediate feedback on their actions and decisions, either through the successful completion of a task or the need to reassess their approach. This feedback helps learners understand the consequences of their actions and adjust their strategies, promoting reflection and self-regulation (Nadolny et al., 2017).

Escape rooms can involve both competitive and collaborative elements, encouraging learners to work together as a team while also striving for personal achievement. This balance of competition and cooperation can enhance motivation and social interactions, fostering a positive learning environment (Chen & Chang, 2020). They also often incorporate a narrative or storyline that provides context and meaning to the tasks and challenges. This immersive storytelling can enhance learner engagement by appealing to their emotions and imagination, making the learning experience more memorable and enjoyable (Breien & Wasson, 2021). Additionally, escape rooms provide a safe, controlled environment for learners to experiment, take risks, and learn from their mistakes. This encourages learners to think creatively and try new strategies without fear of failure, fostering a growth mindset and resilience (Westera, 2015).

Self-Efficacy

In education, self-efficacy theory refers to an individual's belief in their ability to successfully perform a specific task or achieve a particular goal. The theory suggests that individuals with high levels of self-efficacy are more likely to approach challenging tasks with enthusiasm and persistence and are more likely to view failures as opportunities for growth and learning (Bandura & Adams, 1977). In contrast, individuals with low levels of self-efficacy may feel overwhelmed by challenging tasks and may give up more easily when faced with difficulties. Educators can help to promote self-efficacy in their students by providing opportunities for success, offering constructive feedback, and helping students to set achievable goals (van Dinther et al., 2011).

Educational escape rooms can align with self-efficacy theory by offering a variety of experiences that contribute to learners' belief in their abilities to succeed. As learners successfully complete puzzles and challenges, they gain mastery experiences that boost their confidence (Schunk, 1995). Teamwork and collaboration within escape rooms allow learners to observe their peers' successes, providing vicarious experiences that further enhance self-efficacy. Verbal persuasion, such as encouragement and positive feedback from peers, instructors, or the game itself, can also help increase learners' confidence in their abilities (van Dinther et al., 2011). The engaging and immersive environment of escape rooms evokes emotions that motivate and energize learners, contributing to their self-efficacy. Escape rooms often present incremental challenges, allowing learners to build their confidence as they progress through increasingly complex tasks. Additionally, these activities encourage goal setting and self-regulation, fostering a sense of control and ownership over the learning experience, ultimately leading to increased motivation, persistence, and improved learning outcomes (Schunk, 1995).

TIPS AND RECOMMENDATIONS

It is clear that educational escape rooms have the potential to be an effective tool for promoting cognitive, affective, and social outcomes among students. However, designing and implementing a successful escape room experience requires careful planning and consideration. In this section, we provide some tips and recommendations for educators who are interested in using educational escape rooms in their classrooms or educational programs. These top ten tips are based our own experiences with designing and implementing escape rooms for educational purposes. By following these recommendations, educators can create engaging and effective escape room experiences that promote learning and student engagement.

1. **Define your learning objectives**: These objectives should guide your design decisions and ensure that the room is aligned with your educational goals.
2. **Align with curriculum:** This will help reinforce the concepts being taught in the classroom and provide students with a more cohesive and integrated learning experience.
3. **Choose a theme:**. A well-chosen theme not only makes the room more immersive, but also helps students connect with the learning objectives.
4. **Create puzzles that are challenging but achievable:** To achieve this balance, you can incorporate puzzles that have multiple solutions or offer clues and hints to help participants along the way.
5. **Use a variety of puzzle types**: This can help prevent boredom and ensure that there is something for everyone in the room. Table 1 explores some different types of puzzles, some examples, and their leaning outcomes.
6. **Incorporate technology:** Technology can add an extra level of excitement and engagement to your escape room.
7. **Be mindful of accessibility and inclusivity:** Make sure that the room and puzzles are accessible to all learners, including those with physical disabilities, sensory impairments, or learning differences.
8. **Test the room**: Testing the room allows you to identify and address any potential issues, fine-tune the puzzles and challenges, and make adjustments to the room's design or layout as needed. Observe the test run, gather feedback, analyze the results, and make any necessary adjustments.
9. **Provide a debriefing session:** This can include a discussion of the learning objectives, a review of the puzzles and challenges, and an opportunity for participants to ask questions.
10. **Monitor and adapt the escape room over time:** This may involve updating puzzles, incorporating new technology, or modifying the room's design to better meet the needs of your students and achieve your learning objectives.

In addition to these general escape room tips, integrating micro-learning with escape rooms can be a powerful approach to enhance the overall learning experience and promote effective knowledge retention. To achieve this, educators can follow a few practical tips that synergize both methods seamlessly. Firstly, designing short and concise micro-learning modules that align with each micro-lesson is essential. These modules can be crafted in various engaging formats, such as bite-sized videos, interactive quizzes, visually appealing infographics, or succinct readings, facilitating learners to grasp key concepts efficiently. Secondly, embedding micro-learning content into the escape room's challenges and puzzles can create a dynamic and immersive learning environment. By strategically incorporating micro-learning modules within the escape room, students are compelled to interact with the content to progress through the challenges and find solutions. This integration ensures that learners not only enjoy the thrill of the escape room but also actively engage with relevant micro-learning content, reinforcing their understanding of the subject matter. As a result, the correlation between micro-learning and escape rooms can empower learners with comprehensive and impactful learning experiences, fostering a deeper understanding of the concepts and encouraging critical thinking and problem-solving skills.

Puzzles are undoubtedly the backbone of the escape room experience, as they require players to use diverse skills to progress through the challenges. However, what makes escape rooms truly unique is the ability to tailor puzzles to any theme or context. This flexibility allows for endless creativity and innovation in the creation of new and exciting escape room experiences. By incorporating puzzles into different contexts and themes, escape rooms can engage players in a wide range of interests and appeal to diverse audiences. Table 1 provides a wide range of puzzle types, examples of how they can be incorporated in educational escape rooms, and their learning outcomes.

In addition to understanding the benefits and strategies of educational escape rooms, it is also important to consider the best implementation methods for these activities. One key decision that needs to be made is whether to use a physical or digital escape room. Both options have their own advantages and disadvantages, and the choice ultimately depends on factors such as available resources, learning goals, and student preferences. Table 2 highlights some of these differences. When planning to incorporate educational escape rooms, it is important to carefully consider these factors in order to make the best decision for your specific educational context.

FUTURE RESEARCH DIRECTIONS

The use of educational escape rooms as a tool for promoting cognitive, affective, and social outcomes is a relatively new and emerging trend in education. As technology

Table 1. Puzzle types and examples

Puzzle Type	Description	Example	Learning Outcomes
Logic Puzzles	Puzzles that require learners to use logical reasoning and critical thinking to solve problems.	Deduce a password based on a series of clues or riddles.	Develop logical reasoning, critical thinking, and problem-solving skills.
Spatial Puzzles	Puzzles that involve the arrangement or manipulation of objects in space.	Rearrange a set of objects to reveal a hidden message.	Enhance spatial awareness, pattern recognition, and visual problem-solving skills.
Physical Challenges	Tasks that require learners to use their physical skills and coordination to overcome obstacles.	Complete an obstacle course or move objects in a specific way.	Develop physical skills, coordination, and teamwork.
Code Breaking	Puzzles that involve deciphering codes, ciphers, or encrypted messages.	Decode a message using a provided cipher or key.	Improve pattern recognition, attention to detail, and analytical skills.
Riddles	Puzzles that involve solving a question or statement that requires creative thinking and interpretation.	Solve a riddle to reveal the location of a hidden key.	Enhance creative thinking interpretation, and problem-solving abilities.
Trivia	Questions or challenges related to specific knowledge or facts in a particular domain.	Answer a series of questions about a historical event.	Reinforce subject-specific knowledge and recall abilities.
Visual Puzzles	Puzzles that require learners to analyze and interpret visual information.	Identify a pattern in a series of images to reveal a clue.	Develop visual analysis, pattern recognition, and interpretation skills.
Audio Puzzles	Puzzles that involve listening to and interpreting audio information.	Listen to a recording and identify specific words or phrases.	Improve listening skills, auditory memory, and attention to detail.
Mathematical Puzzles	Puzzles that require learners to apply mathematical concepts and operations to solve problems.	Solve a series of math problems to unlock a combination lock.	Enhance mathematical reasoning, problem-solving, and computational skills.
Role-Playing	Scenarios that involve learners taking on specific roles or characters and interacting with others.	Act as a diplomat negotiating a peace treaty between nations.	Develop communication, negotiation, empathy, and perspective-taking abilities.
Technology-Based	Puzzles that require learners to use technology or digital tools to solve problems or complete tasks.	Use a computer to retrieve information from a simulated database.	Improve digital literacy, technology problem-solving, and information retrieval skills.
Hidden Objects	Tasks that involve searching for hidden objects or clues within the escape room environment.	Find a hidden key in a bookshelf to unlock a door.	Enhance observation, attention to detail, and search strategies.
Association Puzzles	Puzzles that require learners to recognize connections or relationships between different items or pieces of information.	Match historical figures with their corresponding achievements.	Develop pattern recognition, memory, and the ability to identify connections between concepts.
Sequencing Puzzles	Puzzles that involve arranging items or events in a specific order based on a set of criteria or relationships.	Arrange a series of events in chronological order.	Improve understanding of relationships, sequencing, and cause-and-effect.
Language Puzzles	Puzzles that involve using language skills, such as reading, writing, and comprehension.	Decode a message written in a foreign language or unscramble a series of letters to form a word.	Improved reading comprehension, vocabulary development, and linguistic problem-solving skills.

continues to advance, it is likely that educational escape rooms will continue to evolve as well. One potential trend is the increased use of virtual and augmented reality technology in escape rooms, which can create more immersive and engaging experiences for participants. This can allow for a wider range of scenarios and puzzles

Table 2. Comparison of the use of physical vs online educational escape rooms

	Physical Escape Rooms	Online Escape Rooms
When	When access to physical space is available and participants can gather in person	When participants are geographically dispersed, access to physical space is limited, or remote participation is preferred
Why	Offers a unique and engaging way to teach different subjects and skills, promotes teamwork and communication, and provides a fully immersive experience	Provides a convenient and accessible alternative to traditional escape rooms, allows for a wider range of participants, and encourages online collaboration
How	Participants physically enter a themed room and solve puzzles and challenges to escape	Participants interact with the game through a digital platform, such as a website or app, and solve puzzles and challenges to escape
Advantages	Provides a fully immersive and interactive experience that engages multiple senses and promotes teamwork and communication, more memorable and engaging	Offers flexibility and convenience, accessible from anywhere with an internet connection, easier to update and modify, potentially more inclusive
Disadvantages	Requires access to physical space, higher costs, limited scalability, may not be accessible for individuals with disabilities	Less immersive than physical rooms, limited social interaction, may require more robust technology and stable internet connection
Challenges	Logistical considerations such as booking and setup, maintaining and updating physical props and room design, ensuring accessibility for all participants	Designing engaging and interactive virtual puzzles, facilitating effective online collaboration and communication, managing technical issues and platform compatibility

to be explored, as well as greater flexibility in terms of location and accessibility. Additionally, the use of digital technology can provide real-time feedback to players, allowing them to track their progress and adjust their strategies accordingly.

Another potential trend is the integration of educational escape rooms into online and distance learning environments. With the shift towards remote learning due to the COVID-19 pandemic, there has been an increased demand for engaging and interactive online learning experiences. Educational escape rooms can provide a unique and exciting way to engage students in online learning, as well as promoting teamwork and collaboration. Additionally, the use of digital tools and platforms can allow for greater customization and personalization of escape rooms to meet the needs and interests of individual learners.

In terms of research opportunities, there is still much to be explored in terms of the effectiveness of educational escape rooms for promoting cognitive and affective outcomes. Further research can help to identify the most effective design elements and strategies for promoting learning outcomes, as well as exploring the potential benefits for diverse populations of learners. Additionally, there is an opportunity to explore the potential use of educational escape rooms for promoting social and emotional learning outcomes, such as empathy, communication, and resilence.

Overall, the future of educational escape rooms is promising, with potential for continued innovation and growth in the field. As technology continues to advance and the demand for engaging and interactive learning experiences increases, educational escape rooms have the potential to become an even more widely used tool for promoting cognitive and affective development in learners of all ages.

CONCLUSION

In conclusion, educational escape rooms offer a unique and engaging approach to teaching and learning, with the potential to promote cognitive, affective, and social outcomes. The current literature provides evidence of their effectiveness in enhancing problem-solving, critical thinking, creativity, decision-making, motivation, engagement, and self-efficacy. However, it is essential to understand how to choose and implement digital or physical escape rooms effectively to optimize the benefits of these immersive learning experiences. While there are still some challenges and limitations to overcome, the future of educational escape rooms appears promising, with emerging trends and opportunities for further research and development. As educators continue to seek innovative ways to enhance student learning, educational escape rooms offer a valuable tool for promoting academic success and preparing students for future career opportunities.

REFERENCES

Adams, P. (2006). Exploring social constructivism: theories and practicalities. Education 3-13, 34(3), 243-257. https://doi.org/ doi:10.1080/0300427060898893

Adams, V., Burger, S., Crawford, K., & Setter, R. (2018). Can You Escape? Creating an Escape Room to Facilitate Active Learning. *Journal for Nurses in Professional Development*, 34(2), E1–e5. doi:10.1097/NND.0000000000000433 PMID:29481471

Alonso, G., & Schroeder, K. T. (2020). Applying active learning in a virtual classroom such as a molecular biology escape room. *Biochemistry and Molecular Biology Education*, 48(5), 514–515. doi:10.1002/bmb.21429 PMID:32812701

Anderson, M., Lioce, L., & Robertson, M., J., O. Lopreiato, J., & A. Díaz, D. (. (2021). Toward Defining Healthcare Simulation Escape Rooms. *Simulation & Gaming*, 52(1), 7–17. doi:10.1177/1046878120958745

Ang, J. W. J., Ng, Y. N. A., & Liew, R. S. (2020). Physical and digital educational escape room for teaching chemical bonding. *Journal of Chemical Education*, *97*(9), 2849–2856. doi:10.1021/acs.jchemed.0c00612

Arnseth, H. C. (2008). Activity theory and situated learning theory: Contrasting views of educational practice. *Pedagogy, Culture & Society*, *16*(3), 289–302. doi:10.1080/14681360802346663

Avargil, S., Shwartz, G., & Zemel, Y. (2021). Educational Escape Room: Break Dalton's Code and Escape! *Journal of Chemical Education*, *98*(7), 2313–2322. doi:10.1021/acs.jchemed.1c00110

Bado, N. (2022). Game-based learning pedagogy: A review of the literature. *Interactive Learning Environments*, *30*(5), 936–948. doi:10.1080/10494820.2019.1683587

Bandura, A., & Adams, N. E. (1977). Analysis of self-efficacy theory of behavioral change. *Cognitive Therapy and Research*, *1*(4), 287–310. doi:10.1007/BF01663995

Berthod, F., Bouchoud, L., Grossrieder, F., Falaschi, L., Senhaji, S., & Bonnabry, P. (2020). Learning good manufacturing practices in an escape room: Validation of a new pedagogical tool. *Journal of Oncology Pharmacy Practice*, *26*(4), 853–860. doi:10.1177/1078155219875504 PMID:31566110

Brady, S. C., & Andersen, E. C. (2021). An escape-room inspired game for genetics review. *Journal of Biological Education*, *55*(4), 406–417. doi:10.1080/00219266. 2019.1703784

Breien, F. S., & Wasson, B. (2021). Narrative categorization in digital game-based learning: Engagement, motivation & learning. *British Journal of Educational Technology*, *52*(1), 91–111. https://doi.org/https://doi.org/10.1111/bjet.13004. doi:10.1111/bjet.13004

Bretz, S. L. (2001). Novak's Theory of Education: Human Constructivism and Meaningful Learning. *Journal of Chemical Education*, *78*(8), 1107. doi:10.1021/ ed078p1107.6

Brown, N., Darby, W., & Coronel, H. (2019). An Escape Room as a Simulation Teaching Strategy. *Clinical Simulation in Nursing*, *30*, 1–6. https://doi.org/https:// doi.org/10.1016/j.ecns.2019.02.002. doi:10.1016/j.ecns.2019.02.002

Buchner, J., Rüter, M., & Kerres, M. (2022). Learning with a digital escape room game: Before or after instruction? *Research and Practice in Technology Enhanced Learning*, *17*(1), 10. doi:10.118641039-022-00187-x PMID:35310067

Cai, S. (2022). Harry Potter Themed Digital Escape Room for Addressing Misconceptions in Stoichiometry. *Journal of Chemical Education*, 99(7), 2747–2753. doi:10.1021/acs.jchemed.2c00178

Cain, J. (2019). Exploratory implementation of a blended format escape room in a large enrollment pharmacy management class. *Currents in Pharmacy Teaching & Learning*, 11(1), 44–50. https://doi.org/https://doi.org/10.1016/j.cptl.2018.09.010. doi:10.1016/j.cptl.2018.09.010 PMID:30527875

Chen, R. (2022). Investigating the Audio-Visual Psychological Effects in a Horror Game Northeastern University].

Chen, S. Y., & Chang, Y.-M. (2020). The impacts of real competition and virtual competition in digital game-based learning. *Computers in Human Behavior*, 104, 106171. https://doi.org/https://doi.org/10.1016/j.chb.2019.10617. doi:10.1016/j.chb.2019.106171

Christopoulos, A., Mystakidis, S., Cachafeiro, E., & Laakso, M.-J. (2022). Escaping the cell: Virtual reality escape rooms in biology education. *Behaviour & Information Technology*, •••, 1–18. doi:10.1080/0144929X.2022.2079560

Clarke, S. J., Peel, D. J., Arnab, S., Morini, L., Keegan, H., & Wood, O. (2017). EscapED: A Framework for Creating Educational Escape Rooms and Interactive Games to For Higher/Further Education. *International Journal of Serious Games*, 4(3). Advance online publication. doi:10.17083/ijsg.v4i3.180

Clauson, A., Hahn, L., Frame, T., Hagan, A., Bynum, L. A., Thompson, M. E., & Kiningham, K. (2019). An innovative escape room activity to assess student readiness for advanced pharmacy practice experiences (APPEs). *Currents in Pharmacy Teaching & Learning*, 11(7), 723–728. doi:10.1016/j.cptl.2019.03.011 PMID:31227096

Cohen, T. N., Griggs, A. C., Kanji, F. F., Cohen, K. A., Lazzara, E. H., Keebler, J. R., & Gewertz, B. L. (2021). Advancing team cohesion: Using an escape room as a novel approach. *Journal of Patient Safety and Risk Management*, 26(3), 126–134. doi:10.1177/25160435211005934

Connelly, L., Burbach, B. E., Kennedy, C., & Walters, L. (2018). Escape room recruitment event: Description and lessons learned. *The Journal of Nursing Education*, 57(3), 184–187. doi:10.3928/01484834-20180221-12 PMID:29505080

Cruz, M. (2019). Escaping from the traditional classroom-The'Escape Room Methodology'in the Foreign Languages Classroom. Babylonia-Rivista svizzera per l'insegnamento delle lingue, 3, 26-29.

da Cruz, M. R. D. F. (2019). 'Escapando de la clase tradicional': The escape rooms methodology within the spanish as foreign language classroom. *Revista Lusófona de Educação*, *46*(46), 117–137. doi:10.24140/issn.1645-7250.rle46.08

Dugnol-Menéndez, J., Jiménez-Arberas, E., Ruiz-Fernández, M. L., Fernández-Valera, D., Mok, A., & Merayo-Lloves, J. (2021). A collaborative escape room as gamification strategy to increase learning motivation and develop curricular skills of occupational therapy students. *BMC Medical Education*, *21*(1), 544. doi:10.118612909-021-02973-5 PMID:34706713

Egan, J. D., Banter, J. N., & Sorgen, C. H. (2021). Assessing Escape Rooms as a Teaching Strategy for Leadership Competency Development. *Journal of Leadership Education*, *20*(1).

EMMENEGGER, S. (2020). Pressure escape: a trade pop up escape room with career orientation purposes.

Ennis, R. (1991). Critical Thinking. *Teaching Philosophy*, *14*(1), 4–18. doi:10.5840/teachphil19911412

Eukel, H., Frenzel, J., Frazier, K., & Miller, M. (2020). Unlocking Student Engagement: Creation, Adaptation, and Application of an Educational Escape Room Across Three Pharmacy Campuses. *Simulation & Gaming*, *51*(2), 167–179. doi:10.1177/1046878119898509

Ferns, J., Hawkins, N., Little, A., & Hamiduzzaman, M. (2022). The escape room experience: Exploring new ways to deliver interprofessional education. *Innovations in Education and Teaching International*, 1–12. doi:10.1080/14703297.2022.2158900

Foltz-Ramos, K., Fusco, N. M., & Paige, J. B. (2021). Saving patient x: A quasi-experimental study of teamwork and performance in simulation following an interprofessional escape room. *Journal of Interprofessional Care*, 1–8. doi:10.1080/13561820.2021.1874316 PMID:33587007

Fotaris, P., & Mastoras, T. (2019). Escape rooms for learning: A systematic review. Proceedings of the European Conference on Games Based Learning, Friedrich, C., Teaford, H., Taubenheim, A., Boland, P., & Sick, B. (2019). Escaping the professional silo: an escape room implemented in an interprofessional education curriculum. *Journal of Interprofessional Care*, *33*(5), 573–575. doi:10.1080/13561820.2018.1538941 PMID:30362849

Fuentes-Cabrera, A., Parra-González, M. E., López-Belmonte, J., & Segura-Robles, A. (2020). Learning Mathematics with Emerging Methodologies—The Escape Room as a Case Study. *Mathematics*, 8(9), 1586. https://www.mdpi.com/2227-7390/8/9/1586. doi:10.3390/math8091586

Gardner, H. (1993). *Multiple intelligences: The theory in practice*. Basic Books/ Hachette Book Group.

Glavaš, A., & Stašcik, A. (2017). Enhancing positive attitude towards mathematics through introducing Escape Room games. Mathematics Education as a Science and a Profession, 281-293.

Gomez, M. (2020). A COVID-19 intervention: Using digital escape rooms to provide professional development to alternative certification educators. *Journal of Technology and Teacher Education*, 28(2), 425–432.

Goodman, J. T., & Landgren, A. (2021). Escape Into a Nursing Career: An Active Recruitment Strategy for Prospective Students. *Nursing Education Perspectives*, 42(6), E147–E148. doi:10.1097/01.NEP.0000000000000312 PMID:33896923

Guckian, J., Eveson, L., & May, H. (2020). The great escape? The rise of the escape room in medical education. *Future Healthcare Journal*, 7(2), 112–115. doi:10.7861/fhj.2020-0032 PMID:32550277

Hartt, M., Hosseini, H., & Mostafapour, M. (2020). Game On: Exploring the Effectiveness of Game-based Learning. *Planning Practice and Research*, 35(5), 589–604. doi:10.1080/02697459.2020.1778859

Hawkins, J. E., Wiles, L. L., Tremblay, B., & Thompson, B. A. (2020). Behind the Scenes of an Educational Escape Room. *The American Journal of Nursing*, 120(10), 50–56. doi:10.1097/01.NAJ.0000718636.68938.bb PMID:32976152

Heim, A. B., Duke, J., & Holt, E. A. (2022). Design, discover, and decipher: Student-developed escape rooms in the virtual ecology classroom. *Journal of Microbiology & Biology Education*, 23(1), e00015–e00022. doi:10.1128/jmbe.00015-22 PMID:35784618

Ho, A. M. (2018). Unlocking ideas: Using escape room puzzles in a cryptography classroom. *PRIMUS (Terre Haute, Ind.)*, 28(9), 835–847. doi:10.1080/10511970.2018.1453568

Horn, M. A. (2023). Design and evaluation of a new consolidation exercise for students studying cardiac physiology: A digital escape room. *Advances in Physiology Education*, 47(1), 82–92. doi:10.1152/advan.00176.2022 PMID:36476116

Hursman, A., Richter, L. M., Frenzel, J., Viets Nice, J., & Monson, E. (2022). An online escape room used to support the growth of teamwork in health professions students. *Journal of Interprofessional Education & Practice*, *29*, 100545. doi:10.1016/j. xjep.2022.100545 PMID:35991695

International Escape Room Markets Analysis. (2019). The Logic Escapes Me.

Kezar, A. (2001). Theory of Multiple Intelligences: Implications for Higher Education. *Innovative Higher Education*, *26*(2), 141–154. doi:10.1023/A:1012292522528

Kinio, A. E., Dufresne, L., Brandys, T., & Jetty, P. (2019). Break out of the Classroom: The Use of Escape Rooms as an Alternative Teaching Strategy in Surgical Education. *Journal of Surgical Education*, *76*(1), 134–139. https://doi.org/https://doi.org/10.1016/j.jsurg.2018.06.030. doi:10.1016/j.jsurg.2018.06.030 PMID:30126728

Kolb, D. A., Boyatzis, R. E., & Mainemelis, C. (2014). Experiential learning theory: Previous research and new directions. In *Perspectives on thinking, learning, and cognitive styles* (pp. 227–248). Routledge. doi:10.4324/9781410605986-9

Kwok, S., & Childers, R. (2023). Escaping the Laboratory: An Escape Room to Reinforce Biomedical Engineering Skills. *Biomedical Engineering Education*, *3*(1), 75–86. doi:10.100743683-022-00089-w PMID:36348693

Lepp, G. A., Fierke, K. K., Friedrich, C., & Sick, B. (2023). How intention/reflection fosters student learning in an interprofessional experiential escape room activity. *Journal of Interprofessional Education & Practice*, *30*, 100589. doi:10.1016/j. xjep.2022.100589

Löffler, E., Schneider, B., Zanwar, T., & Asprion, P. M. (2021). Cysecescape 2.0—A virtual escape room to raise cybersecurity awareness. *International Journal of Serious Games*, *8*(1), 59–70. doi:10.17083/ijsg.v8i1.413

López, Á. G. (2019). The use of escape rooms to teach and learn English at university. Research, technology and best practices in education, 94-101.

López-Pernas, S., Gordillo, A., Barra, E., & Quemada, J. (2019a). Analyzing Learning Effectiveness and Students' Perceptions of an Educational Escape Room in a Programming Course in Higher Education. *IEEE Access: Practical Innovations, Open Solutions*, *7*, 184221–184234. doi:10.1109/ACCESS.2019.2960312

López-Pernas, S., Gordillo, A., Barra, E., & Quemada, J. (2019b). Examining the Use of an Educational Escape Room for Teaching Programming in a Higher Education Setting. *IEEE Access: Practical Innovations, Open Solutions*, *7*, 31723–31737. doi:10.1109/ACCESS.2019.2902976

Lundholm, M. D., Simpson, K. P., & Ozark, L. (2022). A medical escape room to build intern workplace social capital in an internal medicine residency program. *Medical Teacher*, *44*(5), 546–550. doi:10.1080/0142159X.2021.2005243 PMID:34822314

Macías-Guillén, A., Díez, R. M., Serrano-Luján, L., & Borrás-Gené, O. (2021). Educational Hall Escape: Increasing Motivation and Raising Emotions in Higher Education Students. *Education Sciences*, *11*(9), 527. https://www.mdpi.com/2227-7102/11/9/527. doi:10.3390/educsci11090527

Makri, A., Vlachopoulos, D., & Martina, R. A. (2021). Digital Escape Rooms as Innovative Pedagogical Tools in Education: A Systematic Literature Review. *Sustainability (Basel)*, *13*(8), 4587. https://www.mdpi.com/2071-1050/13/8/4587. doi:10.3390u13084587

McCarthy, M. (2010). Experiential learning theory: From theory to practice. [JBER]. *Journal of Business & Economics Research*, *8*(5). Advance online publication. doi:10.19030/jber.v8i5.725

Mello-Stark, S., VanValkenburg, M. A., & Hao, E. (2020). Thinking outside the box: Using escape room games to increase interest in cyber security. Innovations in Cybersecurity Education, 39-53.

Moore, L., & Campbell, N. (2021). Effectiveness of an escape room for undergraduate interprofessional learning: A mixed methods single group pre-post evaluation. *BMC Medical Education*, *21*(1), 220. doi:10.118612909-021-02666-z PMID:33879150

Morrell, B. L. M., Eukel, H. N., & Santurri, L. E. (2020). Soft skills and implications for future professional practice: Qualitative findings of a nursing education escape room. *Nurse Education Today*, *93*, 104462. https://doi.org/https://doi.org/10.1016/j.nedt.2020.104462. doi:10.1016/j.nedt.2020.104462 PMID:32791421

Nadolny, L., Alaswad, Z., Culver, D., & Wang, W. (2017). Designing With Game-Based Learning: Game Mechanics From Middle School to Higher Education. *Simulation & Gaming*, *48*(6), 814–831. doi:10.1177/1046878117736893

Nelson, V., & Crea, J. (2021). The Data Science Instructional Escape Room-a Successful Experiment. *Chance*, *34*(2), 53–58. doi:10.1080/09332480.2021.1915034

Nicholson, S. (2015). Peeking Behind the Locked Door: A Survey of Escape Room Facilities. White Paper. https://scottnicholson.com/pubs/erfacwhite.pdf

Pan, R., Lo, H., & Neustaedter, C. (2017). Collaboration, Awareness, and Communication in Real-Life Escape Rooms Proceedings of the 2017 Conference on Designing Interactive Systems, Edinburgh, United Kingdom. https://doi.org/10.1145/3064663.3064767

Patel, C. (2018). An Analysis of Jean Lave and Etienne Wenger's Situated Learning: Legitimate Peripheral Participation. Taylor & Francis. https://books.google.com. au/books?id=GEFNDwAAQBAJ

Peleg, R., Yayon, M., Katchevich, D., Moria-Shipony, M., & Blonder, R. (2019). A Lab-Based Chemical Escape Room: Educational, Mobile, and Fun! *Journal of Chemical Education*, *96*(5), 955–960. doi:10.1021/acs.jchemed.8b00406

Pérez, P., González-Sosa, E., Kachach, R., Pereira, F., & Villegas, Á. (2021). Ecological validity through gamification: An experiment with a mixed reality escape room. 2021 IEEE International Conference on Artificial Intelligence and Virtual Reality (AIVR), Plass, J. L., Homer, B. D., & Kinzer, C. K. (2015). Foundations of Game-Based Learning. *Educational Psychologist*, *50*(4), 258–283. doi:10.1080/00461520.2015.1122533

Reeves, T. C. (2006). How do you know they are learning? The importance of alignment in higher education. *International Journal of Learning Technology*, *2*(4), 294–309. doi:10.1504/IJLT.2006.011336

Ritzko, J., & Robinson, S. (2011). Using Games To Increase Active Learning. [TLC]. *Journal of College Teaching and Learning*, *3*(6). Advance online publication. doi:10.19030/tlc.v3i6.1709

Ross, R., & Bell, C. (2019, August 20-23). 2019). Turning the classroom into an escape room with decoder hardware to increase student engagement. 2019 IEEE Conference on Games (CoG), Ross, R., & Bennett, A. (2020). Increasing engagement with engineering escape rooms. *IEEE Transactions on Games*, *14*(2), 161–169. doi:10.1109/TG.2020.3025003

Sarage, D., O'Neill, B. J., & Eaton, C. M. (2021). There is no I in escape: Using an escape room simulation to enhance teamwork and medication safety behaviors in nursing students. *Simulation & Gaming*, *52*(1), 40–53. doi:10.1177/1046878120976706

Schunk, D. H. (1995). Self-efficacy, motivation, and performance. *Journal of Applied Sport Psychology*, *7*(2), 112–137. doi:10.1080/10413209508406961

Seebauer, S., Jahn, S., & Mottok, J. (2020). Learning from escape rooms? A study design concept measuring the effect of a cryptography educational escape room. 2020 IEEE Global Engineering Education Conference (EDUCON), Shepard, L. A., Penuel, W. R., & Davidson, K. L. (2017). Design principles for new systems of assessment. *Phi Delta Kappan*, *98*(6), 47–52.

Shi, Y.-R., & Shih, J.-L. (2015). Game factors and game-based learning design model. *International Journal of Computer Games Technology*, *2015*, 11. Advance online publication. doi:10.1155/2015/549684

Stohlmann, M. S. (2020). Escape room math: Luna's lines. Mathematics Teacher: Learning and Teaching PK-12, 113(5), 383-389.

Sundsbø, K. (2018). Open Access Escape Room. figshare (2018): https://figshare. com/projects/Open Access Escape Room/56915 (accessed January 24, 2019).

Taraldsen, L. H., Haara, F. O., Lysne, M. S., Jensen, P. R., & Jenssen, E. S. (2022). A review on use of escape rooms in education – touching the void. *Education Inquiry*, *13*(2), 169–184. doi:10.1080/20004508.2020.1860284

Tercanli, H., Martina, R., Ferreira Dias, M., Wakkee, I., Reuter, J., Amorim, M., Madaleno, M., Magueta, D., Vieira, E., & Veloso, C. (2021). Educational escape rooms in practice: research, experiences, and recommendations.

Terrasi, B., Badoux, L., Abou Arab, O., Huette, P., Bar, S., Leviel, F., Amsallem, C., Ammirati, C., Dupont, H., & Lorne, E. (2020). Escape game training to improve non-technical team skills in the operating room. *Medical Teacher*, *42*(4), 432–482. doi:10.1080/0142159X.2019.1638505 PMID:31304836

Valdes, B., Mckay, M., & Sanko, J. S. (2021). The Impact of an Escape Room Simulation to Improve Nursing Teamwork, Leadership and Communication Skills: A Pilot Project. *Simulation & Gaming*, *52*(1), 54–61. doi:10.1177/1046878120972738

van Dinther, M., Dochy, F., & Segers, M. (2011). Factors affecting students' self-efficacy in higher education. *Educational Research Review*, *6*(2), 95–108. https://doi.org/https://doi.org/10.1016/j.edurev.2010.10.003. doi:10.1016/j.edurev.2010.10.003

Veldkamp, A., van de Grint, L., Knippels, M.-C. P., & van Joolingen, W. R. (2020). Escape education: A systematic review on escape rooms in education. *Educational Research Review*, *31*, 100364. doi:10.1016/j.edurev.2020.100364

Vergne, M. J., Smith, J. D., & Bowen, R. S. (2020). Escape the (remote) classroom: An online escape room for remote learning. *Journal of Chemical Education*, *97*(9), 2845–2848. doi:10.1021/acs.jchemed.0c00449

Vestal, M. E., Matthias, A. D., & Thompson, C. E. (2021). Engaging Students with Patient Safety in an Online Escape Room. *The Journal of Nursing Education*, *60*(8), 466–469. https://doi.org/doi:10.3928/C1484834-20210722-10. doi:10.3928/01484834-20210722-10 PMID:34346812

Warmelink, H., Mayer, I., Weber, J., Heijligers, B., Haggis, M., Peters, E., & Louwerse, M. (2017). AMELIO: Evaluating the team-building potential of a mixed reality escape room game. Extended abstracts publication of the annual symposium on computer-human interaction in play, Westera, W. (2015). Games are motivating, aren't they? Disputing the arguments for digital game-based learning. *International Journal of Serious Games*, 2(2). Advance online publication. doi:10.17083/ijsg.v2i2.58

Wilby, K. J., & Kremer, L. J. (2020). Development of a cancer-themed escape room learning activity for undergraduate pharmacy students. *International Journal of Pharmacy Practice*, 28(5), 541–543. doi:10.1111/ijpp.12622 PMID:32307797

Zhang, X. C., Lee, H., Rodriguez, C., Rudner, J., Chan, T. M., & Papanagnou, D. (2018). Trapped as a Group, Escape as a Team: Applying Gamification to Incorporate Team-building Skills Through an 'Escape Room' Experience. *Cureus*, 10(3), e2256. doi:10.7759/cureus.2256 PMID:29725559

ADDITIONAL READING

Bartlett, K. A., & Anderson, J. L. (2019). Gaming to learn: Bringing escape rooms to the classroom. In *Handbook of Research on Innovative Digital Practices to Engage Learners* (pp. 1–27). IGI Global. doi:10.4018/978-1-5225-9438-3.ch001

Fotaris, P., & Mastoras, T. (2019). Escape rooms for learning: A systematic review. *Proceedings of the European Conference on Games Based Learning*

Makri, A., Vlachopoulos, D., & Martina, R. A. (2021). Digital Escape Rooms as Innovative Pedagogical Tools in Education: A Systematic Literature Review. *Sustainability (Basel)*, 13(8), 4587. https://www.mdpi.com/2071-1050/13/8/4587. doi:10.3390u13084587

Ouariachi, T., & Van Dam, M. (2022). Educational innovation to address climate change issues: The emerging trend of (online) escape rooms. In *Handbook of Research on Using Disruptive Methodologies and Game-Based Learning to Foster Transversal Skills* (pp. 263–278). IGI Global. doi:10.4018/978-1-7998-8645-7.ch013

Ross, R., Hall, R., & Ross, S. L. (2022). Converting Course Material to Educational Escape Room Formats. In Handbook of Research on the Influence and Effectiveness of Gamification in Education (pp. 164-188). IGI Global. doi:10.4018/978-1-6684-4287-6.ch009

Taraldsen, L. H., Haara, F. O., Lysne, M. S., Jensen, P. R., & Jenssen, E. S. (2022). A review on use of escape rooms in education – touching the void. *Education Inquiry*, *13*(2), 169–184. doi:10.1080/20004508.2020.1860284

Tercanli, H., Martina, R., Ferreira Dias, M., Wakkee, I., Reuter, J., Amorim, M., Madaleno, M., Magueta, D., Vieira, E., & Veloso, C. (2021). Educational escape rooms in practice: research, experiences, and recommendations.

Tricarico, M. (2021). The Educational Value of the Escape Room in Virtual Environments. In Handbook of Research on Teaching With Virtual Environments and AI (pp. 341-372). IGI Global. doi:10.4018/978-1-7998-7638-0.ch015

Veldkamp, A., van de Grint, L., Knippels, M.-C. P., & van Joolingen, W. R (2020). Escape education: A systematic review on escape rooms in education. *Educational Research Review*, *31*, 100364. doi:10.1016/j.edurev.2020.100364

KEY TERMS AND DEFINITIONS

Active learning: An instructional approach that involves students actively participating in the learning process, rather than passively receiving information.

Affective outcomes: Emotional and attitudinal aspects of learning, such as motivation, engagement, and self-efficacy.

Cognitive outcomes: The mental skills and abilities that are developed through learning, such as problem-solving, critical thinking, and memory.

Educational escape room: Escape room designed for educational purposes.

Escape room: Live-action team-based game where players discover clues, solve puzzles, and accomplish tasks in one or more rooms to accomplish a specific goal (usually escaping from the room) in a limited time.

Game-based learning: The use of games and game-like elements in education to enhance learning, engagement, and motivation.

Puzzle: A problem or enigma designed to test a person's ingenuity, knowledge, or problem-solving skills.

Social outcomes: The development of interpersonal skills and social competencies, such as communication, teamwork, and collaboration.

Section 3
Technology and Learning Environments

Chapter 8
Enhancing Learning Experiences Through Artificial Intelligence:
Classroom 5.0

Luis Coelho
https://orcid.org/0000-0002-5673-7306
Instituto Superior de Engenharia do Porto, Portugal

Sara Reis
https://orcid.org/0000-0002-3416-2257
Instituto Superior de Engenharia do Porto, Portugal

ABSTRACT

Artificial Intelligence (AI) has evolved rapidly since its inception in the 1950s, from simple rule-based systems to today's advanced deep learning models. AI has impacted society in many ways, ranging from revolutionizing the way we live, work, and interact with technology, to creating new job opportunities, improving decision-making and automating tasks, and solving complex problems in fields like healthcare, finance, and transportation. However, it has also raised concerns about job displacement, privacy and security, and ethical considerations. The evolution of AI is ongoing, and it is expected to continue to shape and transform society in new and profound ways. The impact of AI in education has also been substantial, offering new and innovative ways to personalize learning, enhance educational resources, and improve educational outcomes. In this chapter we will cover the most important aspects related with the teaching-learning process, from a physiological perspective to the different strategies.

DOI: 10.4018/978-1-6684-8656-6.ch008

1. THE COMPLEXITY OF LEARNING

Learning is a process of acquiring knowledge, skills, behaviors, or attitudes through experience, study, or instruction. It involves a change in an individual's cognitive, affective, or behavioral patterns, and may occur consciously or unconsciously. Learning can take place through various methods, including observation, experience, imitation, and instruction, and may involve both formal and informal settings. The process of learning is dynamic and ongoing, and individuals continue to acquire new knowledge and skills throughout their lives. Individuals differ in the way they prefer to receive and process information, as well as the methods they use to retain and apply knowledge. Some people may learn best through visual aids, such as diagrams, videos, or pictures, while others may prefer auditory information, such as lectures or podcasts. Some individuals may learn best through hands-on experience, such as experiments or practical applications, while others may prefer to read and reflect on information. Understanding one's own learning style can be helpful in optimizing the learning process and improving educational outcomes.

1.1 Learning Styles

A learning style refers to the way in which an individual prefers to receive and process information. It involves the combination of cognitive, affective, and physiological factors that influence how individuals perceive, organize, retain, and use information. While there are many different models of learning styles, some of the most referenced are:

1. Visual: learners who prefer to process information through visual aids such as pictures, diagrams, and videos.
2. Auditory: learners who prefer to process information through spoken words, either by listening to others or by talking to themselves.
3. Kinesthetic or tactile: learners who prefer to process information through physical sensations and experiences, such as touching, moving, and doing.
4. Verbal: learners who prefer to process information through words, either written or spoken.
5. Logical: learners who prefer to process information through reasoning and problem-solving activities.
6. Social: learners who prefer to process information through interaction with others, such as group discussions and collaboration.

The first four, are known as the VARK model, after (Fleming, 2006), which has then been expanded to the presented six. All these categories can additionally be influenced by factors such as the selection of colors (Diachenko et al., 2022; Liu et al., 2021), the teacher's prosody (Coelho et al., 2011; Sikveland et al., 2021), the underlying presentation narrative/story-telling (Banerjee et al., 2020; McQuiggan et al., 2008), or even cultural factors. When considering the VARK categories, it is important to note that, despite their popularity and physiological basis, there is limited empirical evidence to support the idea that individuals have different learning styles and that teaching methods that match these styles are more effective than other methods. In fact, some studies have shown that matching teaching methods to learning styles may not improve learning outcomes at all. For example, in (Pashler et al., 2008) the concept of learning styles and the evidences supporting it are discussed. The authors conclude that any credible validation of learning-styles-based instruction requires robust documentation and a very particular type of experimental finding with several necessary criteria. First, students must be divided into groups based on their learning styles, and then, students from each group must be randomly assigned to receive one of multiple instructional methods. Next, students must then sit for a final test that is the same for all students. Finally, to demonstrate that optimal learning requires that students receive instruction tailored to their putative learning style, the experiment must reveal a specific type of interaction between learning style and instructional method: Students with one learning style achieve the best educational outcome when given an instructional method that differs from the instructional method producing the best outcome for students with a different learning style. Additionally, in (Hatami, 2013), it is plead that a learning style is not in itself an ability but rather a preferred way of using one's abilities. Individuals have different learning styles, that is, they differ in their 'natural, habitual, and preferred way(s) of absorbing, processing, and retaining new information and skills'. Learning styles are typically bipolar entities (for example reflective versus impulsive, random versus sequential), representing two extremes of a wide continuum; however, where a learner falls on the continuum is value neutral because each extreme has its own potential advantages and disadvantages. Moreover, although individuals may have some strong style preferences and tendencies, learning styles are not fixed modes of behavior, and, based on different situations and tasks, styles can be extended and modified. However, the extent to which individuals can extend or shift their styles to suit a particular situation varies.

Therefore, it's important for educators to focus on evidence-based teaching practices that are grounded in research rather than relying on learning styles as a guiding principle (Coelho et al., 2021; Reis et al., 2018). While there are individual differences in cognitive processing and brain activity, these differences are not strongly correlated with specific learning style preferences.

Research suggests that the concept of learning styles may be more related to individuals' personal preferences and experiences rather than underlying physiological or cognitive factors. For example, an individual may have a preference for visual learning because they find it easier to remember information that is presented in a visual format, but this preference may be shaped by their previous experiences and learning environments rather than a fundamental difference in brain function.

Additionally, it's important to note that the brain is highly adaptable and capable of changing in response to learning experiences. This means that individuals can develop and improve their abilities to process information through different sensory modalities with practice and exposure.

Nevertheless, while there may be individual differences in cognitive processing and brain activity, there is limited empirical confirmations to suggest that these differences are strongly correlated with specific learning style preferences or distinct physiological reasons. Instead, learning style preferences may be more related to individual experiences and personal preferences.

1.2 Learning Strategies

There are several learning approaches that have proven to be effective for different types of learners and educational settings. In the following paragraphs we will cover the most popular strategies.

Active learning is a widely used strategy that emphasizes hands-on, interactive learning experiences, such as groups discussions, problem-solving activities, and project-based learning. The main goals of active learning are to engage learners in the learning process, encourage critical thinking and problem-solving skills, promote collaboration and teamwork (Hernández-de-Menéndez et al., 2019). Active learning is a student-centered approach that emphasizes the importance of learners taking an active role on their own education. By engaging students in the learning process, active learning can help to improve student motivation and retention, deepen understanding of concepts, and prepare learners for lifelong learning (Saunders and Wong, 2020).

In a complementary way, *inquiry-based learning* can be used, an approach often contrasting with traditional didactic approaches where information is presented to learners in a more passive manner. This type of learning style emphasizes active and self-directed learning through exploration, investigation, and problem-solving. In inquiry-based learning, the learner takes an active role in constructing their own knowledge and understanding by asking questions, investigating problems, and drawing conclusions based on evidence. Inquiry-based learning may involve individual or group activities and can be applied across a wide range of subject areas and disciplines. By engaging in inquiry-based learning, students develop critical thinking skills, creativity, and a deeper understanding of the subject matter. The goal of inquiry-based learning is to encourage students to become independent, self-directed learners who are able to transfer their knowledge and skills to new situations.

As an alternative, *experiential learning* can be used. It is a type of learning style that emphasizes learning through direct experience and reflection. It involves a process of active experimentation, reflection, and application, where learners engage in hands-on activities and use their own experiences to gain knowledge and skills. Experiential learning can occur in a variety of settings, including classrooms, workplaces, and communities, and can involve both individual and group activities. Examples of experiential learning activities include internships, service learning, simulations, and outdoor education. The goal of experiential learning is to help learners develop a deeper understanding of the subject matter and to apply their knowledge and skills to real-world situations. By engaging in experiential learning, learners can develop critical thinking skills, problem-solving abilities, and a greater sense of personal and social responsibility.

The learning experience specifically adjusted to an individual, using *personalized learning* that involves tailoring the instruction process to meet the learners' needs, interests, knowledges and competences. It can include self-paced instruction, adaptative learning techniques, or individualized coaching and feedback (Shemshack and Spector, 2020). Materials, approaches, and activities can be adjusted to maximize the compatibility with the learner's profile.

But working in group has its underlying benefits. *Collaborative (or cooperative) learning*, another popular approach (Laal and Ghodsi, 2012), is focused on working with others to learn and achieve common goals. It can take many forms, including group projects, peer review, and others, providing learning opportunities for learners to discuss and analyze complex problems, share their perspectives, and develop innovative solutions (Reis et al., 2020). By working together, in groups that ensure that everyone participates, learners can leverage each other's strengths and learn from diverse perspectives, leading to improved critical and solving problem (Shaik, 2022). Additionally, collaborative learning promotes communication and collaboration skills, as learners must work together to accomplish tasks, share ideas, and provide feedback to each other. These are skills that are highly valued in many professional settings and are essential for effective work (Le et al., 2013).

In most cases traditional face-to-face instruction can be combined with online learning activities, consisting in a *blended learning* approach (Davis and Fill, 2007). The goal of blended learning is to create a more flexible and engaging learning environment that combines the benefits of both traditional and online learning approaches (Morais and Raposo, 2021). It has been found to be effective in improving learning outcomes, increasing student engagement and motivation, and promoting greater student autonomy and independence (Stacey and Gerbic, 2009).

1.3 The Teaching Process

When planning a teaching strategy, it is important to follow a set of key steps to ensure that the strategy is effective and meets the needs of the learners. From the several frameworks that exist to support the teaching process we will be inspired by the 5E (Balci et al., 2006; Wilder and Shuttleworth, 2005), since it is simple and covers the most essential aspects. The 5E learning cycle is a student-centered instructional model widely used in science education to promote active learning and engagement. It consists of five phases, each beginning with the letter "E." The first phase is "Engage," where the teacher captures students' interest and curiosity with intriguing questions or real-world scenarios related to the topic. In the "Explore" phase, students participate in hands-on activities and experiments to discover and gather data on the subject matter. Next, in the "Explain" phase, students discuss their findings and articulate their understanding with the teacher's guidance. The "Elaborate" phase extends learning by applying concepts to real-world situations, fostering higher-order thinking skills. Finally, in the "Evaluate" phase, students and teachers assess learning outcomes through various forms of evaluation, guiding future instruction and promoting deeper comprehension. The 5E learning cycle empowers students to construct their knowledge actively, fostering motivation and critical thinking skills throughout the learning process.

With this in mind, for our purposes, we define a first step to identify learning objectives and determine what learners should know or be able to do by the end of the learning experience, as depicted in the pipeline of Figure 1. Next, it is important to analyze and plan the strategy starting from an assumed student's knowledge state to correctly determine appropriate instructional strategies. If the students' level is unknown, then it is necessary to pre-assess learners' needs. This involves determining their prior knowledge, skills, and learning styles. Identifying the student's strengths and weaknesses is crucial for the success of the process, helping to tailor instruction to their needs.

Figure 1. Pipeline with general stages for the teaching process

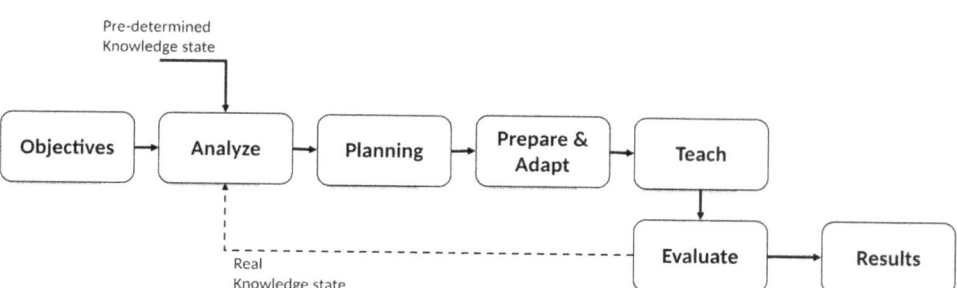

The next step, preparation, is to select and adapt instructional materials and resources that support the learning objectives, and to determine appropriate instructional methods, such as lectures, discussions, demonstrations, or group activities. The best way to adapt a lesson to a specific student and maximize their learning is to use evidence-based teaching practices that are grounded in research on effective instructional strategies (Coelho et al., 2021; Kharb et al., 2013). Using a variety of teaching strategies can help you engage students who have different learning preferences and maximize their learning. For example, considering the learning styles theory, visual aids can be used in combinations with hands-on activities, and group work to present information in multiple modalities.

While applying the defined strategies and using the selected materials, support and instant feedback should be provided, helping students to identify areas where they need to improve and build their skills. It is also important to do micro-planning for ongoing evaluation and feedback to continuously assess the teaching strategy and adjust as necessary.

After the teaching stage has ended it is necessary to assess its effectiveness and evaluation must be applied. It should be developed to measure whether learners have met the initially defined learning objectives. Once the teaching strategy has been implemented, it is important to reflect on its effectiveness and, if required, redefine the initial strategy to make improvements, either for the current process or for future teaching. It is also important to build communication strategies to provide feedback for the students. By following these key steps, the teaching strategy can be well-planned, effective, and meet the needs of the learners.

During the described process, evaluating or monitoring has a critical role since they convey the information to define what to do next. If the evaluation process only takes place at the end of the teaching process, it is possible to establish improvement guidelines for the next process. But, if monitoring is performed during the process, the learning progress can be evaluated, helping to identify areas where students are struggling and adjust instruction accordingly. By this means, a feedback loop is established, allowing adjustments during the teaching process and correct deviations from the desired trajectory.

To adapt a lesson to a specific student or group while maximizing their learning, evidence-based practices should be used to create a learning environment that supports their growth and development. Such practices can help establish a sense of trust and rapport with learners, while also ensuring that instruction is tailored to their needs and learning styles. Ultimately, this approach can lead to more successful learning outcomes for students.

2. LEARNING AND ENGAGEMENT INDICATORS AND BIOMARKERS

Monitoring learning during the teaching process is critical for ensuring that students are making progress toward the learning objectives. It provides teachers with an opportunity to provide feedback to students on their progress, adjust their instruction to meet the needs of individual students or groups of students, and identify areas where their instruction may need improvement. By tracking student performance data, teachers can identify patterns of misunderstanding or areas where students may need more or different types of instruction. This information can then be used to adjust instruction and provide additional support and resources to students who need it. In addition, monitoring learning can help support student motivation by providing students with a sense of progress and accomplishment. By recognizing and celebrating student achievements, teachers can help motivate students to continue their learning and strive for further success. Overall, monitoring learning during the teaching process is essential for ensuring student success and supporting their ongoing learning and development.

Motivation and engagement should also be matter of attention, since they are crucial for the effectiveness of the learning process (Singh et al., 2022) and bring several benefits for both teachers and students. When focusing on the group, it creates the opportunity for teachers to adjust their instruction to make it more engaging and relevant to students' interests and needs. When focusing of the student, it allows teachers to identify students who may be struggling or disengaged from the learning process, which enables them to provide additional support and resources. In both cases, monitoring engagement helps teachers build better relationships with students by paying attention to their interests and needs. This also helps to build a positive classroom environment that promotes active learning and encourages students to participate in classroom discussions and activities. Finally, when using this information, the teacher can provide feedback and recognition for active participation and effort, helping students feel more connected to their learning and motivated (Steinmayr et al., 2019).

To assess motivation and learning several methods are available. With the evolution of technology, classic methods, requiring manual intervention, are now evolving to semi-automatic and automatic approaches, with some examples shown in Table 1. It

Table 1. Examples of student learning and engagement monitoring approaches

Manual	Semi-Automatic	Automatic
• Student observation • Self-reporting • Exam	• Question answering time • Question raising • Question time to answer	• Facial analysis • Gesture and Posture • Speech analysis • Study time

is also possible to establish direct and indirect relations with personalized patterns or indicators. For example, using learning biomarkers, biological or behavioral measures that indicate changes in the brain and body, it is possible to assess the effectiveness of educational interventions and to identify specific areas where learners may be struggling or excelling. These can be changes in physiological measures such as heart rate, or simple EEG (Apicella et al., 2022), or based on behavioral measures such as response times or accuracy on learning tasks. Similarly, engagement can also be objectively estimated, during an educational activity. Examples of engagement biomarkers include the observation of pupil dilation or body movements (Uçar and Özdemir, 2022). By monitoring these biomarkers, educators and researchers can gain a better understanding of how engaged learners are during the learning process and how to optimize teaching strategies to improve the learning outcomes.

2.1 Behavior indicators

Facial monitoring using machine learning has the potential to provide valuable insights into student engagement and attention in the classroom. By identifying and analyzing a set of facial features that are indicative of attention or focus, machine learning algorithms can track visual cues to detect when students are paying attention to the teacher's explanation or to the material being presented. Possible facial features that could be indicative of attention include eye movements, eyebrow position, head tilt, facial muscle tension, and mouth position. For example, in (Sunagawa et al., 2020) a multimodal approach, combining gaze analysis, lip detection and eye blinking to detect drowsiness. In (Kumar et al., 2022), the eyeball movement alone is successfully used for the detection of drowsiness in the classroom. In (Mo, 2021) a similar approach is used to detect fatigue in on-line classes, due to the comfort of the home environment. Facial features are also used to classify attention level in (Chen, 2012; Koshti et al., 2022) with very good results. The authors report positive correlation between learning improvement and attention, pointing that facial-recognition technology can be used to provide immediate warning and adjusted contents, reenforcing the educational benefits of on-line classes.

Nevertheless, it's important to note that the specific facial features that are indicative of attention may vary depending on the individual and the context, and cultural and individual differences may affect the interpretation of facial cues. Nonetheless, facial monitoring using machine learning has the potential to provide teachers and educators with a new tool for assessing student engagement and identifying areas where additional support or intervention may be needed.

There has been an increasing interest towards computer vision and camera-based solutions as technology that overcomes the limits of both human observations and expensive equipment used to measure student engagement and learning. One approach to measure student engagement levels in real time is to combine and analyze three modalities representing students' behaviors: emotions from facial expressions, keyboard keystrokes, and mouse movements. Such a solution operates in real time while providing the exact level of engagement and using the least expensive equipment possible. In (Altuwairqi et al., 2021) a multimodal approach is explored. The authors estimate emotions from facial expression, using computer vision techniques to detect changes in facial expressions that may indicate changes in the student's emotional state during learning. Keyboard keystrokes and mouse movements were be used to track the student's interactions with the online learning environment and to provide insights into their level of engagement. Machine learning is the used to fuse the collected information and provide an integrated perspective of the student's learning stage.

Another advantage of computer-vision and machine learning techniques is that they can easily tackle large groups. For example, in (Vanneste et al., 2021) the authors explore the complexity of measuring the engagement of students and its strong interpretative component. They describe a methodology to measure students' engagement, taking both an individual (student-level) and a collective (classroom) approach. The reported results show that students' individual behavior, such as note-taking or hand-raising, is challenging to recognize and does not correlate with students' self-reported engagement. Interestingly, students' collective behavior can be quantified in a more generic way using measures for students' symmetry, reaction times and eye-gaze intersections. Nonetheless, the evidence for a connection between these collective measures and engagement is rather weak. Although this study does not succeed in providing a proxy of students' self-reported engagement, their approach sheds light on the needs for future research. More concretely, they suggest that not only the behavioral but also the emotional and cognitive component of engagement should be captured. These techniques can be used to develop a smart online learning system that can automatically adapt to learners' emotions and provide feedback about their motivations (Vanneste et al., 2021).

The use of eye-tracking technology to evaluate students' visual attention during computer-based learning activities is explored in (Pabba and Kumar, 2022). The authors argue that eye-tracking can provide valuable insights into students' learning behaviors and can help identify areas where students may be struggling. The paper presents a case study where eye-tracking was used to evaluate students' visual attention during a computer-based science lesson. The results showed that eye-tracking data can be used to identify specific areas of the lesson where students may be experiencing difficulty and can be used to improve the design of the lesson. A similar approach is used in (Sharma et al., 2023). In this paper, the authors present a system to detect the engagement level of students using only information provided by the typical built-in web-camera present in a laptop computer. The system combines information about the movements of the eyes and head, and facial emotions to produce a concentration index with three classes of engagement: "very engaged", "nominally engaged" and "not engaged at all". The system was tested in a typical e-learning scenario and the results show that it correctly identifies each period of time where students were "very engaged", "nominally engaged" and "not engaged at all". In both cases, the authors conclude that eye-tracking technology can be a powerful tool for evaluating student engagement and learning in computer-based learning environments and can help teachers and designers create more effective learning experiences.

Eye tracking alone can even be used to estimate the perception of students. For example in (Zlokazov et al., 2018) some of the issues of e-learning are discusses, namely the problems of adaptations of learning materials to the individual opportunities and needs of students. The standardized content of e-learning doesn't take into account individual features of student's cognitive activity, which results in low motivation to study and poor progress. The authors describe an experimental research of hybrid text perception with the help of eye tracking technology where data about behavior and emotions of students when completing learning tasks is estimated. The authors believe that the visual component of a hybrid text influences efficiency of text perception because it may arouse different emotions: negative or positive.

2.2 Physiological Indicators

Advancements in wearable technology have made consumer-grade EEG devices more accessible and reliable, allowing for a variety of real-life applications. Devices like the Emotiv EPOC headset and the Muse S headband have gained popularity as tools for emotion recognition due to their portability and ease of use. In (Moontaha et al., 2023), the authors presents a novel approach for monitoring the emotional state of individuals in real-time using a wearable sensor device. The authors propose a system that uses machine learning algorithms to analyze physiological signals, such as electrocardiography (ECG) and electrodermal activity (EDA), to detect emotional changes (Gazdi et al., 2018, 2016). The system is designed to be used in a variety of real-life scenarios, such as in sports training or in the workplace. The authors tested the system in a pilot study involving participants engaging in a stress-inducing task. The results showed that the system was able to detect changes in the participants' emotional state with high accuracy, demonstrating its potential for real-world applications. The authors suggest that their approach has potential for improving mental health and well-being by providing individuals with real-time feedback on their emotional state and enabling them to take proactive measures to manage stress and negative emotions.

The effectiveness of the learning process mainly depends on the engagement level of the learner. In case of distraction, lack of interest or superficial participation, the teaching strategy could be personalized by an automatic modulation of contents and communication strategies. Concerning engagement, in (Apicella et al., 2022), a wearable system for the personalized EEG-based detection of engagement in learning 4.0 is proposed. The proposed solution is assessed by means of the classification accuracy in predicting engagement. The system can be used to make an automated teaching platform adaptable to the user, by managing eventual drops in cognitive and emotional engagement. The system is validated by an experimental case study on twenty-one students. The experimental task was to learn how a specific human-machine interface works. Both the cognitive and motor skills of participants were involved. De facto standard stimuli were employed to guarantee a metrologically founded reference. In within-subject approach, the proposed signal processing pipeline reaches almost 77% average accuracy in detecting both cognitive and emotional engagement.

Students now wear an extensive set of devices that can monitor several important indicators (Köles et al., 2015). In (Bustos-López et al., 2022) the author cover several student engagement detection initiatives in the educational domain. Their review highlights existing commercial and non-commercial wearables for student engagement monitoring and identifies key physiological signals involved in engagement detection. The authors found that common physiological signals used to measure student engagement include heart rate, skin temperature, respiratory rate, oxygen saturation, blood pressure, and electrocardiogram (ECG) data. Similarly, stress and surprise are key features of student engagement. Appropriate teaching–learning strategies lead to student engagement during learning activities.

3. SMART COMPUTER ASSISTED TEACHING

We have covered in the previous sections the complexity of the teaching-learning process. On the student side, there is a diversity of characteristics that impact the way they learn, from their intrinsic physiology to cultural factors. On the teacher's side, with the aim of imparting knowledge, skills and competence, the challenge is great, with a multitude of variables that can enhance this process. Simultaneously, the effectiveness of the process should be constantly monitored to ensure that there are no deviations and that no one is left behind. Artificial intelligence tools can be a useful asset for educators, since they can easily deal with large amounts of data and provide estimates based on existing patterns.

A general pipeline for a smart computer assisted teaching system is presented in Figure 2 that can be interpreted both in a classroom context, considering short

Figure 2. General pipeline for a smart computer assisted teaching-learning system

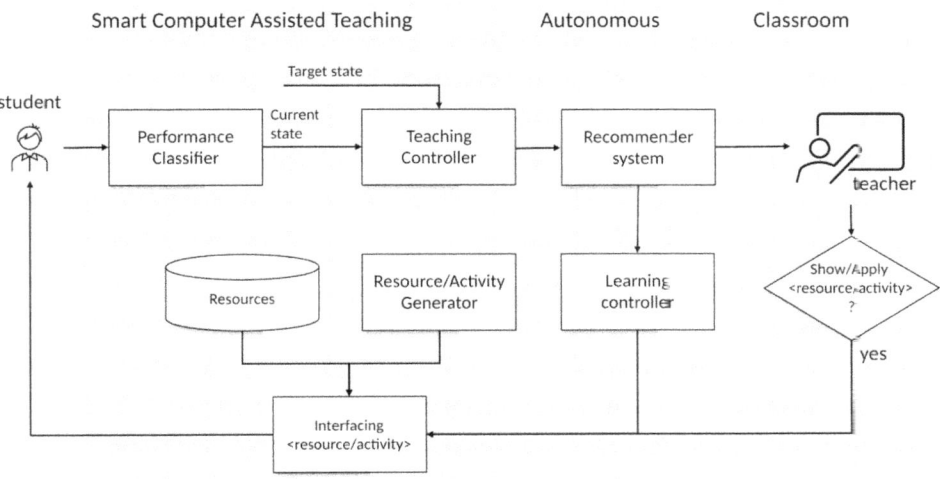

time intervals, but also in a broader context, involving several sessions. Focused on the student, a performance classification must be first estimated, encompassing learning state, motivation state, or other variables that can be useful for the process. In this process, AI has a crucial role in the perception of patterns and trends. This information is then compared with a target state that was pre-defined, with specific learning objectives and timings. After estimating the process error (difference between the current state and the target state), the teaching controller can propose actions, following a given learning strategy or style, targeting the individual or the group, ensuring multimodality and content variety. Then, an AI based recommender system can provide some possibilities within the defined path and guidelines. These can be used by the student, when studying autonomously or by the teacher, when preparing instruction or during the process. In the former case, a learning controller can again observe the student's current state and its learning history, and provide the best content and strategies. In the last case, the teacher can decide how to use these recommendations and how to proceed. Finally, the desired strategies and resource types are interfaced with the student. This process can again be managed by an AI system, with real-time generated contents or from existent resources.

The mediation of this process using AI can be made in several ways. Active learning can be effectively supported by artificial intelligence (AI), for example: AI-powered tools such as chatbots, virtual assistants, and adaptative learning platforms can provide personalized feedback and guidance to learners, allowing them to engage in active learning activities and receive support (Cohn, 2010). AI could generate virtual simulations and environments that provide realistic and interactive learning experiences. Learners can actively engage with these simulations, manipulate variables, and observe outcomes, which can promote active learning in a safe and controlled setting (Dawley and Dede, 2014). Additionally, the use of Natural language processing (NLP), a field of AI, could facilitate active learning by enabling learners to interact with educational content through voice or text-based interfaces. This can include asking questions, engaging in discussions, and obtaining immediate feedback (Shaik, 2022). Also, AI can analyze learners' interests, preferences, and learning resources, activities, and strategies, providing learners with personalized recommendations. AI technologies could support and enhance active learning by providing personalized feedback, adaptive instruction, realistic simulations, and driven insights.

The use of AI tools in collaborative learning can also have a positive impact on the enhancement of the learning experience for individuals or groups. For example, AI can facilitate group learning by analyzing group dynamics and suggesting ways to improve collaboration and communication (Hoey et al., 2018). Another advantage is related to data analysis. AI can be used to analyze large amounts of data on student performance, which can help teachers identify areas where students are struggling and adjust their teaching methods accordingly. This can help teachers to provide targeted support to students and improve overall learning outcomes (Hooda et al., 2022). Also, AI can be used to facilitate creative collaboration in art and design projects. For example, AI tools can be used to generate new ideas or suggest improvements to existing designs, which can be used as a starting point of group collaboration (McCormack et al., 2020). Overall, the interaction between collaborative learning and AI can lead to more personalized and effective learning experiences for students, as well as improved collaboration and communication within groups.

In self-paced instruction, the students can control the pace of their own learning. This means that they can work through learning materials, exercises, and assessments at their own speed (Anurugwo, 2018). One way that AI can support self-paced learning is by providing students with personalized recommendations for learning materials based on their interests, goals, and learning history. For example. An AI-powered platform could use data from a student´s past performance to recommended additional resources or exercises that would help them better understand a concept (Seo et al., 2021).

Adaptative learning is an approach that uses technology to create a personalized learning experience for each individual student. It involves analyzing data about student's performance and using that data to tailor the learning experience to their specific needs and abilities (Xie et al., 2019). Adaptative learning systems use algorithms and machine learning to analyze data on a student's performance and then adjust the content, pace, and difficulty level of the learning materials accordingly (Kabudi et al., 2021). Adaptative learning can be applied to a wide range of educational settings, from elementary schools to universities, and can be used for a variety of subjects, including math, science, and language learning. It has the potential to change education by enabling students to learn at their own pace and in a way that is best suited to their individual needs and abilities.

The use of these techniques can also be combined with gamification approaches, to boost motivation and enrich the learning experience, as in (Frutos-Pascual and Garcia-Zapirain, 2015).

4. OTHER TECHNOLOGIES

In an adjacent area, virtual reality (VR), augmented reality (AR) and extended reality (XR) technologies can revolutionize education by offering students an entirely new dimension of immersive and interactive learning experiences, acting as a powerful supporting tool to complement and enhance AI-driven content (Kamińska et al., 2023). Imagine a classroom where students are not limited to static textbooks or traditional lectures but instead, they are transported to historically significant events, distant planets, or even the microscopic world of cells. Through VR, students can step into these virtual environments, making their learning journey captivating and engaging. For instance, history lessons come alive as students witness historical figures and events in a visually realistic and emotionally impactful way, fostering a deeper understanding and connection to the subject matter. Furthermore, VR technology enables educators to create personalized learning experiences tailored to each student's needs and preferences. AI-driven algorithms can analyze individual learning patterns and strengths, suggesting specific VR modules that align with the student's unique learning style. This personalization not only boosts comprehension but also instills a sense of autonomy and empowerment in students, fostering a love for learning. One of the most significant advantages of VR in education is its capacity to provide hands-on training and simulations for various professions. Students studying fields like medicine, engineering, or aviation can practice procedures and tasks within a safe virtual environment. These simulated experiences enable them to gain practical skills and confidence before entering real-world scenarios, ultimately contributing to better professional competence and reducing potential risks (Zwoliński et al., 2022).

Also important is the ability of VR to facilitate collaborative learning, allowing students to interact and collaborate with their peers and instructors from across the globe, breaking down geographical barriers and promoting cross-cultural exchange. Through virtual classrooms and interactive group projects, students can learn to work effectively in diverse teams, honing vital interpersonal skills essential for success in today's interconnected world.

As mentioned, the role of VR is to complement the role of teachers by providing supplementary content and enriching the overall learning experience. Skilled teachers can curate and guide students through the vast array of VR experiences, ensuring that the technology serves as a pedagogical asset rather than a mere novelty.

As the fields of AI and VR continue to advance, we can expect even more sophisticated and tailored educational experiences. This combination of AI content and VR technology holds the potential to revolutionize education, making it more accessible, engaging, and effective for students of all ages, backgrounds, and learning abilities. By harnessing the power of these cutting-edge tools, we can create a future where learning knows no bounds and knowledge becomes an exciting adventure for every student.

5. CONCLUSION

Additionally, AI is being used to analyze large amounts of student data to identify patterns and insights that can inform decisions and improve educational outcomes. This data can now be very comprehensive, encompassing simple student evaluation reports to complex behavioral patterns. In fact, there are several complementary technologies that can be used to support the teaching/education process and objectively evaluate attention, understanding, cognitive load or memory.

For this, physiological information, such as heart rate, skin conductance, temperature, can be used in adaptive learning to provide insights into a student's physical and emotional state. By monitoring physiological responses, AI algorithms can detect stress, excitement, or boredom, which can be used to personalize the learning experience. This information can be used to adapt the learning experience, for example by adjusting the pace of learning to match the student's emotional state or by providing additional support when the student is feeling stressed. On the other hand, if a student is feeling excited and engaged, the pace of learning can be increased, or more challenging material can be introduced. This information can also be used to provide teachers with feedback on the effectiveness of their teaching, allowing them to adjust support student learning. Brain electrical activity, in a EEG like acquisition, can even be explored to estimate cognitive load or more complex states. Eye-tracking can also be a useful source of information to assess students engagement. However, it is important to consider the privacy and ethical implications of collecting and using physiological information, and to ensure that students' data is collected and used responsibly. The use of physiological information in adaptive learning has the potential to enhance the learning experience by making it more personalized and supportive.

AI can also monitor emotions in education, such as neutrality or happiness, through various techniques such as facial expression recognition, voice analysis, wearable devices, and self-reporting patterns. By analyzing students' facial expressions, speech patterns, physiological responses, and self-reported emotions, AI algorithms can provide guidelines to tailor teaching activities and materials.

The described personalized learning experiences, by utilizing various techniques such as adaptive learning, intelligent recommendation systems, chatbots and virtual tutors, predictive analytics, and personalized testing, will soon become a common practice. Adaptive learning algorithms can analyze student data, such as past performance and learning pace, to personalize learning content and pace. Intelligent recommendation systems can analyze student performance data and suggest personalized learning resources, such as videos, books, and articles. AI-powered chatbots and virtual tutors can provide instant feedback and guidance to students, addressing their individual needs and learning styles. Predictive analytics can analyze student performance data to make predictions about future performance, allowing educators to intervene early to support struggling students. Personalized testing involves using AI to personalize test content based on student learning progress, ensuring that students receive assessments that are appropriate for their level of understanding.

As the fields of AI and VR continue to advance, we can expect even more sophisticated and tailored educational experiences. A combination of AI content and VR technology holds the potential to revolutionize education, making it more accessible, engaging, and effective for students of all ages, backgrounds, and learning abilities.

In all these approaches, it is important not to forget the privacy and ethical implications of student performance monitoring using AI, and to ensure that student data is collected and used responsibly. The use of AI to education has the potential to enhance the learning experience by making it more personalized and supportive but must be done in a responsible and ethical manner.

The future of learning with AI tools is expected to be characterized by highly personalized, efficient, and engaging learning experiences. AI will likely be used to create immersive learning environments through virtual and augmented reality, as well as to provide personalized learning pathways tailored to individual student learning styles and goals. Predictive learning algorithms will likely become more sophisticated, using machine learning techniques to predict student learning outcomes and provide teachers with insights on how to support students who are struggling. Automated assessment using AI will also be implemented, freeing up teacher time to focus on other tasks. However, it is important to ensure that AI is used to support and enhance human teaching, rather than replace it, and that ethical considerations are considered. The future of AI in education promises to be innovative and transformative.

REFERENCES

Altuwairqi, K., Jarraya, S. K., Allinjawi, A., & Hammami, M. (2021). Student behavior analysis to measure engagement levels in online learning environments. *Signal, Image and Video Processing*, *15*(7), 1387–1395. doi:10.100711760-021-01869-7 PMID:34007342

Anurugwo, A. O. (2018). *ICT Tools for Promoting Self-Paced Learning among Sandwich Students in a Nigerian University, Commission for International Adult Education*. Commission for International Adult Education.

Apicella, A., Arpaia, P., Frosolone, M., Improta, G., Moccaldi, N., & Pollastro, A. (2022). EEG-based measurement system for monitoring student engagement in learning 4.0. *Scientific Reports*, *12*(1), 5857. doi:10.103841598-022-09578-y PMID:35393470

Balci, S., Cakiroglu, J., & Tekkaya, C. (2006). Engagement, exploration, explanation, extension, and evaluation (5E) learning cycle and conceptual change text as learning tools. *Biochemistry and Molecular Biology Education*, *34*(3), 199–203. doi:10.1002/bmb.2006.49403403199 PMID:21638670

Banerjee, M., Zlatkin-Troitschanskaia, O., & Roeper, J. (2020). Narratives and Their Impact on Students' Information Seeking and Critical Online Reasoning in Higher Education Economics and Medicine. *Frontiers in Education*, 5.

Bustos-López, M., Cruz-Ramírez, N., Guerra-Hernández, A., Sánchez-Morales, L. N., Cruz-Ramos, N. A., & Alor-Hernández, G. (2022). Wearables for Engagement Detection in Learning Environments: A Review. *Biosensors (Basel)*, *12*(7), 509. doi:10.3390/bios12070509 PMID:35884312

Chen, H.-R. (2012). Assessment of Learners' Attention to E-Learning by Monitoring Facial Expressions for Computer Network Courses. *Journal of Educational Computing Research*, *47*(4), 371–385. doi:10.2190/EC.47.4.b

Coelho, L., Braga, D., Dias, M., & Garcia-Mateo, C. 2011. An Automatic Voice Pleasantness Classification System Based on Prosodic and Acoustic Patterns of Voice Preference, in: Proc. Interspeech. Presented at the Interspeech, Florence. 10.21437/Interspeech.2011-589

Coelho, L., Coelho, F. G., & Reis, S. 2021. Preferences for Teaching Materials: A Survey on a Multimodal World, in: 2021 IEEE Global Engineering Education Conference (EDUCON). Presented at the 2021 IEEE Global Engineering Education Conference (EDUCON). 10.1109/EDUCON46332.2021.9454099

Cohn, D. (2010). Active Learning. In C. Sammut & G. I. Webb (Eds.), *Encyclopedia of Machine Learning* (pp. 10–14). Springer US., doi:10.1007/978-0-387-30164-8_6

Davis, H. C., & Fill, K. (2007). Embedding blended learning in a university's teaching culture: Experiences and reflections. *British Journal of Educational Technology*, *38*(5), 817–828. doi:10.1111/j.1467-8535.2007.00756.x

Dawley, L., & Dede, C. (2014). Situated Learning in Virtual Worlds and Immersive Simulations. In J. M. Spector, M. D. Merrill, J. Elen, & M. J. Bishop (Eds.), *Handbook of Research on Educational Communications and Technology* (pp. 723–734). Springer., doi:10.1007/978-1-4614-3185-5_58

Diachenko, I., Kalishchuk, S., Zhylin, M., Kyyko, A., & Volkova, Y. (2022). Color education: A study on methods of influence on memory. *Heliyon*, *8*(11), e11607. doi:10.1016/j.heliyon.2022.e11607 PMID:36411932

Fleming, N. D. (2006). *Teaching and Learning Styles: VARK Strategies*. N.D. Fleming.

Frutos-Pascual, M., & Garcia-Zapirain, B. (2015). Assessing Visual Attention Using Eye Tracking Sensors in Intelligent Cognitive Therapies Based on Serious Games. *Sensors (Basel)*, *15*(5), 11092–11117. doi:10.3390150511092 PMID:25985158

Gazdi, L., Pomázi, K., Radostyán, B., Szabó, M., Szegletes, L., & Forstner, B. 2016. Experimenting with classifiers in biofeedback-based mental effort measurement, in: 2016 7th IEEE International Conference on Cognitive Infocommunications (CogInfoCom). Presented at the 2016 7th IEEE International Conference on Cognitive Infocommunications (CogInfoCom), pp. 000331–000336. 10.1109/CogInfoCom.2016.7804571

Gazdi, L., Pomázi, K., Szabó, M., & Forstner, B. (2018). An Innovative Model for Adaptive Learning Utilizing Biofeedback and Item Response Theory. *Periodica Polytechnica. Electrical Engineering and Computer Science*, *62*, 90–105. doi:10.3311/PPee.12213

Hatami, S. (2013). Learning styles. *ELT Journal*, *67*(4), 488–490. doi:10.1093/elt/ccs083

Hernández-de-Menéndez, M., Vallejo Guevara, A., Tudón Martínez, J. C., Hernández Alcántara, D., & Morales-Menendez, R. (2019). Active learning in engineering education. A review of fundamentals, best practices and experiences. *Int J Interact Des Manuf*, *13*(3), 909–922. doi:10.100712008-019-00557-8

Hoey, J., Schröder, T., Morgan, J., Rogers, K. B., Rishi, D., & Nagappan, M. (2018). Artificial Intelligence and Social Simulation: Studying Group Dynamics on a Massive Scale. *Small Group Research*, *49*(6), 647–683. doi:10.1177/1046496418802362

Hooda, M., Rana, C., Dahiya, O., Rizwan, A., & Hossain, M. S. (2022). Artificial Intelligence for Assessment and Feedback to Enhance Student Success in Higher Education. *Mathematical Problems in Engineering*, *2022*, e5215722. doi:10.1155/2022/5215722

Kabudi, T., Pappas, I., & Olsen, D. H. (2021). AI-enabled adaptive learning systems: A systematic mapping of the literature. *Computers and Education: Artificial Intelligence*, *2*, 100017. doi:10.1016/j.caeai.2021.100017

Kamińska, D., Zwoliński, G., Laska-Leśniewicz, A., Raposo, R., Vairinhos, M., Pereira, E., Urem, F., Hinic, M. L., Haamer, R. E., & Anbarjafari, G. 2023. Augmented Reality: Current and New Trends in Education. doi:10.20944/preprints202306.1665.v1

Kharb, P., Samanta, P. P., Jindal, M., & Singh, V. (2013). The Learning Styles and the Preferred Teaching—Learning Strategies of First Year Medical Students. *Journal of Clinical and Diagnostic Research : JCDR*, *7*, 1089–1092. doi:10.7860/JCDR/2013/5809.3090 PMID:23905110

Köles, M., Szegletes, L., & Forstner, B. 2015. Towards a physiology based difficulty control system for serious games, in: 2015 6th IEEE International Conference on Cognitive Infocommunications (CogInfoCom). Presented at the 2015 6th IEEE International Conference on Cognitive Infocommunications (CogInfoCom), pp. 323–328. 10.1109/CogInfoCom.2015.7390612

Koshti P. Paryani A. Talreja J. Zope V. 2022. AttenQ- Attention Span Detection Tool for Online Learning. doi:10.2139/ssrn.4096416

JR., D.K., Harish, N., Priyadharsini, K., Gowtham, S., & Gokulraj, G., (2022). Machine Learning based Drowsiness Detection in Classrooms. In *2022 International Conference on Edge Computing and Applications (ICECAA)* (pp. 1186-1191). IEEE.

Laal, M., & Ghodsi, S. M. 2012. Benefits of collaborative learning. Procedia - Social and Behavioral Sciences, World Conference on Learning, Teaching & Administration - 2011 31, 486–490. 10.1016/j.sbspro.2011.12.091

Le, H., Janssen, J., & Wubbels, T. (2018). Collaborative learning practices: Teacher and student perceived obstacles to effective student collaboration. *Cambridge Journal of Education*, *48*(1), 103–122. doi:10.1080/0305764X.2016.1259389

Liu, Y., Ma, W., Guo, X., Lin, X., Wu, C., & Zhu, T. (2021). Impacts of Color Coding on Programming Learning in Multimedia Learning: Moving Toward a Multimodal Methodology. *Frontiers in Psychology, 12*, 12. doi:10.3389/fpsyg.2021.773328 PMID:34925175

McCormack, J., Hutchings, P., Gifford, T., Yee-King, M., Llano, M. T., & D'inverno, M. (2020). Design Considerations for Real-Time Collaboration with Creative Artificial Intelligence. *Organised Sound, 25*(1), 41–52. doi:10.1017/S1355771819000451

McQuiggan, S. W., Rowe, J. P., Lee, S., & Lester, J. C. (2008). Story-Based Learning: The Impact of Narrative on Learning Experiences and Outcomes. In B. P. Woolf, E. Aïmeur, R. Nkambou, & S. Lajoie (Eds.), *Intelligent Tutoring Systems* (pp. 530–539). Lecture Notes in Computer Science. Springer., doi:10.1007/978-3-540-69132-7_56

Mo, Q. (1827). 2021. Fatigue Detection For Online Classes Based on Adaboost. *Journal of Physics: Conference Series, 012121*. Advance online publication. doi:10.1088/1742-6596/1827/1/012121

Moontaha, S., Schumann, F. E. F., & Arnrich, B. (2023). Online Learning for Wearable EEG-Based Emotion Classification. *Sensors (Basel), 23*(5), 2387. doi:10.339023052387 PMID:36904590

Morais, N. S., & Raposo, R. 2021. Blended-Learning in contexts conditioned by the pandemic: the perceptions of higher education students, in: 2021 International Symposium on Computers in Education (SIIE). Presented at the 2021 International Symposium on Computers in Education (SIIE), pp. 1–6. 10.1109/SIIE53363.2021.9583650

Pabba, C., & Kumar, P. (2022). An intelligent system for monitoring students' engagement in large classroom teaching through facial expression recognition. *Expert Systems: International Journal of Knowledge Engineering and Neural Networks, 39*(1), e12839. doi:10.1111/exsy.12839

Pashler, H., McDaniel, M., Rohrer, D., & Bjork, R. (2008). Learning Styles: Concepts and Evidence. *Psychological Science in the Public Interest, 9*(3), 105–119. doi:10.1111/j.1539-6053.2009.01038.x PMID:26162104

Reis, S., Coelho, F., & Coelho, L. (2020). Success Factors in Students' Motivation with Project Based Learning: From Theory to Reality. [iJOE]. *International Journal of Online and Biomedical Engineering, 16*(12), 4–17. doi:10.3991/ijoe.v16i12.16001

Reis, S., Guimarães, P., Coelho, F., Nogueira, E., & Coelho, L. 2018. A framework for simulation systems and technologies for medical training, in: 2018 Global Medical Engineering Physics Exchanges/Pan American Health Care Exchanges (GMEPE/PAHCE). Presented at the 2018 Global Medical Engineering Physics Exchanges/Pan American Health Care Exchanges (GMEPE/PAHCE), pp. 1–4. 10.1109/GMEPE-PAHCE.2018.8400757

Saunders, L., & Wong, M. A. 2020. Active Learning: Engaging People in the Learning Process, in: Instruction in Libraries and Information Centers. Windsor & Downs Press.

Seo, K., Tang, J., Roll, I., Fels, S., & Yoon, D. (2021). The impact of artificial intelligence on learner–instructor interaction in online learning. *International Journal of Educational Technology in Higher Education*, *18*(1), 54. doi:10.118641239-021-00292-9 PMID:34778540

Shaik, T., Tao, X., Li, Y., Dann, C., McDonald, J., Redmond, P., & Galligan, L. (2022). A Review of the Trends and Challenges in Adopting Natural Language Processing Methods for Education Feedback Analysis. *IEEE Access : Practical Innovations, Open Solutions*, *10*, 56720–56739. doi:10.1109/ACCESS.2022.3177752

Sharma, P., Joshi, S., Gautam, S., Maharjan, S., Khanal, S. R., Reis, M. C., Barroso, J., & Filipe, V. M. de J. (2023). *Student Engagement Detection Using Emotion Analysis*. Eye Tracking and Head Movement with Machine Learning., doi:10.48550/arXiv.1909.12913

Shemshack, A., & Spector, J. M. (2020). A systematic literature review of personalized learning terms. *Smart Learning Environments*, *7*(1), 33. doi:10.118640561-020-00140-9

Sikveland, R. O., Solem, M. S., & Skovholt, K. (2021). How teachers use prosody to guide students towards an adequate answer. *Linguistics and Education*, *61*, 100886. doi:10.1016/j.linged.2020.100886

Singh, M., James, P. S., Paul, H., & Bolar, K. (2022). Impact of cognitive-behavioral motivation on student engagement. *Heliyon*, *8*(7), e09843. doi:10.1016/j.heliyon.2022.e09843 PMID:35815149

Stacey, E., & Gerbic, P. 2009. Effective Blended Learning Practices: Evidence-Based Perspectives in ICT-Facilitated Education, https://services.igi-global.com/resolvedoi/resolve.aspx?doi=10.4018/978-1-60566-296-1. IGI Global.

Steinmayr, R., Weidinger, A. F., Schwinger, M., & Spinath, B. (2019). The Importance of Students' Motivation for Their Academic Achievement – Replicating and Extending Previous Findings. *Frontiers in Psychology*, *10*, 10. doi:10.3389/fpsyg.2019.01730 PMID:31417459

Sunagawa, M., Shikii, S., Nakai, W., Mochizuki, M., Kusukame, K., & Kitajima, H. (2020). Comprehensive Drowsiness Level Detection Model Combining Multimodal Information. *IEEE Sensors Journal*, *20*(7), 3709–3717. doi:10.1109/JSEN.2019.2960158

Uçar, M. U., & Özdemir, E. (2022). Recognizing Students and Detecting Student Engagement with Real-Time Image Processing. *Electronics (Basel)*, *11*(9), 1500. doi:10.3390/electronics11091500

Vanneste, P., Oramas, M. J., Verelst, T., Tuytelaars, T., Raes, A., Depaepe, F., & Van den Noortgate, W. (2021). Computer Vision and Human Behaviour, Emotion and Cognition Detection: A Use Case on Student Engagement. *Mathematics*, *9*(3), 287. doi:10.3390/math9030287

Wilder, M., & Shuttleworth, P. (2005). Cell Inquiry: A 5e Learning Cycle Lesson. *Science Activities*, *41*(4), 37–43. doi:10.3200/SATS.41.4.37-43

Xie, H., Chu, H.-C., Hwang, G.-J., & Wang, C.-C. (2019). Trends and development in technology-enhanced adaptive/personalized learning: A systematic review of journal publications from 2007 to 2017. *Computers & Education*, *140*, 103599. doi:10.1016/j.compedu.2019.103599

Zlokazov, K., Voroshilova, M., Pirozhkova, I., & Lapenok, M. V. (2018). Eye Tracking Technology for Assessment of Electronic Hybrid Text Perception by Students. In V. L. Uskov, R. J. Howlett, & L. C. Jain (Eds.), *Smart Education and E-Learning 2017, Smart Innovation, Systems and Technologies* (pp. 245–252). Springer International Publishing., doi:10.1007/978-3-319-59451-4_24

Zwoliński, G., Kamińska, D., Laska-Leśniewicz, A., Haamer, R. E., Vairinhos, M., Raposo, R., Urem, F., & Reisinho, P. (2022). Extended Reality in Education and Training: Case Studies in Management Education. *Electronics (Basel)*, *11*(3), 336. doi:10.3390/electronics11030336

Chapter 9
Designing Metaverse Escape Rooms for Microlearning in STEM Education

Robertas Damaševičius
iD https://orcid.org/0000-0001-9990-1084
Vytautas Magnus University, Lithuania

Tatjana Sidekerskienė
Kaunas University of Technology, Lithuania

ABSTRACT

The use of immersive and interactive learning environments is gaining traction in science, technology, engineering and mathematics (STEM) education, as educators seek to engage students and enhance learning outcomes. We explore the potential of Metaverse for designing immersive and interactive escape rooms that leverage microlearning to teach STEM concepts and skills. We overview Metaverse and its potential as a learning environment, before delving into the use of escape rooms as a strategy for fostering critical thinking, collaboration, and problem-solving in STEM education. We examine the benefits of incorporating microlearning strategies into escape rooms, including the use of bite-sized content and personalized learning paths. Through a case study of a Metaverse escape rooms implemented in Studio Gometa as a smartphone app and aimed at mathematics education, we highlight the learning outcomes achieved and the challenges faced in the design and implementation process.

DOI: 10.4018/978-1-6684-8656-6.ch009

1. INTRODUCTION

The COVID-19 pandemic has disrupted the traditional modes of teaching and learning, forcing educators and instructional designers to explore innovative and flexible approaches to engage students and enhance learning outcomes (Olasina, 2022). The pandemic has also highlighted the importance of digital technologies and virtual learning environments in enabling remote and hybrid learning

(Paulauskas et al., 2023). In this context, Metaverse platforms have emerged as immersive and interactive environments that offer unique opportunities for teaching and learning (López Belmonte et al., 2023). Metaverse platforms are 3D virtual worlds that enable users to create and interact with digital objects and environments. These platforms are increasingly being used for educational purposes, such as simulations, virtual field trips, and collaborative projects. In particular, Metaverse platforms can offer a more engaging and interactive learning experience than traditional online learning platforms, enabling students to explore and experiment with STEM concepts and skills in a more immersive and experiential way (Ahmad et al., 2022).

Escape rooms, on the other hand, are a form of game-based learning that can be used to promote critical thinking, problem-solving, collaboration, and communication skills (Veldkamp et al., 2020). In escape rooms, players are presented with a series of puzzles or challenges that they must solve within a certain time limit in order to escape a virtual room or space. Escape rooms have gained popularity in recent years as an engaging and interactive form of entertainment, and have also been adapted for educational purposes, including in STEM education. When combined with Augmented Reality (AR) and Virtual Reality (VR), escape rooms provide unique immersive and engaging experiences (Lampropoulos, Keramopoulos, Diamantaras, & Evangelidis, 2022; Lampropoulos, Keramopoulos, Diamantaras, & Evangelidis, 2022) which support student motivation and improve learning achievements (Mokmin et al., 2023).

Microlearning is another innovative approach to teaching and learning that has gained traction in recent years (Betancur-Chicue´ & Munoz˜-Repiso, 2023). Microlearning involves the delivery of bite-sized content and learning activities that can be consumed and completed in short periods of time, often using mobile devices

(Yang & Gottlieb, 2023). Microlearning supports adaptive learning (Munoz et al., 2022) and can be more flexible, personalized, and adaptive than traditional forms of learning, enabling learners to access and engage with learning materials at their own pace and on their own terms.

The aim of this study is to explore the potential of Metaverse escape rooms as a gamification strategy that incorporates microlearning principles to enhance student engagement and learning outcomes in STEM education. We will achieve this aim by pursuing the following objectives:

1. To provide an overview of the concepts of Metaverse, escape rooms, gamification, and microlearning, and how they can be combined to create innovative and effective learning experiences.
2. To design and implement Metaverse escape rooms that promote STEM learning objectives and skills while incorporating gamification and microlearning principles, and evaluate their effectiveness in enhancing student engagement and learning outcomes in STEM education.
3. To provide practical insights and guidelines for educators and instructional designers to design and implement effective Metaverse escape rooms that incorporate gamification and microlearning principles in STEM education.

The novelty of this study lies in its exploration of the potential of Metaverse escape rooms as a gamification strategy that incorporates microlearning principles in STEM education. While Metaverse platforms and escape rooms have been used for educational purposes before, there is a lack of research on the use of Metaverse escape rooms that incorporate microlearning principles to enhance STEM learning outcomes. This study aims to bridge this gap by providing insights and guidelines for designing and implementing effective Metaverse escape rooms in STEM education.

The contribution of this study lies in its practical implications for educators and instructional designers seeking innovative and effective ways to engage students in online and hybrid learning environments. Ultimately, this study aims to contribute to the growing body of research on innovative and effective approaches to online and hybrid learning in STEM education.

We begin by overviewing of Metaverse, escape rooms, and microlearning, and how they can be combined to create engaging and immersive learning experiences in Section 2. The chapter then delves into the design and implementation of Metaverse escape rooms that incorporate gamification and microlearning principles to promote STEM learning objectives and skills in Section 3. We present a case study of successful Metaverse escape rooms in mathematics education, highlighting the learning outcomes achieved and the challenges faced in the design and implementation process in Section 4. We conclude with practical insights and guidelines for educators and instructional designers seeking to design and implement effective Metaverse escape rooms in STEM education in Section 5.

2. METAVERSE AND ESCAPE ROOMS IN STEM EDUCATION

2.1 Potential of Metaverse in STEM Education

Metaverse is a term that refers to a collective virtual shared space that is created by the convergence of physical and digital reality. It is a three-dimensional (3D) world that provides a wide range of opportunities for users to interact with digital objects and environments. Metaverse implements active learning (Md Khambari et al., 2021) has the potential to create an immersive and interactive learning environment that enables students to explore and experiment with STEM concepts and skills in a more experiential way. The use of Metaverse in STEM education requires a methodological framework that guides the design and implementation of effective learning experiences. Here are some of the key methodological frameworks that educators and instructional designers can use when incorporating Metaverse into STEM education.

Design-based research (DBR) is a methodology that combines iterative design and evaluation to develop effective learning interventions. In the context of Metaverse in STEM education, DBR can be used to develop and test the effectiveness of Metaverse learning experiences in achieving STEM learning outcomes. This approach involves collaboration between educators and researchers to co-create and refine Metaverse learning experiences based on feedback from students and evaluation data.

Gamification is the use of game design elements and principles in non-game contexts to motivate and engage learners. A gamification design framework can guide the design and implementation of Metaverse learning experiences that incorporate gamification elements to enhance student engagement and motivation (Alsubhi et al., 2021; Ramadhan et al., 2022). This framework involves identifying the learning objectives and challenges, selecting appropriate game mechanics and elements, and evaluating the effectiveness of gamified experience (Khaldi et al., 2023). There are numerous examples of serious educational games implemented using gamification concepts in STEM education (Maulana et al., 2021; Oyesiku et al., 2018; Sharma et al., 2022).

Learning experience design (LXD) is a methodology that focuses on designing and delivering effective learning experiences that engage and motivate learners (Ramli et al., 2022). In the context of Metaverse in STEM education, LXD can guide the design and implementation of Metaverse learning experiences that incorporate microlearning principles, such as delivering bite-sized content and learning activities that can be consumed and completed in short periods of time.

Designing Metaverse Escape Rooms for Microlearning in STEM Education 1-3

The potential of Metaverse in STEM education lies in its ability to create a more engaging and interactive learning experience for students. In Metaverse, students can experience simulations and scenarios that are difficult or impossible to replicate in the physical world. Metaverse can also promote collaboration and teamwork among students. In a Metaverse environment, students can work together on group projects, share ideas and resources, and provide feedback to each other. This collaborative approach can enhance the learning experiences (tom Dieck et al., 2023), boost motivation (Uriarte-Portillo et al., 2023) and enable students to develop important 21ct century skills such as communication, problem-solving, and critical thinking (Wogu et al., 2019).

2.2 Escape Rooms

Escape rooms are immersive and interactive games that require players to solve puzzles and challenges to escape a room or a space within a certain time limit. Escape rooms have gained popularity in recent years as a form of entertainment, but they also offer significant benefits for STEM education. The use of digital escape rooms in STEM education requires a methodological framework that guides the design and implementation of effective learning experiences. Here are some of the key methodological frameworks that educators and instructional designers can use when designing digital escape rooms for STEM education:

Game-based learning (Li & Tsai, 2013) is a methodology that focuses on designing learning experiences that are similar to games. In the context of digital escape rooms, this approach involves creating an immersive and interactive game-like environment that requires players to solve STEM-related puzzles and challenges to escape a room or a space. This framework involves identifying the learning objectives and challenges, selecting appropriate game mechanics and elements, and evaluating the effectiveness of the digital escape room.

Instructional design (Abuhassna & Alnawajha, 2023) is a methodology that focuses on designing learning experiences that are effective and efficient. In the context of digital escape rooms, this approach involves identifying the learning objectives, selecting appropriate content and activities, and evaluating the effectiveness of the digital escape room. This framework involves collaborating with subject matter experts and students to create engaging and effective learning experiences.

Universal design for learning (UDL) (Capp, 2017) is a methodology that focuses on designing learning experiences that are accessible and inclusive to all learners, regardless of their abilities or backgrounds. In the context of digital escape rooms, this approach involves creating a digital escape room that is accessible to all learners, including those with disabilities or language barriers. This framework involves designing the digital escape room with multiple means of representation, expression, and engagement to meet the needs of all learners.

2.3 Microlearning in Escape Rooms

Microlearning is a learning approach that delivers small, focused learning units that can be consumed and completed in short periods of time. When combined with escape rooms, mi-crolearning can enhance the learning experience by breaking down complex concepts into small, manageable parts and providing learners with immediate feedback.

Here are some of the benefits of using microlearning in escape rooms:

- Bite-sized content: Microlearning provides learners with bite-sized content that is easy to digest and remember. In escape rooms, microlearning can present learners with small chunks of information that are directly related to the puzzles and challenges they are solving.
- Immediate feedback: Microlearning provides learners with immediate feedback on their progress and performance. In escape rooms, microlearning can provide learners with instant feedback on their solutions and progress, which can enhance their engagement and motivation.
- Personalized learning: Microlearning can be tailored to the individual needs and preferences of learners. In escape rooms, microlearning can provide learners with personalized challenges and puzzles that are based on their interests and learning styles.

3. DESIGNING METAVERSE ESCAPE ROOMS FOR MICROLEARNING

3.1 Design Principles

Designing Metaverse escape rooms for microlearning in STEM education involves the use of the out-of-the-box learning (Tatjana Sidekerskiene˙ and Robertas Damasevi˘cius˘ et al., 2023) methodological principles that guide the design and implemen-tation of effective learning experiences. Here are some of the key methodological principles that educators and instructional designers can use when designing Metaverse escape rooms for microlearning:

1. **Identify the learning objectives:** The first step in designing a Metaverse escape room for microlearning in STEM education is to identify the learning objectives. This involves defining the specific STEM concepts and skills that the escape room is intended to teach and the learning outcomes that are expected.
2. **Develop microlearning content:** Microlearning content should be developed to support the learning objectives. This content should be delivered in small, focused units that are easy to digest and remember. In the context of Metaverse escape rooms, microlearning content can be presented through digital objects and environments that require students to engage in problem-solving and critical thinking.

3. **Incorporate gamification elements:** Gamification elements should be incorporated into the design of Metaverse escape rooms to promote engagement and motivation. This can include elements such as points, badges, and leaderboards that incentivize students to solve puzzles and challenges.

4. **Provide feedback and assessment:** Feedback and assessment should be provided throughout the Metaverse escape room experience to promote learning and retention. This can include immediate feedback on the solutions to puzzles and challenges, as well as assessment of learning outcomes.

5. **Test and iterate:** The design of Metaverse escape rooms should be tested and iterated based on feedback from students and evaluation data. This iterative process should involve collaboration between educators, instructional designers, and students to co-create and refine the Metaverse escape room experience based on feedback and evaluation data.

Designing Metaverse Escape Rooms for Microlearning in STEM Education 1-5

3.2 Game Mechanics and Elements

Game mechanics and elements are crucial components of the design of Metaverse escape rooms for microlearning in STEM education. Game mechanics are the rules and procedures that govern gameplay, while game elements are the tools and components that are used to enhance the gaming experience. Here are some of the game mechanics and elements that can be used when designing Metaverse escape rooms for microlearning in STEM education:

- **Puzzles and challenges** are the core game mechanics of Metaverse escape rooms. These can take the form of logic puzzles, riddles, or math problems that require players to use critical thinking and problem-solving skills to solve.
- **Time limits** are a game mechanic that adds a sense of urgency and excitement to the Metaverse escape room experience. Players must solve puzzles and challenges within a certain time limit to escape the room or space.
- **Points and scoring** are game mechanics that incentivize players to solve puzzles and challenges. Players can earn points for solving puzzles and challenges, and the scoring can be displayed on a leaderboard to create competition and motivation.
- **Storyline and theme** of Metaverse escape rooms are game elements that can enhance the immersion and engagement of players. A well-crafted storyline and theme can provide context and motivation for solving puzzles and challenges.

- **Avatars and customization** are game elements that allow players to personalize their gaming experience. In Metaverse escape rooms, players can customize their avatars and choose their own paths through the escape room experience.
- **Feedback and rewards** are game elements that provide players with immediate feedback on their progress and performance. In Metaverse escape rooms, feedback can take the form of hints and clues that help players solve puzzles and challenges, while rewards can be in the form of unlocking new rooms or spaces.

By incorporating these game mechanics and elements into the design of Metaverse escape rooms, educators and instructional designers can create engaging and effective learning experi-ences that promote critical thinking, problem-solving skills, and collaboration. The use of game mechanics and elements can enhance the motivation and engagement of players and create a fun and immersive learning experience.

3.2.1 Storyboarding and Prototyping

Storyboarding is a crucial step in the design process of Metaverse escape rooms. Storyboarding is a visual representation of the storyline and design elements of the escape room, while prototyping involves creating a functioning model of the escape room that can be tested and refined. Here are some of the key considerations when storyboarding and prototyping Metaverse escape rooms for microlearning in STEM education: The storyboard should include the storyline, puzzles and challenges, game mechanics and elements, and visual design elements of the Metaverse escape room. Storyboarding should be used to create a visual representation of the escape room experience, to ensure that it is engaging and effective in achieving the learning objectives. Storyboarding can help to identify any gaps in the storyline or design, and ensure that the escape room experience is cohesive and immersive.

3.3 Implementation Strategies

Implementing Metaverse escape rooms for microlearning in STEM education requires a well-planned and executed strategy that takes into acccunt the needs of learners and educators. Here are some of the key implementation strategies for Metaverse escape rooms in STEM education:

- **Choose a Metaverse platform** that is user-friendly and compatible with different devices and operating systems. The platform should also provide the necessary tools and resources for designing and implementing Metaverse escape rooms.

- **Provide training and support** to educators and instructional designers on the design and implementation of Metaverse escape rooms. This can include workshops, online resources, and one-on-one support to ensure that educators and instructional designers are confident in using the Metaverse platform and designing effective escape room experiences.
- **Integrate Metaverse escape rooms** into the STEM curriculum to ensure that the learning objectives are aligned with the curriculum goals. This can help to ensure that students are engaged and motivated to learn the STEM concepts and skills being taught.
- **Evaluate the effectiveness** of the Metaverse escape room experience using both qualitative and quantitative evaluation methods. This can include surveys, focus groups, and assessment of learning outcomes to determine the effectiveness of the Metaverse escape room experience in achieving the learning objectives (Swacha et al., 2023).

By following these implementation strategies, educators and instructional designers can create engaging and effective Metaverse escape rooms for microlearning in STEM education that enhance critical thinking, problem-solving skills, and collaboration among students. The use of Metaverse escape rooms in STEM education offers a promising approach that can provide unique opportunities for students to explore and experiment with STEM concepts and skills in a fun and immersive learning experience.

3.3.1 Platform Selection and Setup

There are a variety of platforms that can be used for designing Metaverse escape rooms for microlearning in STEM education. These platforms provide educators and instructional designers with the necessary tools and resources to design and implement immersive and engaging escape rooms. Here are some platforms that can be used for designing Metaverse escape rooms:

Roblox (Han et al., 2023) is a popular online gaming platform that can be used to create Metaverse escape rooms. It offers a user-friendly interface and a range of tools and resources for creating immersive environments, designing puzzles and challenges, and incorporating game mechanics and elements.

Designing Metaverse Escape Rooms for Microlearning in STEM Education 1-7

Minecraft (Nebel et al., 2016) is a popular game that can be used to create Metaverse escape rooms. It offers a range of tools and resources for designing and building immersive environments, creating puzzles and challenges, and incorporating game mechanics and elements.

CoSpaces (Al-Gindy et al., 2020) is a virtual reality platform that can be used to create Metaverse escape rooms. It offers a range of tools and resources for designing immersive environments, creating puzzles and challenges, and incorporating game mechanics and elements.

VirBELA is a virtual world platform (Jauhiainen, 2021) that can be used to create Metaverse escape rooms. It offers a range of tools and resources for designing immersive environments, creating puzzles and challenges, and incorporating game mechanics and elements.

TaleBlazer is an open-source platform for creating location-based augmented reality (AR) games and educational experiences (Kleftodimos et al., 2022). It was developed at MIT to provide a tool for educators and game designers to create engaging experiences that combine physical and virtual spaces. TaleBlazer allows users to create mobile games and AR experiences by setting up a virtual world and placing digital content, such as characters, objects, and interactive elements, in physical locations. Users can then add logic and rules to the content to create a game or educational experience. TaleBlazer also supports multiplayer games, which enables users to create collaborative experiences that can be played by multiple people at the same time. This makes it possible to create educational experiences that encourage teamwork, communication, and problem-solving skills.

Studio Gometa is a cloud-based platform that allows users to create AR and VR experiences without any coding or technical skills (Kleftodimos et al., 2022). The platform is user-friendly and provides a drag-and-drop interface that allows users to create interactive experiences by simply placing and configuring various virtual elements. Studio Gometa also provides a wide range of templates and pre-made content that users can use as a starting point for their projects. Additionally, users can import their own 3D models and other multimedia assets into the platform to customize their projects. Studio Gometa is particularly useful for creating educational content, such as virtual labs and simulations, as well as for marketing and advertising purposes. With its ease-of-use and versatility, Studio Gometa allows to create engaging AR and VR experiences without extensive technical knowledge or resources.

Table 1 that compares educational AR/VR/Metaverse development platforms based on vari-ous features. By using these platforms, educators and instructional designers can create engaging and effective Metaverse escape rooms that enhance critical thinking, problem-solving skills, and collaboration among students. The choice of platform may depend on the specific needs and preferences of the educators

Table 1. Comparison of educational AR/VR/metaverse development platforms

Features	Roblox	Minecraft	CoSpaces	VirBELA	Gometa	TaleBlazer
Programming language	Lua	Java	Blockly	JavaScript	None	Blockly
Geolocation support	No	No	Yes	Yes	No	Yes
Multiplayer support	Yes	Yes	Yes	Yes	Yes	Yes
Virtual currency system	Yes	No	Yes	No	No	No
3D modeling tools	Yes	Yes	Yes	Yes	Yes	No
Interactive objects	Yes	Yes	Yes	Yes	Yes	Yes
Collaborative creation	Yes	Yes	Yes	Yes	Yes	Yes
Real-time communication	Yes	Yes	Yes	Yes	Yes	Yes
Mobile device support	Yes	Yes	Yes	Yes	Yes	Yes
Educational templates	Yes	Yes	Yes	Yes	Yes	Yes
Gamification elements	Yes	Yes	Yes	Yes	Yes	Yes
Learning analytics	Yes	No	Yes	No	No	No
Open-source	No	No	No	No	No	Yes

and students, as well as the resources available for designing and implementing Metaverse escape rooms.

3.3.2 Content Creation and Integration

Visual content creation and integration is a crucial component of the design of Metaverse escape rooms for microlearning in STEM education. However, this process can present some challenges that need to be addressed to ensure that the visual content is effective in achieving the learning objectives. Here are some of the problems and solutions for visual content creation and integration into Metaverse escape rooms:

Problem: Limited technical skills in content creation tools

Solution: Educators and instructional designers can attend training sessions and workshops to improve their skills in content creation tools. There are also online resources and tutorials available to learn content creation tools such as Blender, SketchUp, and Adobe Photoshop.

Problem: Limited access to high-quality visual assets

Solution: Educators and instructional designers can search for free or low-cost visual assets from online resources such as Sketchfab, TurboSquid, and BlendSwap. They can also create their own visual assets using content creation tools.

Problem: Limited device compatibility for visual content integration

Solution: Educators and instructional designers should ensure that the visual content is com-patible with different devices and operating systems. They can also test the visual content on different devices to ensure that it functions correctly.

By addressing these problems and implementing the solutions, educators and instructional designers can create effective visual content for Metaverse escape rooms that enhance critical thinking, problem-solving skills, and collaboration among students in STEM education. The use of high-quality visual assets can also enhance the immersive and engaging nature of the Metaverse escape room experience, which can motivate and engage students in the learning process.

3.4 UX Design Challenges for AR Interfaces in Metaverse Escape Rooms

The use of augmented reality (AR) interfaces in Metaverse escape rooms presents a unique set of user experience (UX) design challenges that need to be addressed to ensure an effective and engaging learning experience (Cao et al., 2023). Here are some of the key UX design challenges for AR interfaces in Metaverse escape rooms:

- AR interfaces can become cluttered and overwhelming with too much information and too many elements. This can lead to confusion and frustration for users, especially in the fast-paced environment of an escape room.

Designing Metaverse Escape Rooms for Microlearning in STEM Education 1-9

- AR interfaces require user engagement to be effective, which can be challenging in an escape room where users are focused on solving puzzles and challenges.
- AR interfaces require calibration to ensure that they are aligned with the real-world environ-ment, which can be time-consuming and frustrating for users.
- AR interfaces require compatibility with different devices and operating systems, which can limit the accessibility of Metaverse escape rooms.
- AR interfaces require physical space to function effectively, which can be limited in the context of an escape room.

To address these challenges, UX designers can follow these guidelines:

- Simplify AR interfaces by reducing clutter and prioritizing the most important information and elements.
- Gamify engagement with AR interfaces by incorporating game mechanics and elements, such as rewards and achievements, to incentivize user engagement.

- Streamline calibration process by incorporating automatic calibration tools and providing clear instructions for users.
- Ensure compatibility by testing AR interfaces on different devices and operating systems and ensuring that they function correctly.
- Optimize space by designing AR interfaces that require minimal physical space or by providing clear instructions on how to use the space effectively.

By addressing these UX design challenges and incorporating these strategies, UX designers can create effective and engaging AR interfaces for Metaverse escape rooms that enhance critical thinking, problem-solving skills, and collaboration among students in STEM education.

4. CASE STUDY: MATHEMATICS ESCAPE ROOM

The implementation of Metaverse escape rooms for microlearning in STEM education presents both opportunities and challenges. In this section, we will discuss the learning outcomes, challenges and limitations, and future directions of Metaverse escape rooms for microlearning in STEM education.

4.1 Implementation

Creating an AR app for an Escape Room using the Metaverse app, also known as Studio Gometa, involves several steps. Firstly, the creators design the game's scenario, which includes puzzles and challenges that players must solve to escape the room. Next, they create 3D models of the virtual environment, characters, and objects in the game. After this, the creators use the Metaverse app to program the logic of the game using block-based coding or JavaScript to create interactions between the player and the virtual environment. The fragment of gameflow is presented in Figure 1. The

Figure 1. Fragment of gameflow in Metaverse app

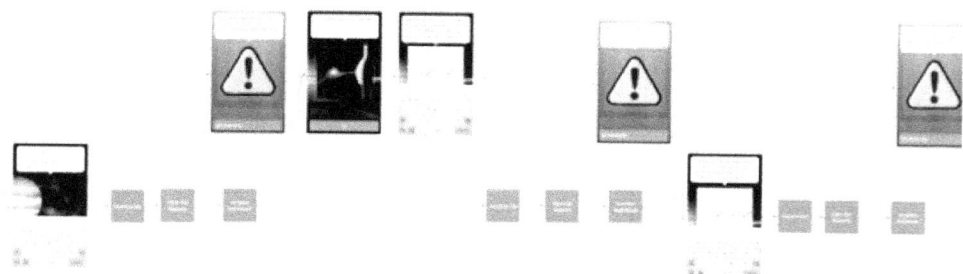

app can include multimedia elements like audio and video that are triggered by the player's actions. Once the game is complete, it can be published on the Metaverse platform. Players can access the game using their smartphones or tablets and can play alone or with others. In real-time, players can interact with each other.

An AR based escape room application named Universe was developed using the Metaverse app to teach differential equation mathematics at the university level. The application presents a scenario where students must travel across the Universe and solve a series of differential equation problems to proceed. The examples of escape room questions presented in Figure 2. The app presents students with various differential equations that they must solve by identifying the equation type and applying the appropriate method. To help students arrive at a solution, the app provides visual aids such as graphs and diagrams. As students solve more complex equations, they can unlock clues to help them escape the current level of the game and proceed to the next level. The game also includes point calculation and a leaderboard as gamification elements that aim to increase student motivation and engagement.

Figure 2. An example of questions in the developed escape room game

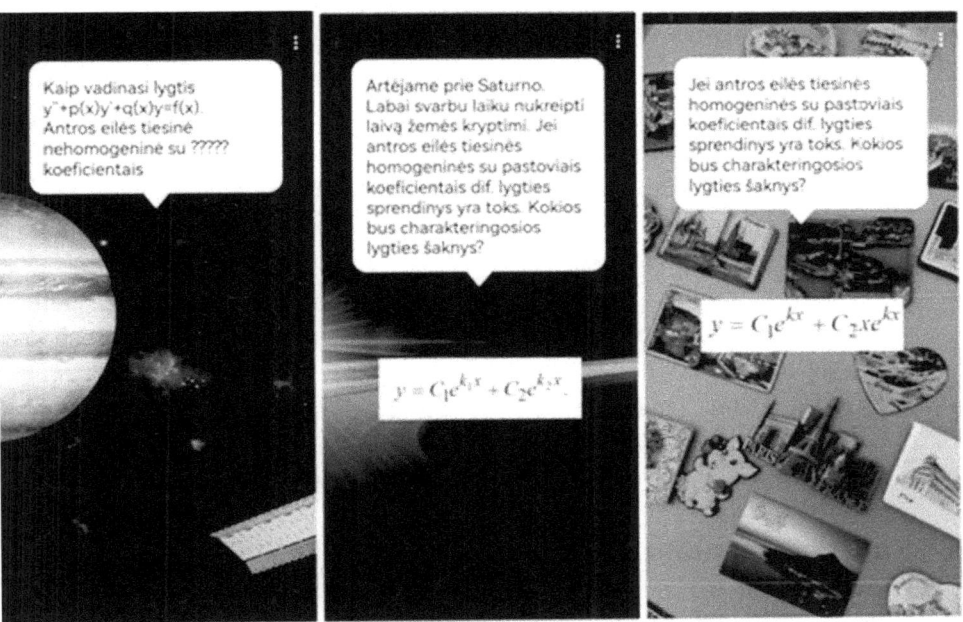

4.2 Learning Outcomes

The use of Metaverse escape rooms for microlearning in STEM education has the potential to enhance critical thinking, problem-solving skills, and collaboration among students. The immersive and interactive nature of Metaverse escape rooms provides students with a fun and engaging learning experience, which can improve motivation and engagement in the learning process. The use of game mechanics and elements, such as puzzles and challenges, can also promote the development of critical thinking and problem-solving skills.

Furthermore, the use of Metaverse escape rooms provides opportunities for students to experiment and explore STEM concepts and skills in a safe and controlled environment. This can improve confidence and competence in STEM education, as well as provide students with a deeper understanding of the relevance of STEM in real-world contexts.

Designing Metaverse Escape Rooms for Microlearning in STEM Education 1-11

4.3 Challenges and Limitations

The implementation of Metaverse escape rooms for microlearning in STEM education also presents some challenges and limitations. These include:

- Technical limitations: The design and implementation of Metaverse escape rooms require technical skills and resources, which may be limited for some educators and instructional designers.
- Content creation: The creation of high-quality visual assets and content can be time-consuming and expensive, which can be a barrier to the implementation of Metaverse escape rooms.
- Device compatibility: The integration of visual content and game mechanics may not be com-patible with all devices and operating systems, which can limit the accessibility of Metaverse escape rooms.
- Assessment and feedback: The design and implementation of effective assessment and feed-back mechanisms can be challenging, which can limit the ability to evaluate the effectiveness of Metaverse escape rooms.

4.4 Future Directions

Future directions for Metaverse escape rooms for microlearning in STEM education can focus on addressing these challenges and limitations. This can include the development of new tools and resources for content creation and integration, as well as the integration of emerging tech-nologies such as artificial intelligence

(Okewu et al., 2021) and virtual reality in the design of Metaverse escape rooms. Future directions can also focus on the development of effective assessment and feedback mechanisms, as well as the exploration of ethical considerations related to immersive and inter-active learning experiences. The implementation of Metaverse escape rooms for microlearning in STEM education offers a promising approach to teaching and learning STEM concepts and skills. While challenges and limitations exist, these can be addressed through continued research and development, which can improve the effectiveness and accessibility of Metaverse escape rooms for microlearning in STEM education.

5. CONCLUSION

Metaverse escape rooms offer a promising approach for engaging and motivating students in STEM education through immersive and interactive learning experiences. This chapter has discussed the design and implementation of Metaverse escape rooms for microlearning in STEM education, including the use of game mechanics and elements, storyboarding and prototyping, and assessment and feedback mechanisms. We have also discussed the potential of Metaverse in STEM education, the benefits of escape rooms in STEM education, and the challenges of visual content creation and integration.

The key points of this chapter include the potential of Metaverse in STEM education, the benefits of escape rooms in STEM education, and the challenges and solutions of visual content creation and integration. The chapter has also discussed the methodological frameworks for designing and implementing Metaverse escape rooms for microlearning in STEM education, in-cluding the use of game mechanics and elements, storyboarding and prototyping, and assessment and feedback mechanisms.

The use of Metaverse escape rooms for microlearning in STEM education offers a unique and engaging approach to teaching and learning STEM concepts and skills. This approach can enhance critical thinking, problem-solving skills, and collaboration among students, as well as improve motivation and engagement in the learning process. The use of Metaverse escape rooms also provides opportunities for students to experiment and explore STEM concepts and skills in a fun and immersive learning experience.

Future research can focus on evaluating the effectiveness of Metaverse escape rooms for microlearning in STEM education, as well as exploring new and innovative approaches to designing and implementing Metaverse escape rooms. Future research can also focus on the development of new tools and resources for content creation and integration, as well as the integration of emerging technologies such as artificial intelligence and virtual reality in the design of Metaverse escape rooms.

REFERENCES

Abuhassna, H., & Alnawajha, S. (2023). Instructional design made easy! instructional design models, categories, frameworks, educational context, and recommendations for future work. *European Journal of Investigation in Health, Psychology and Education*, *13*(4), 715–735. doi:10.3390/ejihpe13040054 PMID:37185907

Ahmad, N. A. N., Suhaimi, A. I. H., & Lokman, A. M. (2022). Conceptual model of augmented reality mobile application design (armad) to enhance user experience: An expert review. *International Journal of Advanced Computer Science and Applications*, *13*(10), 574–582. doi:10.14569/IJACSA.2022.0131067

Al-Gindy, A., Felix, C., Ahmed, A., Matoug, A., & Alkhidir, M. (2020). Virtual reality: Development of an integrated learning environment for education. *International Journal of Information and Education Technology (IJIET)*, *10*(3), 171–175. doi:10.18178/ijiet.2020.10.3.1358

Alsubhi, M. A., Ashaari, N. S., & Wook, T. S. M. T. (2021). Design and evaluation of an engagement framework for e-learning gamification. *International Journal of Advanced Computer Science and Applications*, *12*(9), 411–417. doi:10.14569/IJACSA.2021.0120947

Betancur-Chicue´, V., & Munoz˜-Repiso, A. G. (2023). Microlearning strategy design features in educational settings: A systematic review. *RIED-Revista Iberoamericana de Educacion a Distancia*, *26*(1), 201–222.

Cao, J., Lam, K., Lee, L., Liu, X., Hui, P., & Su, X. (2023). Mobile augmented reality: User interfaces, frameworks, and intelligence. *ACM Computing Surveys*, *55*(9), 1–36. doi:10.1145/3557999

Capp, M. J. (2017). The effectiveness of universal design for learning: A meta-analysis of literature between 2013 and 2016. *International Journal of Inclusive Education*, *21*(8), 791–807. doi:10.1080/13603116.2017.1325074

Han, J., Liu, G., & Gao, Y. (2023). Learners in the metaverse: A systematic review on the use of roblox in learning. *Education Sciences*, *13*(3), 296. doi:10.3390/educsci13030296

Jauhiainen, J. S. (2021). Entrepreneurship and innovation events during the covid-19 pandemic: The user preferences of virbela virtual 3d platform at the shift event organized in finland. *Sustainability (Basel)*, *13*(7), 3802. doi:10.3390u13073802

Khaldi, A., Bouzidi, R., & Nader, F. (2023). Gamification of e-learning in higher education: A systematic literature review. *Smart Learning Environments*, *10*(1), 10.

Kleftodimos, A., Lappas, G., & Vrigkas, M. (2022). Taleblazer vs. metaverse: A com-parative analysis of two platforms for building AR location-based educational games. *International Journal of Entertainment Technology and Management*, *1*(4), 290. doi:10.1504/IJENTTM.2022.129630

Lampropoulos, G., Keramopoulos, E., Diamantaras, K., & Evangelidis, G. (2022). Augmented reality and virtual reality in education: Public perspectives, sentiments, attitudes, and discourses. *Education Sciences*, *12*(11), 798. doi:10.3390/educsci12110798

Lampropoulos, G., Keramopoulos, E., Diamantaras, K., & Evangelidis, G. (2022). Augmented reality and gamification in education: A systematic literature review of research, applications, and empirical studies. *Applied Sciences (Basel, Switzerland)*, *12*(13), 6809. doi:10.3390/app12136809

Li, M., & Tsai, C. (2013). Game-based learning in science education: A review of relevant research. *Journal of Science Education and Technology*, *22*(6), 877–898. doi:10.100710956-013-9436-x

López Belmonte, J., Pozo-Sánchez, S., Moreno-Guerrero, A. J., & Lampropoulos, G. (2023). Metaverse in education. *Systematic Reviews*.

Maulana, F. I., Aldiki Febriantono, M., Raharja, D. R. B., Sofiani, I. R., & Firdaus, V. A. H. (2021). A scientometric analysis of game technology on learning media research study in recent 10 years. In *7th International Conference on Electrical, Electronics and Information Engineering: Technological Breakthrough for Greater New Life, ICEEIE 2021*. 10.1109/ICEEIE52663.2021.9616963

Md Khambari, M. N., Wang, D., Wong, S. L., Moses, P., & Md, M. N., Khambari, R. W. O. K. Rahmat, & Khalid. (2021). Design of customizable gamified augmented reality apps: Towards embracing active learning. *29th International Conference on Computers in Education Conference, ICCE 2021 - Proceedings*, 2, 488–494.

Mokmin, N. A. M., Hanjun, S., Jing, C., & Qi, S. (2023). Impact of an AR-based learning approach on the learning achievement, motivation, and cognitive load of students on a design course. *Journal of Computers in Education*, 1-18.

Munoz, J. L. R., Ojeda, F. M., Jurado, D. L. A., Pena, P. F. P., Carranza. C. P. M., Berr'ios, H. Q., Molina, S. U., Farfan, A. R. M., & Arias-Gonzales, J. L. (2022). Systematic review of adaptive learning technology for learning in higher education. *Eurasian Journal of Educational Research*, *2022*(98), 221–233.

Nebel, S., Schneider, S., & Rey, G. D. (2016). Mining learning and crafting scientific experiments: A literature review on the use of minecraft in education and research. *Journal of Educational Technology & Society*, *19*(2), 355–366.

Okewu, E., Adewole, P., Misra, S., Maskeliunas, R., & Damasevicius, R. (2021). Artificial neural networks for educational data mining in higher education: A systematic literature review. *Applied Artificial Intelligence*, *35*(13), 983–1021. doi :10.1080/08839514.2021.1922847

Olasina, G. (2022). Augmented reality in higher education: The new reality of teaching and learning during and post-covid-19. *Ubiquitous Learning*, *16*(1), 31–54. doi:10.18848/1835-9795/CGP/v16i01/31-54

Oyesiku, D., Adewumi, A., Misra, S., Ahuja, R., Damasevicius, R., & Maskeliunas, R. (2018). An educational math game for high school students in Sub-Saharan Africa. *Applied Informatics: First International Conference, ICAI 2018, Bogotá, Colombia, November 1-3, 2018 Proceedings*, *1*, 228–238.

Paulauskas, L., Paulauskas, A., Blažauskas, T., Damaševičius, R., & Maskeliūnas, R. (2023). Reconstruction of industrial and historical heritage for cultural enrichment using virtual and augmented reality. *Technologies*, *11*(2), 36. doi:10.3390/ technologies11020036

Ramadhan, A. D., Permanasari, A. E., & Wibirama, S. (2022). Gamification opportunity in augmented reality-based learning media: A review. *2022 2nd International Conference on Intelligent Cybernetics Technology and Applications, ICICyTA 2022*, 117–122. 10.1109/ICICyTA57421.2022.10037922

Ramli, R. Z., Sahari, N., Noor, S. F. M., Noor, M. M., Majid, N. A. A., Dahlan, H. A., & Wahab, A. N. A. (2022). Assessing usability of learning experience prototype. *International Journal of Emerging Technologies in Learning*, *17*(9), 20–36. doi:10.3991/ijet.v17i09.29955

Sharma, V., Bhagat, K. K., Huang, H., & Chen, N. (2022). The design and evaluation of an ar-based serious game to teach programming. *Computers & Graphics*, *103*, 1–18. doi:10.1016/j.cag.2022.01.002

Sidekerskienė, T., & Damaševičius, R. (2023, April). Out-of-the-box learning: Digital escape rooms as a metaphor for breaking down barriers in stem education. *Sustainability (Basel)*, *15*(9), 7393. doi:10.3390u15097393

Swacha, J., Queiros, R., & Paiva, J. C. (2023). Gatugu: Six perspectives of evaluation of gamified systems. *Information (Basel)*, *14*(2), 136. doi:10.3390/info14020136 tom Dieck, M. C., Cranmer, E., Prim, A., & Bamford, D. (2023). Can augmented reality (ar) applica-tions enhance students' experiences? gratifications, engagement and learning styles. *Information Technology & People*. Advance online publication. doi:10.1108/ITP-10-2021-0823

Uriarte-Portillo, A., Iba'nez, M. B., Zatarain-Cabada, ˜. R.. & Barron´-Estrada, M. L. (2023). Comparison of using an augmented reality learning tool at home and in a classroom regarding motivation and learning outcomes. *Multimodal Technologies and Interaction*, *7*(3), 23. doi:10.3390/mti7030023

Veldkamp, A., van de Grint, L., Knippels, M. P. J., & van Joolingen, W. R. (2020). Escape education: A systematic review on escape rooms in education. *Educational Research Review*, *31*, 31. doi:10.1016/j.edurev.2020.100364

Wogu, I. A. P., Misra, S., Assibong, P. A., Olu-Owolabi, E. F., Maskeli˜unas, R., & Damasevicius, R. (2019). Artificial intelligence, smart classrooms and online education in the 21st century: Implications for human development. *Journal of Cases on Information Technology*, *21*(3), 66–79. doi:10.4018/JCIT.2019070105

Yang, L., & Gottlieb, M. (2023). Gamification Mobile Applications: A Literature Review of Empirical Studies. In *International Conference on Interactive Collaborative Learning* (pp. 933-946). Springer.

Chapter 10
Transition Towards Hybrid Learning Environments in Higher Education Institutions:
How to Use Metaverse to Support Active Learning

Marjo Joshi
Turku University of Applied Sciences, Finland

Werner Ravyse
Turku University of Applied Sciences, Finland

Timo Haavisto
ⓘ https://orcid.org/0000-0003-2306-4069
Turku University of Applied Sciences, Finland

Mika Luimula
Turku University of Applied Sciences, Finland

Vesa Taatila
ⓘ https://orcid.org/0000-0002-7050-5130
Turku University of Applied Sciences, Finland

ABSTRACT

The recent COVID-19 pandemic forced organizations to find new solutions for remote collaboration and refine hybrid education in the context of applied, praxis-based learning. Various tech giants have started investing in more immersive remote communication technologies, such as metaverse. This paper discusses hybrid environments and metaverse in education at Turku University of Applied Sciences (Turku UAS) as the site of the study. The new strategy of the university aims to support people and organizations in a hybrid world where physical and virtual worlds are merged. At Turku UAS, VR environment is seen as a platform that uses social communication for real-life integration through both hands-on skill development and theoretical knowledge transfer. The metaverse technology and collaborative learning environments can be seen as testbeds for future pedagogy and work life. Examples of implementations of interactive technologies in different fields of education are presented. In addition, a revised hybrid education model with future possibilities is introduced.

DOI: 10.4018/978-1-6684-8656-6.ch010

1. INTRODUCTION

The recent COVID-19 pandemic has forced organizations to seek new solutions for remote collaboration from training to design and operations. Teleconferencing seems to be currently the most common solution for remote collaboration. At the same time, various tech giants have started investing in more immersive remote communication technologies, such as metaverse. Metaverse appeared for the first time in Gartner hype curve for emerging technologies in 2022 (Gartner, 2022). The global metaverse market size was $ 60 billion in 2021 and is expected to reach a revenue CAGR of 43,2% until 2030 (Emergen Research, 2022). Metaverse economy could be worth $13 trillion by 2030 (Citibank, 2022). These curves show maturities and business potentials of future technologies. However, it is likely we need to wait until the 2030s before metaverse will be widely available, similar to the early use of the VR glasses and their widespread use.

Virtual and augmented reality have been seen to be efficient tools to train and test students' behavior, for example in fire safety (Somerkoski et al., 2022; Oliva et al., 2019). Virtual training solutions have been developed and assessed in several research, development, and innovation (RDI) projects conducted in close cooperation with local industry (Izullah et al., 2022; Luimula et al., 2022). Experiments in national and international RDI projects, VR can already be seen as a robust technology that can be widely applied in many fields of training. Based on the experiences and feedback from the industry, it can be concluded that virtual training markets are fragmented and there is a need for collaborative training solutions which require the use of metaverse technologies.

This paper discusses hybrid learning environments and presents examples of the use of the metaverse at Turku University of Applied Sciences (Turku UAS) as the site of the study. The topic is approached from several research perspectives. Turku UAS has started developing their own metaverse technology, with the intention to introduce various collaborative learning environments developed using the metaverse technology to support the active learning methods of the university virtually. The metaverse technology and these collaborative learning environments can be seen as testbeds for the university's researchers who are investigating what kind of changes are needed in pedagogy, and to determine how to design and implement these new hybrid learning environments to meet the future requirements in the working life. Examples of implementations of interactive technologies in different fields of education are presented. Lessons learned and recommendations are made. In addition, a modified future hybrid education model is introduced. Finally, future possibilities and directions are discussed.

1.1. Changes in Today's Higher Education

Several challenges were seen in higher education during COVID-19 (OECD, 2021). The universities were unprepared for the sudden shift to online education, the teachers lacked competence, equipment, or facilities to provide quality education online, and students were left without the social and collaborative element of studying together on campus. Online learning during the pandemic was often described as emergency remote teaching as opposed to well-designed education (Hodges & Fowler, 2020) that focused more on the use of the platforms rather than pedagogically designed learning situations. In the field of applied higher education, there is a need to also consider how to implement practical, hands-on training in online and virtual environments. The entry of new technological solutions impacts the HEIs, bringing new competence needs for teachers and students, possibly changing what we currently consider to be online learning and teaching (Joshi, 2023).

Several changes are needed in education following the pandemic. In several aspects, education and especially higher education have changed very little in their methods over the years, decades, and centuries. While individual practices, group sizes, emphasis on the contents and the dialogical methods have transformed according to contemporary societal needs and desires (see, for example, Compayré & Payne, 1885), in most cases there has been a teacher interacting with a student or a group of students, passing the skills and information accumulated during the teacher's own learning career. In a higher education setting this has often been done in a lecture setting, with the teacher passing oral information to the learners in a more or less active way. The more vocational the subject, the more there has been hands-on guidance and feedback on the artefacts.

The other path to learning, self-study, has also always existed, most likely before the teacher-led learning activities emerged. In the end, humans are often self-directed learners with a desire to improve their actions and better understand the phenomena in their surroundings. When comparing self-study and teacher-led processes, one major aspect is that the first ones take place in an open environment while the latter often use somehow simplified examples or cases for the learner to focus on the predesignated learning topic. In an open learning process, it is more difficult to pinpoint the goal of learning as the number of variables that may have to be considered is theoretically limitless. There are also cross-sections between these two extremes of the educational spectrum. For example, pragmatism (see, for example, Dewey 1925/1988) and its numerous off-springs like Learning by Developing (Taatila & Raij, 2012) or innovation pedagogy (Keinänen & Kairisto-Mertanen, 2019; Lappalainen, 2020), or different problem-based learning methods combine relatively open inquiry with the teacher-guided learning paths.

Taatila (2017) presented from several points of view that today's higher education is experiencing a moment of a major paradigm shift. Financial restraints, need for accountability, mass education and e-enhanced global marketplace for learning are transforming the millennia long status quo of education. Today it is easier than ever in human history to get access to the utmost experts in any field of life and to seek their guidance and instructions, whether face to face or via more passive methods. Whatever the learning needs, the path is available for an active learner.

1.2 National Collaboration in the Digitalization of Education

In Finland, a national project Digivision 2030 brings together all the 38 Finnish higher education institutions (HEIs). The program was established as the institutions recognized the need for improving the digital learning environment and experience of the students and that it would be more operationally and financially beneficial to create a shared national approach instead of several competing systems. Its aim, *"... is to create a future for learning that benefits higher education institutions, learners and our society as a whole."* (Digivisio, 2021).

The main parts of the project are creating a national digital service platform and support for change management at HEIs. However, from the point of view of this paper, the most interesting set of goals lies within the third one, a guidance-system based on digital pedagogy, the learner's path and shared data. In it, the first sub-goal is to support *"...studies and students' well-being regardless of time and place and in an accessible manner"* (Digivisio, 2021).

Within Digivision 2030, the pedagogical solutions will be decided autonomously by the independent institutions. The national program will agree on the shared platforms and interfaces, enabling the students to acquire learning through a number of digital sources. The program will create a national marketplace through which the students will be able to easily navigate to the learning opportunity of their choice. Each institute, each professor and each digital learning tool will thus have wider access to potential learners eliminating the traditional access barriers of time and place.

1.3 University Strategy Defining New Direction for Education

This paper presents a case from a university of applied sciences in Turku, Finland, that provides higher education in both Bachelor and Master level (Ministry of Education and Culture, 2014). Turku UAS actively develops the region and with its 12,000 students, is the fourth largest technical university in Finland (Turku UAS, n.d.). The philosophy supports the praxis-oriented education (Taatila & Raij, 2012) where the aim is to improve working life and support internationalization and digitalization through teaching and learning solutions (ARENE, 2018). Turku UAS uses a pedagogical strategy that focuses on active, team-based learning (Joshi, 2022).

At the beginning of this year, the university published their new strategy for the next ten years (Turku UAS, 2023). In the strategy, this disruptive era has been illustrated as an opportunity to design and implement products and services for a better (working) life. The aim of the university is to support people and organizations in a hybrid world where physical and virtual worlds are merged. In this context, metaverse is seen as one of the key technologies to make this change happen.

The process to create a new strategy started in early spring 2022 (Turku UAS, 2022a). It was defined that during the process the expectations and the needs of the regional organizations will be mapped through a series of 360-degree analysis and in-depth interviews. The data accumulated through these studies worked as a basis on which the strategic choices were made in a series of internal discussions with the staff and the students of the community. The draft versions were discussed with the owners and the board, and the new strategy was decided to be put into action in the board meeting at the end of 2022 (Turku UAS, 2022b).

The new strategy defined four strategic themes and three internal operating programs (Turku UAS, 2023). The most relevant strategic theme for this article is titled "**At home in the hybrid world**". It is defined as follows: "*For us, change is an opportunity for a better (working) life. We study and develop products and services, so that people and companies can operate in the hybrid world with ease. The physical and virtual world seamlessly overlap with each other in people's everyday lives, both at work and in spare time.*" (Turku UAS, 2023). Similarly, the most relevant operating program in the context of this paper is "**We learn in a changing world**". It is defined as: "*High-quality competence is the foundation of our existence. We respond to the needs of the changing world proactively by providing versatile pedagogic solutions. We offer a good, personal study experience both in degree studies and in smaller entities. We provide genuine encounters on the campuses and online. Change is here to stay, competence will last.*" (Turku UAS, 2023).

Through these strategic themes and programs, Turku UAS wants to transform both itself and the organizations within its operating region into active agents of the hybrid world. The future is seen as a blend between physical and digital and the main question is the interaction between these two environments. Thus, the focus is on learning, especially in relation to the practical skills required from the graduates of a university of applied sciences.

1.4 Moving to Hybrid and VR Modes of Education

Turku UAS started offering their first online degree programs in 2017. To respond to the university's needs of using their specific pedagogical strategy in the digital context of online degree education, a model was created for the pedagogically informed holistic design of online degree programs in higher education. (Joshi, 2023.) The experiences of the online degree programs were useful during the pandemic to transfer teaching from the campus-based mode to the online and hybrid modes.

During the pandemic, it became necessary to define and redefine the concept of hybrid teaching in the context of applied, praxis-based learning. At Turku UAS, hybrid teaching term was defined to refer to teaching that takes place both as campus-based teaching and online teaching. As such, it includes both synchronous and asynchronous teaching sessions as part of a course. A course can be implemented as a blended course, using an asynchronous hybrid approach where some of the teaching is implemented on campus (e.g., labs) and some online (e.g., lectures). A teaching session on a course can be implemented as a synchronous hybrid (e.g., teacher and some of the students on campus, and some students and a visiting lecturer online). The objective of hybrid teaching is to enable equal participation, engagement and experience, whilst considering the limitations. It is important for the teacher to consider how they can support the students in the hybrid mode and plan the teaching accordingly.

The teaching sessions can take place either on campus, learning laboratories, online learning platforms, virtual environments or teleconferencing systems. Teachers design their teaching to fit the hybrid teaching implementation plan that is suitable for their subject and learning objectives of the course. They can conduct the teaching either in the specified teaching studios on campus, or remotely from home. The students join the sessions as either on campus or remotely, using their own laptops according to the bring-your-own-device (BYOD) method. This type of hybrid does not mean that the students can choose whether to attend onsite or online, instead they will participate either on campus or online according to the course plan. The university provides the facilities for both campus-based and remote-based teaching and offers technical and pedagogical support for teachers in the design and implementation of hybrid teaching. Figure 1 below illustrates the current hybrid teaching model at Turku UAS.

Because of the pandemic, the actions of the university were forced to be moved fully online. The disruption offered a possibility to start engaging the university staff and other stakeholders in a virtual reality (VR) environment, giving push to the creation of the new technology and VR solution at Turku UAS.

In March 2021 Turku UAS opened their new campus premises that had been under construction already before the pandemic. The opening ceremony was organized remotely due to the lock-down by the Futuristic Interactive Technologies (FIT) Turku Competence Center (Turku UAS (2021) that is in charge of the VR technologies at Turku UAS (Luimula et al., 2021). For the opening ceremony, Microsoft's AltspaceVR technology was chosen as the virtual reality social platform and as such, worked as a

Figure 1. Hybrid teaching model at Turku UAS
(Joshi, 2021)

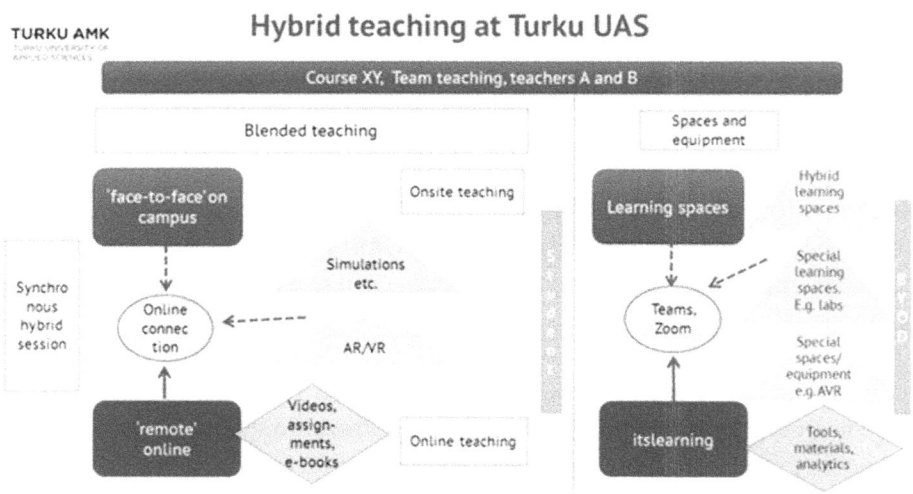

precursor for what would later become the Turku UAS's own metaverse technology solution, with a working title of 'Turku UAS VR Social Platform'. The opening ceremony engaged hundreds of participants to be present in our virtual exhibition hall and gave a possibility to test the use of VR technology on a wider scale. In total there were around 200 participants, of which around 80 of them with avatars, and over 40 joining the YouTube live stream. As a result of this test, the technology was found to contain several challenges in organizing massive virtual events. Some of the challenges included a limited number of users, complicated registration and no hands-on-experiencing. Based on this experience, FIT Turku Competence Center started developing its first own metaverse prototypes in the spring 2021.

In the first experiments, Unreal and Unity game engines were tested and compared (Österman, 2021). During summer 2021, FIT Competence Centre decided to focus on Unity game engine because it is widely used among industrial partners businesses and because it can be used with limited and unlimited resources. This technology supports the Turku UAS vision by including features for social communication, hands on experiencing and digital twin integration (Luimula et al., 2022). The existing technologies typically have challenges such as update management, number of simultaneous users, usability, user experience, license policies, customization but also limited user interaction and user data gathering.

In 2021, Turku UAS formed a team for AR/VR solutions and support with involvement from all faculties. The purpose of this team was to leverage know-how and best practices. The team started internal activities to increase awareness and expand the piloting opportunities of VR technologies in other internal units. This included holding staff meetings, conducting surveys and evaluating needs for equipment, with the aim of gaining a better understanding of how VR and metaverse could be used on a wider scale in the transition towards hybrid learning environments. Based on the results, the immediate needs were identified to be professional development of teachers, investment in physical and virtual spaces, internal and external collaboration with project partners, benchmarking other universities and their solutions, and finally, internal communication to increase awareness of utilizing VR in teaching and learning in higher education.

2. DEVELOPING THE METAVERSE TECHNOLOGY

Metaverse approach presented in this paper can be seen as a continuum for Virtual Continuum (VC) presented by Milgram & Kishino (1994). In their visions, an ideal virtual space with reality essential for communication will be needed within the same visual display environment. According to XR4All (2020) eXtended Reality (XR) can be seen as an umbrella term used for Virtual Reality (VR), Augmented Reality (AR), and Mixed Reality (MR), covering terms used in the VC taxonomy. Virtual reality is defined as a method of interacting with a computer-simulated environment (Das et al., 1994). Augmented reality, in turn, is a technology which allows computer generated virtual imagery to exactly overlay physical objects in real time (Zhou et al., 2008). Metaverse describes a virtual universe shared amongst its users allowing them to interact with each other within the boundaries of the platform (Nevelsteen, 2017). During the year 2021 the metaverse became a more frequently used term. Microsoft's CEO Nadella (Microsoft, 2021) illustrated their visions of an enterprise metaverse as a platform layer bringing together IoT, digital twins, and mixed reality. Facebook in turn described their organization's transition from a social media company to a metaverse company called Meta. This transition will require around 10-15 years before metaverse products will be fully realized (Bosworth and Clegg, 2021).

New investments in consumer metaverse (e.g., Epic Games) and consumer metaverse software development tool (e.g., Lego) are being made (Verdict, 2022). However, Nokia's CEO Pekka Lundberg suggests that the future of metaverse is not for consumers (Lundmark, 2022). Indeed, Nokia (2023) has classified metaverse business in three categories, consumer, enterprise, and industrial metaverse. In this paper, the focus is on the metaverse technology designed for a higher education institution. In this context, it can be seen as the fourth category because 1) users are not consumers, but teachers and students, 2) educational institutions are not enterprises, but typically public owned organizations, and 3) users and institutions are not factories, but rather designing next generation solutions to improve productivity and efficiency. All in all, the approach at Turku UAS is closest to the industrial metaverse.

Turku University of Applied Sciences started the development of its own metaverse technology in spring 2021. The main development work related to metaverse at Turku UAS has been conducted at the FIT Competence Centre with laboratory facilities for augmented and virtual reality technology research and development (Turku UAS, 2021). In Luimula et al. (2022), metaverse is defined as a technology which consists of features for social communication, hands on experiencing and digital twin integration. These features are lacking in many current metaverse technologies (e.g., MootUp, Breakroom, Facebook Horizon, Mozilla Hub), and although some attempts have been seen to combine digital and physical worlds (e.g., Microsoft's Hololens version 3), they have suffered from cancellations or plummeting earnings (e.g., Meta's stocks in 2022). Nevertheless, one future prediction by Nokia suggests that metaverse will replace smartphones in the second half of this decade (Dallas News, 2022).

2.1 Collaboration in A Virtual Environment

Metaverse is, at best, an abstract term used in various interpretations of social and collaborative platforms. At Turku UAS, VR environment is seen as a platform that uses social communication for real-life integration through both hands-on skill development and theoretical knowledge transfer. In other words, at Turku UAS, the metaverse drive is earmarked by the notion of a community of practice. The aim is to transition into an era where technology brings massive groups of trainees, such as students or industry experts updating their competences, together without straining the global carbon footprint, but not merely in the format of remote lecturing through teleconference systems, but instead, by utilizing VR technology. Teleconferencing systems do not activate in the learning sufficiently—in fact, less than in traditional classroom situations (PricewaterhouseCoopers, 2022).

Putting aside the problem of under-engagement through teleconference teaching and training, most online learning platforms also suffer from content-related matters. Teaching efforts concentrate primarily on knowledge content and actual execution, rather than understanding the dynamic of the human dimensions of the associated learning context. Content training, whether in real-life or virtually, is fundamentally disconnected from the dynamic of community if there is no cause and effect. As a response to this, several advances in XR technologies have started to enable more interactive solutions and offer participation in cause-and-effect hands-on-training activities that can contain real-life integration by means of digital twins. Although the use of XR in simulation training undeniably brings about the possibility of communicating cause and effect of human-environment interaction, it still does not address the wider social aspects of meaningful collaborative practices.

Metaverse approaches are not only suitable for hands-on training environments. The current state-of the-art knowledge sharing platforms available to HEIs are limited to traditional LMS platforms that suffer from lagged communication or insufficient feedback loops, instead of encouraging dialogue with corrective, discussive and reflective feedback. Metaverse technology promotes fluid communication through immediate voice communication with peer learners and teachers alike. Furthermore, a real teacher presence in a metaverse environment gives the true sense of being in a virtual classroom where discussion can be initiated. In addition, the metaverse technology is well-capable of collecting metrics and analytics beyond that of traditional LMS platforms, providing a strong catalyst for debriefing activities—often hyped to be the most powerful learning mechanism of all.

2.2 Turku UAS Metaverse Approach

At Turku UAS, metaverse is defined as a technology which consists of features for social communication, hands-on-training, and digital twins (Luimula et al., 2022). In this paper, the name 'Turku UAS VR Social Platform' is used to describe the Turku UAS metaverse technology. Turku UAS approach offers collaborative virtual interaction to facilitate learning from each other and learning with each other to enable a comprehensive community impact experience. Turku UAS aims to promote communication and collaboration through a metaverse platform, whereby anybody anywhere (also beyond national borders) can update their knowledge and skill across all education levels, academic institutions, and workplace environments.

Several experiments by Turku UAS research groups have been conducted on the use of metaverse in education. Some of the experiments have been developed using Microsoft AltspaceVR technology. These experiments have shown that many of the existing virtual reality social platforms, a sort of precursors of metaverse, are still missing several relevant features needed in the education field, and at the moment offer only a limited number of users, complicated registrations, limitations in hands-on-training and links to physical world objects (Luimula et al., 2021). Due to this, Turku UAS decided to start developing its own metaverse technology which would better fulfill the identified needs. After a rigorous design and development period, the technology is ready to meet the requirements set by the university.

Based on the current understanding, there is only a limited number of metaverse technologies designed for B2B markets with realistic simulations and behavioral monitoring (incl. eye tracking, biosensors). This development demands multidisciplinary research activities conducted through R&D projects requiring expertise from both academic and other working life. One example of an industry collaboration at Turku UAS is Kiwa, one of the leading Testing, Inspection and Certification organizations in Europe, that has launched so-called virtual training centers and competence cards with VR add-ons. International collaboration is important, and one example is a current project conducting effectiveness studies in virtual certified training with Nanyang Technological University Singapore.

Turku UAS VR Social Platform can be seen as a multi-user environment which is not only hosting multiple users remotely or locally, but which is combining several or all multi-user environments into unified seamless platform as shown below in Figure 2.

Figure 2. Turku UAS VR Social Platform: a metaverse technology with a common platform combining several multi-user environments

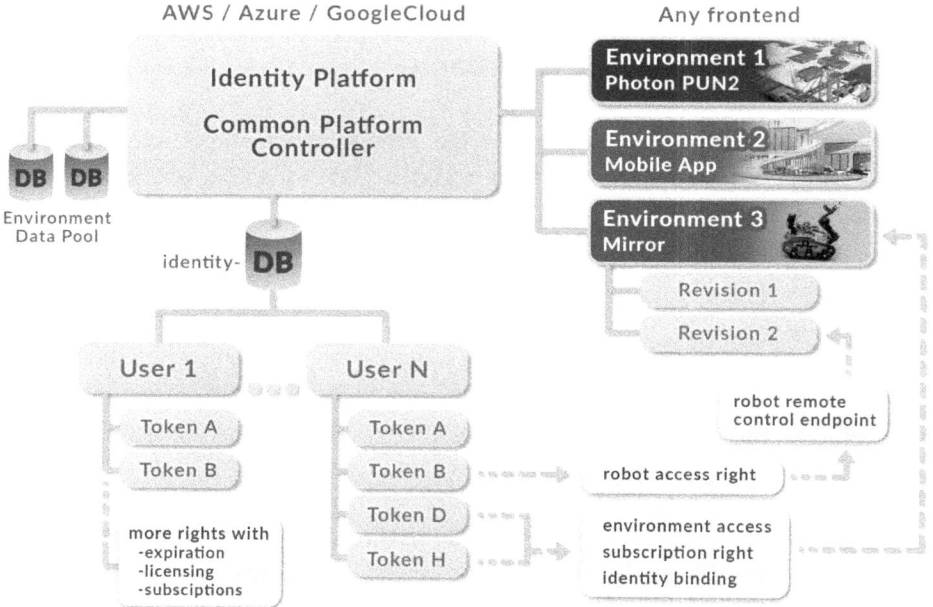

The platform architecture is designed to handle modular and extensible token-based account control. Each user's rights can be expanded by redeeming tokens of respectable accesses. Each token in turn has redemption count and also expiration, so the rights may be assigned per specific feature, duration or only to allow right during certain periods of time.

One benefit from common platform architecture is the unique user identification across all environments, building a foundation for seamless progress and action logging of a single user operating through the environments. Data collection of individual users who complete tasks and assignments in several environments can be combined into reporting. The unique user identification can be connected to external identity providers, which bring strong authentication and strong authorization features as possibility. Common identity is essential for role-based feature sets and also access credential management throughout the Turku UAS VR Social Platform.

Common identity also allows the setting of user individual quotas across the platform. One early example of such user-specific extension would be an avatar system: the same user's representation is available in all environments of the platform, which in turn makes the user more easily identifiable. Strong user verification methods can be used to ensure that the avatar is indeed representing the user it claims to represent.

Implementation of the Turku UAS VR Social Platform identity management has already been tested in various RDI projects with end-users from the technology industry, maritime, and universities. For theory-based courses, an environment with tasks and exercises given by cues has been developed at Turku UAS. With the common platform, the data of each task and exercise attempt is collected in the backend system. These theory courses can run 24/7 and courses can be organized at the same time for hundreds of students from different universities all around the world.

Turku UAS VR Social Platform can provide access to several environments and training scenarios, where the courses can vary from theory to practice. Tasks and exercises are done in a virtual environment, supervised by a certified trainer or neural network. The students' progress can be followed and reviewed even for audits, such as in the case of competence certificates in the industry. Monitoring of each task and exercise attempt is collected in the backend system, and attempts can be fully reconstructed in the virtual environment. The course trainer can move freely in the environment, gaining any required perspective of the attempts, also allowing real-time communication between the trainer and trainee. The trainer can also switch to the trainee's view at any moment when required. Statistics of the exercise environment are provided for course supervisors in real time if required.

Environment isolation is one of the core features of the Turku UAS VR Social Platform. The architecture could be maintained in its launch state indefinitely, without need of regular downtime from updates. Several instances of the same environment can run in parallel, providing redundancy, and traffic can be diverted into another instance during maintenance. The feature set is locked into the environment and future development can be integrated to an environment on-demand. Also, several different feature-sets can be provided for the same environment, separated by instantiation. This allows an active environment to continue operation in parallel while a new feature set version of the same environment is opened. The Turku UAS VR Social Platform is built and structured to be modular from functionality and graphical representation of the environment perspective. Any graphical assets and functionalities created into the base platform feature set are available as core features for all environments, which provides significant improvement to development and prototyping cycles.

2.3 Practical Examples Implemented in Turku UAS VR Social Platform

To demonstrate the metaverse technology in practice, a harbor area was selected in autumn 2021 as a test environment. In the first test, AltspaceVR technology was used to develop the environment itself with features needed in virtual exhibition called Match XR (XR Center, 2021). This was followed by an experiment where the harbor environment with same functionalities was moved to the Turku UAS VR Social Platform (Figure 3 below).

Figure 3. Turku UAS VR Social Platform (left column) and Microsoft AltspaceVR (right column) containing similar features such as posters, holograms, and 360 photos

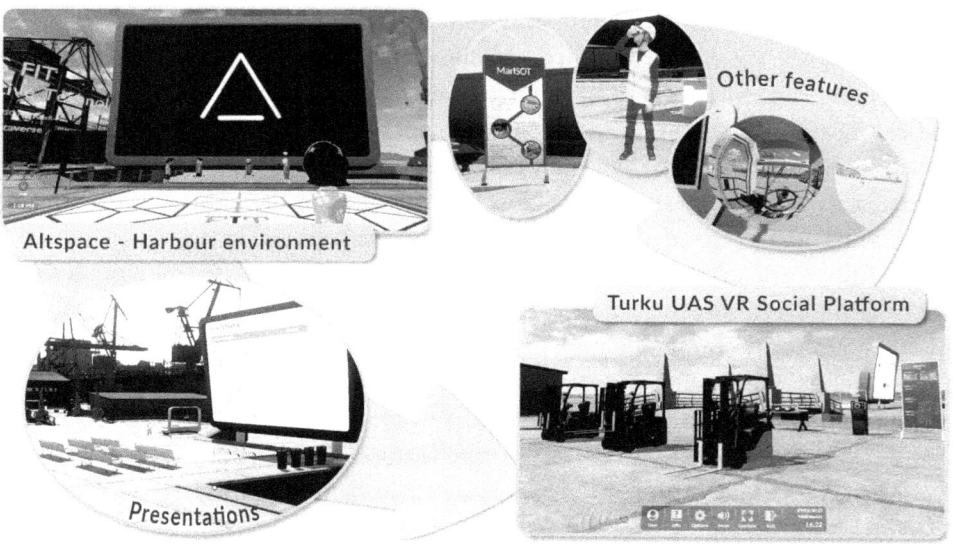

Unity environment conversion from AltspaceVR technology into Turku UAS VR Social Platform is directly supported with minimal development effort requirements, which has become relevant aspect recently, due to the discontinuation of AltspaceVR in March 2023.

Once the conversion is completed, the use of our metaverse technology enables bringing hands-on-training inside the harbor environment. One practical example of hands-on-training is creating exercises for various drivers with operations of forklifts, gantry cranes, and trucks and for seafarers with operations of deck cranes and on command bridge (Figure 4 below).

Figure 4. Collaborative training environment for professionals in harbors

Collaborative training in such a demanding industrial environment such as harbor is quite challenging using traditional training methods. Harbor operations cannot be stopped for training purposes and typical training simulators do not support collaborative training between various professionals in the whole logistic chain. Turku UAS collaborative approach enables tens of professionals to solve logistic challenges in a digitalized version of the harbor without causing any disturbance for the real-life operations. As a long-term objective, the collaborative training environments, such as the harbor environment above, can be further developed towards remote controlled environments. Most recent revisions of the training environments also consider extensions towards AI instructors and AI evaluators. These include integrations to existing models and readily available neural network inference providers, like OpenAI, as well as support for in-house data collection and neural network training based on data gathered from the environments. Multi-user environment and activities provide high variance in the behavioral data, reinforcing the neural network training data set.

One conundrum that many neglect to address appropriately in hands-on training is the requirement of prior theoretical knowledge. Traditionally, the training process starts with a typical classroom briefing on the necessary theoretical aspects of the training before learners move to their respective practical engagements. To keep the theory and practice more closely coupled in terms of delivery mode (platform) and physical movement, Turku UAS has started to explore the potential of serving theory content through a collaborative metaverse environment. In an RDI project called Artificial Intelligence and Society (AIIS) funded by Erasmus+, we developed a collaborative learning interface on the Turku UAS VR Social Platform architecture for teaching medical students how artificial intelligence and soft skills feature in their future healthcare professions.

The AIIS learning interface is a validated 3 ECTS course. It comprises a 3D environment where students can move around to various task dispensers where they select the theory tasks, they must complete about specific AI and soft-skills topics (Figure 5 below).

Figure 5. Students doing theory exercises in the environment created for AIIS

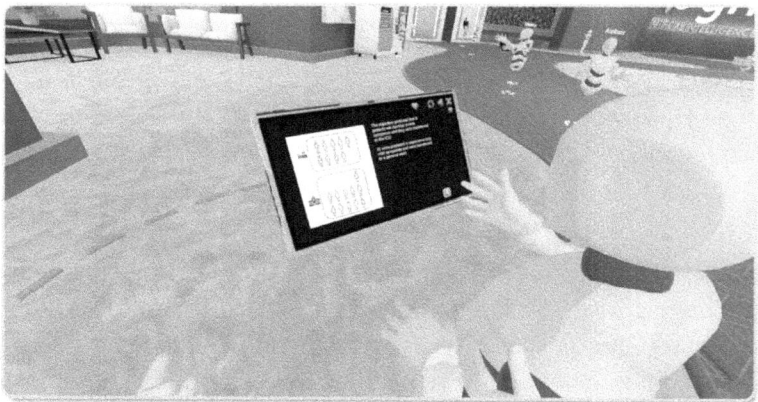

The AIIS pedagogy requires students to make use of the Turku UAS VR Social Platform's collaborative features to complete the course. The environment also hosts reflection zones, where students are encouraged to explore topics independently more deeply, and a practical challenges selection area, where students select one of several practical group assignments that puts their newly acquired theoretical knowledge into practice.

In the autumn of 2022, an extensive pilot with 125 medical students from five European universities was conducted, and out of them, 92 students completed the theoretical components and successfully applied their theory knowledge to their respective practical group challenges. The project outcome was stable in public testing using operational environment and load for several months, with 24/7 accessibility. This experience was one of the steppingstones to start utilizing the metaverse technology more widely at Turku UAS. Turku UAS is looking to offer its own first Turku UAS VR Social Platform course on Gamification and Serious Games theory (as part of the Games and Interactive Technologies formal curriculum) in the Autumn of 2023.

In recent years, advancements in AI and machine learning have made the integration of these technologies into various neural networks increasingly essential. Turku UAS VR Social Platform has incorporated interfaces for widely used machine learning model platforms, such as OpenAI, enabling the integration of ChatGPT and other Large Language Models. This development facilitates the creation of responsive and AI-driven hybrid learning environments with modular machine learning integrations.

Figure 6. Users in the Turku UAS VR Social Platform environment using ChatGPT integration (left) and five avatars interacting in a training warehouse featuring realistic avatars (right)

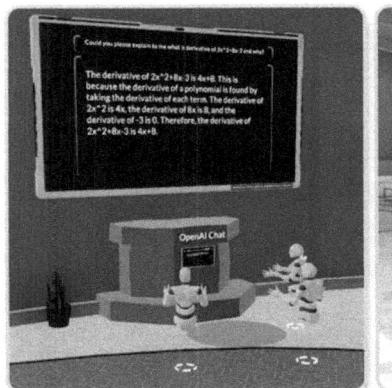 

Figure 6 above (left) depicts a group of students engaging with basic mathematical questions within the Turku UAS VR Social Platform environment. The user interface features a small panel for individual users, while a larger panel displays the question and ChatGPT-generated answer for all users in the environment. The interface is accessible for both desktop and VR users.

To ensure fair resource allocation and cost control, each user's profile includes a predetermined quota of available interactions. This approach prevents a single user from exhausting the neural network inference quota and helps manage costs associated with various neural network API endpoints. Additionally, users can regulate their quota consumption by specifying the desired length of the neural network-generated responses. Longer answers tend to consume more quota at many available OpenAI endpoints.

To enhance user experience and personalization, the Turku UAS VR Social Platform incorporates a comprehensive avatar system, offering both customizable and pre-designed avatar sets. This feature enables practical exercises with appropriate attire for scenarios that necessitate specific clothing for task assignments. Realistic avatars also allow easier identification and interaction among students within the virtual environment.

Figure 6 (right) illustrates the most recent revision of avatar customization implemented into training facility modeled in Turku UAS VR Social Platform. The avatar movements are fully animated and natural. For desktop users, hand animations are pre-recorded, while for VR users, the hand animations follow the user's hand movements via VR controller's movement tracking.

Currently the training facility is used to run experiments of Virtual Training Certification project regarding theory content delivery and effectiveness practical exercises, as well as engaging the trainees into social interaction while completing their training courses. The training facility environment uses Turku UAS VR Social Platform as a base, and the concurrent user count during the experiments is 60-75.

The digitalized version of an environment can also consist of digital twins with specific functionalities that can be integrated into the platform. With fully customizable API support of the platform, the digital twins and their sensors could be coupled to real world machinery and equipment, providing access to executing remote operations. With data collection, this functionality could be further developed to user-assisted autonomous systems and to gather training data for neural network operated autonomous systems.

The platform registrations are limited by expiration of tokens, which occurs automatically after certain enrollment date has been exceeded. However, public anonymous access rights can be granted for specific time periods, allowing remote control right for example to presentation crowd. One implementation of this feature was presented in the European Robotics Forum 2023, where the participants of conference demonstration in Denmark could control a robot in Finland using their mobile phones. The mobile device interface was attached as an external source to the platform, and access to control the robot was granted only for the duration of the demonstration.

Recently the Turku UAS VR Social Platform has been expanded towards digital twins and remote robot control. Extensive user right management with tokens naturally enforces queueing and reservation of physical robots: students can control specific robot only at specific times, and their right will then automatically expire after the token allowing that access has expired. In Figure 7 above, the user is controlling a robot in real-world via a digital twin from Turku UAS VR Social Platform. The robot remote controls are assigned based on the environment location: as user enters the remote-control area, he gains control of the robot, which in turn is visualized in VR as a digital twin inside the environment.

Figure 7. Remote controlling a real robot via VR using digital twin

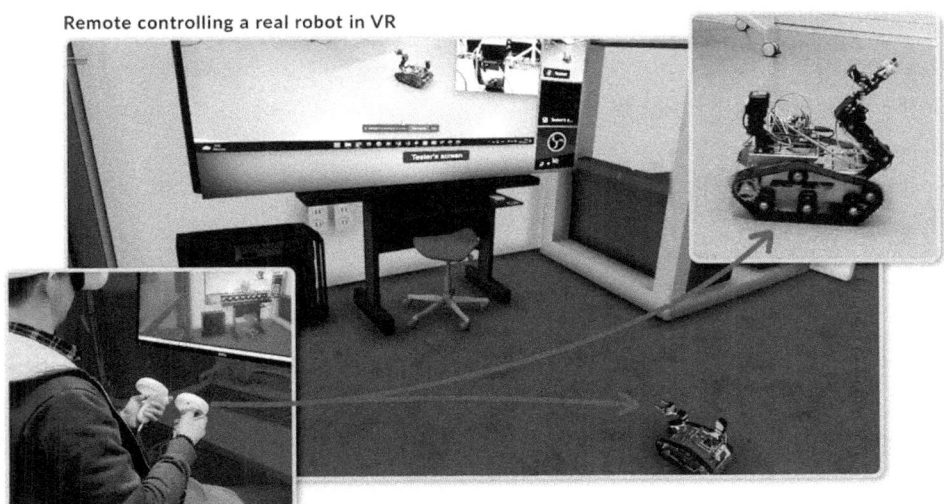

Remote controlling a real robot in VR

2.4 Students as Designers and Developers

The role of engineering faculty and engineering students is essential in the design and development work. At Turku UAS, the CDIO principles of conceive, design, implement, operate (CDIO, n.d.) are used in the engineering education in the school of ICT. Since autumn 2012, a new Capstone Innovation Project course based on the CDIO framework was piloted at Turku UAS (Kulmala et al., 2014). At Turku UAS, the CDIO approach is widened to include different stakeholders in the design process. The RDI projects funded by funding agents will enable an efficient use of staff members in various roles. This is complemented by the final year students and student assistants. This gives the possibility to have 30-50 developers working collaboratively to develop metaverse environments with specialists from different degree programs and competence tracks.

Figure 8 below illustrates how the students are used in the planning, developing, and testing phases of designing and developing a VR learning environment in a RDI project.

Figure 8. Students' role in the design and development of VR environments

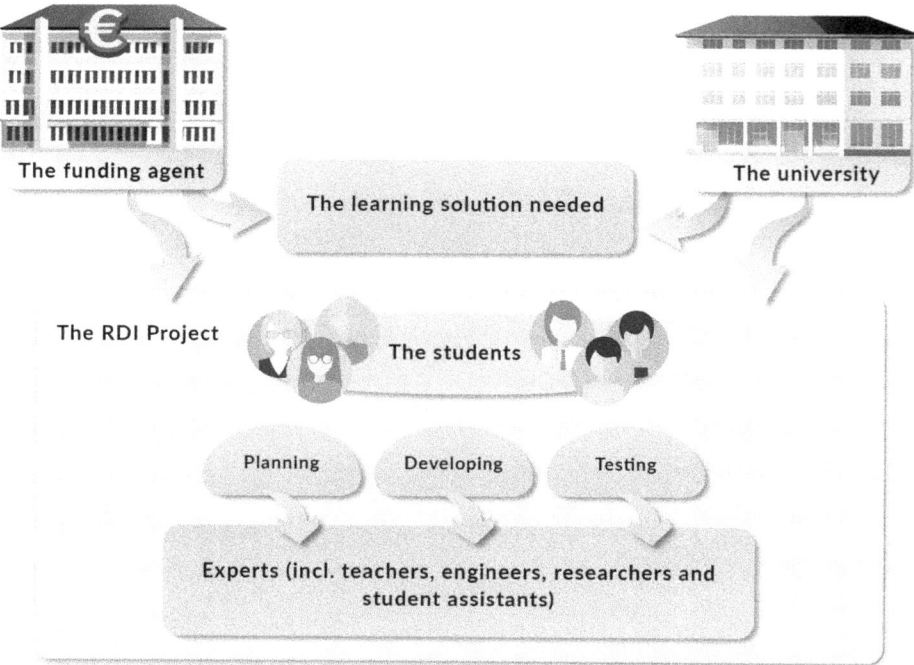

It is important to note that training in a VR environment does not compete with the practical training that is part of the university curricula but instead offers a complementary way to practice the hands-on practical skills needed in the profession. VR offers a possibility for endless repetitive drills of special situations that are either rarely encountered in real life or are otherwise difficult to replicate repeatedly in a real environment, due to high cost, lack of access to equipment, or distant locations, to name a few. The users can also observe pre-recorded operations in 3D repeatedly from a freely chosen angle, providing flexibility and point of views, which would be impossible in the real world.

Since autumn 2021, Turku UAS has offered ICT students new courses called 'Serious Games Project' and 'R&D Project', which have both given the students better chances to participate in the research group's RDI projects with promising results to design and develop VR solutions. An example of an ongoing student project at Turku UAS is a project where the students are experimenting if the collaboration in a virtual reality environment can increase the sense of belonging and the ability to work in teams, thus increasing the students' wellbeing in a fully online study environment. Collaborating in a virtual environment can increase active learning possibilities in a more authentic way than in a traditional online learning environment through a feeling of immersion.

One example of a student design and development is XR solutions for medication training (Figure 9 below, left), which was done as part of an ongoing project that focuses on extended reality and pedagogy in education (PedaXR, n.d.). Another example of a student group design and development is a set of immersive serious games for forklift driving using VR headsets (Figure 9 below, right). Both of these examples show the potential of student projects. Typically, student projects have been used as the first step in industrial cooperation and, in the best-case scenario, the cooperation has continued using public funding instruments with industrial partners.

Figure 9. XR solutions developed by student groups for medication and forklift training

 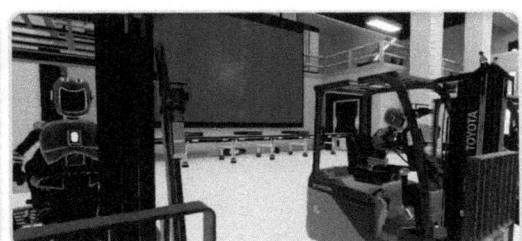

The experiences of working closely in multidisciplinary teams show that HEIs have unused potential to produce next generation learning content in a way where latest interactive technologies, especially XR, metaverse, and artificial intelligence, can be used efficiently in courses which require hands-on-training and collaboration. The practical examples illustrated above show that when specialists from certain subject areas, such as medical field, will give their contribution in the form of writing manuscripts, giving feedback, and testing students' prototypes in a close cooperation with engineers from interactive technologies, it is possible to efficiently create immersive and highly motivated learning content, not only for the students of the HEI but also for third parties.

3. THE FUTURE HYBRID EDUCATION MODEL

The new strategy of the Turku UAS emphasizes operating fluently between physical and digital worlds in a so-called hybrid world. In the revised hybrid education model, VR could replace the teleconferencing technologies, and redefine the understanding of hybrid world in the university strategy where hybrid is a combination of where we are simultaneously in the physical and online mode, moving towards XR (Extended reality).

The following steps are required to scale up and realize the new hybrid education model in practice:

1) The university can be considered a factory to produce next generation learning content and solutions,
2) teacher groups are involved as pedagogical leaders and producers to create content for the global markets and,
3) students gain opportunities for hands-on learning and collaboration in a VR environment.

Furthermore, this model may generate financial profits for content creators (both students and staff members involved) through new startups. In this model, student teams are used in the prototyping, which is a sort of idea generation phase where students are asked to bring fresh ideas from gaming. In addition, teacher groups develop pedagogical solutions and pilot metaverse in education. These active pioneers will be in the key role to leverage these next generation virtual learning environments to be widely used in the whole university. The importance of participants from working life is a significant part of this hybrid model. The integration of the research group's competences in metaverse development to the learning analytics into these new learning environments can help create solutions for global markets in close cooperation with industrial partners.

As a result of this paper, the hybrid education model has been revised to reflect the future changes brought about by the Turku UAS VR Social Platform solution (Figure 10 below).

To be able to scale up, it is important to select the most appropriate solutions to be further developed in the form where teachers can easily author the content. These solutions should be brought in one compact package on a metaverse platform which will contain all required tools to do the authoring, to be able to easily interact with students where best practices from real and digital worlds will be combined for immersive learning experiences, and to be able to evaluate students' performance efficiently.

This can be achieved by involving early adapters to define requirement specifications. Once the platform is ready for the scaling up phase, the next challenge is to change the mindset – people need to be convinced why the use of

Figure 10. The future hybrid education model

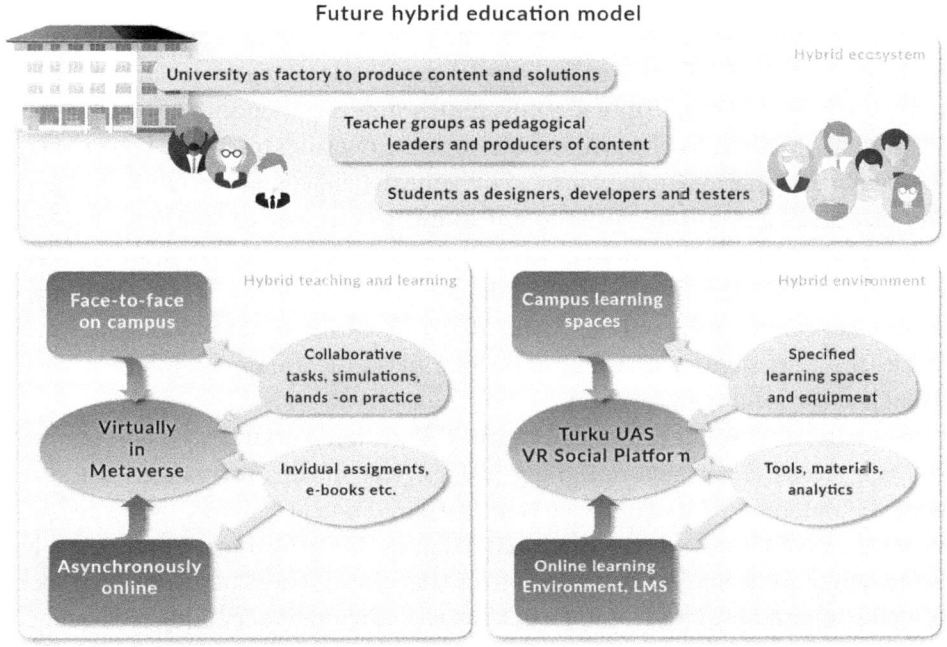

interactive technologies with metaverse platform will be a better solution than the teleconferencing systems used during the pandemic and at least as good a solution as the traditional classroom teaching.

The question of how to make the mindset change happen will require consideration for the role of individual teachers in this new hybrid education model, for example in the design of the pedagogical solutions and learning materials. It has been a tradition that some of the teachers have had private business publishing books as teaching material. This business has been mainly a national level business and only a handful of teachers have been able to engage in this kind of business. Entering global markets requires efforts which are most of the time not realistic neither for individual teachers as authors nor publishing houses in Finland. This era where physical and digital worlds will be merged will open totally new markets for players who understand the technology but also about the new way of teaching, i.e., new pedagogy, where teachers can produce efficiently new immersive and highly engaging learning content for own students but also for global markets.

The new strategy of Turku UAS defines that we learn in a changing world, where we aim to bring versatile solutions to create personalized study experiences in a hybrid world, where virtual and real worlds are intertwined (Turku UAS, 2023). Virtual reality has already shown possibilities for collaboration and co-operation training situations in observed and repeatable scenarios (Luimula et al., 2022) and in developing gamified applications for complex physical learning environments, where the experiences reveal realistic and enjoyable learning experiences to the participants (Oliva et al., 2019). It has been a suitable strategic decision for Turku UAS to build their own metaverse technology instead of being dependent on available short-term solutions, and since writing this article, Turku UAS metaverse technology has been commercialized by ProVerse Interactive Ltd. Turku UAS already has experience in designing and implementing online degree programs where all the studies and services are offered fully online (Joshi, 2023). The transition to metaverse can be seen as the next step to offer education in a hybrid learning environment where virtual and physical realities meet.

In pursuit of ensuring high-quality hybrid education, Turku UAS is continuously exploring, researching, and designing pedagogical models for various use cases under the potential of metaverse-driven learning content delivery. Most recently (through an R&D project called Virtual Training Certifications, Turku UAS has started a rigorous scientific investigation into the effectiveness of combining theory and hands-on training by means of a 3D virtual collaborative learning environment with the aim to define a pedagogy framework for metaverse-directed vocational training. Moreover, the importance of API integrations, modularity and extensibility; those, even though technical, are core requirements for future massive multi-user hybrid platform. Especially important is the seamless integration of the platform as an additional service, not (yet) replacing but extending legacy systems during the transition, helping with adaptation and coping with the changes. The three requirements of API integrations, modularity and extensibility are essential to avoid having "multiple metaverses" which are incompatible with each other, thus posing a risk of creating isolated environments of varying specifications instead of one common metaverse.

As a conclusion, it can be suggested that the transition towards hybrid learning environments at Turku UAS can work as an example on how to use metaverse in higher education to create new possibilities for active and enjoyable learning experiences. Given the vast array of metaverse application potential, if higher education institutions want to put metaverse widely into use within the next decade, they should not just passively wait but instead, start researching their potential application and making strategic plans as to how they can utilize a metaverse effectively to enable students and stakeholders to gain better learning results in VR environments.

REFERENCES

AIIS Artificial Intelligence. Innovation & Society. (No date). A project website. https://aiis.usal.es/

Bosworth, A., & Clegg, N. (2021) Building the Metaverse Responsibly, Meta Newsroom (September 27, 2021), DOI = https://about.fb.com/news/2021/09/buildingthe-metaverse-responsibly/

CDIO. (No date). About CDIO. http://www.cdio.org/about

Compayré, G., & Payne, W. H. (1885). *The History of Pedagogy*. Routledge.

Dallas News. (2022). Nokia's vision of the future is a world where the metaverse replaces smartphones. https://www.dallasnews.com/business/technology/2022/10/13/nokias-vision-of-the-future-is-a-world-where-the-metaverse-replaces-smartphones/

Das, S., Franguiadakis, T., Papka, M., Defanti, T. A., & Sandin, D. J. A genetic programming application in virtual reality. In *Proceedings of the 1994 IEEE 3rd International Fuzzy Systems Conference*, Orlando, FL, USA, 26–29 June 1994, pp. 480–484.

Dewey, J. (1988). The development of American Pragmatism. In J. Dewey & J. A. Boydston (Eds.), *The Middle Works of John Dewey* (Vol. 10, pp. 320–365). Southern Illinois University Press. (Original work published 1925)

Digivisio (2021). Basic information of the Digivisio 2030 program. https://digivisio2030.fi/en/basic-information-on-the-digivisio-2030-programme/

Emergen Research. (2022). Metaverse Market, By Component (Hardware), By Platform (Desktop and Others), By Offering (Avatars), By Technology (Mixed Reality (MR) and Others), By Application, (Gaming and Others) By End-Use Vertical, and By Region Forecast to 2030. https://www.emergenresearch.com/industry-report/metaverse-market

Fortune (2022). Citi says metaverse economy could be worth $13 trillion by 2030. https://fortune.com/2022/04/01/citi-metaverse-economy-13-trillion-2030/

Hodges, C. B., & Fowler, D. J. (2020). The COVID-19 Crisis and Faculty Members in Higher Education: From Emergency Remote Teaching to Better Teaching through Reflection. *International Journal of Multidisciplinary Perspectives in Higher Education*, 5(1), 118–122. https://ojed.org/jimphe. doi:10.32674/jimphe.v5i1.2507

Izullah, F. P., Koivisto, M., Nieminen, V., Luimula, M., & Hämäläinen, H. (2022) Aging and sleep deprivation affect different neurocognitive stages of spatial information processing during a virtual driving task – An ERP study, Transportation Research Part F: Psychology and Behaviour, 89, Elsevier, August, pp. 399–406.

Joshi, M. (2021). *Hybrid teaching at Turku UAS.* A Blog post. Turku UAS intranet.

Joshi, M. (2023). *Holistic Design of Online Degree Programmes in Higher Education – A Pedagogically Informed Design Framework. A doctoral dissertation.* University of Lapland., https://urn.fi/URN:ISBN:978-952-337-349-5

Joshi, M. S. (2022). Holistic design of online degree programmes in higher education – a case study from Finland. *International Journal of Educational Management*, *36*(1), 32–48. doi:10.1108/IJEM-12-2020-0588

Keinänen, M., & Kairisto-Mertanen, L. (2019). Researching learning environments and students' innovation competences. *Education + Training*, *61*(1), 17–30. doi:10.1108/ET-03-2018-0064

Kulmala, R., Luimula, M., & Roslöf, J. (2014) Capstone Innovation Project – Pedagogical Model and Methods, In *Proceedings of the 10th International CDIO Conference* (CDIO 2014), June 15-19, Barcelona, Spain, p. 10.

Lappalainen, H. (2020) Innovation Pedagogy in the Era of Industrial Revolution 4.0. In *Proceedings of the 6th International Conference on Education and Technology* (ICET 2020) 10.2991/assehr.k.201204.005

Luimula, M., Haavisto, T., Pham, D., Markopoulos, P., Aho, J., Markopoulos, E., & Saarinen, J. (2022). The use of metaverse in maritime sector – a combination of social communication, hands on experiencing and digital twins. In: Evangelos Markopoulos, Ravindra S. Goonetilleke and Yan Luximon (eds.). Creativity, Innovation and Entrepreneurship. AHFE International Conference 2022. *AHFE Open Access, 31.* AHFE International, USA. http://doi.org/10.54941/ahfe1001513

Luimula, M., Markopoulos, E., Österman, M., Markopoulos, P., Aho, J., Ravyse, W., Saarinen, J., & Reunanen, T. (2021). Avatar Based Multiplayer Functionalities in Next Generation Communication and Learning in Virtual Reality Social Platforms – Case MarISOT Room, In *Proceedings of the 12th IEEE International Conference on Cognitive Infocommunications CogInfoCom*, 23-25 Sept 2021, online, pp. 447-452.

Luimula, M., Pitkäkangas, P., Saarenpää, T., Bulatovic Trygg, N., & Pyae, A. (2016). Students' Role in Gamified Solutions in Healthcare RDI Project, In *Proceedings of the 12th International CDIO Conference* (CDIO 2016), Turku, Finland, pp. 219-227.

Lundmark, P. (2022). The real future of the metaverse is for consumers. *Financial Times,* 2022. https://www.ft.com/content/af0c9de8-d36e-485b-9db5-5ee1e57716cb

MatchX. R. Event, https://helsinkixrcenter.com/events/match-xr-2021/

Microsoft. (2021). CEO Satya Nadella's keynote Speech. Microsoft Inspire, July 15, 2021. https://news.microsoft.com/wp-content/uploads/prod/2021/07/Microsoft-Inspire-2021-Satya-Nadella.pdf

Milgram, P., & Kishino, F. (1994). A Taxonomy of Mixer Reality Visual Displays. *IEICE Transactions on Information and Systems, E77-D*(12), 1321–1329.

Ministry of Education and Culture. (2014). Universities of Applied Sciences Act. https://www.finlex.fi/fi/laki/kaannokset/2014/en20140932_20200000.pdf

Nevelsteen, K.J. (2017) Virtual world, defined from a technological perspective, and applied to video games, mixed reality and the metaverse. *Computer Animation and Virtual Worlds, 29*(1) / e1752. https://doi.org/ doi:10.1002/cav.1752

Nokia (2023). Metaverse Explained. https://www.nokia.com/about-us/newsroom/articles/metaverse-explained/

OECD. (2021). *The state of higher education: One year in to the COVID-19 pandemic.* OECD Publishing., doi:10.1787/83c41957-

Oliva, D., Somerkoski, B., Tarkkanen, K., Lehto, A., & Luimula, M. (2019). *Virtual reality as a communication tool for fire safety – Experiences from the VirPa project.* GamiFIN Conference, Levi, Finland, April 8-10, 2019.

Österman, M. (2021). *Development of a virtual reality conference application.* Bachelor's Thesis in Information and Communications Technology. Turku University of Applied Sciences.

PricewaterhouseCoopers. (2022). Emerging Technology - What does virtual reality and the metaverse mean for training? https://www.pwc.com/us/en/tech-effect/emerging-tech/virtual-reality-study.html

Somerkoski, B., Tarkkanen, K., Oliva, D., Lehto, A., & Luimula, M. (2022). Pedagogic solutions and results in designing a mobile game for fire safety teaching. In *Proceeding of the 6th GamiFIN conference*, online, pp. 44-53.

Taatila, V. (2017). Paradigm Shift in Higher Education? On The Horizon, 25(2), pp. 103-108. https://doi.org. doi:10.1108/OTH-06-2016-0030

Taatila, V., & Raij, K. (2012). Philosophical Review of Pragmatism as a Basis for Learning by Developing Pedagogy. *Educational Philosophy and Theory*, *44*(8), 831–844. doi:10.1111/j.1469-5812.2011.00758.x

The Rectors' Conference of Finnish Universities of Applied Sciences ARENE (2018). Towards the World's Best Higher Education System. The structural development working group report. https://www.arene.fi/julkaisut/raportit/rake-selvitys/

Turku, U. A. S. (2021). FIT Turku Competence Center (Futuristic Interactive Technologies. https://www.tuas.fi/en/services/products/fit-turku-competence-center/

Turku, U. A. S. (2022a). The minutes of the meeting of the board of Turku University of Applied Sciences March 17th, 2022. https://www.turkuamk.fi/media/filer_public/f4/6c/f46c94de-7481-4d9d-98e3-9cadc0385bef/turun_amk_oy_hallitus_1732022_poytakirja.pdf

Turku, U. A. S. (2022b). The minutes of the meeting of the board of Turku University of Applied Sciences, December 12, 2022. https://www.turkuamk.fi/media/filer_public/44/e0/44e02fb3-249f-499c-987e-2b0d5ea7e0b5/turun_amk_oy_hallitus_12122022_poytakirja.pdf

Turku, U. A. S. (2023). Turku UAS - impact across the world of work. https://www.tuas.fi/en/about-us/operations-and-organization/values-and-strategy/

TurkuU. A. S. (n.d.). https://www.tuas.fi/en/about-us/tuas/

Verdict (2022) Leading game companies in the metaverse theme. https://www.verdict.co.uk/top-ranked-gaming-companies-in-metaverse/

XR4All (2022). Definition – What is XR? XR4All Horizon, 2020. https://xr4all.eu/xr/

Zhou, F., Duh, H. B.-L., & Billinghurst, M. (2008) Trends in augmented reality tracking, interaction and display: A review of ten years of ISMAR. In *Proceedings of the 7th IEEE/ACM International Symposium on Mixed and Augmented Reality*, Cambridge, UK, 15–18 September 2008, pp. 193–202.

Section 4

Creative Learning Strategies and Assessment

Chapter 11

Autonomous Creative Learning Strategy Directed to Higher Education Students in Health Area

Paulo Veloso Gomes
 https://orcid.org/0000-0002-3975-2395
*LabRP, CIR, School of Health,
Polytechnic of Porto, Portugal*

Renato Magalhães
 https://orcid.org/0000-0002-8488-0943
*LabRP, CIR, School of Health,
Polytechnic of Porto, Portugal*

João Donga
 https://orcid.org/0000-0002-8701-2113
*LabRP, CIR, School of Media Arts and
Design, Polytechnic of Porto, Portugal*

Vítor J. Sá
 https://orcid.org/0000-0002-4982-4444
*FFCS, Universidade Católica
Portuguesa, Portugal & ALGORITMI/
LASI, University of Minho, Portugal*

Sandra Ferreira
*Group of Schools of Perafita,
Matosinhos, Portugal*

ABSTRACT

As digital native learners, Z and Alpha generation students upcoming new challenges for Higher Education Institutions. Their early contact with technological devices does not in itself confer the necessary digital skills to correctly apply technology in academic or professional contexts. Digital skills are fundamental to the future health professionals, improving their academic performance and prepares them for their integration into the labor market. The integration of information and communication technologies in the curricula of higher education courses in the health area is a differentiating factor for academic and professional enhancement. The Autonomous Creative Learning Strategy directed to higher education students in the health area is based on project-oriented approaches, combined with interactive and immersive based-gaming learning activities that appeal to creativity, autonomy and encourage proactivity, self-learning, and the constant search for continuous improvement.

DOI: 10.4018/978-1-6684-8656-6.ch011

INTRODUCTION

Higher Education Institutions must be prepared to face Z and Alpha generation students upcoming new challenges. As digital native learners, they present different capabilities and different needs. Early contact with technological devices and permanent access to heterogeneous sources of information means that their relationship with large volumes of information is established from childhood. However, being familiar with technology by using technological devices such as mobile phones, computers, or game consoles daily, or using social networks and streaming platforms, does not in itself confer the necessary digital skills to correctly apply technology in academic or professional contexts.

The integration of Information and Communication Technologies (ICT) teaching in the curricula of higher education health courses gives students and future health professionals a significant added value in terms of curriculum, gives them the digital skills necessary for better academic performance in the various course units and prepares them for their integration into the labor market.

Teaching information and communication technologies to health higher education students face significant challenges. In addition to generational challenges, the profile of these students lacks basic technological training. Often, they have difficulties in clearly understanding the technology and its potential applications, as well as the ability to effectively communicate and integrate it into academic and research work.

It is important to develop pedagogical strategies that motivate students to learn, practice, and integrate ICT into academic activities. These strategies should take a multidimensional approach, addressing aspects that reveal the importance of ICT as a differentiating factor, for academic and professional enhancement, which allows students to have the perception that the time invested in developing this type of skills will be largely compensated throughout the course because they start to do tasks more effectively and efficiently, and that activities and tasks are defined and integrated into motivating projects capable of mobilizing students to actively participate in the teaching/learning process and that simultaneously encourage the development of certain soft skills.

As part of education and professional development, ICT can provide students and future professionals with a wide range of resources, including digital libraries, online journals, and databases. The ICT provides virtual spaces that allow students to establish bridges between face-to-face and virtual interaction. tools for real-time collaboration and communication allowing students to work together on projects and assignments enable the creation of interactive and engaging learning experiences which can lead to better learning.

First, this work analyzes the relation between the generations Z and Alpha with technology, highlights the importance of acquiring ICT skills for future health professionals. Then, addresses the potential of using Based-Gaming Learning and the Project-Oriented Approach in learning environments. Finally, proposes the elaboration of a differentiating strategy (Autonomous Creative Learning Strategy) for Teaching information and communication technologies to higher education students in health courses, based on the mapping between the characteristics of students, who belong to the Z and Alpha generation, and the expected digital skills that those students and future health professionals should achieve during their bachelor's and master's courses in the health area.

HOW GENERATIONS Z AND ALPHA RELATE TO TECHNOLOGY

Generations Z and Alpha students are digital natives, have grown up with technology and are comfortable using it in their daily lives (Reyes et al., 2020), they are fast decision makers, and highly connected (Cilliers, 2017). They have a keen social and politically aware and are actively engaged in social and political issues, they are more diverse and inclusive than previous generations (Schenarts, 2019; Seemiller & Meghan, 2017). These students are conscious and have a strong desire to learn new skills and gain practical experience. They appreciate independence, value their autonomy and are not afraid to question authority. They are creative and deal well with innovation. However, many of them are exposed to a high level of stress and anxiety.

As Alpha, Generation Z have multitasking behavior between activities and technological devices (Shatto & Erwin, 2017). They complete homework, watch television and play mobile games simultaneously, they are continually being stimulated by digital content. Generation Z students are observers, before applying the learning themselves they like to watch others complete tasks (Seemiller & Meghan, 2017), they are customed to learning independently, team-work could be a serious challenge for them.

Generation Z students prefer engaging and exciting experiences (Reyes et al., 2020), they tend to reject merely expository lectures, preferring pragmatic, immersive, interactive and sensorial learning experiences (Cilliers, 2017; Schenarts, 2019). For them, gamification is a must, and appreciate to use their own methods to meet educational objectives (Schenarts, 2019).

Generation Z is technologically advanced, pragmatic, risk adverse, individualistic and better behaved than preceding generations (Schenarts, 2019), they expect that their educators be innovative (Reyes et al., 2020). These students prefer to engage in hands-on learning tasks in which they can immediately apply what they learn to real context (Seemiller & Meghan, 2017). The thinking of Generation Z are structurally different than those of earlier generations as a result of the external environment and how the brains respond to such stimuli (Cilliers, 2017).

As a result of the frequent use of digital content, their visual perception is very sharp, which makes the visual forms of learning more effective for them (Cilliers, 2017). The perceptions of these students regarding their own technology know-how is very high (Cilliers, 2017), this imply that they have a great expectation in integrating technology as part of teaching-learning creative process, with more visual-teaching methods and interesting, quick-result participatory methods (Cilliers, 2017). Generation Z students tends to be impatient and instant minded, they prefer stimulants and flexible learning environments that cultivate mentoring (Singh & Dangmei, 2016).

Being familiar with the daily use of technology in a social context does not mean knowing how to take advantage of its potential in an academic and work context. According to the American Library Association (2000), "Information literacy is a set of abilities requiring individuals to recognize when information is needed and have the ability to locate, evaluate, and use effectively the needed information". Taking into account this definition, Geck (2007) considers that Generation Z students are not information literate. Although technology is a part of their identity and they are tech savvy, show lack problem-solving skills and have not demonstrated the ability to look at a situation, put in context, analyze it and make a decision (Singh & Dangmei, 2016). For this reason Mohor & Mohr (2017) recommend teachers to promote informational literacy and help students select and critically consume online resources.

THE IMPORTANCE OF ACQUIRING ICT SKILLS FOR HEALTH PROFESSIONALS

Information and Communication Technologies (ICT) have been having a significant impact on health, allowing to improve the quality and efficiency of health care, as well as communication between professionals and patients. Using information systems, healthcare professionals can quickly access patient data, facilitating the diagnosis and treatment of diseases.

The implementation of ICT in health requires that all people working in the health system, such as doctors, nurses, pharmacists, but also computer scientists, managers, among others (Magalhães, 2022), have adequate skills to effectively use and manage technologies. Kostkova (2015) defines digital health as the "use of information and communication technologies to improve human health, health services and well-being for individuals and among populations". When the healthcare professional needs digital resources, such as information and technology, they are considered a "digital health professional" (Brice & Almond, 2020).

Technology will be present in all areas of healthcare. Across the board, health professionals should have basic knowledge in ICT, which includes knowledge of software, hardware, information security and data privacy, as well as the ability to work with health information systems. For healthcare professionals, they should be able to use communication technologies to communicate with other healthcare professionals and patients, use electronic health systems such as electronic health records, telemedicine systems and other information management tools.

With the arrival of emerging technologies in healthcare, clinicians will use artificial intelligence (AI), in particular Deep Learning, to help analyze large volumes of patient data, enabling more accurate and personalized diagnoses, assisting practitioners in decision making (Topol, 2019). We are witnessing a growth of the digital transformation of health, through the implementation of AI systems, one of the most powerful instruments of transformation in the different areas of the hospital (Fernandes, 2022). Other emerging technologies are appearing to health professionals and have the potential to revolutionize healthcare, of which we highlight:

1. Robotics, used for less invasive surgeries.
2. Virtual reality, augmented reality and mixed reality, can be used to provide real-time information to healthcare professionals during surgeries and medical procedures, as well as in patient rehabilitation.
3. the Internet of Things, which can be used to monitor remote patients in real time and alert healthcare workers in the event of an emergency.
4. 3D printing, which can be used to create custom prosthetics for patients.

The use of ICT in health requires digital skills on the part of the professionals of a health unit, namely:

- Medicine: Use of clinical software, such as electronic medical records and diagnostic imaging systems. Knowledge of big data and data analysis. So that physicians can use all available information to make more informed clinical decisions.
- Nursing: Use of nursing management software, such as nursing record systems and. Knowledge in telemedicine.
- Pharmacy: Use of pharmacy management software, such as stock management systems and electronic prescribing systems. Knowledge in safety systems for drug control. So that pharmacists can protect their patients' data, ensuring the security and privacy of information.
- Physiotherapy: Use of exercise management software and patient assessment systems. Knowledge in wearable and remote monitoring technologies. So that

physiotherapists can monitor and evaluate their patients remotely, improving the efficiency of treatments.

- Public health: Use of epidemiological analysis software and management systems of public health programs. Knowledge in geographic information systems. So that public health professionals can map and monitor the evolution of diseases and epidemics, allowing a more effective response.
- ICT Professionals: Advanced knowledge in information systems, networks, security, software development. Knowledge in emerging technologies (AI, Big Data, IoT). The IT professional is responsible for the management and maintenance of health information systems, information security, software development and the implementation of emerging technologies. Must have an advanced knowledge in information systems, networks, security and software development, as well as in emerging technologies to improve the efficiency of health information systems.

Therefore, it will be necessary a continuous training program in hospital organizations, to ensure an adequate update in emerging technologies in the health area (Eta Berner, 2020), both for new health professionals and those who are already active, both for the systems in production that are evolving, as well as the new ones that will be introduced, as well as in cybersecurity, ethics, roboethics and data protection. All skills acquisition must be accompanied with the implementation of knowledge management, considered an essential element of good governance (Mesquita, Santos, & Raposo, 2021).

GAME-BASED LEARNING

Game-based learning is an approach to education that involves using games to teach or reinforce concepts and skills. It is a form of experiential learning that engages students in an interactive and fun way, and it is often used in educational settings to supplement or enhance traditional teaching methods (Jan & Gaydos, 2016).

The concept of game-based learning has been around for centuries, but it wasn't until the rise of digital technology in the 20th century that it gained traction as a modern educational approach. Here is a brief history of game-based learning (Jaiswal, 2021; Pan et al., 2021):

- Ancient civilizations, such as the Greeks and Romans, used games to teach subjects such as strategy, history, and philosophy.
- In the 18th and 19th centuries, board games and puzzles were used as teaching tools in schools.

- In the 1960s, computer games began to emerge as a means of entertainment, but they were not yet widely used in education.
- In the 1970s, educational games such as The Oregon Trail and Lemonade Stand were developed to teach students about history and economics.
- In the 1980s, educational games continued to grow in popularity with the introduction of console games such as Math Blaster and Reader Rabbit.
- In the 1990s, with the widespread adoption of personal computers, educational software became a common tool in schools, with games and simulations used to teach a variety of subjects.
- In the 2000s, the rise of mobile devices and the internet led to a proliferation of educational games and gamified learning experiences.

Game-based learning can take many forms, from simple educational games that reinforce basic concepts like math or language skills, to more complex simulations that immerse students in real-world scenarios and challenge them to solve problems and make decisions.

The idea behind game-based learning is that it can increase student motivation and engagement, as well as provide opportunities for students to practice critical thinking, problem-solving, collaboration, and decision-making skills (Hartt, Hosseini, & Mostafapour, 2020). Games can also be designed to provide immediate feedback, which can help students better understand their strengths and weaknesses and improve their learning outcomes.

Game-based learning can be applied in a variety of educational settings, from early childhood education to higher education, as well as in corporate training and professional development (Dimitra, Konstantinos, Christina, & Katerina, 2020).

Here are some examples of where game-based learning can be applied:

- Basic education: Game-based learning can be used to teach a wide range of subjects, from math and science to history and language arts. Games can be designed to reinforce basic concepts, such as counting or vocabulary, or to teach more complex skills, such as critical thinking and problem-solving.
- Higher education: Game-based learning can be used in higher education to engage students in complex subject matter, such as business strategy, engineering, or medical diagnosis. Games can provide students with hands-on experience in applying theoretical concepts to real-world scenarios.
- Corporate training: Game-based learning can be used in corporate training and professional development to teach employees new skills, such as customer service or project management. Games can provide a safe and fun environment for employees to practice new skills and receive immediate feedback.

- Healthcare: Game-based learning can be used in healthcare to train medical professionals in patient diagnosis and treatment. Games can provide medical professionals with an opportunity to practice their skills in a safe and realistic environment, improving patient outcomes.

Game-based learning can be used in any context where there is a requirement to teach new abilities or strengthen existing knowledge in an entertaining and captivating manner.

There are several approaches to using game-based learning, depending on the learning goals and the target audience (Al-azawi, Al-faliti, & Al-blushi, 2016; Martens, Diener, & Malo, 2008; Randi & Carvalho, 2013). Here are a few examples:

- Gamification: This approach involves adding game elements to non-game activities, such as quizzes or assignments. For example, a quiz may include points or badges that are earned for correct answers, or a course may include a leaderboard that tracks student progress.
- Simulation: This approach involves creating realistic scenarios that allow learners to practice skills or decision-making in a safe and controlled environment. For example, a simulation game may allow healthcare professionals to practice diagnosing and treating patients, or a business simulation may allow students to practice running a company.
- Role-playing: This approach involves assigning learners specific roles or characters to play, which helps to create a more immersive and engaging learning experience. For example, a language learning game may involve role-playing as a tourist navigating a foreign city, or a history game may involve role-playing as a historical figure.
- Game-based assessments: This approach involves using games as a form of assessment to measure learning outcomes. For example, a math game may include questions that assess the learner's understanding of math concepts, or a language game may assess the learner's ability to use vocabulary and grammar correctly.

Game-based learning strategies can be customized to match the learning objectives and demands of the audience, resulting in increased engagement, motivation, and improved learning results.

Game-based learning offers several advantages over traditional forms of teaching and learning. Here are a few key advantages (Hawlitschek & Köppen, 2013):

- Increased engagement and motivation: Games are inherently fun and engaging, which can increase student motivation and interest in learning.

When students are more engaged, they are more likely to retain information and be active participants in the learning process.

- Active learning: Games require active participation and problem-solving, which can help students develop critical thinking and decision-making skills. Active learning is also more effective at promoting long-term retention of information.

- Personalized learning: Games can be designed to adapt to the learner's individual needs and learning style, providing a personalized learning experience. This can help to address gaps in knowledge and provide additional support to struggling learners.

- Immediate feedback: Games can provide immediate feedback on performance, which can help learners understand their strengths and weaknesses and adjust their learning strategies accordingly. Immediate feedback is also more effective at promoting learning than delayed feedback.

- Safe environment for experimentation: Games can provide a safe and controlled environment for learners to experiment with new ideas and strategies. This can help to build confidence and reduce the fear of failure, which can be a barrier to learning.

Game-based learning can be an effective way to promote engagement, motivation, and learning outcomes, and can provide a fun and immersive learning experience for learners of all ages.

Here are some strategies to follow when using game-based learning (Ifenthaler, Eseryel, & Ge, 2012; Pan et al., 2021):

- Set clear learning goals: Identify specific learning goals and objectives that align with the curriculum or training objectives. Games should be designed to reinforce these learning goals and help learners achieve them.

- Design for the target audience: Games should be designed with the target audience in mind, taking into consideration their age, interests, and learning needs. Design elements, such as graphics and language, should be appropriate for the target audience.

- Ensure games are aligned with the curriculum: Games should be aligned with the curriculum or training objectives and should complement, not replace, traditional teaching methods. Games should be used to reinforce learning, not as a standalone teaching method.

- Provide clear instructions: Games should have clear instructions and objectives, and learners should be given guidance on how to play the game. Instructions should be concise and easy to understand, and learners should have access to tutorials or help guides if needed.

- Provide feedback and rewards: Games should provide immediate feedback on performance and rewards for progress and achievement. Feedback should be constructive and provide guidance on how to improve, and rewards should be motivating and aligned with the learning goals.
- Test and refine: Games should be tested and refined to ensure they are effective at achieving the learning goals. Feedback from learners should be solicited and used to make improvements to the game.

Educators and trainers can utilize game-based learning as a potent method to enhance engagement and learning results. These strategies can be implemented to create games that consolidate learning while providing an exciting and captivating learning experience suitable for learners of all ages.

Augmented Reality (AR) and Virtual Reality (VR) can enhance game-based learning experiences by providing immersive and interactive environments that allow learners to engage with digital content in new and exciting ways. Here are some ways that AR and VR can be used in game-based learning (Oyelere et al., 2020; Pellas, Fotaris, Kazanidis, & Wells, 2019):

1. Simulation-based learning: AR and VR can be used to create realistic simulations that allow learners to practice skills or decision-making in a safe and controlled environment. For example, a VR simulation game may allow healthcare professionals to practice surgical procedures, or a safety training game may allow workers to practice handling hazardous materials.
2. Interactive exploration: AR and VR can be used to create interactive environments that allow learners to explore and interact with digital content in 3D. For example, an AR game may allow learners to explore a historical site, or a VR game may allow learners to explore a virtual laboratory.
3. Gamified assessments: AR and VR can be used to create gamified assessments that measure learning outcomes in a fun and engaging way. For example, an AR game may include questions that assess the learner's understanding of scientific concepts, or a VR game may assess the learner's ability to apply critical thinking skills in a specific scenario.
4. Personalized learning: AR and VR can be used to provide learners with personalized learning experiences by adapting the game to their individual learning needs and preferences. For example, an AR game may adjust the level of difficulty based on the learner's performance, or a VR game may provide additional support for struggling learners.

AR and VR can significantly enhance the game-based learning experience by creating immersive and interactive environments that excite and engage learners.

Integrating AR and VR into game-based learning enables educators and trainers to develop dynamic and effective learning experiences that promote learning outcomes, resulting in improved engagement and motivation for learners.

PROJECT-ORIENTED APPROACH IN LEARNING ENVIRONMENTS

Project-based learning (PBL) consists in a methodology where students learn by actively engaging in real-world, personally meaningful projects. It involves a structured approach to learning, which typically includes defining the problem or challenge, planning and implementing a solution, and evaluating and reflecting on the outcomes of the project (DeFillippi, 2001). PBL is characterized by being a teaching strategy where students gain knowledge and skills by working over a long period of time to investigate and respond to an authentic, engaging, and complex question, problem, or challenge. There are several studies highlighting evidence about its efficacy in engagement and outcomes (Almulla, 2020; Guo, Saab, Post, & Admiraal, 2020).

Project-based learning main characteristics are the existence of a time frame, as in any project-oriented activity, and the engagement in solving a real-world problem or answering a complex question, but also the demonstration of knowledge and skills by creating a public product or presentation for a real audience. In a broader view of education, it can also be seen as an educational opportunity for equity, diversity and inclusion (Lantada, 2022).

In addition to develop in-depth content knowledge, this teaching-learning methodology has as its main results the development of the skills of critical thinking, problem solving, collaboration, creativity and communication (Wurdinger & Qureshi, 2015), also known as the students 21st-century skills (Stehle & Peters-burton, 2019).

The well-known Project Management Institute, through its Educational Foundation, established, with other partners, the Framework for High Quality Project Based Learning, which describes six criteria that characterize student experiences in high quality projects (PMIEF, 2018):

1. Intellectual challenge and accomplishment: To complete a project successfully, students need to learn important academic content, concepts, and skills. Therefore, projects should not just be "fun activities" or "hands-on experiences" requiring minimal intellectual effort.
2. Authenticity: Projects should be experienced as "real" to motivate students an also to show them the relevance of what they are learning.

3. Public product: In a high-quality project, students should make their work public by sharing with a diverse audience (with each other, experts, and other people beyond the classroom), not only with the teacher in private relationship.
4. Collaboration: There are always individual activities, which are necessary, but it is also very important to learn the skill of collaboration. Students should work in teams to complete complex tasks and should learn to become effective team members and leaders.
5. Project management: The culture of project management is very important because people work on projects whether it's on the job or in their personal lives. The use of project management processes, tools, and strategies like those used in the world is very benefic and didactic. Students start earlier experiencing how to manage time, tasks, and resources efficiently.
6. Reflection: Reflection is a tool to increase students own personal agency. Learning is reinforced when they reflect on what they know and do. Reflection on what was accomplished allows a longer retention of project content and skills, develop a greater sense of control over education, and build confidence.

United Nations, European Union and Organisation for Economic Co-operation and Development regularly reflect on the quality of higher education institutions and the need to promote students' skills and teachers' practices. PBL is one of the most frequently denoted as a reference of student-centered methodology (Ravitz, Hixson, English, & Mergendoller, 2012).

An important topic, current and of enormous importance in the coming decades is digitization. In the context of PBL the dichotomous view of technologies as a risk for learning or a distraction should be well thought out (Dias & Mergendoller, 2019). In fact, it can be integrated in planning and in promoting richer learning environments, freeing the teacher from the role of information provider and allowing new and more stimulant roles (Sarkar, 2012).

Implementing project-based can be challenging, but also very rewarding, for teachers and students alike. Some of the steps that can help implement this learning approach are as follows (Kokotsaki, Menzies, & Wiggins, 2016):

1. Define the learning objective: Defining the learning objectives that will be achieved through this learning approach is an important step. It is necessary to choose a project that is relevant and challenging for the students, and at the same time that is aligned with the skills and content that must be learned.
2. Organize students into teams: It is important to form teams of students who work together to solve the problem or carry out the project. This allows students to develop team collaboration, communication, and problem-solving skills.

3. Identify resources: Identifying resources and materials needed to carry out the project or solve the problem is crucial. Resources can include books, articles, videos, interviews, software tools and other topic-related materials.
4. Accompanying and guiding students: The teacher's role is to guide students, offering support and guidance during the learning process. Teachers must be available to help students identify sources of information, plan their activities, and provide constructive feedback.
5. Evaluate performance: Evaluating student performance is important to monitor progress, check understanding of concepts, and identify opportunities for improvement. The evaluation can be done through presentations, reports, group work and other forms of demonstration of the acquired knowledge.

Implementing project-based learning takes time, dedication, and careful planning, but it can be an exciting and enriching experience for students and teachers alike. In fact, it generates a contagious and creative energy among students and teachers, if it is well prepared. A basic characteristic is that project contains and frames curriculum and instruction, being the vehicle for teaching the important knowledge and skills that the student needs to learn. It should be emphasized here that this is different from the situation where a (usually lighter) project is launched after the teacher has taught the content of a unit in the "usual" way.

AUTONOMOUS CREATIVE LEARNING STRATEGY

Information and Communication Technologies have become an essential part of education, training, and professional development of the future health care professionals. ICTs provide the necessary tools for academic and professional development, making it easier to acquire knowledge and skills. The empowerment of future health professionals will be reflected in their professional performance, increasing their productivity and efficiency.

The acquisition of digital skills is an added value for the academic path of future health professionals. The development of these skills will provide a greater competitive advantage, which is reflected in the entry into the job market and in their future professional progression.

In the academic field, digital skills facilitate access to information, allowing to identify and select appropriate information sources, giving students access to a wide range of resources, including digital libraries, online journals, and databases. The use of collaboration and communication tools allow students to work together on projects and assignments. Distance Learning platforms enable online and distance learning, which allows students to access to educational resources from anywhere. ICTs can also be used to create interactive and engaging learning experiences, which can lead to better learning outcomes.

On a professional level, ICTs provide access to professional development resources, such as webinars and online courses, which can help individuals improve their skills and advance their careers. Remote working, teleconferencing, and virtual collaboration can increase productivity, and provide access to specialized health care for disadvantaged populations due to their geographic location or access difficulties.

Teaching information and communication technologies to health higher education students is fundamental for the acquisition of digital skills, however it can present significant challenges. One of the challenges is the lack of knowledge or experience with the technology among both students and teachers of curricular units that are not related to ICT. The cost and availability of the necessary equipment and resources is also a limitation to the use of ICTs in the classroom context. But the most significant challenge is perhaps the clear understanding of the technology and its potential applications, as well as the ability to effectively communicate and integrate it into the curriculum, and it is essential that teachers keeping up with the rapid pace of technological advancements and ensuring that the curriculum stays current.

For a sustainable use of ICTs in the academic path of students, institutions must consider some fundamental aspects, such as, ensure that students have access to the appropriate equipment and software, and that they develop the necessary technical skills to use them, avoid the digital divide by ensuring that students from disadvantaged backgrounds have access to the same resources and opportunities as their peers, integrate technology into the curriculum in meaningful and relevant ways that enhance the learning experience and ensure that the use of technology increases student productivity and is not a distraction.

During the teaching/learning process for the acquisition of digital skills, the approach on the potential of technology to complement human interaction in healthcare environments must consider that students should be aware about the impact of technology on patient privacy and confidentiality.

A project oriented Autonomous Creative Learning Strategy (ACLS) allows students to learn and adapt on their own, taking an active role in their learning and minimizing teacher intervention. This method empowers students with autonomous and creative learning capabilities to come up with a solution. During the project they receive feedback and guidance from experts to improve their performance.

Project-oriented learning is an approach where students learn by working on projects or real-world problems. Gamification can be used as a motivation strategy in learning strategies and knowledge transmission (Veloso Gomes, Donga, & Sá, 2021). Innovative teaching using different forms of technology may be required to fully engage new generations (Shatto & Erwin, 2017). The implementation of gamification in project development is a motivating factor for students and helps them to set goals and deadlines.

Immersive environments create impactful experiences. The use of virtual reality is highly motivating for students, captures attention, stimulates the senses, and awakens creativity. The contact with immersive environments, which they are not used to, breaks down epistemological obstacles and promotes the search for more creative and unconventional solutions to problems.

The proposal as a development challenge is a transversal team project, which crosses the area of ICT with the area of the course, allowing the student to feel the relationship between the potential of technology and their future professional area. To carry out the project, divided by steps, it will be necessary to apply different contents that are part of discipline. This problem-solving approach, using specific software tools, allows to explore the potential of information technologies in health sciences.

It is intended that students achieve some fundamental objectives, such as, identify the different features provided by new ICTs; understand the importance of information technologies in health activities and research; recognize and understand the social, professional, and scientific implications of the use of Information Technologies to support communication and transmission of knowledge, and apply Information Technology as support tools for the development of activities and teamwork.

To respond to the proposed challenge, students must develop skills in several ICT areas, such as:

- Collaborative Tools: Communicating, collaborating, sharing and managing work information are essential skills. All team members must have, at any time, access to all the information that is being produced about the work.
- Health Information Sources Management: Identify different types of information sources and apply information validation technics.
- Search and Information Retrieval on the Internet: Understand the semantic and technical aspects and design an adequate information search strategy using knowledge bases. The use of concept maps is an added value for this item.
- Documentation Management in Health Sciences: Content Analysis, bibliographic management software and information security.
- Plan and organize multimedia presentations: Use software for image, sound and video processing. The construction of a multimedia animation is an excellent task where all these items can be applied. Narratives and storytelling can be especially useful to understand varying viewpoints and use critical thinking (Shatto & Erwin, 2017).
- Writing scientific documents: Word Processor, spreadsheet.

In this project, the teacher assumes a mentorship role in the learning process, after defining the general lines of the project and establishing the main objectives, his role will be to monitor, follow up and be available to respond to students' requests. In addition to transmitting the theoretical concepts, accompanied by a demonstrative aspect that allows students to understand the practical application of knowledge, the teacher should be a facilitator and should promote critical thinking.

Students are given the autonomy to self-motivate and build their own self-directed learning. It is important that they identify their knowledge needs and look for the ways that they consider most appropriate for solving problems. The search for creative solutions should be strongly encouraged and decision-making processes must always be well-founded.

Encouraging students to use their own technology is very important, they bringing their own devices (mobile phones, tablets) into the learning environment increase their involvement and it facilitates the way they manage information (Shatto & Erwin, 2017).

Generation Z students are "compulsive" video consumers (Shatto & Erwin, 2017). Video-based learning can be used to explain a theory or concept or to demonstrate a challenging process (Schenarts, 2019; Seemiller & Meghan, 2017). Visual forms of learning are more effective for them (Cilliers, 2017).

Knowing how to deal with information is vital. Identify the more reliable information sources, analyze summarize, and synthesize the content are fundamental skills (Mohr & Mohr, 2017). Comparing information from different sources allows validation and encourages critical thinking. Representing the same information in different ways is a challenge. Exploring different formats, text, visual formats (diagrams, infographics), video, as well as directing the same information to different target audiences, forces the search for creative solutions and develops critical thinking.

The final presentation of the work to the whole class is an enriching moment of knowledge sharing. At this stage, in addition to communication skills, students have the opportunity to learn about the projects developed by other teams, develop a critical thinking and share creative solutions (Seemiller & Meghan, 2017).

FUTURE RESEARCH DIRECTIONS

Nowadays, any area of activity depends to a large extent on information and communication technologies, the health area is no exception. Technology by itself is not of great value. Its true value emerges in its application in information systems and integration in human activity systems.

Some challenges are identified in this area, the volume of knowledge needed to train a health professional is ever-increasing, and the degree of specialization required is extremely high. The training time and the number of curricular units' condition and limit the choices of syllabus contents. Specific content is often prioritized to the detriment of other skills, for this reason, many course programs choose not to include ICT skills in their curricula. This type of decision occurs when there is no awareness that ICT skills are fundamental and enhance the acquisition of information and knowledge in all other areas.

The inclusion of ICT curricular units in the course curriculum must be done in such a way as to integrate ICT skills with the different areas of knowledge of the courses.

CONCLUSIONS

Teaching information and communication technologies to students who belong to the Z and Alpha generation is a complex and dynamic process. It involves human, technological, cultural, and procedural factors. This group of students has some specific characteristics that must be considered when designing teaching/learning strategies. As digital native learners, they demonstrate a keen affinity for using technology in their daily tasks, on the other hand, too much confidence can be an obstacle to the predisposition to acquire new knowledge and skills.

The teaching of information and communication technologies can be integrated into different multidisciplinary projects that take place throughout the course. This integration enhances the different areas of knowledge, on the one hand students have a real perception of the importance and usefulness of ICT skills, on the other hand, the development of these skills will be a facilitator for the acquisition of knowledge in the specific areas of the course.

The Autonomous Creative Learning Strategy directed to higher education students in the health area is a project-oriented approach. This strategy uses interactive and immersive game-based learning activities, develops different soft skills through teamwork, appeal to creativity, autonomy encourage proactivity, self-learning, and the constant search for continuous improvement. This method allows students to identify their needs for knowledge and apply in practice the knowledge gained to achieve the proposed objectives, it is an effective way to engage students and promote deeper understanding of the subject matter.

REFERENCES

Al-azawi, R., Al-faliti, F., & Al-blushi, M. (2016). Educational Gamification Vs. Game Based Learning : Comparative Study. *International Journal of Innovation, Management and Technology*, *7*(4), 131–136. doi:10.18173/ijimt.2016.7.4.659

Almulla, M. A. (2020). The Effectiveness of the Project-Based Learning (PBL) Approach as a Way to Engage Students in Learning. *SAGE Open*, *10*(3). Advance online publication. doi:10.1177/2158244020938702

Brice, S., & Almond, H. (2020). Health Professional Digital Capabilities Frameworks: A Scoping Review. *Journal of Multidisciplinary Healthcare*, *2*(13), 1375–1390. doi:10.2147/JMDH.S269412 PMID:33173300

Cilliers, E. J. (2017). The Challenge of Teaching Generation Z. *The International Journal of Social Sciences (Islamabad)*, *3*(1), 188–198. doi:10.20319/pijss.2017.31.18819

DeFillippi, R. (2001). Introduction: Project-Based Learning, Reflective Practices and Learning Outcomes. *Management Learning*, *32*(1), 5–10. doi:10.1177/1350507601321001

Dias, P., & Mergendoller, J. (2019). Plagiarism vs. Pedagogy: Implications of Project-Based Learning Research for Teachers in the 21st Century. In D. Velliaris (Ed.), Scholarly Ethics and Publishing: Breakthroughs in Research and Practice (pp. 247–266). IGI Global. doi:10.4018/978-1-5225-8057-7.ch026

Dimitra, K., Konstantinos, K., Christina, Z., & Katerina, T. (2020). Types of Game-Based Learning in Education : A brief state of the art and the implementation in Greece. *The European Educational Researcher*, *3*(2), 87–100. doi:10.31757/euer.324

Eta Berner. (2020). *Informatics Education in Healthcare. Lessons Learned* (E. S. Berner, Ed.; 2nd ed.). Springer Cham., doi:10.1007/978-3-030-53813-2

Fernandes, A. C. (2022). *Saúde em Portugal: pensar o futuro*. Coimbra: Editora D'Ideias.

Geck, C. (2007). The generation Z connection: Teaching information literacy to the newest net generation. In E. Rosenfeld & D. Loertscher (Eds.), *Toward a 21st-century school library media program* (pp. 807–828).

Guo, P., Saab, N., Post, L. S., & Admiraal, W. (2020). A review of project-based learning in higher education: Student outcomes and measures. *International Journal of Educational Research*, *102*, 101586. doi:10.1016/j.ijer.2020.101586

Hartt, M., Hosseini, H., & Mostafapour, M. (2020). Game On: Exploring the Effectiveness of Game-based Learning. *Planning Practice and Research*, *35*(5), 589–604. doi:10.1080/02697459.2020.1778859

Hawlitschek, A., & Köppen, V. (2013). Analyzing Player Behavior in Digital Game - Based Learning: Advantages and Challenges. In *8th European conference on games based learning. Academic Conferences and Publishing International* (pp. 199–206). Retrieved from https://wwwiti.cs.uni-magdeburg.de/iti_db/publikationen/ps/auto/HK14.pdf

Ifenthaler, D., Eseryel, D., & Ge, X. (2012). Assessment for Game-Based Learning. In X. Ifenthaler, D., Eseryel, D., Ge (Ed.), Assessment in Game-Based Learning (pp. 1–8). Springer, New York, NY. doi:10.1007/978-1-4614-3546-4_1

Information Literacy Competency Standards for Higher Education. (2000). Retrieved from https://alair.ala.org/handle/11213/7668

Jaiswal, A. (2021). Revisiting the Historical Roots of Game-Based Learning. *TechTrends*, *65*(3), 243–245. doi:10.100711528-021-00603-x

Jan, M., & Gaydos, M. (2016). What Is Game-Based Learning? Past, Present, and Future Learning with Games. *Educational Technology*, *56*(3), 6–11. https://www.jstor.org/stable/44430486

Kokotsaki, D., Menzies, V., & Wiggins, A. (2016). Project-based learning: A review of the literature. *Improving Schools*, *19*(3), 267–277. doi:10.1177/1365480216659733

Kostkova, P. (2015). Grand challenges in digital health. *Frontiers in Public Health*, *3*(134). Advance online publication. doi:10.3389/fpubh.2015.00134 PMID:26000272

Lantada, A. D. (2022). Engineering Education 5.0: Strategies for a Successful Transformative Project-Based Learning. In M. Bouezzeddine (Ed.), *Insights Into Global Engineering Education After the Birth of Industry 5.0* (p. 19)., doi:10.5772/intechopen.102844

Magalhães, T. (2022). *Transformação Digital em Saúde*. Almedina.

Martens, A., Diener, H., & Malo, S. (2008). Game-based Learning with Computers – Learning, Simulations, and Games Alke Martens University of Rostock Department of Computer Science and Electrical Engineering Holger Diener, Steffen Malo. In A. Pan, Z., Cheok, A.D., Müller, W., El Rhalibi (Ed.), Transactions on Edutainment I. Lecture Notes in Computer Science (Vol. 5080, pp. 172–190). Springer, Berlin, Heidelberg. doi:10.1007/978-3-540-69744-2_15

Mesquita, A., Santos, D., & Raposo, V. (2021). A gestão do conhecimento em contexto hospitalar: Uma scoping review. *Revista De Investigação & Inovação Em Saúde*, *4*(2), 99–110. doi:10.37914/riis.v4i2.172

Mohr, K., & Mohr, E. (2017). Understanding Generation Z Students to Promote a Contemporary Learning Environment. *Journal on Empowering Teaching Excellence*, *1*(1). Advance online publication. doi:10.1016/j.ijhm.2018.01.016

Oyelere, S. S., Bouali, N., Kaliisa, R., Obaido, G., Yunusa, A. A., & Jimoh, E. R. (2020). Exploring the trends of educational virtual reality games: A systematic review of empirical studies. *Smart Learning Environments*, *7*(31), 31. Advance online publication. doi:10.118640561-020-00142-7

Pan, L., Tlili, A., Li, J., Jiang, F., Shi, G., Yu, H., & Yang, J. (2021). How to Implement Game-Based Learning in a Smart Classroom? A Model Based on a Systematic Literature Review and Delphi Method. *Frontiers in Psychology*, *12*(December), 1–13. doi:10.3389/fpsyg.2021.749837 PMID:34925153

Pellas, N., Fotaris, P., Kazanidis, I., & Wells, D. (2019). Augmenting the learning experience in primary and secondary school education : A systematic review of recent trends in augmented reality game - based learning. *Virtual Reality (Waltham Cross)*, *23*(4), 329–346. doi:10.100710055-018-0347-2

PMIEF. (2018). Framework for high quality project based learning. *Project Management Institute Educational Foundation*, 1–6. Retrieved from https://hqpbl.org/wp-content/uploads/2018/03/FrameworkforHQPBL.pdf

Randi, M., & Carvalho, H. (2013). Learning Through Role-Playing Games: An Approach for Active Learning and Teaching. *Revista Brasileira de Educação Médica*, *37*(1), 80–88. doi:10.1590/S0100-55022013000100012

Ravitz, J., Hixson, N., English, M., & Mergendoller, J. (2012). Using project based learning to teach 21 st century skills : Findings from a statewide initiative. In *Annual Meetings of the American Educational Research Association.* Vancouver, BC.

Reyes, A. Jr, Galvan, R. Jr, Navarro, A., Velasquez, M., Soriano, D. R., Cabuso, A. L., David, J. R., Lacson, M. L., Manansala, N. T., & Tiongco, R. E. (2020). Across Generations: Defining Pedagogical Characteristics of Generation X, Y, and Z Allied Health Teachers Using Q-Methodology. *Medical Science Educator*, *30*(4), 1541–1549. doi:10.100740670-020-01043-7 PMID:34457822

Sarkar, S. (2012). The role of information and communication technology (ICT) in higher education for the 21st century. *Science*, *1*(1), 30–41.

Schenarts, P. J. (2019). Now Arriving: Surgical Trainees From Generation Z. *Journal of Surgical Education*, *77*(2), 246–253. doi:10.1016/j.jsurg.2019.09.004 PMID:31562032

Seemiller, C., & Meghan, G. (2017). Generation Z: Educating and Engaging the Next Generation of Students. *About Campus: Enriching the Student Learning Experience*, *22*(3), 21–26. doi:10.1002/abc.21293

Shatto, B., & Erwin, K. (2017). Teaching Millennials and Generation Z: Bridging the Generational Divide. *Creative Nursing*, *23*(1), 24–28. doi:10.1891/1078-4535.23.1.24 PMID:28196564

Singh, A. P., & Dangmei, J. (2016). Understanding the generation Z: The Future Workforce. *South -. Asian Journal of Multidisciplinary Studies*, *3*(3), 1–5.

Stehle, S. M., & Peters-burton, E. E. (2019). Developing student 21 st Century skills in selected exemplary inclusive STEM high schools. *International Journal of STEM Education*, *6*(39), 1–15. doi:10.118640594-019-0192-1

Topol, E. (2019). High-performance medicine: The convergence of human and artificial intelligence. *Nature Medicine*, *25*(1), 44–56. https://doi.org/https://doi.org/10.1038/s41591-018-0300-7. doi:10.103841591-018-0300-7 PMID:30617339

Veloso Gomes, P., Donga, J., & Sá, V. J. (2021). Software requirements definition processes in gamification development for Immersive environments. In R. A. P. de Queirós & A. J. Marques (Eds.), *Handbook of Research on Solving Modern Healthcare Challenges With Gamification* (pp. 68–78). IGI Global., doi:10.4018/978-1-7998-7472-0.ch005

Wurdinger, S., & Qureshi, M. (2015). Enhancing College Students' Life Skills through Project Based Learning. *Innovative Higher Education*, *40*(3), 279–286. doi:10.100710755-014-9314-3

Chapter 12
Using Web Tools in Lecture:
Example of Micro Teaching Lesson

Fatma Alkan
🆔 https://orcid.org/0000-0003-2784-875X
Hacettepe University, Turkey

Fatma Merve Mustafaoğlu
Hacettepe University, Turkey

ABSTRACT

New technologies have been widely used in educational environments, as in every field. Web tools attract attention to make learning processes more efficient and to make students active. The microteaching method offers pre-service teachers the opportunity to apply new teaching. The purpose of this research is to determine the pre-service teachers' perception of web tools in micro-teaching and to analyze them according to various variables. The research was designed in a quasi-experimental design model. 75 pre-service teachers studying at the faculty of education participated in the research. Teachers' perceptions towards using web 2.0 tools in lectures scale was used as a data collection tool. As a result of the research, it was determined that micro teaching applications had a significant effect on the pre-service teachers' perception of web tools competence. Pre-service teachers stated that the use of web tools while teaching is beneficial in terms of drawing attention to the lesson and attracting the attention of the students.

INTRODUCTION

The most basic goal of successful teacher education is to enable teacher candidates to gain effective learning strategies and experiences. According to Mishra and Koehler, improving preservice teachers' technological pedagogical content knowledge should

DOI: 10.4018/978-1-6684-8656-6.ch012

be one of the important goals of teacher education (Mishra & Koehler, 2006). In the 21st century, great developments have emerged in information and communication technologies. As a result of these developments, the use of technology in the learning-teaching process has become inevitable in order to increase efficiency in learning environments (Gaviria et al., 2015; Valencia-Arias et al., 2019). With the inclusion of technology in learning environments, it has become necessary for teachers to acquire the skills to use technology and to use technology efficiently/effectively at the same time (Küçükgöz, 2019). In this context, it can be stated that teachers have an important role in the integration of technology into learning environments (Suharwoto, 2006). In addition, teachers are expected to use technology in a way that increases the effectiveness of their lessons and integrates them with a correct pedagogical method (Ertmer & Ottenbreit-Leftwich, 2010; Şad & Göktaş, 2014).

Web 2.0 tools, which have become widespread in recent years, appear as tools that can be used with constructivist learning (Horzum, 2010). Web 2.0 tools can easily be used in learning environments as a technological innovation that supports the change in the education system. In various studies, one of the principles of being a constructivist teacher is the ability to use interactive materials (Brooks, 1999). It is recommended to use technological tools integrating with pedagogical methods to prepare such materials and course contents (Ertmer & Ottenbreit-Leftwich, 2010; Şad & Göktaş, 2014). One of these syntheses is microteaching applications supported by Web 2.0 tools. The application of interactive materials prepared using Web 2.0 tools in microteaching method offers preservice teachers the opportunity to both learn to use technology and evaluate their own teaching performance (Walker & White, 2013). Fırat and Köksal (2019) stated that the use of Web 2.0 technologies by preservice teachers strengthens their level of integration into the teaching processes in their future classes, and in this context, it is a necessity to support teacher training programs with Web 2.0 technologies.

Micro-teaching is a method that offers preservice teachers the opportunity to practice, experience and self-evaluate the skill to be developed before they show their teaching skills in the real classroom environment (Atav et al., 2014). Microteaching is a process in which the preservice teacher prepares a short lecture (planning), presents this lecture to a group of preservice teachers (teaching), and then evaluates herself/himself (reflection) through reflection and feedback (Diana, 2013; Peker, 2009). Diana (2013) emphasizes that integrating technology tools into microteaching applications at any or all of the planning, teaching and reflection steps of microteaching will enrich the method. Microteaching through audio-visual web tools increases preservice teachers' self-confidence and provides a safe, threat-free environment for them to reflect on their practices (Dixon et al., 2019). In this study, it was aimed to determine the effect of microteaching applications supported by

Web 2.0 technology on the perceptions of preservice teachers using Web 2.0 tools and their concerns about microteaching. The research questions are as follows:

1. What is the effect of microteaching applications supported by Web 2.0 technology on preservice teachers' perceptions of using Web 2.0 tools?
2. What are the reasons for preservice teachers' concerns about microteaching practices?

BACKGROUND

For many years, it has been tried to determine whether teacher candidates have acquired the targeted professional competencies in their learning processes or not. It has been argued that whether preservice teachers have achieved these competencies should be supported by performance measurements ((Darling-Hammond, 2010; Kavas & Özdener, 2012). In the training programs, the opportunity to apply the knowledge of the field that they have learned should be provided to the preservice teachers, and they should be given the opportunity to receive feedback, re-apply and continue to develop during this application process (Darling-Hammond, 2010). Based on this, Allen et al. used microteaching as a tool to train teachers in terms of a few teaching skills determined in the 1960s (Higgins & Nicholl, 2003; Şahinkayası, 2009). The microteaching model developed by Allen et al. at Stanford University is designed to serve three main purposes. The identified objectives are as follows:

1. To enable preservice teachers to practice to improve their teaching skills,
2. To investigate the effects of education in controlled learning environments,
3. Providing in-service training support to experienced teachers (Allen, 1967)

While micro-teaching provides preservice teachers with the opportunity to transform theoretical knowledge into practice (Ostrosky, et al., 2013), on the other hand, it enables them to notice the correct and wrongs made in practice and correct their mistakes (Fisher & Burrell, 2011). Micro-teaching can only be possible if preservice teachers make an effort towards learning goals (Prediger et al., 2022). Feedback and reflection are key concepts in microteaching method (Farris, 1991; Karlström & Hamza, 2019; Thomas, 2023). It is important for preservice teachers to receive feedback after the application in terms of the effectiveness of micro-teaching and promoting reflection (Estaban et al., 2016; Ping, 2013). According to Kourieos (2016), video technology is the most effective among the different techniques used to support microteaching, due to its usefulness in reflection. The use of video recording in microteaching practices enables the preservice teacher to do self-reflection by watching herself/himself and supports her/his professional development (Birney et al., 2017).

It has been determined that micro-teaching, which is used as a teaching tool in teacher education, is a useful method to identify preservice teachers' deficiencies and misconceptions in content knowledge (Bahçivan, 2017; Gödek, 2016), increasing their self-efficacy (Arsal, 2014) and reducing their teaching anxiety (Peker, 2009). Besides, micro-teaching offers teachers and preservice teachers the opportunity to evaluate the learning-teaching approaches used in the process of transferring knowledge and to use different strategies for further teaching (Crichton et al., 2021).

Application of Microteaching in Teacher Education

The microteaching environment has been designed to simplify the difficulties encountered in the learning-teaching process. Class size, teaching time, teaching content, and tasks have been scaled down to give preservice teachers the most appropriate experience (He & Yan, 2011). Since the microteaching method is a small group application, it is limited in terms of course time and number of students. Attention is paid that the duration (time) of the lesson is between 5-20 minutes, and the number of students should not be less than 4 and more than 20 (Demirel, 1999; Fernandez, 2005; Huber & Ward, 2009; Ping, 2013; Wragg, 1999). In microteaching, lectures can be video-recorded during the teaching period or the counselor can take notes on the preservice teacher's lecture. After the lecture, the preservice teacher can evaluate herself/himself by watching/listening to herself/himself or by examining the notes of the guidance teacher. In addition, the preservice teacher receives feedback and suggestions from the guidance teachers and other preservice teachers (Ryan & Cooper, 1980; Teague et al., 1994). After the evaluations, the preservice teacher can re-teach the same lesson to another small group or to the same group in order to improve the determined teaching skill. Based on the repetition of the teaching skill determined in micro-teaching until it reaches the desired level, the number of times this application will be repeated depends on the decision of the guidance teacher (Demirel, 1999).

Current and Potential Advantages of Microteaching

Microteaching is a method that contributes to teacher education in basic aspects and has the potential to contribute. Microteaching facilitates the tracking of preservice teachers' progress in pedagogical content knowledge and subject matter knowledge (Baştürk, 2016); Fernandez, 2010). Micro teaching is a method that enables preservice teachers to adapt to the profession before starting the profession. With this method, it is ensured that preservice teachers gain experience and improve themselves before starting the profession in their own classes (Demirel, 1999). While microteaching helps preservice teachers overcome the difficulties and problems they may encounter in the classroom environment, it also provides them with the opportunity to increase their self-confidence (Brown, 1975).

In the micro-teaching process, preservice teachers may face situations that they may encounter in a real classroom environment. The aim of micro-teaching is to give prospective teachers an experience by lecturing to their peers away from the chaos of the classroom (Upadhyay, 2017). Microteaching method is used especially to improve the pedagogical skills of preservice teachers (Agyei & Voogt, 2012; Kafyulilo et al., 2015). Micro-teaching is a useful method in developing preservice teachers' skills in choosing instructional objectives, preparing lesson plans and presenting the lesson, and in solving the problems they encounter on these issues (Birney et al., 2017; Ng, 2017; Umuzdaş, 2010). In addition, it enables preservice teachers to realize the importance of planning, decision-making and implementation. (Gess-Newsome ve Lederman, 1990). Although microteaching is an effective method for the training of preservice teachers, it seems that it is not fully understood what it means (Bell, 2007). Digital technologies are considered to have the potential to improve microteaching applications. An implementation process using digital technologies that enable interactive reflection is needed. According to Tondeur et al., (2012), teacher education should focus on how to use technology in the teaching and learning process. Effectively integrating technology into teacher education offers great opportunities for preservice teachers to practice using technology when they begin their careers as classroom teachers (Dawson et al., 2003; Diana, 2013).

Using Web 2.0 Technology in Education

Today, new technologies have been widely used in learning environments, as in every field. One of the newest technologies that has attracted the attention of many educators worldwide is Web 2.0. Web 2.0 technology attracts attention as a term coined by O'Reilly in 2004 to explain the concept of grouping a set of design and functional features for web pages (O'Reilly, 2005). Web 2.0 is defined by McLoughlin and Lee (2007) as the second generation or more personalized communicative form of the World Wide Web, where users can develop content, collaborate with each other, and support the exchange of information and ideas among users. According to Deperlioğlu & Köse (2010), Web 2.0 is user-oriented web environments that can interact with the user, allow collaboration, and share easily. Web 2.0 includes web technologies that are widely used today, offer the opportunity to access information quickly and comfortably, include the user in the information creation process and are dynamic in structure (Çekinmez, 2009). Web 2.0 technologies, which motivate collaborative work, ensure the continuation of social interaction in the digital environment, and support different types of information sharing, are of interest to education (Deperlioğlu & Köse, 2010; Faizi et al., 2015). Studies reveal that Web 2.0 tools improve individuals' communication skills (Çalışkan et al., 2019), problem-solving skills (Koehler et al., 2017), and also have positive effects on individuals such as writing skills (Hartshorne & Ajjan, 2009) and collaboration (Zou et al., 2016).

These benefits of Web 2.0 technologies have made its integration into educational environments a necessity. By using Web 2.0 tools that can be easily integrated into every course, a course content can be created and learning environments suitable for this course content can be provided (Rich, 2008). The features of Web 2.0 tools such as easy content creation, sharing, social interaction and collaboration can be used in the organization of learning environments (Gül, 2022). Many Web 2.0 tools, especially wiki, blog and social media, are widely used in educational environments. In addition, many animation, communication and collaborative word processing tools used in educational environments that can attract students' attention are among Web 2.0 tools (Koehler et al., 2017). Some of the Web 2.0 tools used in learning environments are as follows (Avcı & Atik, 2020; Elmas & Geban, 2012);

- VoiceThread, which is used as a tool for preparing presentations containing audio and video,
- Google Drive as a file sharing and saving tool,
- Kahoot as an online assessment and evaluation tool,
- Powtoon as a digital story making tool,
- Wordpress as a blogging tool,
- Voki as an online meeting tool

Web 2.0 tools provide many advantages such as enriching the teaching processes in terms of interaction and quality, and developing positive attitudes and behaviors towards learning. However, the use of Web 2.0 tools in the lesson should be carried out in a controlled manner by the guidance counselor/preservice teacher, considering the problems that may arise such as the lack of knowledge of the preservice teachers about the use of technology (Lee et al., 2008) and security problems (Grosseck, 2009). It is thought that micro-teaching applications with feedback and video recording will be effective in providing this control.

MAIN FOCUS OF THE CHAPTER

Methodology

In the research, a single group pre-test post-test experimental design was used. The single-group pretest-posttest design is a type of research design often used by behavioral researchers to determine the impact of a treatment or intervention on a given sample. This research design is characterized by two features. The first feature is the use of a single group of participants (ie, single group design). This property indicates that all participants are part of a single condition; that is, all participants are given the same application and assessments. The second feature is a linear sequence (ie, a pretest-posttest design) that requires evaluation of a dependent variable before and after an implementation. In the pretest-posttest research designs, the effect of the application is determined by calculating the difference between the first evaluation and the final (Cranmer, 2017).

The single group pretest-posttest pattern is often carried out to reveal the importance of a new teaching method or to draw attention to an innovation in the curriculum. Here, the researcher measures the relevant characteristic of a group, such as attitude and achievement. Then it performs an experimental operation. This process is designed to increase the group's attitude or success. After an experimental procedure, the researcher measures the relevant characteristic of the group again. It examines the differences between pre-test and post-test scores by drawing attention to the effects of the applied experimental procedure (Cohen et al., 2007, p.282-284). Before starting the application process, students or participants are given a pre-test. The teaching is carried out by the teacher, the effectiveness of which will be examined, followed by a post-test. Here, the change in scores is examined (Mertler, 2022, p.129). In this research, the participants were determined on a voluntary basis. Before starting the applications, each participant was informed that the right to withdraw from the research at any time. In order to protect the privacy of the participants, the real names of the participants are not used in the research, and the participants are referred to as PT/number.

Participants

The sample of the research consists of 75 preservice teachers studying at the education faculty of a state university in Turkey. The sample of the study was determined by the purposive sampling method, which is one of the non-random sampling methods. Purposeful sampling is a sample selection using the personal judgments of researchers to select a sample based on a group's previous knowledge and the specific purpose of the research (Fraenkel et al. 2012). Purposive sampling is preferred because it is a widely used technique in qualitative research for identifying and selecting information-rich situations for the most effective use of limited resources (Patton, 2002). Preservice teachers who took the Micro Teaching course were included in the sample group. The preservice teachers who took the course and wanted to participate in the research were informed in advance about the purpose of the study. The research started with 75 preservice teachers. Six preservice teachers were excluded from the study because they did not continue later (n=6). The preservice teachers filled out a voluntary participation form before participating in the research. The sample of the research consists of 69 preservice teachers. Demographic information of the sample group is given in Table 1.

Table 1. Demographic details and characteristics of sampling

Categories		f	%
Gender	Female	50	72,5
	Male	19	27,5
Age	18-19	7	10,15
	20-21	25	36,23
	22-23	37	53,62
Programme	Primary Education	16	23,2
	Science Education	4	5,8
	Mathematics Education	3	4,3
	Biology Education	2	2,9
	Chemistry Education	7	10,1
	Physics Education	1	1,4
	Foreign Language Education	5	7,2
	Computer Education and Instructional Technology	4	5,8
	Turkish Education	5	7,2
	Physical Education	2	2,9
	Elementary Mathematics Education	6	8,7
	Early Childhood Education	5	7,2
	Guidance and Psychological Counseling	9	13
Grade	2. class	11	15,9
	3. class	25	36,2
	4. class	33	47,8
Total		69	100

Data Collection Tools

Quantitative data collection tool: Teachers' perceptions towards using Web 2.0 tools in lectures scale was used as a data collection tool in the research. The scale was developed by Yıldırım and Akkuş (2020). It consists of 22 items in 5-point Likert type. According to exploratory factor analysis, the scale has a two-factor structure. The first factor is perception towards using 12 items, and the second factor is professional competence perception 10 items. The Cronbach's alpha internal consistency coefficient of the scale was found to be .95. The Cronbach alpha internal consistency coefficient obtained from the sample data is .96.

Qualitative data collection tool: Two open-ended questions were prepared to examine in detail the opinions of preservice teachers about micro teaching application supported by web tools. In this form, "Does the lecturer in the micro-teaching class worry you?" and the second question "Explain the reason for your concern." has been asked. Preservice teachers were given approximately 20 minutes to answer the questions.

Application Process

The research was carried out in the Micro teaching course during the 2021-2022 fall semester. Micro teaching course is an elective course, it is carried out for two hours per week. Each preservice teacher's lectures twice in micro teaching. Within the scope of the course, information about microteaching is given during the first 5 weeks. This information includes the history of micro teaching, micro teaching and its applications in the world and in Turkey, etc. contains titles. For the next 9 weeks, preservice teachers do microteaching. Preservice teachers choose a topic, prepare for the topic and explain the lesson in 15 minutes. The first lecture is conducted as a classical teacher center. The second lecture was made using Web 2.0 tools. Before the lectures started, all preservice teachers completed the teachers' perceptions towards using Web 2.0 tools in lectures scale. After the second lecture was completed, that is, after the application was completed, the scale was filled as a posttest.

Data Analyses

Analysis of Quantitative Data

SPSS23 was used in the analysis of the data obtained from the study. After micro teaching applications supported by Web 2.0 tools, the difference between pre-test and post-test scores was examined with the paired samples t-test. First, the assumption of normality was checked. Whether the data of a research show a normal distribution or not is determined by using descriptive, graphical and statistical methods (Ghasemi & Zahediasl, 2012; Abbott, 2011).

In this direction, the assumption of normality of teachers' perceptions towards using Web 2.0 tools in lectures scale data was taken into descriptive, graphical and statistical analysis. Some statistics such as arithmetic mean, standard deviation, mode, median, kurtosis and skewness coefficients were analyzed in descriptive methods (Kirk, 2008).

In graphical methods for the assumption of normality, the position of the scale pretest-posttest data is presented visually according to whether it is on a line or not (McKillup, 2012). In graphical methods, the normal Q-Q, detrended normal Q-Q graph are examined, and normality is commented on by looking at the histogram and box-line graph.

The assumption of normality was finally examined by statistical methods. It is generally used here with the Shapiro-Wilks Test or the Kolmogorov-Smirnov Test (Abbott, 2011). In order for the data set to show a normal distribution, non-significant values should be obtained from these tests. Shapiro-Wilks Test results are taken into account when the number of people in the examined group is less than 50, and Kolmogorov-Smirnov Test results when it is more than 50 (Büyüköztürk, 2006). Teachers' perceptions towards using Web 2.0 tools in lectures scale, the assumption of normality was tested statistically with the significance level of the Kolmogorov Smirnov test.

Analysis of Qualitative Data

The qualitative data of the research were collected with two open-ended questions. The answers to the questions were analyzed by descriptive and content analysis. Descriptive analysis was carried out on the answers given to the first question. To the first question, "Does the lecturer in the microteaching class worry you?" Answers to this question were given as "yes" or "no". Here, yes-no answers were analyzed descriptively before and after the application. The second question is "Explain the reason for your concern." The answers to the question were analyzed by content analysis. Content analysis was carried out by following the steps of coding the data (1), creating the themes (2), organizing the codes and themes (3), identifying and interpreting the findings (4) (Yıldırım & Şimşek, 2013).

1. Coding the data: While coding the data, open coding technique was used. In the open coding technique, the data is analyzed word for word, sentence by sentence. In this way, the data are interpreted within the framework of their similarities and differences (Charmaz, 2006).
2. Finding the themes: The coded data is collected under themes, thematic coding is done.
3. Organizing the data according to themes and codes: Code and themes are defined with the data in the data set, and a meaningful relationship is created between codes and themes.

4.   Interpretation of the findings: The data are interpreted by the researcher and inferences are made.

In this study, the themes were presented with sample expressions directly quoted from the preservice teachers' sentences (eg [PT3]). For reliability studies, the percentage of agreement of the data submitted to the opinion of 2 experts was calculated. The data were analyzed independently by two researchers. The percentage of agreement between the raters was calculated as 0.92. This similarity rate also determines the reliability of qualitative analysis (Patton, 2002). It can be calculated using the Miles and Huberman formula (Miles & Huberman, 1994). This value indicates high reliability. An example of open coding and theme on a piece taken from the data set is given in Table 2.

Table 2. Example of coding based on qualitative data collection tool data

Data	Encoding	Themes
"It was worrying to be presenting in front of my other friends and lecturer in the class."	Excitement-anxiety	Affective domains

Findings

Quantitative Findings

Results on the normality assumption

The normality assumption of the teachers' perceptions towards using Web 2.0 tools in lectures scale data was taken into descriptive, graphical and statistical analysis. In descriptive methods, some statistics such as arithmetic mean, standard deviation, mode, median, kurtosis and skewness coefficients obtained from scale data were examined. The results are given in Table 3.

When the descriptive analysis results of Table 3 teachers' perceptions towards using Web 2.0 tools in lectures scale pretest-posttest dataset are examined, it is seen that mode and median values are similar to each other. When the kurtosis and skewness values of the data set are checked, it is noticed that they are between -1.5 and +1.5 recommended in the literature. Accordingly, the scale data set shows a descriptively normal distribution.

The normality assumption is secondly examined by graphical methods. In graphical methods, normal Q-Q, trend-free Q-Q graph is examined, and normality is interpreted

Table 3. Descriptive statistics for the observed variables

Observed variables		Mean	SD	Mode	Median	Min	Max	Skew.	Kurt.
Perception towards using	Pre-test	4.08	.64	4.00	4.00	2.00	5.00	-.713	.676
	Post-test	4.37	.47	5.00	4.33	3.33	5.00	-.275	-.694
Professional competence perception	Pre-test	3.56	.79	3.30	3.60	1.00	5.00	-.636	1.167
Perception towards using	Post-test	4.03	.71	4.00	4.00	2.00	5.00	-.527	-.137
	Pre-test	4.08	.64	4.00	4.00	2.00	5.00	-.713	.676

Note: Skew. = Skewness; Kurt. = Kurtosis.

by looking at histogram and box-line graph. For the normal distribution, a straight line is expected on the Q-Q graph, while there will be no point around the zero line in the trendless Q-Q graph. Teachers' perceptions towards using Web 2.0 tools in lectures scale pretest-posttest data were analyzed one by one with the normal Q-Q graph and the bias-free Q-Q graph. When the pre-test-post-test distributions of the sub-dimensions of the scale were examined, it was noticed that there were very few deviations from the normal when the normal Q-Q and the trend-free Q-Q graphs were examined. This situation is not at a level to prevent normal distribution. The scale pretest-posttest data show a normal distribution graphically.

The assumption of normality was examined statistically in a third method. For this, both the Shapiro-Wilks Test and the Kolmogorov-Smirnov Test were performed. In order for the data set obtained from the scale to show a normal distribution, non-significant values should be obtained from these tests. Statistical method results of Teachers' perceptions towards using web 2.0 tools in lectures scale are shown in Table 4.

Table 4. Teachers' perceptions towards using web 2.0 tools in lectures scale pretest-posttest tests of normality results

Observed variables		Kolmogorov-Smirnov			Shapiro-Wilk		
		Statistic	df	Sig.	Statistic	df	Sig.
Perception towards using	Pre-test	.101	69	.077(*)	.942	69	.003
	Post-test	.109	69	.055(*)	.933	69	.001
Professional competence perception	Pre-test	.094	69	.200(*)	.964	69	.046
	Post-test	.096	69	.194(*)	.955	69	.014

*p>0.05

Since the sample of the study was more than 50, Kolmogorov-Smirnov Test results were evaluated while examining statistical methods. This value is not significant in all sub-dimensions of the scale (p>0.05). According to the results of the statistical analysis, it is accepted that the data do not deviate from the normal distribution and statistically normality is assumed.

Perceptions Towards Using Web 2.0 Tools Pre-test Post-test Results.

As a result of the preliminary examinations, the data set meets the normality assumption descriptively, graphically and statistically. The effect of micro teaching application supported by Web 2.0 tools on the perception of web tools of teacher candidates was investigated. The dependent sample t-test was used to determine whether there was a significant difference between the teacher candidates' teachers' perceptions towards using Web 2.0 tools in lectures scale pretest and posttest findings. The results of the examination are given in Table 5.

Table 5. Paired Samples Test results perception towards using web 2.0 tools scale pretest-posttest scores

Observed variables		Mean	SD	df	t	p
Perception towards using	Pre-test	4.08	.64	68	-3.511	.001*
	Post-test	4.37	.47			
Professional competence perception	Pre-test	3.56	.79	68	-5.081	.001*
	Post-test	4.02	.71			

*p<0.05

When the table is examined, it is seen that there is a statistically significant difference between the pretest scores and posttest scores of teachers' perceptions towards using Web 2.0 tools in lectures scale's perception towards using and professional competence perception sub-dimensions (t=- 3.511, -5.081, p<0, 05). It is noteworthy that the preservice teachers' mean perception towards using dimension was (X: 4.08) before the micro-teaching application, while it was (X: 4.37) after the application. While the other dimension, professional competence perception, is average (X: 3.56), it is seen after the application (X: 4.02). Based on these results, it can be interpreted that the micro teaching application supported by Web 2.0 tools has a significant impact on the development of preservice teachers' perceptions towards using Web 2.0 tools in lectures.

Qualitative Findings

In this part of the findings, descriptive and content analysis of the data obtained from the qualitative data collection tool is given. The preservice teachers were first asked whether they were worried about giving lectures in the microteaching lesson. "Does the lecturer in a microteaching class worry you?" Answers to this question were given as "yes" or "no". The answers to this question before and after the application are shown in the Table 6.

Table 6. Descriptive statistics towards micro teaching anxiety

		f	%
Before application	Yes	34	49.3
	No	35	50.7
After application	Yes	16	23.2
	No	53	76.8

When the table is examined, it is noticed that half of the teacher candidates (f:34, 49.3%) were worried before the micro teaching application supported by Web 2.0 tools. The decrease in the number of people with anxiety after the application is remarkable (f:16, 23.2%).

Content Analysis on the Cause of Micro Teaching Anxiety

The second question directed to teacher candidates is "Explain the reason for your concern." The answers to this question were analyzed by content analysis. Content analysis was completed in 4 steps. These steps are; coding the data, finding the themes, organizing the data according to the themes and codes, and interpreting the findings. The coding of the data was done according to the open coding technique. After the application, 16 preservice teachers continued to worry. The data obtained from the answers of these people were gathered under three themes. These themes are Affective domains, Learning environment, Lack of using ICT/technology competence.

When the table is examined, it is seen that three themes emerged. These are Affective domains, Learning environment and Lack of using ICT/technology competence.

The first theme is affective domains. In this theme, preservice teachers are concerned about lecturing in micro teaching; they focused on affective characteristics such as uneasiness, anxiety, and fear of making mistakes, caused by being lecturing

Table 7. Themes and codes of micro teaching anxiety

Themes	Code
Affective domains	Excitement-Anxiety
	Inexperience
	Anxiety of making mistakes
Learning environment	Artificial class environment
	Time management
Lack of using ICT/technology competence	Anxiety of using web tools

for the first time. Affective domains are described by three codes. The codes in the Affective domains theme are "Excitement-Anxiety", "Inexperience" and "Anxiety of making mistakes".

Statements regarding the excitement-anxiety code are as follows: *"It was worrying to be presenting in front of my other friends and lecturer in the class [PT22], Lecture in front of the class was a concern in itself [PT35]"*. The statements of the second code, inexperience, are as follows with direct quotations: *"I didn't have much experience in presentation before and it wasn't very promising, that was the reason for my main concern [PT17], I think I would be excited because I had no experience [PT42]"*. The expressions of the anxiety of making mistakes code are as follows: *"I am afraid of the problems that may arise during the lecture [PT8], I am afraid of not being able to do my job properly [PT52]"*.

The second theme is learning environment. This theme is defined by artificial class environment and time management codes. In this theme, preservice teachers stated that lecturing to their peers in micro teaching does not create the real classroom environment, therefore it raises concerns. Another concern is time management. In micro teaching, teaching the planned lesson in a limited time creates anxiety. Statements related to the code of artificial class environment *"I was a little nervous and stressed by putting older people in the place of children and telling them about secondary school [PT23], I am comfortable talking to children, but I get too excited when presenting to adults [PT61]"*. The expressions related to the second code, the time management code, are as follows with direct quotations: *"The short duration of time and not being able to bring up the subject I will talk about [PT17]"*.

The third theme is Lack of using ICT/technology competence. This theme content is defined by anxiety of using web tools code. Preservice teachers generally have concerns about adapting technology tools to the lesson and using web tools in teaching. The expressions of this code are *"Using web 2.0 tool instead of using blackboard in my lesson frightens me [PT35], I was worried that I might have technological difficulties with web tools [PT22]".*

Discussion

This research was conducted to examine the effect of micro teaching application supported by Web 2.0 tools on the perception of preservice teachers to use web tools. In microteaching, a preservice teacher teaches a chosen topic twice. Each lecture takes a maximum of 15 minutes. In this study, the first lecture was made as face-to-face lecture in the classroom environment. The second lecture was supported by Web 2.0 tools and was carried out on pre-recorded video. The preservice teacher benefited from Web 2.0 tools at any stage of the second microteaching application (for example, introduction to the course, evaluation).

As a result of the research, it was determined that microteaching had a positive effect on improving the perception of teacher candidates towards using web tools. In the study conducted by Babacan & Şaşmaz Ören (2017), findings supporting the result of this research were obtained. In the research, it was concluded that technology-supported micro-teaching practices had a positive effect on the technology use perceptions of science teacher candidates. In the study conducted by Bang and Luft (2013), it was determined that the perceptions of newly graduated preservice teachers regarding the ability to use Web 2.0 technologies increased as a result of technology-supported applications. It is assumed that preservice teachers' perceptions of technology are important in terms of giving an idea about how they will use technology in their future careers (Babacan & Şaşmaz Ören, 2017). For this reason, it can be said that it is important to investigate the effects of technology-supported microteaching practices on preservice teachers' perceptions of technology use.

In the literature, there are studies examining the effects of microteaching practices supported by different technology tools on some cognitive, affective and behavioral characteristics of pre-service teachers. In the study conducted by Karalar & Altan (2018), the effect of microteaching applications supported by Web 2.0 tools on preservice teachers' web pedagogical content knowledge and teacher self-efficacy was investigated. According to the researchers, web pedagogical content knowledge includes the use of appropriate pedagogical models and web tools in teaching the subject area. As a result of the study, it was determined that the web pedagogical content knowledge and teacher self-efficacy levels of the preservice teachers changed positively at the end of the microteaching applications. In addition, it was concluded that micro-teaching applications supported by Web 2.0 tools increased the motivation of preservice teachers and their participation in the course. In her study, Cavin (2007) investigated the change in the technological pedagogical content knowledge (TPCK) of preservice teachers with the technology-supported microteaching method. As a result of the research, it was revealed that microteaching practices facilitated the technology integration of the preservice teachers and increased their TPCK levels. Microteaching is a method that produces effective results in improving that skill when it is focused and applied on a skill (Francis, 1997). Subramaniam (2006) emphasizes the importance of supporting the microteaching method with technological tools, video recording, expert criticism, and written/oral feedback for the microteaching method to be effective.

As a result of this research, when the sub-dimensions of the teachers' perceptions towards using Web 2.0 tools in lectures scale were examined, it was determined that the difference between the pre-test/post-test scores in the perception towards using and professional competence perception sub-dimensions was statistically significant. According to the results of the research, higher averages were obtained in the dimension of perception of using Web 2.0 tools. In other studies, preservice teachers stated that the use of web tools in the course makes the classroom environment fun, creates an interactive learning environment and contributes to the development of students' creativity (Akkaya, 2019; Babacan & Şaşmaz Ören, 2017).

According to the results of the research, it has been revealed that the professional competence perceptions of the preservice teachers are at a lower level than the perceptions of using Web 2.0 tools. This sub-factor examines preservice teachers' perceptions of their competence in using Web 2.0 tools effectively and adapting these tools to the course. Microteaching is accepted as a method that strengthens the steps that preservice teachers will take in the profession, increases their teaching quality and self-confidence by eliminating their professional deficiencies, and helps their professional development (Diana, 2013; Marulcu & Dedetürk, 2014; Tok, 2007). Having a lower mean in this dimension indicates that preservice teachers' perceptions of professional competence need to be improved. It can be said that the professional development perceptions of preservice teachers will change positively by increasing microteaching practices.

In the qualitative part of the research, preservice teachers were asked what their concerns about microteaching were and content analysis was conducted on the data obtained. As a result of the analysis, it was determined that preservice teachers had concerns about affective domains, learning environment and inadequacy of using technology. Preservice teachers stated that they had difficulty in the implementation process because they felt inexperienced, excited and worried about making mistakes during the implementation. In addition, it has been revealed that time management, unrealistic learning environment and anxiety about not being able to use web tools affect the implementation processes. The results obtained in this study are similar to the results of other researches in which preservice teachers have similar concerns (Karataş et al., 2020). In this direction, the researchers added a pre-micro-teaching step to the microteaching application process in order to reduce the negative effect of the anxiety factor and tried to evaluate the effectiveness of the developed microteaching application from the perspective of preservice teachers. As a result of the research, it was concluded that pre-micro teaching practices reduced the anxiety of pre-service teachers during the implementation process and increased their performance (Marulcu & Dedetürk, 2014; Karataş et al., 2020). Cho (2017) determined that preservice teachers have difficulties in planning and implementing micro-teaching practices. The preservice teachers' concerns about making mistakes and not being able to use web tools may have resulted from their inadequate perception of professional competence.

CONCLUSION

In this study, the effect of technology supported microteaching on preservice teachers' perceptions of the use of Web 2.0 tools was examined. The results obtained show that the perceptions of the preservice teachers changed positively after the applications. However, it was determined that their perceptions of professional competence for using web tools were lower than their perceptions for using Web 2.0 tools. Perception of professional skill in using Web 2.0 tools is evaluated as the ability to use web tools effectively and adapt these tools to the course. It was determined in line with the questions asked to them that the preservice teachers with a low perception of professional competence had anxiety about different reasons during the application process. Anxiety types of teacher candidates were classified and coded as affective domains, learning environment and lack of technology competence. Based on this study, more emphasis should be placed on supporting the development of pre-service teachers' professional competence in using web tools. In order to contribute to improving their perceptions of professional competence, targeted training that addresses the challenges they face can be provided and technical/academic support can be provided to use web tools effectively. And it is recommended to carry out studies to reduce the anxiety of preservice teachers in the microteaching process.

REFERENCES

Abbott, M. L. (2011). *Understanding educational statistics using Microsoft Excel and SPSS*. John Wiley & Sons, Inc.

Agyei, D., & Voogt, J. (2012). Developing technological pedagogical content knowledge in pre-service mathematics teachers, through collaborative design teams. *Australasian Journal of Educational Technology*, 28(4), 547–564. doi:10.14742/ajet.827

Akkaya, A. (2019). *The effect of the activities developed by Web 2.0 tools on computer hardware on student success* [Unpublished master's thesis]. Balıkesir University.

Allen, D. W. (1967). Microteaching, A description. Retrieved from https://files.eric.ed.gov/fulltext/ED019224.pdf

Arsal, Z. (2014). Microteaching and pre-service teachers' sense of self-efficacy in teaching. *European Journal of Teacher Education, 37*(4), 453–464. doi:10.1080/02619768.2014.912627

Atav, E., Kunduz, N., & Seçken, N. (2014). Pre-service teachers' views about micro teaching practices in biology education. *Hacettepe University Journal of Faculty of Education, 29*(4), 01-15.

Avcı, F., & Atik, H. (2020). Metaphoric perceptions and views of preschool and elementary teachers on the concept of "web 2.0 tools". *Qualitative Social Sciences, 2*(2), 142–165. doi:10.47105/nsb.800117

Babacan, T., & Şaşmaz Ören, F. (2017). The effect of technology assisted micro teaching practices on prospective science teachers' perceptions of technology usage. [Teknoloji destekli mikro öğretim uygulamalarının fen bilimleri öğretmen adaylarının teknoloji kullanım algıları üzerine etkisi]. *Educational Technology Theory and Practice, 7*(2), 193–214. doi:10.17943/etku.300412

Bahçivan, E. (2017). Implementing microteaching lesson study with a group of preservice science teachers: An encouraging attempt of action research. *International Online Journal of Educational Sciences, 9*(3), 591–602. doi:10.15345/iojes.2017.03.001

Bang, E., & Luft, J. A. (2013). Secondary science teachers' use of technology in the classroom during their first 5 years. *Journal of Digital Learning in Teacher Education, 29*(4), 118–126. doi:10.1080/21532974.2013.10784715

Baştürk, S. (2016). Investigating the effectiveness of microteaching in mathematics of primary pre-service teachers. *Journal of Education and Training Studies, 4*(5). Advance online publication. doi:10.11114/jets.v4i5.1509

Bell, N. D. (2007). Microteaching: What is it that is going on here? *Linguistics and Education, 18*(1), 24–40. doi:10.1016/j.linged.2007.04.002

Birney, L. B., Kong, J., Evans, B. R., Danker, M., & Grieser, K. (2017). Microteaching: An introspective case study with middle school teachers in New York City Public Schools. *Journal of Curriculum and Teaching, 6*(2), 1–5. doi:10.5430/jct.v6n2p1

Brown, G. (1975). *Micro-teaching: A program of teaching skills*. Harper & Row.

Bulut, K., Açık, F., & Çiftçi, Ö. (2016). The Effect of microteaching on pre-service Turkish language teachers' speaking skills. *Journal of Mother Tongue Education*, *4*(1), 134–150. doi:10.16916/aded.36249

Büyüköztürk, Ş. (2006). *Manual of data analysis for social sciences* [Sosyal Bilimler İçin Veri Analizi El Kitabı]. PegemA Yayınları.

Çalışkan, S., Güney, Z., Sakhieva, R. G., Vasbieva, D. G., & Zaitseva, N. A. (2019). Teachers' views on the availability of Web 2.0 tools in education. *International Journal of Emerging Technologies in Learning*, *14*(22), 70–81. doi:10.3991/ijet. v14i22.11752

Cavin, R. M. (2007). *Developing technological pedagogical content knowledge in preservice teachers through microteaching lesson study* [Unpublished doctoral dissertation]. The Florida State University.

Charmaz, K. (2006). *Constructing Grounded Theory: A practical guide through qualitative analysis*. Sage.

Cho, M. (2017). Pre-service L2 teacher trainees' reflection: What do they focus on? *English Teaching*, *72*(1), 105–129. doi:10.15858/engtea.72.1.201703.105

Cohen, L., Manion, L., & Morrison, K. (2007). Research methods in education (6th ed.). Routledge/Taylor & Francis Group. doi:10.4324/9780203029053

Cranmer, G. (2017). One-group pretest–posttest design. In M. Allen (Ed.), *The sage encyclopedia of communication research methods* (pp. 1125–1126). SAGE Publications, Inc., doi:10.4135/9781483381411.n388

Crichton, H., Valdera Gil, F., & Hadfield, C. (2021). Reflections on peer micro-teaching: Raising questions about theory informed practice. *Reflective Practice*, *22*(3), 345–362. doi:10.1080/14623943.2021.1892621

Darling-Hammond, L. (2010). Teacher education and the American future. *Journal of Teacher Education*, *61*(1–2), 35–47. doi:10.1177/0022487109348024

Dawson, K., Pringle, R., & Adams, T. L. (2003). Providing links between technology integration, methods courses, and school-based field experiences: A curriculum-based and technology-enhanced microteaching. *Journal of Computing in Teacher Education*, *20*(1), 41–47.

Demirel, O. (1999). *Didactics* [[*Öğretme sanatı*]]. Pegem Press.

Deperlioğlu, Ö., & Köse, U. (2010). Effects of Web 2.0 technologies on the education and an example learning experience. [Web 2.0 teknolojilerinin eğitim üzerindeki etkileri ve örnek bir öğrenme yaşantısı]. XII. *Akademik Bilişim Konferansı Bıldirileri*, 237-242.

Diana, T. J. Jr. (2013). Microteaching revisited: Using technology to enhance the professional development of pre-service teachers. *The Clearing House: A Journal of Educational Strategies, Issues and Ideas*, *86*(4), 150–154. doi:10.1080/00098655.2013.790307

Dixon, R. A., Hall, C., & Shawon, F. (2019). Using virtual reality and web conferencing technologies: Exploring alternatives for microteaching in a rural region. *Northwest Journal of Teacher Education*, *14*(1), 1–18. doi:10.15760/nwjte.2019.14.1.4

Elmas, R., & Geban, Ö. (2012). Web 2.0 tools for 21st century teachers. *International Online Journal of Educational Sciences*, *4*(1), 243–254.

Ertmer, P. A., & Ottenbreit-Leftwich, A. T. (2010). Teacher technology change: How knowledge, confidence, beliefs, and culture intersect. *Journal of Research on Technology in Education*, *42*(3), 255–284. doi:10.1080/15391523.2010.10782551

Esteban, S.G., Laborda, J.G., & Llamas, M.R. (2016). ICTs, ESPs and ZPD through microlessons in teacher education. *New Perspectives on Teaching and Working with Languages in the Digital Era*, 105-113. . doi:10.14705/rpnet.2016.tislid2014.426

Faizi, R., Chiheb, R., & El Afia, A. (2015). Students' perceptions towards using Web 2.0 technologies in education. *International Journal of Emerging Technologies in Learning*, *10*(6), 32–36. doi:10.3991/ijet.v10i6.4858

Farris, R. A. (1991). Micro-peer teaching: Organization and benefits. *Education*, *111*(4), 559–562.

Fernandez, M. L. (2005). Learning through microteaching lesson study in teacher preparation. *Action in Teacher Education*, *26*(4), 37–47. doi:10.1080/01626620.2005.10463341

Fernandez, M. L. (2010). Investigating how and what prospective teachers learn through micro teaching lesson study. *Teaching and Teacher Education*, *26*(2), 351–362. doi:10.1016/j.tate.2009.09.012

Fırat, E. A., & Köksal, M. S. (2019). Effects of instruction supported by web 2.0 tools on prospective teachers' biotechnology literacy. *Computers & Education*, *135*, 61–74. doi:10.1016/j.compedu.2019.02.018

Fisher, J., & Burrell, D. N. (2011). The value of using micro teaching as a tool to develop instructors. *Review of Higher Education and Self-Learning, 4*(11), 86–94.

Fraenkel, J. R., Wallen, N. E., & Hyun, H. H. (2012). *How to design and evaluate research in education* (8th ed.). Mc Graw Hill.

Francis, D. (1997). Reconceptualising Microteaching as Critical Inquiry. *Asia-Pacific Journal of Teacher Education, 25*(3), 207–223. doi:10.1080/1359866970250302

Gaviria, D., Arango, J., & Valencia-Arias, A. (2015). Reflections about the use of information and communication technologies in accounting education. *Procedia: Social and Behavioral Sciences, 176*, 992–997. doi:10.1016/j.sbspro.2015.01.569

Gess-Newsome, J., & Lederman, N. G. (1990). The preservice microteaching course and science teachers' instructional decisions: A qualitative analysis. *Journal of Research in Science Teaching, 27*(8), 717–726. doi:10.1002/tea.3660270802

Ghasemi, A., & Zahediasl, S. (2012). Normality tests for statistical analysis: A guide for non-statisticians. *International Journal of Endocrinology and Metabolism, 10*(2), 486–489. doi:10.5812/ijem.3505 PMID:23843808

Gödek, Y. (2016). Science teacher trainees' microteaching experiences: A focus group study. *Educational Research Review, 11*(16), 1473–1493. doi:10.5897/ERR2016.2892

Grosseck, G. (2009). To use or not to use web 2.0 in higher education? *Procedia: Social and Behavioral Sciences, 1*(1), 478–482. doi:10.1016/j.sbspro.2009.01.087

Gül, R. (2022). *The effect of online education supported by web 2.0 tools on the conceptual achievement, attitudes and self-regulation perceptions of 5th grade middle school students in the sun, earth and moon unit* [Unpublished master's thesis]. Yıldız Teknik University.

Hartshorne, R., & Ajjan, H. (2009). Examining student decisions to adopt Web 2.0 technologies: Theory and empirical tests. *Journal of Computing in Higher Education, 21*(3), 183–198. doi:10.100712528-009-9023-6

He, C., & Yan, C. (2011). Exploring authenticity of micro-teaching in pre-service teacher education programmes. *Teaching Education, 22*(3), 291–302. doi:10.1080/10476210.2011.590588

Higgins, A., & Nicholl, H. (2003). The experiences of lecturers and students in the use of microteaching as a teaching strategy. *Nurse Education in Practice, 3*(4), 220–227. doi:10.1016/S1471-5953(02)00106-3 PMID:19038126

Horzum, M. B. (2010). Investigating teachers' Web 2.0 tools awareness, frequency and purposes of usage in terms of different variables. [Öğretmenlerin Web 2.0 araçlarından haberdarlığı, kullanım sıklıkları ve amaçlarının çeşitli değişkenler açısından incelenmesi]. *Uluslararası İnsan Bilimleri Dergisi, 7*(1), 603–634.

Huber, J., & Ward, B. E. (2009). Pre-service confidence through micro-teaching. *Education Journal, 90*(1), 65–68.

Kafyulilo, A., Fisser, P., Pieters, J., & Voogt, J. (2015). ICT use in science and mathematics teacher education in Tanzania: Developing technological pedagogical content knowledge. *Australasian Journal of Educational Technology, 31*(4), 381–399. doi:10.14742/ajet.1240

Karataş, F. Ö., Cengiz, C., & Uludüz, Ş. M. (2020). Re-designing micro-teaching to lessen anxiety in the process: The pre-service teachers' views. *Necatibey Faculty of Education Electronic Journal of Science and Mathematics Education, 14*(1), 30–56.

Karlström, M., & Hamza, K. (2019). Preservice science teachers' opportunities for learning through reflection when planning a microteaching unit. *Journal of Science Teacher Education, 30*(1), 44–62. doi:10.1080/1046560X.2018.1531345

Kavas, G., & Özdener, N. (2012). Effects of video-supported web-based peer assessment on microteaching applications: Computer teacher candidates sample. *Creative Education, 3*(7), 1221–1230. doi:10.4236/ce.2012.37181

Kirk, R. E. (2008). *Statistics an introduction* (5th ed.). Thomson Higher Education.

Koehler, A. A., Newby, T. J., & Ertmer, P. A. (2017). Examining the role of Web 2.0 tools in supporting problem solving during case-based instruction. *Journal of Research on Technology in Education, 49*(3–4), 182–197. doi:10.1080/15391523.2017.1338167

Kourieos, S. (2016). Video-mediated microteaching-A stimulus for reflection and teacher growth. *The Australian Journal of Teacher Education, 41*(1), 65–80. doi:10.14221/ajte.2016v41n1.4

Küçükgöz, A. B. (2019). *Perceptions of prospective classroom teachers on using interactive whiteboards through micro-teaching* [Unpublished doctoral dissertation]. Hacettepe University.

Marulcu, İ., & Dedetürk, A. (2014). Pre-service science teachers' micro-teaching practices: An action research. *Mustafa Kemal University Journal of Graduate School of Social Sciences, 11*(25), 353–372.

McKillup, S. (2012). *Statistics explained: An introductory guide for life scientists* (2nd ed.). Cambridge University Press.

McLoughlin, C., & Lee, M.J.W. (2007). Social software and participatory learning: Pedagogical choices with technology affordances in the Web 2.0 era. *Proceedings ascilite Singapore*, 664-675.

Mertler, C. A. (2022). Introduction to educational research (Third edition). Chapter 7 quantitative research methods. Los Angeles: SAGE Publications.

Miles, M. B., & Huberman, A. M. (1994). *Qualitative data analysis: An expanded Sourcebook* (2nd ed.). Sage.

Mishra, P., & Koehler, M. J. (2006). Technological Pedagogical content knowledge: A framework for teacher knowledge. *Teachers College Record*, *108*(6), 1017–1054. doi:10.1111/j.1467-9620.2006.00684.x

Ng, C. H. (2017). Pre-service teachers teaching critical literacy through microteaching: Possibilities and constraints. *Changing English*, *24*(1), 81–90. doi:10.1080/13586 84X.2016.1273759

O'Reilly, T. (2005). *Web 2.0: Compact definition*. Retrieved from http://radar.oreilly.com/2005/10/web-20-compact-definition.html

Ostrosky, M. M., Mouzourou, C., Danner, N., & Zaghlawan, H. Y. (2013). Improving teacher practices using microteaching: Planful video recording and constructive feedback. *Young Exceptional Children*, *16*(1), 16–29. doi:10.1177/1096250612459186

Patton, M. Q. (2002). *Qualitative research & evaluation methods* (3rd ed.). Sage Publications, Inc.

Peker, M. (2009). The use of expanded microteaching for reducing pre- service teachers' teaching anxiety about mathematics. *Scientific Research and Essays*, *4*(9), 872–880.

Ping, W. (2013). Micro-teaching: A powerful tool to embedding the English teacher certification testing in the development of English teaching methodologies. *International Journal of English Language and Literature Studies*, *2*(3), 163–175.

Prediger, S., Quabeck, K., & Erath, K. (2022). Conceptualizing micro-adaptive teaching practices in content-specific ways: Case study on fractions. *Journal on Mathematics Education*, *13*(1), 1–30. doi:10.22342/jme.v13i1.pp1-30

Rich, M. (2008). Millennial students and technology choices for information searching. *Electronic Journal of Business Research Methods*, *6*(1), 73–76.

Ryan, K., & Cooper, J. M. (1980). *Those who can, teach.* Houghton Miffling Company.

Şad, S. N., & Göktaş, Ö. (2014). Preservice teachers' perceptions about using mobile phones and laptops in education as mobile learning tools. *British Journal of Educational Technology, 45*(4), 606–618. doi:10.1111/bjet.12064

Şahinkayası, H. (2009). *Contributions and challenges of cognitive tools and microteaching for preservice teachers' instructional planning and teaching skills* [Unpublished doctoral dissertation]. Middle East Technical University, Ankara, Turkey.

Subramaniam, K. (2006). Creating a microteaching evaluation form: The needed evaluation criteria. *Education, 126*(4), 666–677.

Suharwoto, G. (2006). *Secondary mathematics preservice teachers' development of technology pedagogical content knowledge in subject-specific, technology-integrated teacher preparation program* [Unpublished doctoral dissertation]. Oregon State University, Oregon.

Teague, F. A., Rogers, D. W., & Tipling, R. N. (1994). *Technology and media.* Kendall / Hunt.

Thomas, G. E. (2023). *Micro-teaching with video-reflection in education* [Unpublished doctoral dissertation]. Indiana State University.

Tok, T. N. (2007). Methods and techniques for effective teaching. In A. Doğanay (Ed.), *Teaching principles and methods* (pp. 161–214). Pegem A Press.

Tondeur, J., Braak, J., Sang, G., Voogt, J., Fisser, F., & Otterbreit-Leftwich, A. (2012). Preparing preservice teachers to integrate technology in education: A synthesis of qualitative evidence. *Computers & Education, 59*(1), 134–144. doi:10.1016/j.compedu.2011.10.009

Upadhyay, S. K. (2017). Microteaching, an efficient technique for learning effective teaching. *International Research Journal of Multidisciplinary Studies, 3*(1), 252–270.

Valencia-Arias, A., Chalela-Naffah, S., & Bermúdez-Hernández, J. (2019). A proposed model of e-learning tools acceptance among university students in developing countries. *Education and Information Technologies, 24*(2), 1057–1071. doi:10.100710639-018-9815-2

Walker, A., & White, G. (2013). *Technology Enhanced Language Learning: connecting theory and practice-Oxford Handbooks for Language Teachers.* Oxford University Press.

Yıldırım, A., & Şimşek, H. (2013). *Qualitative research methods in the social sciences* (9th ed.). Seçkin Press.

Yıldırım, B., & Akkuş, A. (2020). Developing a scale to assess teachers' perceptions towards using web 2.0 tools in lectures (TPUWL scale). *Participatory Educational Research*, 7(3), 124–138. doi:10.17275/per.20.38.7.3

Zou, B., Wang, D., & Xing, M. (2016). Collaborative tasks in wiki-based environment in EFL learning. *Computer Assisted Language Learning*, 29(5), 1001–1018. doi:10.1080/09588221.2015.1121878

KEY TERMS AND DEFINITIONS

Content Analysis: The act of examining and evaluating recurring themes in any product such as speech, literature, article. Analysis to reveal the meaning, purpose and impact of a content.

Micro Teaching: Micro teaching is a teaching technique. It is especially used in pre-service training for prospective teachers to experience teaching behaviors.

Qualitative Data Analysis: Qualitative data analysis is the process of organizing, analyzing, and interpreting qualitative data—non-numeric, conceptual information and user feedback—to capture themes and patterns, answer research questions, and identify actions to take to improve your product or article.

Quantitative Data Analysis: Quantitative data analysis is an analysis method based on the collection of numerical data and the evaluation of these data using various mathematical and statistical methods.

Teachers' Perceptions: The thoughts or mental images that teachers have about their professional activities or any other subject that influence their background information and professional behavior.

Web 2.0 Tools: They are user-oriented web environments that allow users to interact, collaborate, and share easily.

Chapter 13
Designing Alternative Assessment Activities and Adaptive Learning Scenarios to Cover Various Learning Styles in Higher Education

Antonios S. Andreatos

iD https://orcid.org/0000-0002-2271-8764
Hellenic Air Force Academy, Greece

ABSTRACT

Teaching should have a pluralism, containing a variety of alternative educational activities and supporting various learning styles. If so, then assessment should also have a pluralism, testing not only knowledge but also skills and attitudes (where applicable). This is mandatory in practical courses which are common in engineering and science disciplines. In this chapter we draw from our experience and research, and propose ways for designing authentic educational activities and adaptive learning scenarios to cover various learning styles in Higher Education in order to revitalize the learning process. The idea is to put students in action by assigning them authentic and meaningful tasks, individually and in groups, leaving the teams to self-organize by undertaking or assigning specific roles and tasks. Case studies from Computer Networking and Cyber Security are presented. We shall also present alternative assessment for these activities and scenarios. This is a fieldwork, hence, quantitative data from real classes, as well as interviews will be presented.

DOI: 10.4018/978-1-6684-8656-6.ch013

1. INTRODUCTION

Teaching is not an easy profession. Teaching is a complex process and teachers need a wide set of skills to be effective and efficient in the classroom. Teaching assumes a full-duplex (two-way) communication channel between the educator and the learner; in order for the communication to be effective, it is necessary that both ends are synchronized in the same frequency and the noise is suppressed. This assumes that the teacher is properly prepared and his/her message is clear on the one hand, but also that the student is receptive and concerted to the teacher (and vice-versa). Students use their senses, each to a varying degree, to receive messages. This is what we call "Learning Style". We can think of the senses as different frequencies of a communication channel. A good teacher uses all frequencies in order to communicate with his/her students effectively. According to "the pyramid of learning" (see Fig. 1), we remember 10 percent of what we read, 20 percent of what we hear, 30 percent of what we see, 50 percent of what we see and hear, 75 percent of what we see, hear and talk about, and 90 percent what we see, hear, discuss, and do (Letrud, 2012; Subramony, 2003; Molenda, 2004; Lalley & Miller, 2007). Lectures cover only a small percentage of the pyramid of learning; for this reason, homework is assigned to students, as a complement to teaching, but in most cases they are not authentic,

Figure 1. The pyramid of learning
Source: https://en.wikipedia.org/wiki/Learning_pyramid

in the sense that they resemble previous academic years' assignments or textbook problems, and they are the same for all the students.

In order to achieve best learning outcomes, we must use authentic educational activities which ask students to see, hear, discuss, and do, in other words, engage them deeply in the learning process. This chapter is about the design and evaluation of Educational Scenarios. Ways of student assessment are also proposed. As a case study, two Educational Scenarios about Computer Networking and Cybersecurity will be presented.

2. LEARNING STYLES

Learning styles refer to the different ways that individuals prefer to use in order to receive, process and retain information. Different students have different learning styles, meaning that each one learns best in his/her own way. If a teacher always uses an unchanged, monotonous, invariant teaching method resulting from his/her own learning/teaching style, this favors always the same students, i.e., those adapted to the teacher's teaching style, but does not favor the rest of the students.

While there are many different models and theories of learning styles, some of the most commonly recognized models closely related to our discussion are the VARK model, Kolb's Learning Styles Model, and Honey & Mumford's model (Bay, 2023; Cambridge, 2023; wikipedia-Learning_styles, 2023; Dunn & Dunn, 1992). Brief presentations of each model follow:

David Kolb was the first to introduce the learning styles in the 1970s. He approached learning as an experiential activity, i.e., how experiencing the materials facilitates learning (Kolb, 2015). According to Kolb, as individuals try to use all possible approaches in the learning process, they may tend to develop a preference for an experience-capturing approach and an experience-transforming approach, leading them to prefer one of the following four learning styles:

a)   Kolb's four learning styles are (Kolb, 1984):
   ◦   Accommodators (those who prefer hands-on learning),
   ◦   Convergers (those who understand abstract theory but tend to put it into practice),
   ◦   Divergers (those who use personal experiences to form theories), and
   ◦   Assimilators (those who love theory and use theories to create their own abstractions).
b)   Honey & Mumford's model. Honey and Mumford developed their four learning styles as a variation of Kolb's learning styles (Cambridge, 2023). Their learning styles are: Activist (Accommodator), Theorist (Assimilator),

Pragmatist (Converger) and Reflector (Diverger) (Mumford, 1997; Pratchett et al., 2016).

c)   The "VARK" model learning styles are: visual, auditory, kinesthetic and reading/ writing (BAU, 2021; wikipedia-Learning_styles, 2023). This model proposes that there are four main types of learners: visual learners (who prefer to learn through visual aids such as diagrams or charts), auditory learners (who prefer to learn through listening to lectures or discussions), reading/writing learners (who prefer to learn through reading and writing activities), and kinesthetic learners (who prefer to learn through hands-on activities and movement) (VARK, 2021).

Examples of how these learning styles might manifest in a classroom setting include visual learners preferring to see diagrams and charts rather than listening to a lecture, auditory learners preferring to listen to a recorded lecture or a video rather than reading a textbook, kinesthetic learners preferring to engage in hands-on activities such as labs or experiments, and so on.

It is worth noting that while learning styles remain a popular concept, there is some debate about their validity and effectiveness as a means of improving educational outcomes. Some researchers argue that the evidence for learning styles is limited or inconclusive, and that other factors such as motivation, interest, and prior knowledge may be more important in determining how learners process and retain information.

Figure 2 presents the VARK model learning styles of a typical engineering class in our institution. These results were collected from a special questionnaire comprising 16 questions, which was delivered to twelve junior engineering students of our institution in March 2023.

From Figure 2 we can see that:

- Each student has his/her own style; even with only 16 questions, each answer is unique;
- Most students have a dominant learning style (which is the 'kinesthetic' followed by the 'auditory');
- All students have a 'mixed learning style', fact which implies that teaching should have a pluralism.

3. LESSONS LEARNED DURING THE LOCKDOWN PERIODS

The pandemic and the evolution of e-learning technologies facilitated the transition from face-to-face learning to distance learning. In this context, there are two different actors, each with its own issues:

Figure 2. VARK model learning styles of a typical engineering class in our institution

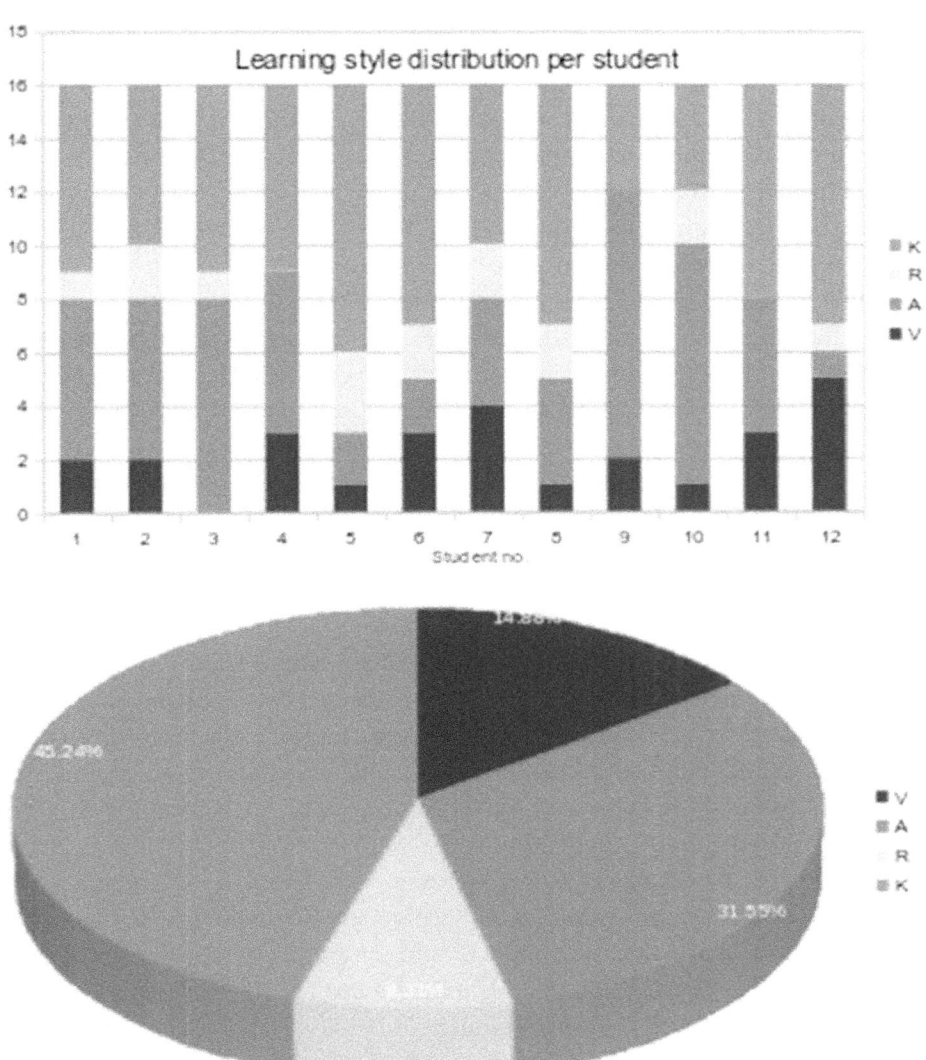

a) the teachers, many of whom had no experience of distance learning and faced unknown challenges.

b) the students, a digital generation, connected, self-sufficient and with a great ability to create and adapt. But also, a generation that also needs to be constantly stimulated and challenged, engaged and guided in personalized learning scenarios where peer collaboration and teacher support are vital.

In this context, the selection of the most appropriate pedagogical practices and tools, as well as the design of personalized learning scenarios for this generational participation are more important than the challenge of the transition from face-to-face to distance education.

Traditionally, in our Institution, oral grades are derived from homework assignments and/or midterm exams, based on the textbook problems or similar problems from the bibliography.

During the lockdown periods, we had to look for new assessment methods, focused on adaptive and personalized learning to cover heterogeneous learning profiles and, at the same time, to prevent cheating (Andreatos, 2021).

After the return to face-to-face learning, personalized assessment methods remained in use in our courses, in order to help these generations acquire knowledge and informal learning in micro-project and multi-disciplinary frameworks.

4. EDUCATIONAL SCENARIOS

4.1 Definition of Educational Scenarios

Educational scenarios are carefully designed and structured learning experiences. An educational scenario typically presents a hypothetical situation or problem that students must work through or solve. We can think of a scenario (script) as a series of scenes. Educational scenarios may involve simulations, lab exercises or other interactive tools (Spector et al., 2021; Spitzer et al., 2016; van der Meijden & Veenman, 2018).

The objective of educational scenarios is to create a more engaging and interactive learning experience that encourages students to think critically and apply their knowledge to real-world situations. By presenting students with a problem or challenge to solve, scenarios can help learners to see the relevance and practical application of the concepts they are learning.

An educational scenario defines the form and the content of the teaching experience, prerequisite background, learning outcomes, pedagogical theories, orientation, etc. and provides the sequence of the learning activities and learning material for each scene (UMI-Sci-Ed project, 2023).

Educational scenarios can take many different forms depending on the subject matter and learning goals. For example, a scenario in a science class might involve a simulated laboratory experiment in which students must collect and analyze data, while a scenario in a language class might involve a virtual conversation with a native speaker. Educational scenarios can also utilize storytelling and narratives (Leskowski, 2023). Overall, educational scenarios are a powerful tool for promoting active learning and engaging students in the learning process. They can be used in a variety of educational settings, from traditional classroom instruction to online and hybrid learning environments.

Another advantage of using educational scenarios is that they often require background from different courses. Splitting a major (such as computer science) in courses is only a crutch facilitating the management of knowledge; however, the students must finally integrate all the knowledge offered in separate courses, and educational scenarios can help in this.

Designing effective educational scenarios requires vision, time, experience, careful planning, good preparation and attention to detail. The teacher must prepare a plan and must be ready to cope with unexpected situations in order to prepare alternative solutions in advance. During the execution the teacher should use a diary and keep notes of unforseen problems and improvements. The scenario must be relevant to the learning objectives, engaging and motivating for students, and aligned with the level of the learners' prior knowledge and skills. It is also important to provide clear instructions and feedback throughout the scenario to ensure that students are on track and learning the intended concepts. In the end, the scenario should be evaluated, corrected, improved and augmented for next usage.

Two **types of educational scenarios** are common: standalone scenarios and branching scenarios. Standalone scenarios are series of consecutive scenes, with the learners engaging in one objective per scene. This is the type of scenarios that we consider in this chapter. Branching scenarios on the other hand, offer branching possibilities based on the choices made by learners in a given situation.

Branching scenarios typically cover more complex situations with multiple decision points, where the outcome changes depending on the decisions made by the learners. Such scenarios are used when we want learners to find the best choice among several good options (Leskowski, 2023).

4.2 Scenario-Based Learning

Scenario-based learning is an interactive instructional strategy that simulates real-life situations to engage learners. While a traditional examination tests a learner's memory (such as recalling or recognizing information), a scenario tests the learner's ability to apply concepts.

5. APPLYING ALTERNATIVE ASSESSMENT

The use of examinations as assessment tools does not suit all students, in the same way that a teaching style does not support all students. This is the reasoning behind different learning styles; using a variety of alternative activities will cater for more learning styles.

Alternative assessment refers to a variety of methods used to evaluate student learning that differs from traditional assessment approaches like standardized testing and multiple-choice exams. Alternative assessment techniques can be more engaging, authentic and comprehensive than traditional assessments, and are often used to measure higher-order thinking skills like analysis, synthesis and evaluation (Wiggins, 1989).

Alternative assessment has some advantages over examination-based assessment (Pascoe et al., 2020):

- Students are not stressed;
- Students behave normally and can perform better;
- Students have the chance to act, cultivate and demonstrate their personal skills.

For this and other reasons (Andreatos, 2021), from Fall 2019 onward, oral grades in our Computer Networking, Cybersecurity courses are derived from a set of academic activities offered throughout the semester, which are also used as alternative assessment. These activities typically include lab exercises, simulations (using programs like Packet Tracer), network traffic analysis (using tools like Wireshark), etc., but not exams or tests. The oral grades arise from various academic activities during the whole semester and take place in a classroom or the lab. The set of activities changes every year as it adapts to technological developments, as well as the interests of the students. As a result, differences were observed in student performance between the alternative assessment activities grades and in the final written exams grades.

After this change in assessment policy, a significant difference between oral grades and final examination scores was observed; there were students who performed well on the oral grades but poorly on the final exam and vice versa. Because of this observation, correlation and predictive modeling between oral and final grades were studied. A quantitative, correlational approach utilizing linear regression analysis to describe any predictive relationship between the examination types was employed. The results indicated that when assessment is based on exams, oral and final grades are correlated. This implies that assessment based on exams favors always the same students, those whose learning style matches best the exam style. Therefore, we decided to use alternative assessment activities to derive the oral grades.

6. CASE STUDIES

Case studies from our teaching experience will be presented, especially from the Computer Networking and Network Security courses.

The Hellenic Air Force Academy (HAFA) offers an undergraduate program on Telecommunications and Electronics Engineering (TEE). This specialization is equivalent to a Bachelor's degree in Electrical Engineering. During the fourth year of studies, the Division of Computer Engineering and Information Science offers the following courses to TEE students:

- Computer Networks I is offered during the 7th semester.
- Computer Networks II is offered during the 8th (last) semester
- Network Security (which is in essence Cyber Security) is offered during the 8th semester (Andreatos, 2017).

These courses are taught by the same instructor (the author), fact which enables him to build the necessary background, as well as, administrate the time needed for the educational scenarios by taking class hours from the aforementioned courses without compromising the syllabus (Andreatos, 2023).

The scenarios presented here use use low-cost equipment and open source software. These scenarios combine the following learning activities:

- Project-based learning: Students work on real-world projects requiring them to use critical thinking, problem-solving and collaboration skills to find solutions.
- Collaborative team work: Small groups of students work together to complete a task or project, sharing knowledge, skills, and resources, and learning from each other.
- Microlearning: Short, focused learning episodes, typically lasting between 3-10 minutes, cover a single concept or skill, making it easy for students to digest and retain the information.
- Competition-based learning: a student-centered pedagogy that combines project-based learning and competitions.

Students are advised to keep notes and screenshots during the educational activities. In the end of each weekly activity they have to submit a report which is used by the teacher to check and assess their achievements. The reports are also useful to the students because they describe the construction of their knowledge throughout the scenarios and will remind them of their achievements at later times. In addition, writing is important for reading/writing learners of the VARK model, as well as occupies an enviable position in the pyramid of learning (fig. 1).

6.1 Scenario A

In 2017 we implemented a competition-based learning scenario to teach some basic network security concepts. The scenario was run on an ad-hoc LAN using Linux and Windows operating systems running on real and virtual machines (Andreatos, 2017).

Scenario A intended to increase students' hands-on experience, integrate topics taught during the past years in various courses, as well as, prepare students for the annual cyber defense exercise. The lab was competition-based, fact which made it more challenging (Lee et al., 2011; Andreatos, 2017).

The scenario was implemented during the academic year 2015-2016, in the 8th semester, in the Computer Networking II and Network Security courses. The scenario spanned from March to April 2016. Twelve 22 years old students participated. Most of this time period was spend in preparation; the competition took place the last two weeks during the class hours of the Network Security course.

Scenario A had two phases: The preparation phase and the competition phase. The preparation phase was executed during the class hours of Computer Networking II and Network Security courses and included a combination of homeworks, demonstrations and lab exercises. The instructor demonstrated the necessary methods and tools (microteaching). At the end of the preparation phase each team should end up with a real or a virtual machine running an Ubuntu server that offers at least three services from the default options (Andreatos, 2017). The purpose of the preparation phase for the students was to build the necessary background, as well as familiarize with the tools. The purpose of the preparation phase for the instructor was to design the implementation of the scenario. Project-based learning and Microlearning were the principal learning methodologies used in this phase.

During the competition phase the students were split into two groups, A and B assuming the role of the "red team" (attackers) and the "blue team" (defenders) in turns. The objective was for the red team to put out of service the blue team's server deploying a DDoS attack from their laptops. Collaborative group work and competition-based learning were the principal learning methodologies used in this phase.

Educational Objectives of Scenario A

Students were expected to learn how to:

1.   Set up a wired or wireless ad-hoc LAN and connect to it;

2.   Run Linux and Windows operating systems on VirtualBox and connect the virtual machines to the ad-hoc LAN;

3.   Install an Ubuntu server with at least three services, one of which was the Apache web server.

4.   Set up the required services on an Apache web server and tools for attack and defense, as well as, traffic monitoring;

5.   Deploy a DDoS attack from their Linux and Windows platforms against the server of the opponent team;

6.   Run packet capture tools to monitor the volume of DDoS traffic against the server;

7.   Verify the result of the attack, and

8.   Explore defense mechanisms.

During this scenario the instructor assumed multiple roles. In the preparation phase he acted as a teacher building the necessary background, designing, modifying and applying the educational scenario. In the execution phase he acted as coach and motivator offering advice and technical support; he also acted as a researcher, observing student participation, decision-making and initiatives, in order to assess the scenario as well as the students. The students' performance in the scenario contributed 10 percent of the oral grade of the course. Students' evaluation of this lab exercise was positive. Lessons learned from this effort will help the instructor to improve the scenario and incorporate additional tools as well as more types of cyber attacks in the future (Andreatos, 2017).

6.2 Scenario B

Scenario B was implemented during the academic year 2021-2022. It was a 10-12 class hours scenario including several successive hands-on exercises. It was implemented in parts and spanned ten weeks from both the Fall 2020 and Spring 2021 semesters. For this reason, the equipment had to be minimal, portable and fast to set up.

In the Fall 2020 semester the scenario was executed during the Computer Networks I hours; in Spring 2021 it was executed during the Computer Networks II and Network Security lecture hours, approximately two hours per week, in parallel with theoretical lectures, so that the students had enough time to get familiar with the prerequisite theoretical background (Andreatos, 2023). The design and preparation time is not included in these 10-12 class hours. Eleven 22 years old senior students participated.

The experimental configuration used an ad-hoc wireless and wired network, and a Raspberry Pi implementing a Web server and an SSH server. Students were connected using their own devices (laptops, tablets). Initially the students performed

DDoS attacks against the Web server using various tools. The students had to create SSH accounts to the server and a pair of RSA keys; using their SSH accounts, the students had to transfer their public keys to the server. Finally, students had to attack the SSH service from Kali Linux running on virtual machines in teams, each team using a different tool. The scenario was implemented in parts during a series of lessons and was positively accepted and evaluated by the students, who got familiar with a number of concepts and tools of computer networking and network security. In the end the students informally assessed the Kali Linux SSH attack tools. Lab exercises used a series of open source software, as well as low-cost equipment (Andreatos, 2023).

Educational Objectives of Scenario B

In scenario B students were expected to learn how to:

- Set up an ad-hoc LAN;
- Monitor LAN users and network traffic;
- Connect to a remote machine using SSH;
- Use virtualization; how to connect a virtual machine (VM) to a LAN;
- Generate a pair of RSA keys for public-key encryption;
- Copy a user's public key to a server and disable username/password authentication;
- Find the configuration files of the SSH server (sshd_config, known_hosts) and how to access them;
- Launch a DoS attack against a web server;
- Prepare a dictionary for a brute-force attack;
- Brute-force attack an SSH server using a dictionary.

The first four objectives are taught in Computer Networking; the rest are taught in Network Security. This is an example of how an Educational scenario may require knowledge from different courses, unifying the science.

6.3 Student Assessment

In such educational scenarios, the students may be assessed both qualitatively and quantitatively, based on their participation and achievements. As an example we present the student assessment for scenario B (Andreatos, 2023). We begin with the **quantitative** assessment. Milestones that were taken into account included:

1. Assessment of DoS attacks: each student had to use one of the suggested DoS attack tools against the Web server of Raspberry Pi, until a proper message showing that the page was not available appeared on their screen. The instructor could observe the packet floods in the packet capture (given the students' IP and MAC addresses).
2. The creation of SSH user accounts in the Raspberry Pi SSH server was verified by exploring the students' home directories.
3. The brute-force attacks on the SSH server were verified through the Wireshark packet capture files.
4. The students had to submit a report with their activities as an assignment in the Computer Networks course, describing their activities and supporting them with screenshots.
5. Generating an RSA key pair and uploading the public key to the server was verified by exploring the students' home directories in Raspberry Pi.
6. The students had to submit another report as an assignment in the Network Security course.

The teacher could check student activity during the various stages of the scenario, using a variety of tools and methods:

1. The instructor could check which students were connected to the network by means of monitoring tools (Angry IP Scanner and Advanced IP Scanner). From these tools he could also get their MAC addresses.
2. The instructor could check which students participated in the attacks using the packet captures and their MAC addresses.
3. The instructor could also check the students' activity on Raspberry Pi (account, public key, etc).

Monitoring student progress during the scenario ensures that no student is left behind.

Qualitative assessment was based on the teacher's observations on student participation and interest, as well as their roles in the team activities (leaders, followers or observers).

6.4 Evaluation of the Educational Scenarios

Educational scenarios are complex procedures and there are always things to be improved or added. Scenario evaluation is based on student acceptance, student opinions, as well as the educator's retrospective thinking; towards this goal, keeping a diary might prove a good practice. Questionnaires and interviews may also be used.

We generally consider a scenario successful if it has complexity and realism, in the sense that it resembles a real case. Considering the students' side, a scenario is consider successful if it engages the students, achieves its educational objectives and promotes students' knowledge and skills in an enjoyable manner, within the predefined time schedule. The instructor must be sure that the students have the necessary background and are able to carry out the complex tasks required by the scenario.

In order to participate in scenario A for instance, the students should have a background covering:

- Bash commands;
- Installation of a Linux server;
- Installation of a wired LAN;
- Use of virtualization and connection of VMs to the LAN;
- Network traffic monitoring;
- DoS attacks, penetration testing basics, etc.

Before engaging students in a complex, multi-discipline scenario assuming knowledge and skills taught in past courses by other teachers, the instructor must make sure that they have the background necessary in order to successfully curry out the scenario.

Finally, the scenarios should be adapted to the students' background, interests, and technological evolution.

7. DISCUSSION

Figure 3 presents the oral and final grades, as well as the graduation order for the class where the aforementioned educational scenario for teaching cyber security using low-cost equipment and open source software was taught.

From Figure 3 we can see that the oral grades differ from the final grades for most students, but there is an increased similarity between final grades and graduation order. In fact, the correlation between oral and final grades is 0.3002 (low), while the correlation between final grades and graduation order is 0.6237 (high). This is because in most courses, both oral and final grades are derived from exams. The problem is that students who cannot perform well in exams due to stress or anxiety, will always be wronged (Struthers et al., 2000; Bernal-Morales et al., 2015), because students' academic stress is inversely related to their course grade (Chapell et al., 2005; Renk & Smith, 2007; Pascoe, 2020; Robotham & Julian, 2006; Zajacova et al., 2005).

Figure 3. Oral and final grades, and graduation order of a typical engineering class in our institution. Oral grades resulted from alternative assessment.

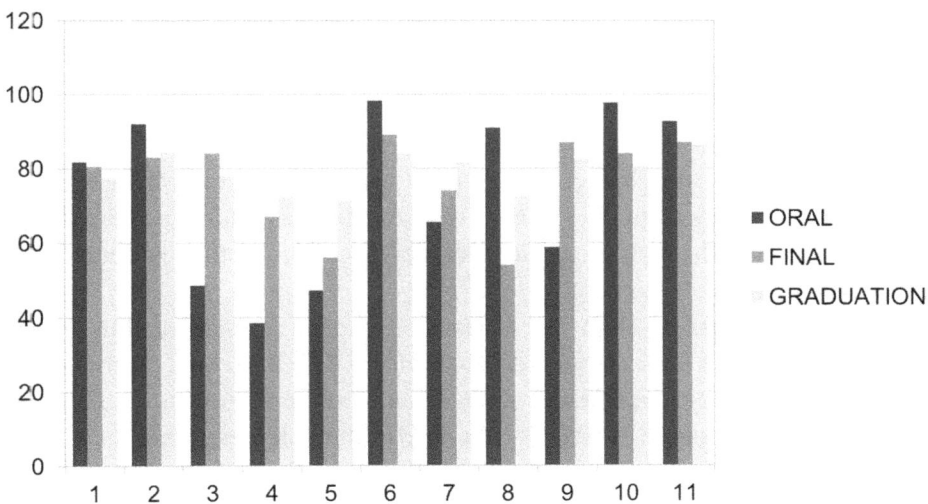

In Figure 3 we can see some cases where students performing well in exams did not get a high oral grade, and vice-versa: students performing well in Oral grades resulting from alternative assessment, but poorly in exams (student no. 8 for instance). Student 8 is an exceptional case because he performed very well in the educational activity but not in the written tests. We interviewed student no. 8 after graduation. From this interview we present his opinion about his participation in scenario B:

"At work so far, I found very useful some things from my involvement in your course (Computer Networking), especially useful in a Cisco school I took on networking essentials!

In your course I liked the labs and the exercises because there I actually learned (several) things and the theory! So I focused on what I knew I liked and where I knew I would do well; I could not perform well in exams.' I didn't like theory, I had a hard time trying to memorize what I should in order to perform well! However, I always did my best, no matter if in the end my anxiety swallowed me up!"

According to Honey & Mumford's model he considers himself as Activist and Pragmatist. It comes out that the aforementioned educational scenario gave this student the chance to learn Computer Networking and Cyber security and inspired him to study further by attending a MOOC.

8. CONCLUSION AND FUTURE DIRECTIONS

This chapter discussed the design and use of active learning scenarios in the classroom. Active learning scenarios are complex learning activities that aim to involve students deeply in the learning process, cover all possible learning styles and cultivate a set of skills considered necessary for succeeding in the current landscape. As a case study we presented two educational scenarios for teaching Computer Networking and Cyber Security using low-cost equipment and open source software and we proposed quantitative and qualitative ways to assess students. Looking back at Figure 1 we can verify that the educational scenarios presented urge students act in all the layers of the pyramid of learning.

Educational scenarios allow for alternative student assessment; this is both important and fair for students who do not perform well in written exams or tests due to anxiety. Our brief experience revealed that there were students with bad rank (due to poor performance in exams) who thrieved in alternative assessment activities, and vice-versa. This is a first direction for future research.

A proposed flowchart for designing standalone educational scenarios in ten steps is the following:

1. Get to know your students, their needs, their learning styles and their background;
2. Select a real-world case to simulate; set the educational objectives and expected results of the scenario;
3. Write the scenario as a set of scenes;
4. Select the objective of each scene, the methods and tools to be demonstrated (microteaching), the students' tasks, the resources (e.g. equipment), the bibliography and the learning activities to be used (e.g. PBL, group work, etc.); make sure that all learning styles are supported;
5. Select the milestones (expected results) and the student assessment criteria for each scene;
6. Make the time schedule;
7. Check for unexpected situations and prepare alternative solutions;
8. Procure the required equipment, including some extra to cover unexpected situations and alternatives;
9. Design metrics for assessing the scenario by the teachers and the students;
10. Test, revise and improve the scenario.

Care should also be taken to ensure that the contents of the scenario are aligned with the course(s) syllabus.

In the future we would like to develop additional scenarios but with increased complexity. Another direction for future research is to develop metrics for evaluating the scenarios by both the teachers and the students.

The educator's role is critical in the whole process of designing and scheduling the scenario, setting the objectives, supporting the students, assessing the students, providing solutions and alternatives, assessing the educational outcomes, and finally, revising and updating the scenario. These assume several skills beyond knowledge of the subject, such as creativity, critical thinking, judgment, complex decision-making, time management, curiosity and continual learning, lifelong learning, etc. But it's worth it because the effect that teachers have on students' personality and career can never be sidelined.

REFERENCES

Andreatos, A. (2023). An Educational Scenario for Teaching Cyber Security Using low-cost Equipment and Open Source Software. In *Proc. of ECCWS 2023, 22nd European Conference on Cyber Warfare and Security*. Hellenic Air Force Academy. 10.34190/eccws.22.1.1113

Andreatos, A. & Leros, A. (2023). Can Oral Grades Predict Final Examination Scores? Case Study in a Higher Education Military Academy. *MDPI Analytics*.

Andreatos, A. S. (2021, January). Redesigning Engineering Assessment during the Covid-19 Lockdown – A case study in Computer Networking and Network Security. *Technium Social Sciences Journal*, *15*, 108–124.

Antonios, S. (2017). Designing educational scenarios to teach network security. *Proc. of IEEE Educon 2017..* https://ieeexplore.ieee.org/document/7943063

Bay Atlantic University. (2021). *8 Types of Learning Styles | The Definitive Guide.* https://bau.edu/blog/types-of-learning-styles/

Bernal-Morales, B., Rodríguez-Landa, J. F., & Pulido-Criollo, F. (2015). *Impact of anxiety and depression symptoms on scholar performance in high school and university students, a fresh look at anxiety disorders*. IntechOpen.

Black, P., & Wiliam, D. (1998). Assessment and classroom learning. *Assessment in Education: Principles, Policy & Practice, 5*(1), 7–74. doi:10.1080/0969595980050102

Cambridge. (2023). https://www.cambridge.org/core/books/abs/practical-tips-for-developing-your-staff/honey-and-mumford-learning-styles/2BA8 CBFC6476F6C3252396CFB7705F8C

Chapell, M. S., Blanding, Z. B., Silverstein, M. E., Takahashi, M., Newman, B., Gubi, A., & McCann, N. (2005). Test anxiety and academic performance in undergraduate and graduate students. *Journal of Educational Psychology*, *972*(2), 268–274. doi:10.1037/0022-0663.97.2.268

Darling-Hammond, L., & Adamson, F. (2014). *Beyond the bubble test: How performance assessments support 21st century learning*. Jossey-Bass.

Kolb, D. A. (1984). *Experiential learning: Experience as the source of learning and development*. Prentice-Hall.

Lalley, J. P., & Miller, R. H. (2007). The learning pyramid: Does it point teachers in the right direction? *Education*, *128*(1), 64–79.

Lee, M. J., & McLoughlin, C. (2007). Teaching and learning in virtual worlds: A review of the educational research. *Educational Research Review*, *2*(2), 69–87.

Leskowski, A. (2023). *How to Write a Scenario That Actually Engages Your Learners*. https://maestrolearning.com/blogs/how-to-write-a-scenario/

Letrud, K. (2012). A rebuttal of NTL Institute's learning pyramid. *Education*, (133), 117–124.

McKenzie, K., & Schweitzer, R. (2001). Who Succeeds at University? Factors predicting academic performance in first year Australian university students. *Higher Education Research & Development*, *20*(1), 21–33. doi:10.1080/07924360120043621

McTighe, J., & Wiggins, G. (2013). *Essential questions: Opening doors to student understanding*. ASCD.

Molenda, M. (2004). Cone of experience. In A. Kovalchik & K. Dawson (Eds.), *Education and Technology* (pp. 161–165). ABCCLIO.

Mumford, A. (1997). Putting learning styles to work. In *Action learning at work* (pp. 121–135). Gower.

Pascoe Michaela, C., Hetrick Sarah, E., & Parker Alexandra, G. (2020). The impact of stress on students in secondary school and higher education. *International Journal of Adolescence and Youth*, *25*(1), 104–112. doi:10.1080/02673843.2019.1596823

Pratchett, T., Young, G., Brooks, C., Jeskins, L., & Monagle, H. (2016). Honey and Mumford – learning styles. In *Practical Tips for Developing Your Staff* (pp. 8–11). Facet. doi:10.29085/9781783301812.005

Renk, K., & Smith, T. (2007). Predictors of academic-related stress in college students: An examination of coping, social support, parenting, and anxiety. *NASPA Journal*, *44*(3), 405–431. doi:10.2202/1949-6605.1829

Robotham, D., & Julian, C. (2006). Stress and the higher education student: A critical review of the literature. *Journal of Further and Higher Education*, *30*(2), 107–117. doi:10.1080/03098770600617513

Spector, J. M., Ifenthaler, D., Sampson, D. G., & Yang, L. (Eds.). (2021). *Educational scenarios: From dreams to action*. Springer.

Spitzer, K. L., & Brinkley-Etzkorn, K. E. (2016). Designing authentic educational experiences in online courses through scenario-based learning. *Online Learning : the Official Journal of the Online Learning Consortium*, *20*(3), 98–114.

Stiggins, R. J. (2010). *An introduction to student-involved assessment FOR learning*. Pearson.

Struthers, C. W., Perry, R. P., & Menec, V. H. (2000). An examination of the relationships among academic stress, coping motivation, and performance in college. *Research in Higher Education*, *41*(5), 581–592. doi:10.1023/A:1007094931292

Subramony, D. P. (2003). Dale's Cone revisited: Critically examining the misapplication of a nebulous theory to guide practice. *Educational Technology*, *7-8*(25-30).

van der Meijden, H., & Veenman, M. V. (2018). *Designing scenario-based learning: A practical guide for teachers*. Routledge.

VARK. (2021). *A Guide to Learning Styles*. Retrieved from https://vark-learn.com/introduction-to-vark/

Wiggins, G. P. (1989). A true test: Toward more authentic and equitable assessment. *Phi Delta Kappan*, *70*(9), 703–713.

wiki-Learning_styles. (2023). https://en.wikipedia.org/wiki/Learning_styles

Zajacova, A., Lynch, S. M., & Espenshade, T. J. (2005). Self-Efficacy, stress and academic success in college. *Research in Higher Education*, *46*(6), 677–706. doi:10.100711162-004-4139-z

Chapter 14

Experimentation and Creation:
The Critical and Creative Thinking in the (Re)invention of Solutions and the Creation of an Own Work

Geraldo Eanes Soares de Castro
ESE, Polytechnic of Porto, Portugal

Susana Maria Sousa Lopes da Silva
ESE, Polytechnic of Porto, Portugal

Ricardo Jorge da Rocha Gonçalves
ESE, Polytechnic of Porto, Portugal

ABSTRACT

The chapter discusses the introduction of adaptive learning in art education to provide students with personalized educational content. The methodology of project work is important for fostering creative thinking and addressing pedagogical and artistic challenges. The Visual Arts and Artistic Technologies Course has a diverse curriculum that emphasizes the practical dimension of knowledge to stimulate observation and learning by doing. The curricular units adapt to meet the needs, expectations, and preferences of the students. The chapter proposes an analysis of the curriculum organization of the course using adaptive microlearning.

ANALYTICAL FRAMEWORK

The Portuguese education system is regulated by the Framework Law on the Education System and is developed in three levels: basic, secondary, and higher education. In turn, Portuguese higher education is currently organized in a binary[1] system that integrates university and polytechnic education.

DOI: 10.4018/978-1-6684-8656-6.ch014

In this chapter, we take polytechnic education as the scenario/context of our reflection. It is important to highlight that polytechnic education is guided by a perspective of applied research and development, aimed at understanding and solving concrete problems and aims at providing a solid cultural and technical training at a higher level, developing the capacity for innovation and critical analysis and providing scientific knowledge of a theoretical and practical nature and its applications with a view to the exercise of professional[2] activities.

These higher education institutions enjoy scientific, pedagogical, cultural and disciplinary autonomy, as set out in Law No. 62/2007 of 10 September, which establishes the legal framework of higher education institutions, regulating their constitution, duties and organization, the functioning and competence of their bodies, and also the supervision and public oversight of the State over them, within the framework of their autonomy Articles 71 to 75.

Since 1998, the School of Education has been reinforcing its dimension as a Higher Education institution linked to teacher training (Early Childhood Education, 1st and 2nd cycles of Basic Education, Music and Sport), and affirming its cultural and citizenship vocation in the areas of Arts, Culture, Heritage and Social Education, which are now a reference in the national educational offer[3]. Presents in its educational portfolio the degree in Visual Arts and Artistic Technologies, which enables "future graduates with technical, operative and theoretical skills in the fields of arts, preparing them for a professional practice directed to the artistic areas, through the creation of projects of individual responsibility. It also enables graduates for diversified creative professional activities, within the scope of an educational intervention, in non-formal contexts"[4].

The design of its humanistic curriculum is faced in an integral and globalizing way, seeking in the transversality of knowledge, creative processes capable of integrating knowledge from the various Curricular Units.

EXPERIMENTATION AND CREATION

In this course, the potential of each student is understood as an asset in the realization of individual or group projects in a questioning and challenging space of the norm that seeks to unquiet students from the doing, inspiring them.

As the National Arts Plan (2019) states, "the undisciplined power of the arts, by unsettling, disrupting and challenging the usual order and certainties, can open a space of freedom for personal and collective construction: a place and time for questioning and openness" (p. 19), to thus change our view of the world and ourselves - and transform our lives and the lives of others, even if this requires creating spaces for rambling and alternative paths.

For students to be better able to use what they learn other capacities must be trained that will give them the flexibility to transfer the knowledge acquired to life, since life situations are generally new and cannot be solved with pre-defined formulas.

In this sense, it is fundamental that students are able to relate facts, anticipate and solve new situations. This only happens when they are encouraged to relate the subjects of the various Curricular Units, real life and what happens in the world; when the methodologies, the materials and the challenges set seek the valorization of the question and allow for mistakes (learning from them), when they allow for individual solutions, valuing each one.

Thus, in the Visual Arts and Artistic Technologies Course, the systemic principle of the raison d'être of the project work is that it establishes the connection between the knowledge of the parts and that of the whole. As we know, the organization of a whole originates unknown qualities of its constituent elements. Hence the need to work in order to unify analysis and synthesis.

The construction or reconstruction allows to reveal the problem, that is, from perception to scientific theory, all knowledge can be a reconstruction, in a certain culture and in a certain time. In this perspective, it offers the possibility of critical and creative thinking poured into the field of arts, ensured by the pluralism that characterises post-modernity.

On the other hand, we can notice that any process of creation was established - since ancient Greece - from a binomial: *arété* (art), which makes reference to a social concept and is consubstantiated through the notions of conscience, perfection, purity, naturalness; and *técné* (technique) which makes reference to all the artificial and is consubstantiated through the notions of the unnatural, of the lie, of falsity. Thus, we can state that any human work is composed of these two binomials, and it is through the junction of these that we are allowed to achieve or build something: an object, an environment, a life scenario.

However, this does not solve the problem, because it establishes a dialectic between the two extremes and, therefore, according to Plato, it is only from the confrontation of arété and técné, that we can reach the notion of idea. And this reveals itself to be a supreme level of abstraction and, as such, unrealizable if we continue in a state of absolute dialectical confrontation of the two terms.

So how can we reach the realisation of an idea? When we introduce the project value. Therefore, any projectual element implies a state of "where I am" and "where I want to go", it means, therefore, to project.

We start, then, from a structure of the theory of knowledge, in which the whole cognitive process follows certain stages, established in a possible scientific model: Archetype; Type; Model; Example.

So, at a first level we have the idea, the "Archetype", which will be expressed verbally.

At a second level we have the prefiguration (sketch), which we call "Type", (this is the first step towards the formal concretisation of something).

In a third level we will obtain the "Model" - defined by the form, not yet final, that is, prototype - substantial in any scientific model.

Finally, at a fourth level, we obtain the "Example" - which is real, tangible.

The methodological system explained here allows the movement between the various levels, that is, if at a given moment we are at the "Model" level we can go up to the "Archetype" level and generate new knowledge, and this is the added value of this methodological model, applied to artistic creation and in turn, to the artistic project.

HOW WE PROCEED: PEDAGOGICAL APPROACHES AND THE ARTS

Fernando Hernandez's (1998) work projects fit into this conception of teaching, seen as a way to rethink school and as another way to raise students' understanding of the knowledge that circulates in the world. The work projects bring the school closer to the students and allow a strong relationship between their research and interests and the discussion of the proposals. In this process it is fundamental to clearly define the objectives and contents, to expose doubts and to value all ideas and suggestions.

In this way of working, the teacher ceases to be a transmitter of content and becomes a researcher and the student goes from passive receiver to subject of the process. We can say that the different phases of a project help students to become aware of their own learning process.

Projects are based on the proposal and planning of a work, indicating the respective procedures and timing of the action, as well as the objectives, the hypotheses of study and the description of the expected results. In its Latin root, the word project refers to the idea of launching forward and may also be understood as being a set of operations aimed at a specific achievement, carried out in a given context and a certain space of time. In other contexts, it may also be associated with an outline of the future of something that is intended to be achieved.

For learning in higher education, Castejón Oliva et al. (2009) and Cepillo Galvín (2010) indicate projects as instruments that provide the development of a variety of written and oral competences and practical expression, which can be used in a formative way.

When working from projects, everyone's curiosity and questioning are valued and are decisive in the choice of project themes. In this process, it is essential to ensure the appropriation of learning by each student so that it is meaningful and connected to the world.

The methodological approaches we have adopted have the intention to privilege the transversality of knowledge and the students' ideas and intentions, for this reason, the teaching staff found in the project work approach the most adequate answer to the work typology oriented to visual arts.

In the progressive education movement, the project work methodology appears deeply associated with the thought of Dewey (1934), who proposes pedagogical approaches based on experimentalism which relates theory and practice.

In this context, each student has a place where his/her individual expression is respected and where his/her ideas and proposals integrate the teachers' guidelines and questioning. It is, therefore, a kind of project co-authorship that results in plural solutions tailored to each student. The search for a more humanised and individualised approach, necessary for artistic education, implies the creation of stimuli to generate projectual initiatives, creative spontaneity and freedom of artistic expression.

The experience of more than a decade indicates that through artistic experience it is possible to develop critical and creative thinking, sensitivity, temporality, contextualisation, spatiality and cultural diversity. Therefore, artistic experience plays an essential role in the development and integral formation of the individual, not only in the aesthetic-expressive domain, but also in the intellectual and moral domains. The artistic experience provides a kind of philosophical dialogue between teachers and students, and also among peers, which allows:

a)   deepen questions and conceive ideas;
b)   articulate them with transparency and rigour;
c)   open up space for complementary questions and ways of finding answers;
d)   create contexts for listening to the other, so as to be able to verify logical-conceptual relationships between ideas and simultaneously systematise and/or analyse the global result of the work.

We try, therefore, to transcend the mere transmission of knowledge, for a learning sustained in the integral development of the student, promoting significant learning, based on his interests and needs, whether in a pedagogical, technological or artistic level, listed by the different Curricular Units. We understand, therefore, that the relationship between development and learning is something that results from the internal dynamics of the subject in action, with others.

Our perspective is that the teacher should be a guide and a facilitator of learning through the promotion of listening, differentiation and the creation of ideas, namely by requesting different ideas from the students, also inviting them to ask questions, redirecting the dialogues so that the discussion remains relevant and focused on the subject, always seeking the relationship between contradictory or consonant ideas.

In this collaborative process, the promotion of critical thinking is done by offering reasons in the answers; questioning and testing the solidity or fragility of the ideas. Central is also the promotion of attitudes favourable to thought, making room for the error that makes us aware of our emotions and reactions and promotes dialogue with the ideas of others. In these dynamics we seek consensus and the creation of awareness about what we learn, namely through the creation of portfolios and descriptive memories where students record and systematize processes, research, questioning, thoughts and where they base their final answers.

It promotes a commitment that comes from shared learning, that is, a process where teaching and learning take place simultaneously, where each teaching strategy is also a vehicle that reinforces learning. Biggs and Tang (2011) state that this is the best way to learn or, as Beard and Wilson (2006) put it, to learn by discovery and not as mere listeners. Aware of this fact, teachers should improve their condition of mediators in the learning process, instead of being limited to the role of simple transmitters of content. Everything is lived and learnt in a relationship. Learning takes place in the relationship (teacher-student, student-student, teacher-teacher, student-internet, teacher-internet...).

The practice of visual arts suggests a "holistic" approach, an essential reconnection, which allows the use of different theoretical contributions without the risk of incurring in pedagogical fundamentalism.

In the course of the AVTA study plan, and as shown by other researches, the subjects who are guided in the sense of relating their doing with previous learning or other experiences, develop a deeper awareness of knowledge, approaching what Guiller et al. (2008) call authentic and multidimensional learning.

PROMOTION OF OWN WORKING METHODS AND EXTENSION TO THE COMMUNITY

The construction of a competence approach, as Perrenoud (1997) states, is situated on the innovation level, through a triple register: purposes, sense of work, school knowledge, the relationship with knowledge and action and on the didactic and pedagogical register.

This approach allows:

- The transformation of information into knowledge but is concerned with its mobilisation and transfer. According to Le Boterf (2016), there are no competencies without knowledge, as these are the ingredients of competencies;
- The development of competencies that are not identified with the application of exams or tests for the production of answers or execution of tasks;

- The development of a degree of autonomy in relation to the use of knowledge in a variety of situations;
- Viewing the curriculum as a project for learning achievement and competence development which should provide meaningful experiences.

All knowledge is integrated in the holistic evolution of civilizations, so everything we learn or share is part of human culture, from the prehistoric caves of Lascaux, (Cro Magnon, 15,000 years BC) to the experience of the most recent form of digital immersion and altered states of consciousness. We consider that culture includes the most contemplative and the most active components of our relationship with the world, the most metaphysical and the most pragmatic. Teaching an excellent class does not create skills but transmits knowledge. In other words, competences cannot be taught, only conditions that stimulate their construction can be created and, to do so, it is necessary to place the student in complex situations which require and train the mobilisation of their knowledge, as well as decision making: a problem to be solved, a project to be designed and developed.

We therefore point to Howard Gardner's (1995) model of multiple intelligences with regard to the diversity of learning that the visual arts offer and that enable the development of a wide spectrum of students' skills, seeking to respect the different ways of learning. Gardner (1995), in applying his theory to education, values teamwork, project work, creation, appreciation and critique of works of art, self-evaluation and conceiving the school as a small community.

Significant adaptive learning is not limited to an increase in knowledge, but to a penetrating learning that causes a modification in the individual's behaviour, future orientation and attitudes.

The projectual work contemplates the implication, appropriation, and the students' responsibility along their teaching-learning processes. These work processes are directly related to what the student wants to learn.

As Hargreaves (2003) recognises, learning in the knowledge society requires applying knowledge in a creative way, taking risks - because without them there can be no creativity - starting research in response to new demands and problems; but also taking personal responsibility for the achievement of common goals, and developing a sense of understanding of others, awareness of our interdependence, as well as being able to carry out collective projects. In curricular units such as Project, Painting, Drawing or Sculpture, students determine their areas of interest and develop research projects, both collectively and individually. The diversity inherent in each group/class leads us to polysemic answers, aware of the influence that the multiple social and political frameworks have on their answers to the challenges posed. Shouldn't we then take advantage of social transformations to keep students in contact with real problems, in order to promote an artistic and participatory consciousness within the polis? We think so.

As some of the research projects have already shown, there seems to be a more significant appetite and involvement in challenges that involve the resolution of real problems and not just idealised situations. The experiences of Chamithri and Kalkreuter in Scotland or the work led by Seitamaa-Hakkarainen and Kangas in Helsinki were examples of trying to solve problems that actually existed and whose complexity involved not only the students but led them to work collaboratively with experts or members of the community where the projects took place. In addition to forcing themselves to understand the context, these working groups helped each other to learn techniques/processes, reinforcing the sense of community.

The training stage therefore proves to be an appropriate space for exploring and encouraging this appetite, combining education with solving problems in the communities where it takes place. This is a path that allows schools and students to be socially effective, contributing to the establishment and maintenance of relationships with their surroundings. In this sense, collaboration protocols are created and maintained with external organisations, such as the Porto and Maia City Councils, art galleries and other institutions, which have been constituting stages for the action of students, in the field of the arts, either within the scope of certain curricular units or of voluntary access, stimulating learning and involvement with the community.

REFERENCES

Beard, C. M., & Wilson, J. P. (2006). *Experiential learning: A best practice handbook for educators and trainers*. Kogan Page Publishers.

Biggs, J. B. (2011). *Teaching for quality learning at university: What the student does*. McGraw-Hill Education.

Castejón Oliva, J., Capllonch Bujosa, M., González Fernández, N., & López Pastor, V. (2009). Técnicas e instrumentos de evaluación. Evaluación formativa y compartida en educación superior: propuestas, técnicas, instrumentos y experiencias, 65-91.

Cepillo Galvín, M. (2010). Aprendizaje basado en problemas. Técnicas docentes y sistemas de evaluación en educación superior, 31-36.

Chamithri, C., & Kalkreuter, B. (2014). Makers in the Classroom: Knowledge exchange through practice. *Making Futures Journal, 3*. http://www. plymouthart. ac.uk/documents/Greru__C__Kalkreuter__B.pdf?1396862851

Dewey, J. (1916). Democracy and education: An introduction to the philosophy of education. Macmillan.

Dewey, J. (1934). *Art as Experience* (14th ed.). Capricorn Books.

Gardner, H. (1995). Inteligências Múltiplas: A teoria na prática. *The Art of Medication*.

Hargreaves, A. (2003). *Teaching in the Knowledge Society*. Columbia University.

Le Boterf, G. (2016). *Professionnaliser: construire des parcours personnalisés de professionnalisation*. Eyrolles.

Manzini, E. (2006). *Design, ethics and sustainability. Guidelines for a transition phase*. Nantes Cumulus Working Papers. Helsinki: University of Art and Design.

Munari, B. (1981). *Das coisas nascem coisas*. Edições 70.

Munari, B. (2007). *Fantasia*. Edições 70.

Perrenoud, Ph. (1997). *Construire des compétences dès l'école*. ESF.

Plano Nacional das Artes. (2019). *Uma estratégia um manifesto*. PNA. https://www.dge.mec.pt/sites/default/files/Projetos/PNA/Documentos/estrategia_do_plano_nacional_das_artes_2019-2024.pdf

Seitamaa-Hakkarainen, P., & Kangas, K. (2013). Craft education: authentic design constraints, embodied thinking, and craft making. DRS CUMULUS 2013 Design Learning for Tomorrow, Oslo.

ENDNOTES

1 https://universcidade.pt/sistema-binario/
2 https://www.dges.gov.pt/pt/pagina/sistema-de-ensino-superior portugues?plid=371
3 https://www.ese.ipp.pt/ese/historia
4 https://www.ese.ipp.pt/cursos/licenciatura/460

Compilation of References

Abbott, M. L. (2011). *Understanding educational statistics using Microsoft Excel and SPSS.* John Wiley & Sons, Inc.

Abdulwahed, M., & Nagy, Z. K. (2009). Applying Kolb's experiential learning cycle for laboratory education. *Journal of Engineering Education, 98*(3), 283–294. doi:10.1002/j.2168-9830.2009. tb01025.x

Abuhassna, H., & Alnawajha, S. (2023). Instructional design made easy! instructional design models, categories, frameworks, educational context, and recommendations for future work. *European Journal of Investigation in Health, Psychology and Education, 13*(4), 715–735. doi:10.3390/ejihpe13040054 PMID:37185907

Adams, P. (2006). Exploring social constructivism: theories and practicalities. Education 3-13, 34(3), 243-257. https://doi.org/ doi:10.1080/03004270600898893

Adams, V., Burger, S., Crawford, K., & Setter, R. (2018). Can You Escape? Creating an Escape Room to Facilitate Active Learning. *Journal for Nurses in Professional Development, 34*(2), E1–e5. doi:10.1097/NND.0000000000000433 PMID:29481471

Agyei, D., & Voogt, J. (2012). Developing technological pedagogical content knowledge in pre-service mathematics teachers, through collaborative design teams. *Australasian Journal of Educational Technology, 28*(4), 547–564. doi:10.14742/ajet.827

Ahmad, N. A. N., Suhaimi, A. I. H., & Lokman, A. M. (2022). Conceptual model of augmented reality mobile application design (armad) to enhance user experience: An expert review. *International Journal of Advanced Computer Science and Applications, 13*(10), 574–582. doi:10.14569/IJACSA.2022.0131067

AICTE Approved Institutions having NBA Accredited Cources. (2019). https://doi.org/ doi:2019-04-10

AIIS Artificial Intelligence. Innovation & Society. (No date). A project website. https://aiis.usal.es/

Akkaya, A. (2019). *The effect of the activities developed by Web 2.0 tools on computer hardware on student success* [Unpublished master's thesis]. Balıkesir University.

Al Fadda, H. (2019). The Relationship between Self-Regulations and Online Learning in an ESL Blended Learning Context. *English Language Teaching, 12*(6), 87–93. doi:10.5539/elt.v12n6p87

Al-azawi, R., Al-faliti, F., & Al-blushi, M. (2016). Educational Gamification Vs. Game Based Learning : Comparative Study. *International Journal of Innovation, Management and Technology, 7*(4), 131–136. doi:10.18178/ijimt.2016.7.4.659

Al-Gindy, A., Felix, C., Ahmed, A., Matoug, A., & Alkhidir, M. (2020). Virtual reality: Development of an integrated learning environment for education. *International Journal of Information and Education Technology (IJIET), 10*(3), 171–175. doi:10.18178/ijiet.2020.10.3.1358

Alkoudmani, R. M., Elkalmi, R. M., Hassali, M. A., & Apolinário-Hagen, J. (2021). The effect of generic medicines e-learning course via Web 2.0 tools on knowledge of pharmacists and pharmacy students. *Pharmacy Education, 21*, 679–689. doi:10.46542/pe.2021.211.679689

Allen, D. W. (1967). Microteaching, A description. Retrieved from https://files.eric.ed.gov/fulltext/ED019224.pdf

Allen, I. E., & Seaman, J. (2010). Class differences: Online education in the United States, 2010. *Sloan Consortium (NJ1).*

Almulla, M. A. (2020). The Effectiveness of the Project-Based Learning (PBL) Approach as a Way to Engage Students in Learning. *SAGE Open, 10*(3). Advance online publication. doi:10.1177/2158244020938702

Alonso, G., & Schroeder, K. T. (2020). Applying active learning in a virtual classroom such as a molecular biology escape room. *Biochemistry and Molecular Biology Education, 48*(5), 514–515. doi:10.1002/bmb.21429 PMID:32812701

Al-Sakkaf, A., Omar, M., & Ahmad, M. (2019). A systematic literature review of student engagement in software visualization: A theoretical perspective. *Computer Science Education, 29*(2-3), 283–309. Advance online publication. doi:10.1080/08993408.2018.1564611

Alsubhi, M. A., Ashaari, N. S., & Wook, T. S. M. T. (2021). Design and evaluation of an engagement framework for e-learning gamification. *International Journal of Advanced Computer Science and Applications, 12*(9), 411–417. doi:10.14569/IJACSA.2021.0120947

Alsuwaida, N. (2022). Designing and Evaluating the Impact of Using a Blended Art Course and Web 2.0 Tools in Saudi Arabia. *Journal of Information Technology Education, 21*, 25. doi:10.28945/4923

Altuwairqi, K., Jarraya, S. K., Allinjawi, A., & Hammami, M. (2021). Student behavior analysis to measure engagement levels in online learning environments. *Signal, Image and Video Processing, 15*(7), 1387–1395. doi:10.100711760-021-01869-7 PMID:34007342

Álvarez-Marín, A., & Velázquez-Iturbide, J. Á. (2021). Augmented reality and engineering education: A systematic review. *IEEE Transactions on Learning Technologies, 14*(6), 817–831. doi:10.1109/TLT.2022.3144356

Anderson, L. W., Krathwohl, D. R., Airasian, P. W., Cruikshank, K. A., Mayer, R. E., Pintrich, P. R., Raths, R., & Wittrock, M. C. (2001). *A taxonomy for learning, teaching and assessing. A revision of Bloom's taxonomy of educational objectives*. Pearson Education.

Anderson, M., Lioce, L., & Robertson, M., J., O. Lopreiato, J., & A. Díaz, D. (. (2021). Toward Defining Healthcare Simulation Escape Rooms. *Simulation & Gaming*, 52(1), 7–17. doi:10.1177/1046878120958745

Andreatos, A. & Leros, A. (2023). Can Oral Grades Predict Final Examination Scores? Case Study in a Higher Education Military Academy. *MDPI Analytics*.

Andreatos, A. (2023). An Educational Scenario for Teaching Cyber Security Using low-cost Equipment and Open Source Software. In *Proc. of ECCWS 2023, 22nd European Conference on Cyber Warfare and Security*. Hellenic Air Force Academy. 10.34190/eccws.22.1.1113

Andreatos, A. S. (2021, January). Redesigning Engineering Assessment during the Covid-19 Lockdown – A case study in Computer Networking and Network Security. *Technium Social Sciences Journal*, 15, 108–124.

Ang, J. W. J., Ng, Y. N. A., & Liew, R. S. (2020). Physical and digital educational escape room for teaching chemical bonding. *Journal of Chemical Education*, 97(9), 2849–2856. doi:10.1021/acs.jchemed.0c00612

Antonios, S. (2017). Designing educational scenarios to teach network security. *Proc. of IEEE Educon 2017.*. https://ieeexplore.ieee.org/document/7943063

Anurugwo, A. O. (2018). *ICT Tools for Promoting Self-Paced Learning among Sandwich Students in a Nigerian University, Commission for International Adult Education*. Commission for International Adult Education.

Apicella, A., Arpaia, P., Frosolone, M., Improta, G., Moccaldi, N. & Pollastro, A. (2022). EEG-based measurement system for monitoring student engagement in learning 4.0. *Scientific Reports*, 12(1), 5857. doi:10.103841598-022-09578-y PMID:35393470

Arcodia, C., Abreu Novais, M., Cavlek, N., & Humpe, A. (2021). Educational tourism and experiential learning: Students' perceptions of field trips. *Tourism Review*, 76(1), 241–254. doi:10.1108/TR-05-2019-0155

Armstrong, E. K. (2003). Applications of role-playing in tourism management teaching: An evaluation of a learning method. *Journal of Hospitality, Leisure, Sport and Tourism Education*, 2(1), 5–16. doi:10.3794/johlste.21.24

Arnseth, H. C. (2008). Activity theory and situated learning theory: Contrasting views of educational practice. *Pedagogy, Culture & Society*, 16(3), 289–302. doi:10.1080/14681360802346663

Arsal, Z. (2014). Microteaching and pre-service teachers' sense of self-efficacy in teaching. *European Journal of Teacher Education*, 37(4), 453–464. doi:10.1080/02619768.2014.912627

Askren, J., & James, W. (2021). Experiential Learning Methods in Culinary Course Can Bridge the Gap: Student Perceptions on How Hands-On Curriculum Prepares Them for Industry. *Journal of Hospitality \& Tourism Education, 33*(2), 111–125. doi:10.1080/10963758.2020.1791134

Atav, E., Kunduz, N., & Seçken, N. (2014). Pre-service teachers' views about micro teaching practices in biology education. *Hacettepe University Journal of Faculty of Education, 29*(4), 01-15.

Avargil, S., Shwartz, G., & Zemel, Y. (2021). Educational Escape Room: Break Dalton's Code and Escape! *Journal of Chemical Education*, *98*(7), 2313–2322. doi:10.1021/acs.jchemed.1c00110

Avcı, F., & Atik, H. (2020). Metaphoric perceptions and views of preschool and elementary teachers on the concept of "web 2.0 tools". *Qualitative Social Sciences*, *2*(2), 142–165. doi:10.47105/nsb.800117

Baase, S., & van Gelder, A. (2000). *Computer algorithms* (3rd ed.). Addison Wesley Longman.

Babacan, T., & Şaşmaz Ören, F. (2017). The effect of technology assisted micro teaching practices on prospective science teachers' perceptions of technology usage. [Teknoloji destekli mikro öğretim uygulamalarının fen bilimleri öğretmen adaylarının teknoloji kullanım algıları üzerine etkisi]. *Educational Technology Theory and Practice*, *7*(2), 193–214. doi:10.17943/etku.300412

Bado, N. (2022). Game-based learning pedagogy: A review of the literature. *Interactive Learning Environments*, *30*(5), 936–948. doi:10.1080/10494820.2019.1683587

Bahçivan, E. (2017). Implementing microteaching lesson study with a group of preservice science teachers: An encouraging attempt of action research. *International Online Journal of Educational Sciences*, *9*(3), 591–602. doi:10.15345/iojes.2017.03.001

Balci, S., Cakiroglu, J., & Tekkaya, C. (2006). Engagement, exploration, explanation, extension, and evaluation (5E) learning cycle and conceptual change text as learning tools. *Biochemistry and Molecular Biology Education*, *34*(3), 199–203. doi:10.1002/bmb.2006.49403403199 PMID:21638670

Bandura, A., & Adams, N. E. (1977). Analysis of self-efficacy theory of behavioral change. *Cognitive Therapy and Research*, *1*(4), 287–310. doi:10.1007/BF01663995

Banerjee, M., Zlatkin-Troitschanskaia, O., & Roeper, J. (2020). Narratives and Their Impact on Students' Information Seeking and Critical Online Reasoning in Higher Education Economics and Medicine. *Frontiers in Education*, 5.

Bang, E., & Luft, J. A. (2013). Secondary science teachers' use of technology in the classroom during their first 5 years. *Journal of Digital Learning in Teacher Education*, *29*(4), 118–126. doi:10.1080/21532974.2013.10784715

Barab, S., & Squire, K. (2004). Design-based research: Putting a stake in the ground. *Journal of the Learning Sciences*, *13*(1), 1–14. doi:10.120715327809jls1301_1

Baştürk, S. (2016). Investigating the effectiveness of microteaching in mathematics of primary pre-service teachers. *Journal of Education and Training Studies*, *4*(5). Advance online publication. doi:10.11114/jets.v4i5.1509

Bay Atlantic University. (2021). *8 Types of Learning Styles | The Definitive Guide.* https://bau.edu/blog/types-of-learning-styles/

Beam, E. A. (2016). Do job fairs matter? Experimental evidence on the impact of job-fair attendance. *Journal of Development Economics*, *120*, 32–40. https://doi.org/https://doi.org/10.1016/j.jdeveco.2015.11.004. doi:10.1016/j.jdeveco.2015.11.004 PMID:34712002

Beard, C. M., & Wilson, J. P. (2006). *Experiential learning: A best practice handbook for educators and trainers.* Kogan Page Publishers.

Beaumont, T. J., Mannion, A. P., & Shen, B. O. (2012). From the Campus to the Cloud: The Online Peer Assisted Learning Scheme. *Journal of Peer Learning*, *5*(6), 20–31.

Bell, L., & Lygo-Baker, S. (2019). Student-centred learning: A small-scale study of a peer-learning experience in undergraduate translation classes. *Language Learning Journal*, *47*(3), 299–312. doi:10.1080/09571736.2016.1278030

Bell, N. D. (2007). Microteaching: What is it that is going on here? *Linguistics and Education*, *18*(1), 24–40. doi:10.1016/j.linged.2007.04.002

Bernal-Morales, B., Rodríguez-Landa, J. F., & Pulido-Criollo, F. (2015). *Impact of anxiety and depression symptoms on scholar performance in high school and university students, a fresh look at anxiety disorders.* IntechOpen.

Berthod, F., Bouchoud, L., Grossrieder, F., Falaschi, L., Senhaji, S., & Bonnabry, P. (2020). Learning good manufacturing practices in an escape room: Validation of a new pedagogical tool. *Journal of Oncology Pharmacy Practice*, *26*(4), 853–860. doi:10.1177/1078155219875504 PMID:31566110

Betancur-Chicue´, V., & Munoz˜-Repiso, A. G. (2023). Microlearning strategy design features in educational settings: A systematic review. *RIED-Revista Iberoamericana de Educacion a Distancia*, *26*(1), 201–222.

Bezanilla, M. J., Fernández-Nogueira, D., Poblete, M., & Galindo-Domínguez, H. (2019). Methodologies for teaching-learning critical thinking in higher education: The teacher's view. *Thinking Skills and Creativity*, *33*, 100584. https://doi.org/https://doi.org/10.1016/j.tsc.2019.100584. doi:10.1016/j.tsc.2019.100584

Bidder, C., Kibat, S. A., & Johnny, C. (2019). Tourism Education: Students' Perceived Values of Field Trips. In A. N. Mat Noor, Z. Z. Mohd Zakuan, & S. Muhamad Noor (Eds.), *Proceedings of the Second International Conference on the Future of ASEAN (ICoFA) 2017 - Volume 1* (pp. 135–143). Springer Singapore.

Biggs, J. B. (2011). *Teaching for quality learning at university: What the student does.* McGraw-Hill Education.

BIMCO, & ICS. (2015). *Manpower Report Executive Summary 2015*, 6.

Birney, L. B., Kong, J., Evans, B. R., Danker, M., & Grieser, K. (2017). Microteaching: An introspective case study with middle school teachers in New York City Public Schools. *Journal of Curriculum and Teaching*, *6*(2), 1–5. doi:10.5430/jct.v6n2p1

Black, P., & Wiliam, D. (1998). Assessment and classroom learning. *Assessment in Education: Principles, Policy & Practice*, *5*(1), 7–74. doi:10.1080/0969595980050102

Blake, J. (2021). Asynchronous peer teaching using student-created multimodal materials. *International Journal of Information and Education Technology (IJIET)*, *11*(6), 286–291. doi:10.18178/ijiet.2021.11.6.1524

Bosworth, A., & Clegg, N. (2021) Building the Metaverse Responsibly, Meta Newsroom (September 27, 2021), DOI = https://about.fb.com/news/2021/09/buildingthe-metaverse-responsibly/

Boud, D. (2001). Making the move to peer learning. *Peer Learning in Higher Education: Learning from and with Each Other*, *1*, 20.

Brady, S. C., & Andersen, E. C. (2021). An escape-room inspired game for genetics review. *Journal of Biological Education*, *55*(4), 406–417. doi:10.1080/00219266.2019.1703784

Breien, F. S., & Wasson, B. (2021). Narrative categorization in digital game-based learning: Engagement, motivation & learning. *British Journal of Educational Technology*, *52*(1), 91–111. https://doi.org/https://doi.org/10.1111/bjet.13004. doi:10.1111/bjet.13004

Bretz, S. L. (2001). Novak's Theory of Education: Human Constructivism and Meaningful Learning. *Journal of Chemical Education*, *78*(8), 1107. doi:10.1021/ed078p1107.6

Brice, S., & Almond, H. (2020). Health Professional Digital Capabilities Frameworks: A Scoping Review. *Journal of Multidisciplinary Healthcare*, *2*(13), 1375–1390. doi:10.2147/JMDH.S269412 PMID:33173300

Brown, G. (1975). *Micro-teaching: A program of teaching skills*. Harper & Row.

Brown, N., Darby, W., & Coronel, H. (2019). An Escape Room as a Simulation Teaching Strategy. *Clinical Simulation in Nursing*, *30*, 1–6. https://doi.org/https://doi.org/10.1016/j.ecns.2019.02.002. doi:10.1016/j.ecns.2019.02.002

Bruner, J. S. (1960). *The process of education*. Harvard University Press.

Buchner, J., Rüter, M., & Kerres, M. (2022). Learning with a digital escape room game: Before or after instruction? *Research and Practice in Technology Enhanced Learning*, *17*(1), 10. doi:10.118641039-022-00187-x PMID:35310067

Bulut, K., Açık, F., & Çiftçi, Ö. (2016). The Effect of microteaching on pre-service Turkish language teachers' speaking skills. *Journal of Mother Tongue Education*, *4*(1), 134–150. doi:10.16916/aded.36249

Bunts-Anderson, K. (2016). Successful online learning collaboration: Peer feedback and technology integration in English composition courses. *Arab World English Journal (AWEJ) Special Issue on CALL, 3*.

Burazer, M., Ebner, M., & Ebner, M. (2020). Implementation of interactive learning objects for German language acquisition in primary school based on learning analytics measurements. EdMedia+ Innovate Learning, Cao, W., Wang, Q., Sbeih, A., & Shibly, F. (2020) Artificial intelligence based efficient smart learning framework for an education platform. *Inteligencia Artificial*, *23*(66), 112–123.

Burhan-Horasanlı, E. (2022). Digital social reading: Exploring multilingual graduate students' academic discourse socialization in online platforms. *Linguistics and Education*, *71*, 101099. https://doi.org/https://doi.org/10.1016/j.linged.2022.101099. doi:10.1016/j.linged.2022.101099

Burkšaitienė, N. (2022). Translation students' peer feedback for learning English for Specific Purposes (ESP). Findings from a case study in Lithuania. *The Journal of Education, Culture, and Society*, *13*(1), 173–187. doi:10.15503/jecs2022.1.173.187

Bustos-López, M., Cruz-Ramírez, N., Guerra-Hernández, A., Sánchez-Morales, L. N., Cruz-Ramos, N. A., & Alor-Hernández, G. (2022). Wearables for Engagement Detection in Learning Environments: A Review. *Biosensors (Basel)*, *12*(7), 509. doi:10.3390/bios12070509 PMID:35884312

Büyüköztürk, Ş. (2006). *Manual of data analysis for social sciences* [Sosyal Bilimler İçin Veri Analizi El Kitabı]. PegemA Yayınları.

Caesar, L. (2013). Sustaining the Supply of Ship Officers:Making a Case for Succession Planning in Seafarer Recruitment. *Universal Journal of Management*, *1*(1), 6–12. doi:10.13189/ujm.2013.010102

Cain, J. (2019). Exploratory implementation of a blended format escape room in a large enrollment pharmacy management class. *Currents in Pharmacy Teaching & Learning*, *11*(1), 44–50. https://doi.org/https://doi.org/10.1016/j.cptl.2018.09.010. doi:10.1016/j.cptl.2018.09.010 PMID:30527875

Cai, S. (2022). Harry Potter Themed Digital Escape Room for Addressing Misconceptions in Stoichiometry. *Journal of Chemical Education*, *99*(7), 2747–2753. doi:10.1021/acs.jchemed.2c00178

Çalışkan, S., Güney, Z., Sakhieva, R. G., Vasbieva, D. G., & Zaitseva, N. A. (2019). Teachers' views on the availability of Web 2.0 tools in education. *International Journal of Emerging Technologies in Learning*, *14*(22), 70–81. doi:10.3991/ijet.v14i22.11752

Cambridge. (2023). https://www.cambridge.org/core/books/abs/practical-tips-for-developing-your-staff/honey-and-mumford-learning-styles/2BA8CBFC6476F6C3252396CFB7705F8C

Canham, N. (2017). Comparing Web 2.0 applications for peer feedback in language teaching: Google Docs, the Sakai VLE, and the Sakai Wiki. *Writing \& Pedagogy, 9*(3).

Cao, J., Lam, K., Lee, L., Liu, X., Hui, P., & Su, X. (2023). Mobile augmented reality: User interfaces, frameworks, and intelligence. *ACM Computing Surveys*, *55*(9), 1–36. doi:10.1145/3557999

Capp, M. J. (2017). The effectiveness of universal design for learning: A meta-analysis of literature between 2013 and 2016. *International Journal of Inclusive Education*, *21*(8), 791–807. doi:10.1080/13603116.2017.1325074

Card, S. K., Mackinley, J. D., & Shneiderman, B. (1999). *Readings in information visualization.* Morgan Kaufmann.

Carvalho, A. R., & Santos, C. (2022). Developing peer mentors' collaborative and metacognitive skills with a technology-enhanced peer learning program. *Computers and Education Open, 3,* 100070. https://doi.org/https://doi.org/10.1016/j.caeo.2021.100070

Castejón Oliva, J., Capllonch Bujosa, M., González Fernández, N., & López Pastor, V. (2009). Técnicas e instrumentos de evaluación. Evaluación formativa y compartida en educación superior: propuestas, técnicas, instrumentos y experiencias, 65-91.

Cavin, R. M. (2007). *Developing technological pedagogical content knowledge in preservice teachers through microteaching lesson study* [Unpublished doctoral dissertation]. The Florida State University.

CDIO. (No date). About CDIO. http://www.cdio.org/about

Cepillo Galvín, M. (2010). Aprendizaje basado en problemas. Técnicas docentes y sistemas de evaluación en educación superior, 31-36.

Chamithri, C., & Kalkreuter, B. (2014). Makers in the Classroom: Knowledge exchange through practice. *Making Futures Journal, 3.* http://www. plymouthart.ac.uk/documents/Greru__C__ Kalkreuter__B.pdf?1396862851

Chandra, S., & Palvia, S. (2021). Online education next wave: Peer to peer learning. *Journal of Information Technology Case and Application Research*, *23*(3), 157–172. doi:10.1080/15228053.2021.1980848

Chapell, M. S., Blanding, Z. B., Silverstein, M. E., Takahashi, M., Newman, B., Gubi, A., & McCann, N. (2005). Test anxiety and academic performance in undergraduate and graduate students. *Journal of Educational Psychology*, *972*(2), 268–274. doi:10.1037/0022-0663.97.2.268

Charmaz, K. (2006). *Constructing Grounded Theory: A practical guide through qualitative analysis.* Sage.

Chen, J. H. (2021). Augmenting Student and Professional Training with Peer Learning Groups: Results from Focus Group Interviews. Rutgers The State University of New Jersey, Graduate School of Applied and~….

Chen, R. (2022). Investigating the Audio-Visual Psychological Effects in a Horror Game Northeastern University].

Chen, H.-R. (2012). Assessment of Learners' Attention to E-Learning by Monitoring Facial Expressions for Computer Network Courses. *Journal of Educational Computing Research*, *47*(4), 371–385. doi:10.2190/EC.47.4.b

Chen, S. Y., & Chang, Y.-M. (2020). The impacts of real competition and virtual competition in digital game-based learning. *Computers in Human Behavior*, *104*, 106171. https://doi.org/https://doi.org/10.1016/j.chb.2019.10617. doi:10.1016/j.chb.2019.106171

Ching, Y.-H. (2014). Exploring the impact of role-playing on peer feedback in an online case-based learning activity. *International Review of Research in Open and Distance Learning*, *15*(3), 292–311. doi:10.19173/irrodl.v15i3.1765

Cho, M. (2017). Pre-service L2 teacher trainees' reflection: What do they focus on? *English Teaching*, *72*(1), 105–129. doi:10.15858/engtea.72.1.201703.105

Christopoulos, A., Mystakidis, S., Cachafeiro, E., & Laakso, M.-J. (2022). Escaping the cell: Virtual reality escape rooms in biology education. *Behaviour & Information Technology*, ●●●, 1–18. doi:10.1080/0144929X.2022.2079560

Cilliers, E. J. (2017). The Challenge of Teaching Generation Z. *The International Journal of Social Sciences (Islamabad)*, *3*(1), 188–198. doi:10.20319/pijss.2017.31.18819

Clarke, S. J., Peel, D. J., Arnab, S., Morini, L., Keegan, H., & Wood, O. (2017). EscapED: A Framework for Creating Educational Escape Rooms and Interactive Games to For Higher/Further Education. *International Journal of Serious Games*, *4*(3). Advance online publication. doi:10.17083/ijsg.v4i3.180

Clauson, A., Hahn, L., Frame, T., Hagan, A., Bynum, L. A., Thompson, M. E., & Kiningham, K. (2019). An innovative escape room activity to assess student readiness for advanced pharmacy practice experiences (APPEs). *Currents in Pharmacy Teaching & Learning*, *11*(7), 723–728. doi:10.1016/j.cptl.2019.03.011 PMID:31227096

Cochran-Smith, M. (2004). The problem of teacher education. *Journal of Teacher Education*, *55*(4), 295–299. doi:10.1177/0022487104268057

Coelho, L., Braga, D., Dias, M., & Garcia-Mateo, C. 2011. An Automatic Voice Pleasantness Classification System Based on Prosodic and Acoustic Patterns of Voice Preference, in: Proc. Interspeech. Presented at the Interspeech, Florence. 10.21437/Interspeech.2011-589

Coelho, L., Coelho, F. G., & Reis, S. 2021. Preferences for Teaching Materials: A Survey on a Multimodal World, in: 2021 IEEE Global Engineering Education Conference (EDUCON). Presented at the 2021 IEEE Global Engineering Education Conference (EDUCON). 10.1109/EDUCON46332.2021.9454099

Cohen, L., Manion, L., & Morrison, K. (2007). Research methods in education (6th ed.). Routledge/Taylor & Francis Group. doi:10.4324/9780203029053

Cohen, L., Manion, L., & Morrison, K. (2018). *Research Methods in Education* (8th ed.). Routledge.

Cohen, T. N., Griggs, A. C., Kanji, F. F., Cohen, K. A., Lazzara, E. H., Keebler, J. R., & Gewertz, B. L. (2021). Advancing team cohesion: Using an escape room as a novel approach. *Journal of Patient Safety and Risk Management*, *26*(3), 126–134. doi:10.1177/25160435211005934

Cohn, D. (2010). Active Learning. In C. Sammut & G. I. Webb (Eds.), *Encyclopedia of Machine Learning* (pp. 10–14). Springer US., doi:10.1007/978-0-387-30164-8_6

Compayré, G., & Payne, W. H. (1885). *The History of Pedagogy*. Routledge.

Connelly, L., Burbach, B. E., Kennedy, C., & Walters, L. (2018). Escape room recruitment event: Description and lessons learned. *The Journal of Nursing Education*, *57*(3), 184–187. doi:10.3928/01484834-20180221-12 PMID:29505080

Cope, B., Kalantzis, M., & Searsmith, D. (2021). Artificial intelligence for education: Knowledge and its assessment in AI-enabled learning ecologies. *Educational Philosophy and Theory*, *53*(12), 1229–1245. doi:10.1080/00131857.2020.1728732

Cordova, J. (2022). Motivating the study of discrete structures with experiments. *Journal of Computing Sciences in Colleges*, *37*(7), 23–30.

Cormen, T. H., Leiserson, C. E., Rivest, R. L., & Stein, C. (2009). *Introduction to algorithms* (3rd ed.). The MIT Press.

Cranmer, G. (2017). One-group pretest–posttest design. In M. Allen (Ed.), *The sage encyclopedia of communication research methods* (pp. 1125–1126). SAGE Publications, Inc., doi:10.4135/9781483381411.n388

Creed, P. A., Fallon, T., & Hood, M. (2009). The relationship between career adaptability, person and situation variables, and career concerns in young adults. *Journal of Vocational Behavior*, *74*(2), 219–229. doi:10.1016/j.jvb.2008.12.004

Creswell, J. W. (2003). Research design: qualitative, quantitative, and mixed method approaches. In V. Knight (Ed.), Thousand Oaks Calif (Vol. 2nd). Sage Publications. doi:10.2307/3152153

Crichton, H., Valdera Gil, F., & Hadfield, C. (2021). Reflections on peer micro-teaching: Raising questions about theory informed practice. *Reflective Practice*, *22*(3), 345–362. doi:10.1080/14623943.2021.1892621

Cronje, J. (2020). Towards a new definition of blended learning. *Electronic journal of e-Learning*, *18*(2), pp114-121-pp114-121.

Crouse-Machcinski, K. (2019). The Benefits of Utilizing Learning Management Systems in Peer Tutor Training. *Learning Assistance Review*, *24*(2), 73–84.

Cruz, M. (2019). Escaping from the traditional classroom-The 'Escape Room Methodology' in the Foreign Languages Classroom. Babylonia-Rivista svizzera per l'insegnamento delle lingue, 3, 26-29.

Cruz, M. (2019). Escaping from the traditional classroom-The'Escape Room Methodology'in the Foreign Languages Classroom. Babylonia-Rivista svizzera per l'insegnamento delle lingue, 3, 26-29.

Cruz, M. (2021). CLIL Approach and the Fostering of "Creactical Skills" towards a Global Sustainable Awareness. *MEXTESOL Journal*, *45*(2), n2.

Cuban, L. (1986). *Teachers and machines: The classroom use of technology since 1920.* Teachers College Press.

D'Antonio, L. (2003). Incorporating bioinformatics in an algorithms course. In *Proceedings of the 10th annual conference on innovation and technology in computer science education, ITiCSE'05*, pp. 211-214. https://doi.org/10.1145/961511.961569

da Cruz, M. R. D. F. (2019). 'Escapando de la clase tradicional': The escape rooms methodology within the spanish as foreign language classroom. *Revista Lusófona de Educação*, *46*(46), 117–137. doi:10.24140/issn.1645-7250.rle46.08

Dallas News. (2022). Nokia's vision of the future is a world where the metaverse replaces smartphones. https://www.dallasnews.com/business/technology/2022/10/13/nokias-vision-of-the-future-is-a-world-where-the-metaverse-replaces-smartphones/

Darling-Hammond, L. (2010). Teacher education and the American future. *Journal of Teacher Education*, *61*(1–2), 35–47. doi:10.1177/0022487109348024

Darling-Hammond, L., & Adamson, F. (2014). *Beyond the bubble test: How performance assessments support 21st century learning.* Jossey-Bass.

Das, S., Franguiadakis, T., Papka, M., Defanti, T. A., & Sandin, D. J. A genetic programming application in virtual reality. In *Proceedings of the 1994 IEEE 3rd International Fuzzy Systems Conference*, Orlando, FL, USA, 26–29 June 1994, pp. 480–484.

Davis, H. C., & Fill, K. (2007). Embedding blended learning in a university's teaching culture: Experiences and reflections. *British Journal of Educational Technology*, *38*(5), 817–828. doi:10.1111/j.1467-8535.2007.00756.x

Dawley, L., & Dede, C. (2014). Situated Learning in Virtual Worlds and Immersive Simulations. In J. M. Spector, M. D. Merrill, J. Elen, & M. J. Bishop (Eds.), *Handbook of Research on Educational Communications and Technology* (pp. 723–734). Springer., doi:10.1007/978-1-4614-3185-5_58

Dawson, K., Pringle, R., & Adams, T. L. (2003). Providing links between technology integration, methods courses, and school-based field experiences: A curriculum-based and technology-enhanced microteaching. *Journal of Computing in Teacher Education*, *20*(1), 41–47.

De Gagne, J. C., Park, H. K., Hall, K., Woodward, A., Yamane, S., & Kim, S. S. (2019). Microlearning in health professions education: Scoping review. *JMIR Medical Education*, *5*(2), e13997. doi:10.2196/13997 PMID:31339105

Debnath, R. M., & Shankar, R. (2012). Improving service quality in technical education: Use of interpretive structural modeling. *Quality Assurance in Education*, *20*(4), 387–407. doi:10.1108/09684881211264019

DeFillippi, R. (2001). Introduction: Project-Based Learning, Reflective Practices and Learning Outcomes. *Management Learning*, *32*(1), 5–10. doi:10.1177/1350507601321001

Delgado, L., Galvez, D., Hassan, A., Palominos, P., & Morel, L. (2020). Innovation spaces in universities: Support for collaborative learning. *Journal of Innovation Economics Management*, *31*(1), 123–153. doi:10.3917/jie.pr1.0064

Demirel, O. (1999). *Didactics* [[*Öğretme sanatı*]]. Pegem Press.

Deperlioğlu, Ö., & Köse, U. (2010). Effects of Web 2.0 technologies on the education and an example learning experience. [Web 2.0 teknolojilerinin eğitim üzerindeki etkileri ve örnek bir öğrenme yaşantısı]. XII. *Akademik Bilişim Konferansı Bildirileri*, 237-242.

Dewar, B., & Sharp, C. (2006). Using evidence: How action learning can support individual and organisational learning through action research. *Educational Action Research*, *14*(2), 219–237. doi:10.1080/09650790600718092

Dewey, J. (1916). Democracy and education: An introduction to the philosophy of education. Macmillan.

Dewey, J. (1934). *Art as Experience* (14th ed.). Capricorn Books.

Dewey, J. (1988). The development of American Pragmatism. In J. Dewey & J. A. Boydston (Eds.), *The Middle Works of John Dewey* (Vol. 10, pp. 320–365). Southern Illinois University Press. (Original work published 1925)

DGS. (2017). Intake Utilization Matrix. Retrieved July 1, 2019, from https://www.dgshipping.gov. in/WriteReadData/CMS/Documents/201805040624390335728CapacityUtilizationReport.pdf

Diachenko, I., Kalishchuk, S., Zhylin, M., Kyyko, A., & Volkova, Y. (2022). Color education: A study on methods of influence on memory. *Heliyon*, *8*(11), e11607. doi:10.1016/j.heliyon.2022. e11607 PMID:36411932

Diana, T. J. Jr. (2013). Microteaching revisited: Using technology to enhance the professional development of pre-service teachers. *The Clearing House: A Journal of Educational Strategies, Issues and Ideas*, *86*(4), 150–154. doi:10.1080/00098655.2013.790307

Dias, P., & Mergendoller, J. (2019). Plagiarism vs. Pedagogy: Implications of Project-Based Learning Research for Teachers in the 21st Century. In D. Velliaris (Ed.), Scholarly Ethics and Publishing: Breakthroughs in Research and Practice (pp. 247–266). IGI Global. doi:10.4018/978-1-5225-8057-7.ch026

Dicen, K. B., Yodsuwan, C., Butcher, K., & Mingkwan, N. (2019). The institutional context for experiential learning investment in hospitality education: A case study from Thailand. *Tourism Education and Asia*, 143–160.

Digivisio (2021). Basic information of the Digivisio 2030 program. https://digivisio2030.fi/en/basic-information-on-the-digivisio-2030-programme/

Dimitra, K., Konstantinos, K., Christina, Z., & Katerina, T. (2020). Types of Game-Based Learning in Education : A brief state of the art and the implementation in Greece. *The European Educational Researcher*, *3*(2), 87–100. doi:10.31757/euer.324

Dixon, R. A., Hall, C., & Shawon, F. (2019). Using virtual reality and web conferencing technologies: Exploring alternatives for microteaching in a rural region. *Northwest Journal of Teacher Education*, *14*(1), 1–18. doi:10.15760/nwjte.2019.14.1.4

Dollinger, M., Lodge, J., & Coates, H. (2018). Co-creation in higher education: Towards a conceptual model. *Journal of Marketing for Higher Education*, *28*(2), 210–231. doi:10.1080/08841241.2018.1466756

Driscoll, M. (2002). Blended learning: Let's get beyond the hype *E-learning*, *1*(4), 1–4.

Dugnol-Menéndez, J., Jiménez-Arberas, E., Ruiz-Fernández, M. L., Fernández-Valera, D., Mok, A., & Merayo-Lloves, J. (2021). A collaborative escape room as gamification strategy to increase learning motivation and develop curricular skills of occupational therapy students. *BMC Medical Education*, *21*(1), 544. doi:10.118612909-021-02973-5 PMID:34706713

Dunn, R., & Dunn, K. (1992). *Teaching secondary students through their individual learning styles: Practical approaches for grades 7-12*. Allyn and Bacon.

Egan, J. D., Banter, J. N., & Sorgen, C. H. (2021). Assessing Escape Rooms as a Teaching Strategy for Leadership Competency Development. *Journal of Leadership Education*, *20*(1).

Elmas, R., & Geban, Ö. (2012). Web 2.0 tools for 21st century teachers. *International Online Journal of Educational Sciences*, *4*(1), 243–254.

Emergen Research. (2022). Metaverse Market, By Component (Hardware), By Platform (Desktop and Others), By Offering (Avatars), By Technology (Mixed Reality (MR) and Others), By Application, (Gaming and Others) By End-Use Vertical, and By Region Forecast to 2030. https://www.emergenresearch.com/industry-report/metaverse-market

EMMENEGGER, S. (2020). Pressure escape: a trade pop up escape room with career orientation purposes.

Ennis, R. (1991). Critical Thinking. *Teaching Philosophy*, *14*(1), 4–18. doi:10.5840/teachphil19911412

Epp, E. C. (1992). Yet another analysis of algorithms laboratory. *SIGCSE Bulletin*, *24*(4), 11–14. doi:10.1145/141837.141842

Ertmer, P. A., & Ottenbreit-Leftwich, A. T. (2010). Teacher technology change: How knowledge, confidence, beliefs, and culture intersect. *Journal of Research on Technology in Education*, *42*(3), 255–284. doi:10.1080/15391523.2010.10782551

Esteban, S.G., Laborda, J.G., & Llamas, M.R. (2016). ICTs, ESPs and ZPD through microlessons in teacher education. *New Perspectives on Teaching and Working with Languages in the Digital Era*, 105-113. . doi:10.14705/rpnet.2016.tislid2014.426

Eta Berner. (2020). *Informatics Education in Healthcare. Lessons Learned* (E. S. Berner, Ed.; 2nd ed.). Springer Cham., doi:10.1007/978-3-030-53813-2

Eukel, H., Frenzel, J., Frazier, K., & Miller, M. (2020). Unlocking Student Engagement: Creation, Adaptation, and Application of an Educational Escape Room Across Three Pharmacy Campuses. *Simulation & Gaming*, *51*(2), 167–179. doi:10.1177/1046878119898509

Experiential, E. S. for. (1998). *Eight Principles of Good Practice for All Experiential Learning Activities*. Eight Principles of Good Practice for All Experiential Learning Activities - Society for Experiential Education.

Faizi, R., Chiheb, R., & El Afia, A. (2015). Students' perceptions towards using Web 2.0 technologies in education. *International Journal of Emerging Technologies in Learning*, *10*(6), 32–36. doi:10.3991/ijet.v10i6.4858

Farghally, M. F., Kohy, K. H., Ernstz, J. V., & Shaffer, C. A. (2017). Towards a concept inventory for algorithm analysis topics. In *Proceedings of the 48rd SIGCSE technical symposium on computer science education, SIGCSE'17*, pp. 207-212. http://dx.doi.org/10.1145/3017680.3017756

Farris, R. A. (1991). Micro-peer teaching: Organization and benefits. *Education*, *111*(4), 559–562.

Felder, R. M., & Silverman, L. K. (1988). Learning and teaching styles in engineering education. *Engineering Education*, *78*(7), 674–681.

Fenwick, J. B., Norris, C., & Wilkes, J. (2002). Scientific experimentation via the matching game. In *Proceedings of the 33rd SIGCSE technical symposium on computer science education, SIGCSE'02*, pp. 326-303. https://doi.org/10.1145/563340.563469

Fernandes, A. C. (2022). *Saúde em Portugal: pensar o futuro*. Coimbra: Editora D'Ideias.

Fernandez, M. L. (2005). Learning through microteaching lesson study in teacher preparation. *Action in Teacher Education*, *26*(4), 37–47. doi:10.1080/01626620.2005.10463341

Fernandez, M. L. (2010). Investigating how and what prospective teachers learn through micro teaching lesson study. *Teaching and Teacher Education*, *26*(2), 351–362. doi:10.1016/j.tate.2009.09.012

Ferns, J., Hawkins, N., Little, A., & Hamiduzzaman, M. (2022). The escape room experience: Exploring new ways to deliver interprofessional education. *Innovations in Education and Teaching International*, 1–12. doi:10.1080/14703297.2022.2158900

Ferreira, J. (2022, April). Um terço dos docentes que ensinam futuros professores não tem formação no ramo educacional. Pessoas by ECO. Retrieved from [URL]

Fırat, E. A., & Köksal, M. S. (2019). Effects of instruction supported by web 2.0 tools on prospective teachers' biotechnology literacy. *Computers & Education*, *135*, 61–74. doi:10.1016/j.compedu.2019.02.018

Fisher, J., & Burrell, D. N. (2011). The value of using micro teaching as a tool to develop instructors. *Review of Higher Education and Self-Learning*, *4*(11), 86–94.

Flannery, L. P., Kazakoff, E. R., Bontá, P., Silverman, B., Bers, M. U., & Resnick, M. (2013). Designing ScratchJr: Support for early childhood learning through computer programming. In *Proceedings of the 12th International Conference on Interaction Design and Children, IDC '13*, pp. 1-10. 10.1145/2485760.2485785

Fleming, N. D. (2006). *Teaching and Learning Styles: VARK Strategies*. N.D. Fleming.

Foltz-Ramos, K., Fusco, N. M., & Paige, J. B. (2021). Saving patient x: A quasi-experimental study of teamwork and performance in simulation following an interprofessional escape room. *Journal of Interprofessional Care*, 1–8. doi:10.1080/13561820.2021.1874316 PMID:33587007

Fortune (2022). Citi says metaverse economy could be worth $13 trillion by 2030. https://fortune.com/2022/04/01/citi-metaverse-economy-13-trillion-2030/

Fotaris, P., & Mastoras, T. (2019). Escape rooms for learning: A systematic review. Proceedings of the European Conference on Games Based Learning, Friedrich. C., Teaford, H., Taubenheim, A., Boland, P., & Sick, B. (2019). Escaping the professional silo: an escape room implemented in an interprofessional education curriculum. *Journal of Interprofessional Care*, *33*(5), 573–575. doi:10.1080/13561820.2018.1538941 PMID:30362849

Fraenkel, J. R., Wallen, N. E., & Hyun, H. H. (2012). *How to design and evaluate research in education* (8th ed.). Mc Graw Hill.

Francis, D. (1997). Reconceptualising Microteaching as Critical Inquiry. *Asia-Pacific Journal of Teacher Education*, *25*(3), 207–223. doi:10.1080/1359866970250302

Frutos-Pascual, M., & Garcia-Zapirain, B. (2015). Assessing Visual Attention Using Eye Tracking Sensors in Intelligent Cognitive Therapies Based on Serious Games. *Sensors (Basel)*, *15*(5), 11092–11117. doi:10.3390150511092 PMID:25985158

Fuentes-Cabrera, A., Parra-González, M. E., López-Belmonte, J., & Segura-Robles, A. (2020). Learning Mathematics with Emerging Methodologies—The Escape Room as a Case Study. *Mathematics*, *8*(9), 1586. https://www.mdpi.com/2227-7390/8/9/1586. doi:10.3390/math8091586

Gaies, S. J. (1985). *Peer Involvement in Language Learning. Language in Education: Theory and Practice No. 60* (1st ed.). National Institute of Education.

Gambhir, V., & Wadhwa, N. C., & Grover Sandeep. (. (2016a). Quality Assurance in Education Article information. *Quality Assurance in Education*, *24*(1), 2–25. doi:10.1108/QAE-07-2011-0040

Gambhir, V., Wadhwa, N. C., & Grover, S. (2013). Interpretive structural modelling of enablers of quality technical education : An Indian perspective. *International Journal of Productivity and Quality Management, 12*(4), 393–409. doi:10.1504/IJPQM.2013.056734

Gardner, H. (1993). *Multiple intelligences: The theory in practice.* Basic Books/Hachette Book Group.

Gardner, H. (1995). Inteligências Múltiplas: A teoria na prática. *The Art of Medication.*

Garrison, D. R., & Kanuka, H. (2004). Blended learning: Uncovering its transformative potential in higher education. *The Internet and Higher Education, 7*(2), 95–105. doi:10.1016/j.iheduc.2004.02.001

Gassler, G., Hug, T., & Glahn, C. (2004). Integrated Micro Learning–An outline of the basic method and first results. *Interactive computer aided learning, 4,* 1-7.

Gaviria, D., Arango, J., & Valencia-Arias, A. (2015). Reflections about the use of information and communication technologies in accounting education. *Procedia: Social and Behavioral Sciences, 176,* 992–997. doi:10.1016/j.sbspro.2015.01.569

Gazdi, L., Pomázi, K., Radostyán, B., Szabó, M., Szegletes, L., & Forstner, B. 2016. Experimenting with classifiers in biofeedback-based mental effort measurement, in: 2016 7th IEEE International Conference on Cognitive Infocommunications (CogInfoCom). Presented at the 2016 7th IEEE International Conference on Cognitive Infocommunications (CogInfoCom), pp. 000331–000336. 10.1109/CogInfoCom.2016.7804571

Gazdi, L., Pomázi, K., Szabó, M., & Forstner, B. (2018). An Innovative Model for Adaptive Learning Utilizing Biofeedback and Item Response Theory. *Periodica Polytechnica. Electrical Engineering and Computer Science, 62,* 90–105. doi:10.3311/PPee.12213

Geck, C. (2007). The generation Z connection: Teaching information literacy to the newest net generation. In E. Rosenfeld & D. Loertscher (Eds.), *Toward a 21st-century school library media program* (pp. 807–828).

Gencel, I. E., Erdogan, M., Kolb, A. Y., & Kolb, D. A. (2021). Rubric for Experiential Training. *International Journal of Progressive Education, 17*(4), 188–211. doi:10.29329/ijpe.2021.366.13

Gess-Newsome, J., & Lederman, N. G. (1990). The preservice microteaching course and science teachers' instructional decisions: A qualitative analysis. *Journal of Research in Science Teaching, 27*(8), 717–726. doi:10.1002/tea.3660270802

Ghasemi, A., & Zahediasl, S. (2012). Normality tests for statistical analysis: A guide for non-statisticians. *International Journal of Endocrinology and Metabolism, 10*(2), 486–489. doi:10.5812/ijem.3505 PMID:23843808

Gilster, P. (1997). *Digital literacy.* Wiley Computer Pub.

Glavaš, A., & Stašcik, A. (2017). Enhancing positive attitude towards mathematics through introducing Escape Room games. Mathematics Education as a Science and a Profession, 281-293.

Goda, Y., Yamada, M., Matsuda, T., Kato, H., Saito, Y., & Miyagawa, H. (2023). From adaptive learning support to fading out support for effective self-regulated online learning. In *Research Anthology on Remote Teaching and Learning and the Future of Online Education* (pp. 254–274). IGI Global.

Gödek, Y. (2016). Science teacher trainees' microteaching experiences: A focus group study. *Educational Research Review*, *11*(16), 1473–1493. doi:10.5897/ERR2016.2892

Gogus, A. (2012). Peer Learning and Assessment. In N. M. Seel (Ed.), *Encyclopedia of the Sciences of Learning* (pp. 2572–2576). Springer US., doi:10.1007/978-1-4419-1428-6_146

Gomez, M. (2020). A COVID-19 intervention: Using digital escape rooms to provide professional development to alternative certification educators. *Journal of Technology and Teacher Education*, *28*(2), 425–432.

González-Herrera, M.-R., & Giralt-Escobar, S. (2021). Tourism Experiential Learning Through Academic Field Trips in Higher Education: A Case Study of Copper Canyon (Mexico). *Tourism: An International Interdisciplinary Journal*, *69*(4), 471–493. doi:10.37741/t.69.4.1

Goodman, J. T., & Landgren, A. (2021). Escape Into a Nursing Career: An Active Recruitment Strategy for Prospective Students. *Nursing Education Perspectives*, *42*(6), E147–E148. doi:10.1097/01.NEP.0000000000000812 PMID:33896923

Götschi, T., Sanders, I., & Galpin, V. (2003). Mental models of recursion. In *Proceedings of the 34th SIGCSE technical symposium on computer science education, SIGCSE'03*, pp. 346-350. https://doi.org/10.1145/611892.612004

Govender, D. W. (2010). Attitudes of students towards the use of a Learning Management System (LMS) in a face-to-face learning mode of instruction. *Africa Education Review*, *7*(2), 244–262. doi:10.1080/18146627.2010.515394

Graham, C. R. (2006). Blended learning systems. The handbook of blended learning: Global perspectives, local designs, 1, 3-21.

Greenaway, R. (2007). Dynamic debriefing. In M. L. Silberman (Ed.), *The Handbook of Experiential Learning* (pp. 59–80). John Wiley & Sons.

Grosseck, G. (2009). To use or not to use web 2.0 in higher education? *Procedia: Social and Behavioral Sciences*, *1*(1), 478–482. doi:10.1016/j.sbspro.2009.01.087

Guachalla, A., & Gledhill, M. (2019). Co-creating learning experiences to support student employability in travel and tourism. *Journal of Hospitality, Leisure, Sport and Tourism Education*, *25*, 100210. https://doi.org/https://doi.org/10.1016/j.jhlste.2019.100210. doi:10.1016/j.jhlste.2019.100210

Guckian, J., Eveson, L., & May, H. (2020). The great escape? The rise of the escape room in medical education. *Future Healthcare Journal*, *7*(2), 112–115. doi:10.7861/fhj.2020-0032 PMID:32550277

Gudo, C. O., & Olel, M. A. (2011). Students' Admission Policies For Quality Assurance: Towards Quality Education In Kenyan Universities. *International Journal of Business and Social Science*, *2*(8), 177–183.

Gül, R. (2022). *The effect of online education supported by web 2.0 tools on the conceptual achievement, attitudes and self-regulation perceptions of 5th grade middle school students in the sun, earth and moon unit* [Unpublished master's thesis]. Yıldız Teknik University.

Gumennykova, T., Pankovets, V., Liapa, M., Miziuk, V., Gramatyk, N., & Drahiieva, L. (2020). Applying instructional design methods to improve the effectiveness of blended-learning. *International Journal of Management*, *11*(5).

Guo, P., Saab, N., Post, L. S., & Admiraal, W. (2020). A review of project-based learning in higher education: Student outcomes and measures. *International Journal of Educational Research*, *102*, 101586. doi:10.1016/j.ijer.2020.101586

Gyamfi, G., Hanna, B., & Khosravi, H. (2022). Supporting peer evaluation of student-generated content: A study of three approaches. *Assessment & Evaluation in Higher Education*, *47*(7), 1129–1147. doi:10.1080/02602938.2021.2006140

Han, J., Liu, G., & Gao, Y. (2023). Learners in the metaverse: A systematic review on the use of roblox in learning. *Education Sciences*, *13*(3), 296. doi:10.3390/educsci13030296

Harden, R. M., & Stamper, N. (1999). What is a spiral curriculum? *Medical Teacher*, *21*(2), 141–143. doi:10.1080/01421599979752 PMID:21275727

Hargreaves, A. (2003). *Teaching in the Knowledge Society*. Columbia University.

Hartshorne, R., & Ajjan, H. (2009). Examining student decisions to adopt Web 2.0 technologies: Theory and empirical tests. *Journal of Computing in Higher Education*, *21*(3), 183–198. doi:10.100712528-009-9023-6

Hartt, M., Hosseini, H., & Mostafapour, M. (2020). Game On: Exploring the Effectiveness of Game-based Learning. *Planning Practice and Research*, *35*(5), 589–604. doi:10.1080/02697459.2020.1778859

Hatami, S. (2013). Learning styles. *ELT Journal*, *67*(4), 488–490. doi:10.1093/elt/ccs083

Hattie, J., & Clarke, S. (2018). *Visible learning: feedback*. Routledge. doi:10.4324/9780429485480

Havnes, A., Christiansen, B., Bjørk, I. T., & Hessevaagbakke, E. (2016). Peer learning in higher education: Patterns of talk and interaction in skills centre simulation. *Learning, Culture and Social Interaction*, *8*, 75–87. https://doi.org/https://doi.org/10.1016/j.lcsi.2015.12.004. doi:10.1016/j.lcsi.2015.12.004

Hawkins, J. E., Wiles, L. L., Tremblay, B., & Thompson, B. A. (2020). Behind the Scenes of an Educational Escape Room. *The American Journal of Nursing*, *120*(10), 50–56. doi:10.1097/01.NAJ.0000718636.68938.bb PMID:32976152

Hawlitschek, A., & Köppen, V. (2013). Analyzing Player Behavior in Digital Game - Based Learning: Advantages and Challenges. In *8th European conference on games based learning. Academic Conferences and Publishing International* (pp. 199–206). Retrieved from https://wwwiti.cs.uni-magdeburg.de/iti_db/publikationen/ps/auto/HK14.pdf

Haynes, S.M. (1995). Explaining recursion to the unsophisticated. *ACM SIGCSE Bulletin 27*(3), 3-6 and 14. https://doi.org/ doi:10.1145/209849.209850

He, C., & Yan, C. (2011). Exploring authenticity of micro-teaching in pre-service teacher education programmes. *Teaching Education*, *22*(3), 291–302. doi:10.1080/10476210.2011.590588

Heim, A. B., Duke, J., & Holt, E. A. (2022). Design, discover, and decipher: Student-developed escape rooms in the virtual ecology classroom. *Journal of Microbiology & Biology Education*, *23*(1), e00015–e00022. doi:10.1128/jmbe.00015-22 PMID:35784618

Helms, S. A. (2014). Blended/hybrid courses: A review of the literature and recommendations for instructional designers and educators. *Interactive Learning Environments*, *22*(6), 804–810. doi:10.1080/10494820.2012.745420

Hernández-de-Menéndez, M., Vallejo Guevara, A., Tudón Martínez, J. C., Hernández Alcántara, D., & Morales-Menendez, R. (2019). Active learning in engineering education. A review of fundamentals, best practices and experiences. *Int J Interact Des Manuf*, *13*(3), 909–922. doi:10.100712008-019-00557-8

Hertzman, J. L., Moreo, A. P., & Wiener, P. J. (2015). Career Planning Strategies and Skills of Hospitality Management Students. *Journal of Human Resources in Hospitality \& Tourism*, *14*(4), 423–443. doi:10.1080/15332845.2015.1002071

Higgins, A., & Nicholl, H. (2003). The experiences of lecturers and students in the use of microteaching as a teaching strategy. *Nurse Education in Practice*, *3*(4), 220–227. doi:10.1016/S1471-5953(02)00106-3 PMID:19038126

Ho, A. M. (2018). Unlocking ideas: Using escape room puzzles in a cryptography classroom. *PRIMUS (Terre Haute, Ind.)*, *28*(9), 835–847. doi:10.1080/10511970.2018.1453568

Hodges, C. B., & Fowler, D. J. (2020). The COVID-19 Crisis and Faculty Members in Higher Education: From Emergency Remote Teaching to Better Teaching through Reflection. *International Journal of Multidisciplinary Perspectives in Higher Education*, *5*(1), 118–122. https://ojed.org/jimphe. doi:10.32674/jimphe.v5i1.2507

Hoey, J., Schröder, T., Morgan, J., Rogers, K. B., Rishi, D., & Nagappan, M. (2018). Artificial Intelligence and Social Simulation: Studying Group Dynamics on a Massive Scale. *Small Group Research*, *49*(6), 647–683. doi:10.1177/1046496418802362

Honebein, P. C., & Honebein, C. H. (2015). Effectiveness, efficiency, and appeal: Pick any two? The influence of learning domains and learning outcomes on designer judgments of useful instructional methods. *Educational Technology Research and Development*, *63*(6), 937–955. doi:10.100711423-015-9396-3

Honnutagi, A. R. R., Sonar, R., & Babu, A. S. (2016). Achieving quality excellence in Indian engineering education : Modelling and analysis using system dynamics. *Internal Journal of Business Excellence, 10*(1), 90–119. doi:10.1504/IJBEX.2016.077622

Hooda, M., Rana, C., Dahiya, O., Rizwan, A., & Hossain, M. S. (2022). Artificial Intelligence for Assessment and Feedback to Enhance Student Success in Higher Education. *Mathematical Problems in Engineering, 2022*, e5215722. doi:10.1155/2022/5215722

Hoong, L. Y., Kin, H. W., & Pien, C. L. (2015). Concrete-pictorial-abstract: Surveying its origin and charting its future. *The Mathematics Educator, 16*(1), 1–18. http://hdl.handle.net/10497/18889

Horn, M. A. (2023). Design and evaluation of a new consolidation exercise for students studying cardiac physiology: A digital escape room. *Advances in Physiology Education, 47*(1), 82–92. doi:10.1152/advan.00176.2022 PMID:36476116

Horzum, M. B. (2010). Investigating teachers' Web 2.0 tools awareness, frequency and purposes of usage in terms of different variables. [Öğretmenlerin Web 2.0 araçlarından haberdarlığı, kullanım sıklıkları ve amaçlarının çeşitli değişkenler açısından incelenmesi]. *Uluslararası İnsan Bilimleri Dergisi, 7*(1), 603–634.

Hsu, P.-Y. (2021). Academic use of Social Networking Technology for English Learning: Implementing Videotaped Peer Evaluation into English Speech Class. *2021 12th International Conference on E-Education, E-Business, E-Management, and E-Learning*, 248–253.

Huber, J., & Ward, B. E. (2009). Pre-service confidence through micro-teaching. *Education Journal, 90*(1), 65–68.

Huertas-Valdivia, I. (2021). Role-Playing a staffing process: Experiential learning with undergraduate tourism students. *Journal of Hospitality, Leisure, Sport and Tourism Education, 29*, 100334. https://doi.org/https://doi.org/10.1016/j.jhlste.2021.100334. doi:10.1016/j.jhlste.2021.100334

Huisman, B., Saab, N., Van Driel, J., & Van Den Broek, P. (2018). Peer feedback on academic writing: undergraduate students' peer feedback role, peer feedback perceptions and essay performance. *Assessment \& Evaluation in Higher Education, 43*(6), 955–968.

Hursman, A., Richter, L. M., Frenzel, J., Viets Nice, J., & Monson, E. (2022). An online escape room used to support the growth of teamwork in health professions students. *Journal of Interprofessional Education & Practice, 29*, 100545. doi:10.1016/j.xjep.2022.100545 PMID:35991695

Hutchinson, S., Woodford, K., Ellis, A., Hamilton-Hinch, B., Stilwell, C., & Manuel, C. (2022). Exploring the role of peer-assisted learning for professional preparation in recreation. *Leisure/ Loisir, 46*(1), 23–48. doi:10.1080/14927713.2021.1922092

Hyasat, A. S. (2022). The Experiential Learning Theory as Base for Tourism and Hospitality Courses and Internship Programs. *Indian Journal of Economics and Business, 21*(1), 291–303.

Ifenthaler, D., Eseryel, D., & Ge, X. (2012). Assessment for Game-Based Learning. In X. Ifenthaler, D., Eseryel, D., Ge (Ed.), Assessment in Game-Based Learning (pp. 1–8). Springer, New York, NY. doi:10.1007/978-1-4614-3546-4_1

Ihantola, P., Karavirta, V., Korhonen, A., & Nikander, J. (2005). Taxonomy of effortless creation of algorithm visualizations. In *Proceedings of the 1st international computing education research workshop, ICER'05*, pp. 123-133. https://doi.org/10.1145/1089786.1089798

Information Literacy Competency Standards for Higher Education. (2000). Retrieved from https://alair.ala.org/handle/11213/7668

International Escape Room Markets Analysis. (2019). The Logic Escapes Me.

Irwin, B. (2019). Enhancing peer feedback practices through screencasts in blended academic writing courses. *The JALT CALL Journal*, *15*(1), 43–59. doi:10.29140/jaltcall.v15n1.158

Izullah, F. P., Koivisto, M., Nieminen, V., Luimula, M., & Hämäläinen, H. (2022) Aging and sleep deprivation affect different neurocognitive stages of spatial information processing during a virtual driving task – An ERP study, Transportation Research Part F: Psychology and Behaviour, 89, Elsevier, August, pp. 399–406.

Jaiswal, A. (2021). Revisiting the Historical Roots of Game-Based Learning. *TechTrends*, *65*(3), 243–245. doi:10.100711528-021-00603-x

Jamal, T., Taillon, J., & Dredge, D. (2011). Sustainable tourism pedagogy and academic-community collaboration: A progressive service-learning approach. *Tourism and Hospitality Research*, *11*(2), 133–147. doi:10.1057/thr.2011.3

Jan, M., & Gaydos, M. (2016). What Is Game-Based Learning? Past, Present, and Future Learning with Games. *Educational Technology*, *56*(3), 6–11. https://www.jstor.org/stable/44430486

Jarvis, P. (2012). *Adult learning in the social context* (Vol. 78). Routledge. doi:10.4324/9780203802724

Jauhiainen, J. S. (2021). Entrepreneurship and innovation events during the covid-19 pandemic: The user preferences of virbela virtual 3d platform at the shift event organized in finland. *Sustainability (Basel)*, *13*(7), 3802. doi:10.3390u13073802

Jensen, J., Smith, C. M., Bowers, R., Kaloi, M., Ogden, T. H., Parry, K. A., Payne, J. S., Fife, P., & Holt, E. (2022). Asynchronous Online Instruction Leads to Learning Gaps When Compared to a Flipped Classroom. *Journal of Science Education and Technology*, *31*(6), 718–729. doi:10.100710956-022-09988-7 PMID:35971508

Jeong, L., Smith, Z., Longino, A., Merel, S. E., & McDonough, K. (2020). Virtual Peer Teaching During the COVID-19 Pandemic. *Medical Science Educator*, *30*(4), 1361–1362. doi:10.100740670-020-01065-1 PMID:32929390

Joshi, M. (2021). *Hybrid teaching at Turku UAS*. A Blog post. Turku UAS intranet.

Joshi, M. (2023). *Holistic Design of Online Degree Programmes in Higher Education – A Pedagogically Informed Design Framework. A doctoral dissertation.* University of Lapland., https://urn.fi/URN:ISBN:978-952-337-349-5

Joshi, M. S. (2022). Holistic design of online degree programmes in higher education – a case study from Finland. *International Journal of Educational Management, 36*(1), 32–48. doi:10.1108/IJEM-12-2020-0588

JR., D.K., Harish, N., Priyadharsini, K., Gowtham, S., & Gokulraj, G., (2022). Machine Learning based Drowsiness Detection in Classrooms. In *2022 International Conference on Edge Computing and Applications (ICECAA)* (pp. 1186-1191). IEEE.

Kabudi, T., Pappas, I., & Olsen, D. H. (2021). AI-enabled adaptive learning systems: A systematic mapping of the literature. *Computers and Education: Artificial Intelligence, 2*, 100017. doi:10.1016/j.caeai.2021.100017

Kafyulilo, A., Fisser, P., Pieters, J., & Voogt, J. (2015). ICT use in science and mathematics teacher education in Tanzania: Developing technological pedagogical content knowledge. *Australasian Journal of Educational Technology, 31*(4), 381–399. doi:10.14742/ajet.1240

Kamińska, D., Zwoliński, G., Laska-Leśniewicz, A., Raposo, R., Vairinhos, M., Pereira, E., Urem, F., Hinic, M. L., Haamer, R. E., & Anbarjafari, G. 2023. Augmented Reality: Current and New Trends in Education. doi:10.20944/preprints202306.1665.v1

Kanji, G. K., Tambi, A., & Wallace, W. (1999). A Comparative Study of Quality Practices in Higher Education Institutions in the US and Malaysia. *Total Quality Management, 10*(3), 357–371. doi:10.1080/0954412997884

Karataş, F. Ö., Cengiz, C., & Uludüz, Ş. M. (2020). Re-designing micro-teaching to lessen anxiety in the process: The pre-service teachers' views. *Necatibey Faculty of Education Electronic Journal of Science and Mathematics Education, 14*(1), 30–56.

Karlström, M., & Hamza, K. (2019). Preservice science teachers' opportunities for learning through reflection when planning a microteaching unit. *Journal of Science Teacher Education, 30*(1), 44–62. doi:10.1080/1046560X.2018.1531345

Kavas, G., & Özdener, N. (2012). Effects of video-supported web-based peer assessment on microteaching applications: Computer teacher candidates sample. *Creative Education, 3*(7), 1221–1230. doi:10.4236/ce.2012.37181

Keerthirathne, W. K. D. (2020). Peer learning: An overview. *International Journal of Scientific Engineering and Science, 4*(11), 1–6.

Kee, T., & Zhang, H. (2022). Digital Experiential Learning for Sustainable Horticulture and Landscape Management Education. *Sustainability (Basel), 14*(15), 9116. Advance online publication. doi:10.3390u14159116

Keinänen, M., & Kairisto-Mertanen, L. (2019). Researching learning environments and students' innovation competences. *Education + Training, 61*(1), 17–30. doi:10.1108/ET-03-2018-0064

Kerr, P. (2016). Adaptive learning. *ELT Journal*, *70*(1), 88–93. doi:10.1093/elt/ccv055

Kezar, A. (2001). Theory of Multiple Intelligences: Implications for Higher Education. *Innovative Higher Education*, *26*(2), 141–154. doi:10.1023/A:1012292522528

Khaldi, A., Bouzidi, R., & Nader, F. (2023). Gamification of e-learning in higher education: A systematic literature review. *Smart Learning Environments*, *10*(1), 10.

Kharb, P., Samanta, P. P., Jindal, M., & Singh, V. (2013). The Learning Styles and the Preferred Teaching—Learning Strategies of First Year Medical Students. *Journal of Clinical and Diagnostic Research : JCDR*, *7*, 1089–1092. doi:10.7860/JCDR/2013/5809.3090 PMID:23905110

Kim, H. J., & Jeong, M. (2018). Research on hospitality and tourism education: Now and future. *Tourism Management Perspectives*, *25*, 119–122. doi:10.1016/j.tmp.2017.11.025

Kinio, A. E., Dufresne, L., Brandys, T., & Jetty, P. (2019). Break out of the Classroom: The Use of Escape Rooms as an Alternative Teaching Strategy in Surgical Education. *Journal of Surgical Education*, *76*(1), 134–139. https://doi.org/https://doi.org/10.1016/j.jsurg.2018.06.030. doi:10.1016/j.jsurg.2018.06.030 PMID:30126728

Kirk, R. E. (2008). *Statistics an introduction* (5th ed.). Thomson Higher Education.

Kleftodimos, A., Lappas, G., & Vrigkas, M. (2022). Taleblazer vs. metaverse: A com-parative analysis of two platforms for building AR location-based educational games. *International Journal of Entertainment Technology and Management*, *1*(4), 290. doi:10.1504/IJENTTM.2022.129630

Koehler, A. A., Newby, T. J., & Ertmer, P. A. (2017). Examining the role of Web 2.0 tools in supporting problem solving during case-based instruction. *Journal of Research on Technology in Education*, *49*(3–4), 182–197. doi:10.1080/15391523.2017.1338167

Kokotsaki, D., Menzies, V., & Wiggins, A. (2016). Project-based learning: A review of the literature. *Improving Schools*, *19*(3), 267–277. doi:10.1177/1365480216659733

Kolb, A. Y., & Kolb, D. A. (2005). Learning styles and learning spaces: Enhancing experiential learning in higher education. *Academy of Management Learning \& Education*, *4*(2), 193–212.

Kolb, D. A. (2014). Experiential learning: Experience as the source of learning and development (N. Jersey (ed.); 2nd ed.). Pearson Education.

Kolb, D. A. (1984). *Experiential learning: Experience as the source of learning and development*. Prentice-Hall.

Kolb, D. A. (1984). *Experimental learning: experience as the source of learning and development*. Prentice Hall.

Kolb, D. A., Boyatzis, R. E., & Mainemelis, C. (2014). Experiential learning theory: Previous research and new directions. In *Perspectives on thinking, learning, and cognitive styles* (pp. 227–248). Routledge. doi:10.4324/9781410605986-9

Köles, M., Szegletes, L., & Forstner, B. 2015. Towards a physiology based difficulty control system for serious games, in: 2015 6th IEEE International Conference on Cognitive Infocommunications (CogInfoCom). Presented at the 2015 6th IEEE International Conference on Cognitive Infocommunications (CogInfoCom), pp. 323–328. 10.1109/CogInfoCom.2015.7390612

Kompen, R. T., Edirisingha, P., Canaleta, X., Alsina, M., & Monguet, J. M. (2019). Personal learning Environments based on Web 2.0 services in higher education. *Telematics and Informatics*, *38*, 194–206. doi:10.1016/j.tele.2018.10.003

Korhonen, A.-M., Ruhalahti, S., & Veermans, M. (2019). The online learning process and scaffolding in student teachers' personal learning environments. *Education and Information Technologies*, *24*(1), 755–779. doi:10.100710639-018-9793-4

Koshti P. Paryani A. Talreja J. Zope V. 2022. AttenQ- Attention Span Detection Tool for Online Learning. doi:10.2139/ssrn.4096416

Kossen, C., & Ooi, C. Y. (2021). Trialling micro-learning design to increase engagement in online courses. *Asian Association of Open Universities Journal*, *16*(3), 299–310. doi:10.1108/AAOUJ-09-2021-0107

Kostkova, P. (2015). Grand challenges in digital health. *Frontiers in Public Health*, *3*(134). Advance online publication. doi:10.3389/fpubh.2015.00134 PMID:26000272

Kourieos, S. (2016). Video-mediated microteaching-A stimulus for reflection and teacher growth. *The Australian Journal of Teacher Education*, *41*(1), 65–80. doi:10.14221/ajte.2016v41n1.4

Küçükgöz, A. B. (2019). *Perceptions of prospective classroom teachers on using interactive whiteboards through micro-teaching* [Unpublished doctoral dissertation]. Hacettepe University.

Kulkarni, A., Khan, A., Mishra, N., Raikwar, S., & Prajapat, S. (2014). DC-Model for Quality Improvement in Technical Education, 308–312.

Kulmala, R., Luimula, M., & Roslöf, J. (2014) Capstone Innovation Project – Pedagogical Model and Methods, In *Proceedings of the 10th International CDIO Conference* (CDIO 2014), June 15-19, Barcelona, Spain, p. 10.

Kwok, S., & Childers, R. (2023). Escaping the Laboratory: An Escape Room to Reinforce Biomedical Engineering Skills. *Biomedical Engineering Education*, *3*(1), 75–86. doi:10.100743683-022-00089-w PMID:36348693

Laal, M., & Ghodsi, S. M. 2012. Benefits of collaborative learning. Procedia - Social and Behavioral Sciences, World Conference on Learning, Teaching & Administration - 2011 31, 486–490. 10.1016/j.sbspro.2011.12.091

Lahtinen, E., Ala-Mutka, K., & Järvinen, H. M. (2005). A study of the difficulties of novice programmers. In *Proceedings of the 10th annual conference on innovation and technology in computer science education, ITiCSE'05*, pp. 14-18. https://doi.org/10.1145/1067445.1067453

Lalley, J. P., & Miller, R. H. (2007). The learning pyramid: Does it point teachers in the right direction? *Education*, *128*(1), 64–79.

Lampropoulos, G., Keramopoulos, E., Diamantaras, K., & Evangelidis, G. (2022). Augmented reality and gamification in education: A systematic literature review of research, applications, and empirical studies. *Applied Sciences (Basel, Switzerland)*, *12*(13), 6809. doi:10.3390/app12136809

Lampropoulos, G., Keramopoulos, E., Diamantaras, K., & Evangelidis, G. (2022). Augmented reality and virtual reality in education: Public perspectives, sentiments, attitudes, and discourses. *Education Sciences*, *12*(11), 798. doi:10.3390/educsci12110798

Lantada, A. D. (2022). Engineering Education 5.0: Strategies for a Successful Transformative Project-Based Learning. In M. Bouezzeddine (Ed.), *Insights Into Global Engineering Education After the Birth of Industry 5.0* (p. 19)., doi:10.5772/intechopen.102844

Lappalainen, H. (2020) Innovation Pedagogy in the Era of Industrial Revolution 4.0. In *Proceedings of the 6th International Conference on Education and Technology* (ICET 2020) 10.2991/assehr.k.201204.005

Larsen, T., Tabor, L., & Smith, P. (2020). End of the field? Hacking online and hybrid environments for field-based learning in geography education. *The Journal of Geography*, *120*(1), 3–11. doi: 10.1080/00221341.2020.1858325

Latifi, S., & Noroozi, O. (2021). Supporting argumentative essay writing through an online supported peer-review script. *Innovations in Education and Teaching International*, *58*(5), 501–511. doi:10.1080/14703297.2021.1961097

Le Boterf, G. (2016). *Professionnaliser: construire des parcours personnalisés de professionnalisation*. Eyrolles.

Leal, J. P., Queirós, R., Ferreirinha, P., & Swacha, J. (2022). A Roadmap to Convert Educational Web Applications into LTI Tools. In A. Simões & J. C. Silva (Eds.), Third International Computer Programming Education Conference (ICPEC 2022), Open Access Series in Informatics (OASIcs) (Vol. 102, pp. 12:1-12:12). Schloss Dagstuhl -- Leibniz-Zentrum für Informatik.

Lee, M. J., Lee, P. C., Dopson, L. R., & Yoon, S. (2020). What dimensions of career expos have the most impact on student satisfaction? *Journal of Hospitality, Leisure, Sport & Tourism Education*, *27*, 100263. https://doi.org/https://doi.org/10.1016/j.jhlste.2020.100263

Lee, M. J., & McLoughlin, C. (2007). Teaching and learning in virtual worlds: A review of the educational research. *Educational Research Review*, *2*(2), 69–87.

Le, H., Janssen, J., & Wubbels, T. (2018). Collaborative learning practices: Teacher and student perceived obstacles to effective student collaboration. *Cambridge Journal of Education*, *48*(1), 103–122. doi:10.1080/0305764X.2016.1259389

Lepp, G. A., Fierke, K. K., Friedrich, C., & Sick, B. (2023). How intention/reflection fosters student learning in an interprofessional experiential escape room activity. *Journal of Interprofessional Education & Practice*, *30*, 100589. doi:10.1016/j.xjep.2022.100589

Letrud, K. (2012). A rebuttal of NTL Institute's learning pyramid. *Education*, (133), 117–124.

Lewis, M., & Moultrie, J. (2005). The Organizational Innovation Laboratory. *Creativity and Innovation Management*, *14*(1), 73–83. doi:10.1111/j.1467-8691.2005.00327.x

Li, M., & Tsai, C. (2013). Game-based learning in science education: A review of relevant research. *Journal of Science Education and Technology*, *22*(6), 877–898. doi:10.100710956-013-9436-x

Linder, K. E. (2017). Fundamentals of hybrid teaching and learning. *New Directions for Teaching and Learning*, *2017*(149), 11–18. doi:10.1002/tl.20222

Lin, J., Sun, G., Cui, T., Shen, J., Xu, D., Beydoun, G., Yu, P., Pritchard, D., Li, L., & Chen, S. (2020). From ideal to reality: Segmentation, annotation, and recommendation, the vital trajectory of intelligent micro learning. *World Wide Web (Bussum)*, *23*(3), 1747–1767. doi:10.100711280-019-00730-9

Lin, M., Preston, A., Kharrufa, A., & Kong, Z. (2016). Making L2 learners' reasoning skills visible: The potential of Computer Supported Collaborative Learning Environments. *Thinking Skills and Creativity*, *22*, 303–322. https://doi.org/https://doi.org/10.1016/j.tsc.2016.06.004. doi:10.1016/j.tsc.2016.06.004

Liu, M., McKelroy, E., Corliss, S. B., & Carrigan, J. (2017). Investigating the effect of an adaptive learning intervention on students' learning. *Educational Technology Research and Development*, *65*(6), 1605–1625. doi:10.100711423-017-9542-1

Liu, Y., Ma, W., Guo, X., Lin, X., Wu, C., & Zhu, T. (2021). Impacts of Color Coding on Programming Learning in Multimedia Learning: Moving Toward a Multimodal Methodology. *Frontiers in Psychology*, *12*, 12. doi:10.3389/fpsyg.2021.773328 PMID:34925175

Löffler, E., Schneider, B., Zanwar, T., & Asprion, P. M. (2021). Cysecescape 2.0—A virtual escape room to raise cybersecurity awareness. *International Journal of Serious Games*, *8*(1), 59–70. doi:10.17083/ijsg.v8i1.413

López Belmonte, J., Pozo-Sánchez, S., Moreno-Guerrero, A. J., & Lampropoulos, G. (2023). Metaverse in education. *Systematic Reviews*.

López, Á. G. (2019). The use of escape rooms to teach and learn English at university. Research, technology and best practices in education, 94-101.

López-Pernas, S., Gordillo, A., Barra, E., & Quemada, J. (2019a). Analyzing Learning Effectiveness and Students' Perceptions of an Educational Escape Room in a Programming Course in Higher Education. *IEEE Access: Practical Innovations, Open Solutions*, *7*, 184221–184234. doi:10.1109/ACCESS.2019.2960312

López-Pernas, S., Gordillo, A., Barra, E., & Quemada, J. (2019b). Examining the Use of an Educational Escape Room for Teaching Programming in a Higher Education Setting. *IEEE Access: Practical Innovations, Open Solutions*, *7*, 31723–31737. doi:10.1109/ACCESS.2019.2902976

Loughran, J., Keast, S., & Cooper, R. (2016). Pedagogical reasoning in teacher education. In *International handbook of teacher education* (pp. 387–421). Springer. doi:10.1007/978-981-10-0366-0_10

Loughran, J., & Menter, I. (2019). The essence of being a teacher educator and why it matters. *Asia-Pacific Journal of Teacher Education, 47*(3), 216–229. doi:10.1080/1359866X.2019.1575946

Luimula, M., Haavisto, T., Pham, D., Markopoulos, P., Aho, J., Markopoulos, E., & Saarinen, J. (2022). The use of metaverse in maritime sector – a combination of social communication, hands on experiencing and digital twins. In: Evangelos Markopoulos, Ravindra S. Goonetilleke and Yan Luximon (eds.). Creativity, Innovation and Entrepreneurship. AHFE International Conference 2022. *AHFE Open Access, 31.* AHFE International, USA. http://doi.org/10.54941/ahfe1001513

Luimula, M., Pitkäkangas, P., Saarenpää, T., Bulatovic Trygg, N., & Pyae, A. (2016). Students' Role in Gamified Solutions in Healthcare RDI Project, In *Proceedings of the 12th International CDIO Conference* (CDIO 2016), Turku, Finland, pp. 219-227.

Luimula, M., Markopoulos, E., Österman, M., Markopoulos, P., Aho, J., Ravyse, W., Saarinen, J., & Reunanen, T. (2021). Avatar Based Multiplayer Functionalities in Next Generation Communication and Learning in Virtual Reality Social Platforms – Case MarISOT Room, In *Proceedings of the 12th IEEE International Conference on Cognitive Infocommunications CogInfoCom*, 23-25 Sept 2021, online, pp. 447-452.

Lundholm, M. D., Simpson, K. P., & Ozark, L. (2022). A medical escape room to build intern workplace social capital in an internal medicine residency program. *Medical Teacher, 44*(5), 546–550. doi:10.1080/0142159X.2021.2005243 PMID:34822314

Lundmark, P. (2022). The real future of the metaverse is for consumers. *Financial Times,* 2022. https://www.ft.com/content/af0c9de8-d36e-485b-9db5-5ee1e57716cb

Luthuli, S., Nyawo, J. C., & Mashau, P. (2019). Effectiveness of training and development on employees' performance in South African municipalities with special reference to Umzumbe Local Municipality. *African Journal of Development Studies, 9*(Special 1), 117.

Lyu, J., Li, M., & Wang, D. (2016). Experiential learning and its effectiveness from the perceptions of hospitality students. *Journal of Teaching in Travel \& Tourism, 16*(4), 296–315. doi:10.1080/15313220.2016.1213149

Macías-Guillén, A., Díez, R. M., Serrano-Luján, L., & Borrás-Gené, O. (2021). Educational Hall Escape: Increasing Motivation and Raising Emotions in Higher Education Students. *Education Sciences, 11*(9), 527. https://www.mdpi.com/2227-7102/11/9/527. doi:10.3390/educsci11090527

Magalhães, T. (2022). *Transformação Digital em Saúde.* Almedina.

Mahadeven, R., Shivaprakash, N. C., & Bose, S. K. (2013). Quality assessment of technical education in Indian Engineering Institutions. *IEEE Global Engineering Education Conference, EDUCON*, (1), 973–977.

Mahajan, P. T., & Golahit, S. B. (2017). Incorporating 11 P's of Service Marketing Mix and Its Impact on the Development of Technical Education. *Journal of Entrepreneurship Education*, *20*(2), 1–14.

Mahapatra, S. S., & Khan, M. S. (2007). A neural network approach for assessing quality in technical education: An empirical study. *International Journal of Productivity and Quality Management*, *2*(3), 287–306. doi:10.1504/IJPQM.2007.012451

Makri, A., Vlachopoulos, D., & Martina, R. A. (2021). Digital Escape Rooms as Innovative Pedagogical Tools in Education: A Systematic Literature Review. *Sustainability (Basel)*, *13*(8), 4587. https://www.mdpi.com/2071-1050/13/8/4587. doi:10.3390u13084587

Manasrah, A., Masoud, M., & Jaradat, Y. (2021). Short videos, or long videos? A study on the ideal video length in online learning. 2021 international conference on information technology (ICIT), Mayer, R. E. (2002). Multimedia learning. []. Elsevier.]. *Psychology of Learning and Motivation*, *41*, 85–139.

Manzini, E. (2006). *Design, ethics and sustainability. Guidelines for a transition phase*. Nantes Cumulus Working Papers. Helsinki: University of Art and Design.

Marques, J., & Pinto, P. R. (2012). Formação pedagógica de professores do ensino superior--a experiência na universidade nova de Lisboa. Revista Portuguesa de Pedagogia, 129-149.

Marr, B. (2022). *Future Skills: The 20 Skills and Competencies Everyone Needs to Succeed in a Digital World*. Wiley.

Martens, A., Diener, H., & Malo, S. (2008). Game-based Learning with Computers – Learning, Simulations, and Games Alke Martens University of Rostock Department of Computer Science and Electrical Engineering Holger Diener, Steffen Malo. In A. Pan, Z., Cheok, A.D., Müller, W., El Rhalibi (Ed.), Transactions on Edutainment I. Lecture Notes in Computer Science (Vol. 5080, pp. 172–190). Springer, Berlin, Heidelberg. doi:10.1007/978-3-540-69744-2_15

Marton, F., & Tsui, A. B. M. (2004). *Classroom discourse and the space of learning*. Routledge. doi:10.4324/9781410609762

Marulcu, İ., & Dedetürk, A. (2014). Pre-service science teachers' micro-teaching practices: An action research. *Mustafa Kemal University Journal of Graduate School of Social Sciences*, *11*(25), 353–372.

Masseck, T. (2017). Living Labs in Architecture as Innovation Arenas within Higher Education Institutions. *Energy Procedia*, *115*, 383–389. doi:10.1016/j.egypro.2017.05.035

MatchX. R. Event, https://helsinkixrcenter.com/events/match-xr-2021/

Matocha, J. (1992). Laboratory experiments in an algorithms course: Technical writing and the scientific method. In *Proceedings of the 22nd ASEE/IEEE frontiers in education conference, FIE'92*, pp. T1G 9-13. https://doi.org/10.1109/FIE.2002.1157917

Compilation of References

Maulana, F. I., Aldiki Febriantono, M., Raharja, D. R. B., Sofiani, I. R., & Firdaus, V. A. H. (2021). A scientometric analysis of game technology on learning media research study in recent 10 years. In *7th International Conference on Electrical, Electronics and Information Engineering: Technological Breakthrough for Greater New Life, ICEEIE 2021.* 10.1109/ICEEIE52663.2021.9616963

McCarthy, M. (2010). Experiential learning theory: From theory to practice. [JBER]. *Journal of Business & Economics Research*, *8*(5). Advance online publication. doi:10.19030/jber.v8i5.725

McCleary-Gaddy, A., Yu, E. T., & Spears, R. D. (2022). In-Person, Remote, or Hybrid Instruction? A Quality Improvement Assessment of a Six Week Interprofessional Education Pathway Program for Undergraduate Pre-Health Students. *Health Care*, *10*(12), 2399. Advance online publication. doi:10.3390/healthcare10122399 PMID:36553922

McCormack, J., Hutchings, P., Gifford, T., Yee-King, M., Llano, M. T., & D'inverno, M. (2020). Design Considerations for Real-Time Collaboration with Creative Artificial Intelligence. *Organised Sound*, *25*(1), 41–52. doi:10.1017/S1355771819000451

McCracken, D. D. (1989). Three "lab assignments" for an algorithms course. *SIGCSE Bulletin*, *21*(2), 61–64. doi:10.1145/65738.65750

McGeoch, C. C. (2012). *A guide to experimental algorithmics.* Cambridge University Press. doi:10.1017/CBO9780511843747

McKenzie, K., & Schweitzer, R. (2001). Who Succeeds at University? Factors predicting academic performance in first year Australian university students. *Higher Education Research & Development*, *20*(1), 21–33. doi:10.1080/07924360120043621

McKillup, S. (2012). *Statistics explained: An introductory guide for life scientists* (2nd ed.). Cambridge University Press.

McLoughlin, C., & Lee, M.J.W. (2007). Social software and participatory learning: Pedagogical choices with technology affordances in the Web 2.0 era. *Proceedings ascilite Singapore*, 664-675.

McQuiggan, S. W., Rowe, J. P., Lee, S., & Lester, J. C. (2008). Story-Based Learning: The Impact of Narrative on Learning Experiences and Outcomes. In B. P. Woolf, E. Aïmeur, R. Nkambou, & S. Lajoie (Eds.), *Intelligent Tutoring Systems* (pp. 530–539). Lecture Notes in Computer Science. Springer., doi:10.1007/978-3-540-69132-7_56

McTighe, J., & Wiggins, G. (2013). *Essential questions: Opening doors to student understanding.* ASCD.

Md Khambari, M. N., Wang, D., Wong, S. L., Moses, P., & Md, M. N., Khambari, R. W. O. K. Rahmat, & Khalid. (2021). Design of customizable gamified augmented reality apps: Towards embracing active learning. *29th International Conference on Computers in Education Conference, ICCE 2021 - Proceedings*, 2, 488–494.

Mello-Stark, S., VanValkenburg, M. A., & Hao, E. (2020). Thinking outside the box: Using escape room games to increase interest in cyber security. *Innovations in Cybersecurity Education*, 39-53.

Melo, A., Melo, C., & Vasconcelos, S. (2023). 'Rota dos Sabores' – Simulation-Based Learning In Tourism, Hospitality and Catering Education and Training. In L. G. Chova, A. L. Martînez & J. Lees (Eds.) *INTED2023 Proceedings*, (pp. 3384-3390). 10.21125/inted.2023.0920

Melo, A., Melo, C., Vasconcelos, S., Liberato, D., & Lopes, M. C. (2021). Soft skills & turismo: do mercado à academia. In *Fórum Interno 21 Livro de Resumos Desafios do "Novo Normal"*, (p.20). Edições Politema. https://recipp.ipp.pt/bitstream/10400.22/20439/1/livroResumos21.pdf

Melo, C., Mouta, C., & Pereira, P. (2022). Innovation in Tourism Higher Education: A project-based approach to Village Tourism. L. G. Chova, A. L. Martînez & J. Lees (Eds.), EDULEARN 2022 Proceedings, pp. 6283-6288. IATED Academy. doi:10.21125/edulearn.2022.1478

Melo, C., Mouta, C., & Pereira, P. (2023). How cool is collaboration? Students' perceptions on partnering with the tourism industry. In L. G. Chova, A. L. Martînez, & J. Lees (Eds.), *INTED 2023 Proceedings* (pp. 3596–3604). IATED Academy., doi:10.21125/inted.2023.0970

Melo, C., Mouta, C., & Pereira, P. (2023). How do tourim students' feel about interdisciplinarity? In L. G. Chova, A. L. Martînez, & J. Lees (Eds.), *INTED 2023 Proceedings* (pp. 6344–6348). IATED Academy., doi:10.21125/inted.2023.1676

Mendonça, J., Pinto, C., & Babo, L. (2020). Industry 5.0 expectations of engineering critical thinking. In EDULEARN20 Proceedings (pp. 8518-8529).

Mertler, C. A. (2022). Introduction to educational research (Third edition). Chapter 7 quantitative research methods. Los Angeles: SAGE Publications.

Mesquita, A., Santos, D., & Raposo, V. (2021). A gestão do conhecimento em contexto hospitalar: Uma scoping review. *Revista De Investigação & Inovação Em Saúde*, 4(2), 99–110. doi:10.37914/riis.v4i2.172

MHRD. (2018). *AISHE Report 2017-18*. https://doi.org/ doi:29-Sept-2018

Microsoft. (2021). CEO Satya Nadella's keynote Speech. Microsoft Inspire, July 15, 2021. https://news.microsoft.com/wp-content/uploads/prod/2021/07/Microsoft-Inspire-2021-Satya-Nadella.pdf

Miles, M. B., & Huberman, A. M. (1994). *Qualitative data analysis: An expanded Sourcebook* (2nd ed.). Sage.

Milgram, P., & Kishino, F. (1994). A Taxonomy of Mixer Reality Visual Displays. *IEICE Transactions on Information and Systems*, E77-D(12), 1321–1329.

Ministry of Education and Culture. (2014). Universities of Applied Sciences Act. https://www.finlex.fi/fi/laki/kaannokset/2014/en20140932_20200000.pdf

Mishra, P., & Koehler, M. J. (2006). Technological Pedagogical content knowledge: A framework for teacher knowledge. *Teachers College Record*, 108(6), 1017–1054. doi:10.1111/j.1467-9620.2006.00684.x

Mittal, R. K., Garg, N., & Yadav, S. K. (2018). Quality assessment framework for educational institutions in technical education: A literature survey. *On the Horizon, 26*(3), 270–280. doi:10.1108/OTH-08-2017-0066

Mohamed, M. N., Nurizah, N., Nurzarina, A. S., & Powzi, N. F. A. (2019). E-collaboration among students of two regions: Impacts on English language learning through peer learning. *International Journal of Learning. Teaching and Educational Research, 18*(9), 201–215.

Mohr, K., & Mohr, E. (2017). Understanding Generation Z Students to Promote a Contemporary Learning Environment. *Journal on Empowering Teaching Excellence, 1*(1). Advance online publication. doi:10.1016/j.ijhm.2018.01.016

Moiseenko, V. (2015). Encouraging Learners to Create Language-Learning Materials. *English Teaching Forum, 53*(4), 14–23.

Mokmin, N. A. M., Hanjun, S., Jing, C., & Qi, S. (2023). Impact of an AR-based learning approach on the learning achievement, motivation, and cognitive load of students on a design course. *Journal of Computers in Education*, 1-18.

Molenda, M. (2004). Cone of experience. In A. Kovalchik & K. Dawson (Eds.), *Education and Technology* (pp. 161–165). ABCCLIO.

Moontaha, S., Schumann, F. E. F., & Arnrich, B. (2023). Online Learning for Wearable EEG-Based Emotion Classification. *Sensors (Basel), 23*(5), 2387. doi:10.3390/s23052387 PMID:36904590

Moore, L., & Campbell, N. (2021). Effectiveness of an escape room for undergraduate interprofessional learning: A mixed methods single group pre-post evaluation. *BMC Medical Education, 21*(1), 220. doi:10.1186/s12909-021-02666-z PMID:33879150

Moore, M. G., & Kearsley, G. (2011). *Distance education: A systems view of online learning*. Cengage Learning.

Mo, Q. (1827). 2021. Fatigue Detection For Online Classes Based on Adaboost. *Journal of Physics: Conference Series, 012121*. Advance online publication. doi:10.1088/1742-6596/1827/1/012121

Morais, N. S., & Raposo, R. 2021. Blended-Learning in contexts conditioned by the pandemic: the perceptions of higher education students, in: 2021 International Symposium on Computers in Education (SIIE). Presented at the 2021 International Symposium on Computers in Education (SIIE), pp. 1–6. 10.1109/SIIE53363.2021.9583650

Morrell, B. L. M., Eukel, H. N., & Santurri, L. E. (2020). Soft skills and implications for future professional practice: Qualitative findings of a nursing education escape room. *Nurse Education Today, 93*, 104462. https://doi.org/https://doi.org/10.1016/j.nedt.2020.104462. doi:10.1016/j.nedt.2020.104462 PMID:32791421

Morrison, G. R., Ross, S. J., Morrison, J. R., & Kalman, H. K. (2019). *Designing effective instruction*. John Wiley & Sons.

Morris, T. H. (2020). Experiential learning – a systematic review and revision of Kolb's model. *Interactive Learning Environments*, *28*(8), 1064–1077. doi:10.1080/10494820.2019.1570279

Moultrie, J., Nilsson, M., Dissel, M., Haner, U.-E., Janssen, S., & Van der Lugt, R. (2007). Innovation Spaces: Towards a Framework for Understanding the Role of the Physical Environment in Innovation. *Creativity and Innovation Management*, *16*(1), 53–65. doi:10.1111/j.1467-8691.2007.00419.x

Mozahem, N. A. (2020). Using learning management system activity data to predict student performance in face-to-face courses. [IJMBL]. *International Journal of Mobile and Blended Learning*, *12*(3), 20–31. doi:10.4018/IJMBL.2020070102

Mumford, A. (1997). Putting learning styles to work. In *Action learning at work* (pp. 121–135). Gower.

Munari, B. (1981). *Das coisas nascem coisas*. Edições 70.

Munari, B. (2007). *Fantasia*. Edições 70.

Munoz, J. L. R., Ojeda, F. M., Jurado, D. L. A., Pena, P. F. P., Carranza, C. P. M., Berr'ios, H. Q., Molina, S. U., Farfan, A. R. M., & Arias-Gonzales, J. L. (2022). Systematic review of adaptive learning technology for learning in higher education. *Eurasian Journal of Educational Research*, *2022*(98), 221–233.

N.A.A.C. (2017). *NAAC Manual for Self-study Report Affiliated / Constituent Colleges*.

Nadolny, L., Alaswad, Z., Culver, D., & Wang, W. (2017). Designing With Game-Based Learning: Game Mechanics From Middle School to Higher Education. *Simulation & Gaming*, *48*(6), 814–831. doi:10.1177/1046878117736893

Nagao, K., & Nagao, K. (2019). Artificial intelligence in education. *Artificial Intelligence Accelerates Human Learning: Discussion Data Analytics*, 1-17.

Nagendra, A. (2014). Paradigm Shift in HR Practices on Employee Life Cycle Due to Influence of Social Media. *Procedia Economics and Finance*, *11*(14), 197–207. doi:10.1016/S2212-5671(14)00188-9

Nakamura, J., & Csikszentmihalyi, M. (2009). Flow theory and research. Handbook of positive psychology, 195, 206.

Naps, T., Roessling, G., Almstrum, V., Dann, W., Fleischer, R., Hundhausen, C., Korhonen, A., Malmi, L., McNally, M., Rodger, S., & Velázquez-Iturbide, J. Á. (2003). Exploring the role of visualization and engagement in computer science education. *SIGCSE Bulletin*, *35*(4), 131–152. doi:10.1145/782941.782998

Natarajan, R. (2000). The Role of Accreditation in Promoting Quality Assurance of Technical Education. *International Journal of Engineering Education*, *16*(2), 85–96.

National Board of Accreditation. (n.d.). Retrieved May 19, 2019, from https://www.nbaind.org/wa_program.aspx

NBA (2012). *Manual for Accreditation of Undergraduate Engineering Programs.*

Nebel, S., Schneider, S., & Rey, G. D. (2016). Mining learning and crafting scientific experiments: A literature review on the use of minecraft in education and research. *Journal of Educational Technology & Society*, *19*(2), 355–366.

Nelsen, R. B. (1993). *Proofs without words: Exercises in visual thinking*. The Mathematical Association of America.

Nelson, V., & Crea, J. (2021). The Data Science Instructional Escape Room-a Successful Experiment. *Chance*, *34*(2), 53–58. doi:10.1080/09332480.2021.1915034

Nevelsteen, K.J. (2017) Virtual world, defined from a technological perspective, and applied to video games, mixed reality and the metaverse. *Computer Animation and Virtual Worlds, 29*(1) / e1752. https://doi.org/ doi:10.1002/cav.1752

Ng, C. H. (2017). Pre-service teachers teaching critical literacy through microteaching: Possibilities and constraints. *Changing English*, *24*(1), 81–90. doi:10.1080/1358684X.2016.1273759

Nguyen, D. Q. (1998). The Essential Skills and Attributes of an Engineer: A Comparative Study of Academics, Industry Personnel and Engineering Students. *Global Journal of Engineering Education*, *2*(1), 65–75.

Nicholson, S. (2015). Peeking Behind the Locked Door: A Survey of Escape Room Facilities. White Paper. https://scottnicholson.com/pubs/erfacwhite.pdf

Nicola, S., Mendonça, J., Pinto, C., & Pereira, A. (2019). Education by challenge: innovation-driven spirit. In INTED2019 Proceedings (pp. 5182-5190). IATED. MATH-DIGGER. (2022). MATH-DIGGER - MATHematics DiGital Escape Rooms. ERASMUS+ Partnerships for cooperation and exchanges of practices. Project Reference 2021-1-PT01-KA220-HED-000032234. Retrieved from [URL] DrIVE-MATH. (2017). DrIVE-MATH - Development of Innovative Mathematical Teaching Strategies in European Engineering Degrees. ERASMUS+ Cooperation for innovation and the exchange of good practices. Project Reference 2017-1-PT01-KA203-035866. Cruz, M. (2018). Chicos, sacad el móvil de vuestras mochilas porque lo vamos a usar: Empowering Spanish As Foreign Language Students Through Mobile Devices. The Turkish Online Journal of Educational Technology, 1(Special Issue for INTE-ITICAM-IDEC), 282-298 10.21125/inted.2019.1292

Nilsson, S. (2010). Enhancing individual employability: The perspective of engineering graduates. *Education + Training*, *52*(6), 540–551. doi:10.1108/00400911011068487

Nkambou, R., Mizoguchi, R., & Bourdeau, J. (2010). *Advances in intelligent tutoring systems* (Vol. 308). Springer Science & Business Media. doi:10.1007/978-3-642-14363-2

Nokia (2023). Metaverse Explained. https://www.nokia.com/about-us/newsroom/articles/metaverse-explained/

Norman, S., & Porter, D. (2007). Designing Learning Objects for online learning.

Nóvoa, A. (2017). Firmar a posição como professor, afirmar a profissão docente. *Cadernos de Pesquisa, 47*(166), 1106–1133. doi:10.1590/198053144843

O'Reilly, T. (2005). *Web 2.0: Compact definition*. Retrived from http://radar.oreilly.com/2005/10/web-20-compact-definition.html

OECD. (2019). *OECD Future of Education and Skills 2030 - OECD Learning Compass 2030*. https://www.oecd.org/education/2030-project/contact/OECD_Learning_Compass_2030_Concept_Note_Series.pdf

OECD. (2021). *The state of higher education: One year in to the COVID-19 pandemic*. OECD Publishing., doi:10.1787/83c41957-

Okewu, E., Adewole, P., Misra, S., Maskeliunas, R., & Damasevicius, R. (2021). Artificial neural networks for educational data mining in higher education: A systematic literature review. *Applied Artificial Intelligence, 35*(13), 983–1021. doi:10.1080/08839514.2021.1922847

Olasina, G. (2022). Augmented reality in higher education: The new reality of teaching and learning during and post-covid-19. *Ubiquitous Learning, 16*(1), 31–54. doi:10.18848/1835-9795/CGP/v16i01/31-54

Oliva, D., Somerkoski, B., Tarkkanen, K., Lehto, A., & Luimula, M. (2019). *Virtual reality as a communication tool for fire safety – Experiences from the VirPa project*. GamiFIN Conference, Levi, Finland, April 8-10, 2019.

Onofrei, G., & Ferry, P. (2020). Reusable learning objects: A blended learning tool in teaching computer-aided design to engineering undergraduates. *International Journal of Educational Management, 34*(10), 1559–1575. doi:10.1108/IJEM-12-2019-0418

Orehovački, T., Bubaš, G., & Kovačić, A. (2012). Taxonomy of Web 2.0 applications with educational potential. *Transformation in teaching: Social media strategies in higher education*, 43-72.

Österman, M. (2021). *Development of a virtual reality conference application*. Bachelor's Thesis in Information and Communications Technology. Turku University of Applied Sciences.

Ostrosky, M. M., Mouzourou, C., Danner, N., & Zaghlawan, H. Y. (2013). Improving teacher practices using microteaching: Planful video recording and constructive feedback. *Young Exceptional Children, 16*(1), 16–29. doi:10.1177/1096250612459186

Ouyang, F., Wu, M., Zheng, L., Zhang, L., & Jiao, P. (2023). Integration of artificial intelligence performance prediction and learning analytics to improve student learning in online engineering course. *International Journal of Educational Technology in Higher Education, 20*(1), 1–23. doi:10.118641239-022-00372-4 PMID:36683653

Oyelere, S. S., Bouali, N., Kaliisa, R., Obaido, G., Yunusa, A. A., & Jimoh, E. R. (2020). Exploring the trends of educational virtual reality games: A systematic review of empirical studies. *Smart Learning Environments*, 7(31), 31. Advance online publication. doi:10.118640561-020-00142-7

Oyesiku, D., Adewumi, A., Misra, S., Ahuja, R., Damasevicius, R., & Maskeliunas, R. (2018). An educational math game for high school students in Sub-Saharan Africa. *Applied Informatics: First International Conference, ICAI 2018, Bogotá, Colombia, November 1-3, 2018 Proceedings*, 1, 228–238.

Pabba, C., & Kumar, P. (2022). An intelligent system for monitoring students' engagement in large classroom teaching through facial expression recognition. *Expert Systems: International Journal of Knowledge Engineering and Neural Networks*, 39(1), e12839. doi:10.1111/exsy.12839

Pal Pandi, A., Jeyathilagar, D., & Kubendran, V. (2013). A study of integrated total quality management practice in engineering educational institutions. *International Journal of Management Science and Engineering Management*, 8(2), 117–125. doi:10.1080/17509653.2013 798949

Pal Pandi, A., Rajendra Sethupathi, P. V., & Jeyathilagar, D. (2016). The IEQMS model for augmenting quality in engineering institutions – an interpretive structural modelling approach. *Total Quality Management & Business Excellence*, 27(3–4), 292–308. doi:10.1080/14783363. 2014.978647

PalaniNathaRaja, M., Deshmukh, S. G., & Wadhwa, S.PalaniNathaRaja. (2006). Measuring service quality in technical education and healthcare services. *International Journal of Services and Operations Management*, 2(3), 222–236. doi:10.1504/IJSOM.2006.009858

Pan, R., Lo, H., & Neustaedter, C. (2017). Collaboration, Awareness, and Communication in Real-Life Escape Rooms Proceedings of the 2017 Conference on Designing Interactive Systems, Edinburgh, United Kingdom. https://doi.org/10.1145/3064663.3064767

Pandi, A. P., Sethupathi, P. V. R., & Jeyathilagar, D. (2016). Quality sustainability in engineering educational institutions - a theoretical model. *International Journal of Productivity and Quality Management*, 18(2/3), 364–384. doi:10.1504/IJPQM.2016.076715

Pandi, A. P., Sethupathi, P. V. R., Jeyathilagar, D., & Rajesh, R. (2016). Structural equation modelling for analyzing relationship between IEQMS criteria and performance of engineering institutions. *International Journal of Enterprise Network Management*, 7(2), 87–97. doi:10.1504/ IJENM.2016.077525

Pan, L., Tlili, A., Li, J., Jiang, F., Shi, G., Yu, H., & Yang, J. (2021). How to Implement Game-Based Learning in a Smart Classroom? A Model Based on a Systematic Literature Review and Delphi Method. *Frontiers in Psychology*, 12(December), 1–13. doi:10.3389/fpsyg.2021.749837 PMID:34925153

Papastergiou, M., & Mastrogiannis, I. (2021). Design, development and evaluation of open interactive learning objects for secondary school physical education. *Education and Information Technologies*, 26(3), 2981–3007. doi:10.100710639-020-10390-2

Parasuraman, A., Zeithaml, V. A., & Berry, L. L. (1985). A Conceptual Model of Service Quality and Its Implications for Future Research. *Journal of Marketing*, 49(4), 41–50. doi:10.1177/002224298504900403

Pascoe Michaela, C., Hetrick Sarah, E., & Parker Alexandra, G. (2020). The impact of stress on students in secondary school and higher education. *International Journal of Adolescence and Youth*, 25(1), 104–112. doi:10.1080/02673843.2019.1596823

Pashler, H., McDaniel, M., Rohrer, D., & Bjork, R. (2008). Learning Styles: Concepts and Evidence. *Psychological Science in the Public Interest*, 9(3), 105–119. doi:10.1111/j.1539-6053.2009.01038.x PMID:26162104

Patel, C. (2018). An Analysis of Jean Lave and Etienne Wenger's Situated Learning: Legitimate Peripheral Participation. Taylor & Francis. https://books.google.com.au/books?id=GEFNDwAAQBAJ

Patton, M. Q. (2002). *Qualitative research & evaluation methods* (3rd ed.). Sage Publications, Inc.

Paulauskas, L., Paulauskas, A., Blažauskas, T., Damaševičius, R., & Maskeliūnas, R. (2023). Reconstruction of industrial and historical heritage for cultural enrichment using virtual and augmented reality. *Technologies*, 11(2), 36. doi:10.3390/technologies11020036

Peker, M. (2009). The use of expanded microteaching for reducing pre- service teachers' teaching anxiety about mathematics. *Scientific Research and Essays*, 4(9), 872–880.

Peleg, R., Yayon, M., Katchevich, D., Moria-Shipony, M., & Blonder, R. (2019). A Lab-Based Chemical Escape Room: Educational, Mobile, and Fun! *Journal of Chemical Education*, 96(5), 955–960. doi:10.1021/acs.jchemed.8b00406

Pellas, N., Fotaris, P., Kazanidis, I., & Wells, D. (2019). Augmenting the learning experience in primary and secondary school education : A systematic review of recent trends in augmented reality game - based learning. *Virtual Reality (Waltham Cross)*, 23(4), 329–346. doi:10.100710055-018-0347-2

Pérez, P., González-Sosa, E., Kachach, R., Pereira, F., & Villegas, Á. (2021). Ecological validity through gamification: An experiment with a mixed reality escape room. 2021 IEEE International Conference on Artificial Intelligence and Virtual Reality (AIVR), Plass, J. L., Homer, B. D., & Kinzer, C. K. (2015). Foundations of Game-Based Learning. *Educational Psychologist*, 50(4), 258–283. doi:10.1080/00461520.2015.1122533

Perrenoud, Ph. (1997). *Construire des compétences dès l'école*. ESF.

Picciano, A. G. (2002). Beyond Student Perceptions: Issues of Interaction, Presence, and Performance in an Online Course. *Journal of Asynchronous Learning Networks*, 6(1), 21–40.

Ping, W. (2013). Micro-teaching: A powerful tool to embedding the English teacher certification testing in the development of English teaching methodologies. *International Journal of English Language and Literature Studies*, 2(3), 163–175.

Pinto, C., Babo, L., & Mendonça, J. (2020). Engineering students' awareness of their present and future professional expertises. In EDULEARN20 Proceedings (pp. 8360-8369). IATED.

Pinto, C. M. A., Mendonça, J., & Nicola, S. (2022). DrIVE-MATH Project: Case Study from the Polytechnic of Porto, PT. *Open Education Studies, 4*(1), 1–20. doi:10.1515/edu-2022-0001

Plano Nacional das Artes. (2019). *Uma estratégia um manifesto.* PNA. https://www.dge.mec.pt/sites/default/files/Projetos/PNA/Documentos/estrategia_do_plano_nacional_das_artes_2019-2024.pdf

Plomp, T., van den Akker, J., Bannan, B., Kelly, A. E., & Nieveen, N. (2013). *Educational design research: An introduction* (T. Plomp & N. Nieveen, Eds.). SLO.

PMIEF. (2018). Framework for high quality project based learning. *Project Management Institute Educational Foundation*, 1–6. Retrieved from https://hqpbl.org/wp-content/uploads/2018/03/FrameworkforHQPBL.pdf

Pollock, N. B. (2022). Student performance and perceptions of anatomy and physiology across face-to-face, hybrid, and online teaching lab styles. *Advances in Physiology Education, 46*(3), 453–460. doi:10.1152/advan.00074.2022 PMID:35759525

Pool, J., & Laubscher, D. (2016). Design-based research: Is this a suitable methodology for short-term projects? *Educational Media International, 53*(1), 42–52. doi:10.1080/09523987.2016.1189246

Prasad, G., & Bhar, C. (2010). Accreditation system for technical education programmes in India: A critical review. *European Journal of Engineering Education, 35*(2), 187–213. doi:10.1080/03043790903497294

Prasad, U. C., & Suri, R. K. (2011). Modeling of Continuity and Change Forces in Private Higher Technical Education Using Total Interpretive Structural Modeling (TISM). *Global Journal of Flexible Systems Managment, 12*(3 & 4), 31–40. doi:10.1007/BF03396605

Pratchett, T., Young, G., Brooks, C., Jeskins, L., & Monagle, H. (2016). Honey and Mumford – learning styles. In *Practical Tips for Developing Your Staff* (pp. 8–11). Facet. doi:10.29085/9781783301812.005

Prediger, S., Quabeck, K., & Erath, K. (2022). Conceptualizing micro-adaptive teaching practices in content-specific ways: Case study on fractions. *Journal on Mathematics Education, 13*(1), 1–30. doi:10.22342/jme.v13i1.pp1-30

Price, M., Handley, K., Millar, J., & O'donovan, B. (2010). Feedback: all that effort but what is the effect? *Assessment \& Evaluation in Higher Education, 35*(3), 277–289.

Price, B., Baecker, R., & Small, I. (1998). An introduction to software visualization. In J. Stasko, J. Domingue, M. H. Brown, & B. A. Price (Eds.), *Software visualization* (pp. 3–27). The MIT Press.

PricewaterhouseCoopers. (2022). Emerging Technology - What does virtual reality and the metaverse mean for training? https://www.pwc.com/us/en/tech-effect/emerging-tech/virtual-reality-study.html

Puthal, M., Das, J. R., & Dash, M. (2018). An Exploratory Study on Effects of Service Quality on Technical Education in the Indian Context. *International Journal of Mechanical Engineering and Technology*, *9*(8), 1255–1265.

Puthal, M., Rout, P. K., Das, J. R., & Dash, M. (2018). A Model for Service Quality in Indian Technical Education. *International Journal of Mechanical Engineering and Technology*, *9*(6), 1081–1092.

Queirós, R. A. P. (2022). Integration of a Learning Playground into an LMS. In *Proceedings of the 27th ACM Conference on on Innovation and Technology in Computer Science Education* Vol. 2 (pp. 626). ACM. 10.1145/3502717.3532175

Rafique, G. M., Mahmood, K., Warraich, N. F., & Rehman, S. U. (2021). Readiness for Online Learning during COVID-19 pandemic: A survey of Pakistani LIS students. *Journal of Academic Librarianship*, *47*(3), 102346. doi:10.1016/j.acalib.2021.102346 PMID:36536686

Rahimi, M. (2013). Is training student reviewers worth its while? A study of how training influences the quality of students' feedback and writing. *Language Teaching Research*, *17*(1), 67–89. doi:10.1177/1362168812459151

Ramadhan, A. D., Permanasari, A. E., & Wibirama, S. (2022). Gamification opportunity in augmented reality-based learning media: A review. *2022 2nd International Conference on Intelligent Cybernetics Technology and Applications, ICICyTA 2022*, 117–122. 10.1109/ICICyTA57421.2022.10037922

Ramli, R. Z., Sahari, N., Noor, S. F. M., Noor, M. M., Majid, N. A. A., Dahlan, H. A., & Wahab, A. N. A. (2022). Assessing usability of learning experience prototype. *International Journal of Emerging Technologies in Learning*, *17*(9), 20–36. doi:10.3991/ijet.v17i09.29955

Randi, M., & Carvalho, H. (2013). Learning Through Role-Playing Games: An Approach for Active Learning and Teaching. *Revista Brasileira de Educação Médica*, *37*(1), 80–88. doi:10.1590/S0100-55022013000100012

Rao, P. S., Viswanadhan, K. G., & Raghunandana, K. (2015). Best Practices for Quality Improvement—Lessons from Top Ranked Engineering Institutions. *International Education Studies*, *8*(11), 169–183. doi:10.5539/ies.v8n11p169

Rao, U. S., & Pandi, A. P. (2007). Quality Enhancement In Engineering Institutions Through Knowledge Management And Total Quality Management. *The Journal of Engineering Education Transformation*, *20*(3), 10–15.

Rapanta, C., Botturi, L., Goodyear, P., Guàrdia, L., & Koole, M. (2021). Balancing technology, pedagogy and the new normal: Post-pandemic challenges for higher education. *Postdigital Science and Education*, *3*(3), 715–742. doi:10.100742438-021-00249-1

Ravitz, J., Hixson, N., English, M., & Mergendoller, J. (2012). Using project based learning to teach 21 st century skills : Findings from a statewide initiative. In *Annual Meetings of the American Educational Research Association*. Vancouver, BC.

Raymond, A., Jacob, E., Jacob, D., & Lyons, J. (2016). Peer learning a pedagogical approach to enhance online learning: A qualitative exploration. *Nurse Education Today*, *44*, 165–169. https://doi.org/https://doi.org/10.1016/j.nedt.2016.05.016. doi:10.1016/j.nedt.2016.05.016 PMID:27429347

Reeves, T. C. (2006). How do you know they are learning? The importance of alignment in higher education. *International Journal of Learning Technology*, *2*(4), 294–309. doi:10.1504/IJLT.2006.011336

Reigeluth, C. M. (2016). Instructional theory and technology for the new paradigm of education. *Revista de Educación a Distancia (RED)*(50).

Reigeluth, C. M., & An, Y. (2020). *Merging the instructional design process with learner-centered theory: The holistic 4D model*. Routledge. doi:10.4324/9781351117548

Reis, S., Guimarães, P., Coelho, F., Nogueira, E., & Coelho, L. 2013. A framework for simulation systems and technologies for medical training, in: 2018 Global Medical Engineering Physics Exchanges/Pan American Health Care Exchanges (GMEPE/PAHCE). Presented at the 2018 Global Medical Engineering Physics Exchanges/Pan American Health Care Exchanges (GMEPE/PAHCE), pp. 1–4. 10.1109/GMEPE-PAHCE.2018.8400757

Reiser, R. (2012). *A history of instructional desgin and technology In?" from Trends and Issues in Instructional Design and Technology, Saddle River*. Pearson.

Reiser, R. A. (2012). A history of instructional design and technology. In J. V. D. R. A. Reiser (Ed.), *Trends and issues in instructional design and technology* (Vol. 3). Pearson Education.

Reis, S., Coelho, F., & Coelho, L. (2020). Success Factors in Students' Motivation with Project Based Learning: From Theory to Reality. [iJOE]. *International Journal of Online and Biomedical Engineering*, *16*(12), 4–17. doi:10.3991/ijoe.v16i12.16001

Renk, K., & Smith, T. (2007). Predictors of academic-related stress in college students: An examination of coping, social support, parenting, and anxiety. *NASPA Journal*, *44*(3), 405–431. doi:10.2202/1949-6605.1829

Report, A. I. C. T. E. 2018-19. (2019). Retrieved May 19, 2019, from http://www.facilities.aicte-india.org/dashboard/pages/dashboardaicte.php

Reyes, A. Jr, Galvan, R. Jr, Navarro, A., Velasquez, M., Soriano, D. R., Cabuso, A. L., David, J. R., Lacson, M. L., Manansala, N. T., & Tiongco, R. E. (2020). Across Generations: Defining Pedagogical Characteristics of Generation X, Y, and Z Allied Health Teachers Using Q-Methodology. *Medical Science Educator*, *30*(4), 1541–1549. doi:10.100740670-020-01043-7 PMID:34457822

Rich, M. (2008). Millennial students and technology choices for information searching. *Electronic Journal of Business Research Methods*, *6*(1), 73–76.

Rinderknecht, C. (2014). A survey on teaching and learning recursive programming. *Informatics in Education*, *13*(1), 87–119. doi:10.15388/infedu.2014.06

Ritzko, J., & Robinson, S. (2011). Using Games To Increase Active Learning. [TLC]. *Journal of College Teaching and Learning*, *3*(6). Advance online publication. doi:10.19030/tlc.v3i6.1709

Rizvi, S., Rienties, B., & Khoja, S. A. (2019). The role of demographics in online learning; A decision tree based approach. *Computers & Education*, *137*, 32–47. doi:10.1016/j.compedu.2019.04.001

Roberts, M. D. (2022). Secondary School Students' Views of Tourism Education and Tourism Careers. *Journal of Hospitality \& Tourism Education*, 1–12.

Robotham, D., & Julian, C. (2006). Stress and the higher education student: A critical review of the literature. *Journal of Further and Higher Education*, *30*(2), 107–117. doi:10.1080/03098770600617513

Rodis, O. M. M., & Locsin, R. C. (2019). The implementation of the Japanese Dental English core curriculum: Active learning based on peer-teaching and learning activities. *BMC Medical Education*, *19*(1), 256. doi:10.118612909-019-1675-y PMID:31291939

Ross, R., & Bell, C. (2019, August 20-23). 2019). Turning the classroom into an escape room with decoder hardware to increase student engagement. 2019 IEEE Conference on Games (CoG), Ross, R., & Bennett, A. (2020). Increasing engagement with engineering escape rooms. *IEEE Transactions on Games*, *14*(2), 161–169. doi:10.1109/TG.2020.3025003

Rudd, J., Stern, K., & Isensee, S. (1996). Low vs. high-fidelity prototyping debate. *interactions*, *3*(1), 76-85.

Rudolph, C. W., Lavigne, K. N., & Zacher, H. (2017). Career adaptability: A meta-analysis of relationships with measures of adaptivity, adapting responses, and adaptation results. *Journal of Vocational Behavior*, *98*, 17–34. doi:10.1016/j.jvb.2016.09.002

Ruhanen, L. (2005). Bridging the Divide Between Theory and Practice. *Journal of Teaching in Travel \& Tourism, 5*(4), 33–51. https://doi.org/ doi:10.1300/J172v05n04_03

Ryan, K., & Cooper, J. M. (1980). *Those who can, teach*. Houghton Miffling Company.

Şad, S. N., & Göktaş, Ö. (2014). Preservice teachers' perceptions about using mobile phones and laptops in education as mobile learning tools. *British Journal of Educational Technology*, *45*(4), 606–618. doi:10.1111/bjet.12064

Saettler, P. (1990). The evolution of American educational technology. *Englewood, Col.: Libraries unlim.*

Saettler, P. (2004). *The evolution of American educational technology*. IAP.

Şahinkayası, H. (2009). *Contributions and challenges of cognitive tools and microteaching for preservice teachers' instructional planning and teaching skills* [Unpublished doctoral dissertation]. Middle East Technical University, Ankara, Turkey.

Sahni, S. (2004). *Data structures, algorithms, and applications in Java* (2nd ed.). Silicon Press.

Sahu, A. R., Shrivastava, R. L., & Shrivastava, R. R. (2008). Key Factors Affecting The Effectiveness of Technical Education–An Indian Perspective. *Proceedings of the World Congress On Engineering, II*, 2–6.

Sahu, A. R., Shrivastava, R. R., & Shrivastava, R. L. (2012). Development and validation of an instrument for measuring critical success factors (CSFs) of technical education - a TQM approach. *International Journal of Productivity and Quality Management, 11*(1), 29–56. doi:10.1504/IJPQM.2013.050567

Sahu, A. R., Shrivastava, R. R., & Shrivastava, R. L. (2013). Critical success factors for sustainable improvement in technical education excellence - A literature review. *The TQM Journal, 25*(1), 62–74. doi:10.1108/17542731311286432

Saito, D. S., & Ulbricht, V. R. (2012). Learning Managent Systems and Face-to-Face Teaching in Bilingual Modality (Libras/Portuguese). *Revista IEEE América Latina, 10*(5), 2168–2174. doi:10.1109/TLA.2012.6362362

Salvioni, D. M., Franzoni, S., & Cassano, R. (2017). Sustainability in the higher education system: An opportunity to improve quality and image. *Sustainability (Basel), 9*(6), 914–941. doi:10.3390u9060914

Sanders, D., & Armstrong, E. K. (2008). Understanding students' perceptions and experience of a tourism management field trip: The need for a graduated approach. *Journal of Hospitality \& Tourism Education, 20*(4), 29–37.

Sanders, I. (2002). Teaching empirical analysis of algorithms. In *Proceedings of the 33rd SIGCSE technical symposium on computer science education, SIGCSE'02*, pp. 321-325. https://doi.org/10.1145/563340.563468

Sanpanich, N. (2021). Investigating Factors Affecting Students' Attitudes toward Hybrid Learning. *Reflections: The SoL Journal, 28*(2), 208–227.

Sarage, D., O'Neill, B. J., & Eaton, C. M. (2021). There is no I in escape: Using an escape room simulation to enhance teamwork and medication safety behaviors in nursing students. *Simulation & Gaming, 52*(1), 40–53. doi:10.1177/1046878120976706

Sarkar, S. (2012). The role of information and communication technology (ICT) in higher education for the 21st century. *Science, 1*(1), 30–41.

Saunders, L., & Wong, M. A. 2020. Active Learning: Engaging People in the Learning Process, in: Instruction in Libraries and Information Centers. Windsor & Downs Press.

Savickas, M. L. (1997). Career Adaptability - An Integrative Construct for Life-Span, Life-Space Theory. *The Career Development Quarterly, 45*(3), 247–259. doi:10.1002/j.2161-0045.1997.tb00469.x

Sayeda, B., Rajendran, C., & Lokachari, P. S. (2010). An empirical study of total quality management in engineering educational institutions of India: Perspective of management. *Benchmarking, 17*(5), 728–767. doi:10.1108/14635771011076461

Schein, E. H. (1996). Career Anchors Revisited: Implications for Career Development in the 21st Century. *The Academy of Management Perspectives*, *10*(4), 80–88. doi:10.5465/ame.1996.3145321

Schenarts, P. J. (2019). Now Arriving: Surgical Trainees From Generation Z. *Journal of Surgical Education*, *77*(2), 246–253. doi:10.1016/j.jsurg.2019.09.004 PMID:31562032

Schunk, D. H. (1995). Self-efficacy, motivation, and performance. *Journal of Applied Sport Psychology*, *7*(2), 112–137. doi:10.1080/10413209508406961

Seebauer, S., Jahn, S., & Mottok, J. (2020). Learning from escape rooms? A study design concept measuring the effect of a cryptography educational escape room. 2020 IEEE Global Engineering Education Conference (EDUCON), Shepard, L. A., Penuel, W. R., & Davidson, K. L. (2017). Design principles for new systems of assessment. *Phi Delta Kappan*, *98*(6), 47–52.

Seemiller, C., & Meghan, G. (2017). Generation Z: Educating and Engaging the Next Generation of Students. *About Campus: Enriching the Student Learning Experience*, *22*(3), 21–26. doi:10.1002/abc.21293

Seitamaa-Hakkarainen, P., & Kangas, K. (2013). Craft education: authentic design constraints, embodied thinking, and craft making. DRS CUMULUS 2013 Design Learning for Tomorrow, Oslo.

Selber, S., & Selber, S. A. (2004). *Multiliteracies for a digital age*. SIU Press.

Sendurur, E. (2022). Öğretme ve Öğrenme Aracı Olarak Teknolojik Araçlar-Programlar-Projeler. In S. D. K. N. Demirci Saygı (Ed.), *Dijitalleşme ve Eğitim* (Vol. 1). Eğiten Kitap.

Senthil Kumar, M., & Sivakumar, P. (2014). Enhancing the quality of technical education accreditation system using current communication system. *International Journal of Applied Engineering Research: IJAER*, *9*(23), 20421–20432.

Seo, K., Tang, J., Roll, I., Fels, S., & Yoon, D. (2021). The impact of artificial intelligence on learner–instructor interaction in online learning. *International Journal of Educational Technology in Higher Education*, *18*(1), 1–23. doi:10.118641239-021-00292-9 PMID:34778540

Shaik, T., Tao, X., Li, Y., Dann, C., McDonald, J., Redmond, P., & Galligan, L. (2022). A Review of the Trends and Challenges in Adopting Natural Language Processing Methods for Education Feedback Analysis. *IEEE Access : Practical Innovations, Open Solutions*, *10*, 56720–56739. doi:10.1109/ACCESS.2022.3177752

Shail, M. S. (2019). Using micro-learning on mobile applications to increase knowledge retention and work performance: A review of literature. *Cureus*, *11*(8). Advance online publication. doi:10.7759/cureus.5307 PMID:31511813

Sharma, G. D., Uppal, R. S., & Mahendru, M. (2016). Technical education as a tool for ensuring sustainable development: A case of India. *International Conference on Sustainability, Technology and Education 2016*, (December), 229–236.

Sharma, P. (2015). Organizational Commitment Among Faculty Members in India : A Study of Public and Private Technical Schools. *Global Business and Organizational Excellence*, *34*(5), 30–38. doi:10.1002/joe.21624

Sharma, P., Joshi, S., Gautam, S., Maharjan, S., Khanal, S. R., Reis, M. C., Barroso, J., & Filipe, V. M. de J. (2023). *Student Engagement Detection Using Emotion Analysis*. Eye Tracking and Head Movement with Machine Learning., doi:10.48550/arXiv.1909.12913

Sharma, P., & Pandher, J. S. (2018). Quality of teachers in technical higher education institutions in India. *Higher Education. Skills and Work-Based Learning*, *8*(4), 511–526. doi:10.1108/HESWBL-10-2017-0080

Sharma, V., Bhagat, K. K., Huang, H., & Chen, N. (2022). The design and evaluation of an ar-based serious game to teach programming. *Computers & Graphics*, *103*, 1–18. doi:10.1016/j.cag.2022.01.002

Shatto, B., & Erwin, K. (2017). Teaching Millennials and Generation Z: Bridging the Generational Divide. *Creative Nursing*, *23*(1), 24–28. doi:10.1891/1078-4535.23.1.24 PMID:28196564

Shemshack, A., & Spector, J. M. (2020). A systematic literature review of personalized learning terms. *Smart Learning Environments*, *7*(1), 33. doi:10.118640561-020-00140-9

Shindler, M., Goodrich, M. T., Gila, O., & Dillencourt, M. (2022). Beyond big O: Teaching experimental algorithmics. *Journal of Computing Sciences in Colleges*, *37*(10), 23–36.

Shi, Y.-R., & Shih, J.-L. (2015). Game factors and game-based learning design model. *International Journal of Computer Games Technology*, *2015*, 11. Advance online publication. doi:10.1155/2015/549684

Shneiderman, B. (1996). The eyes have it: A task by data type taxonomy for information visualizations. In *Proceedings 1996 IEEE symposium on visual languages, VL'96*, pp. 336-343. https://doi.org/10.1109/VL.1996.545307

Shukla, O. P., & Garg, S. K. (2017). Perception of faculty members on factors affecting quality education and employability skills in technical education sector: An empirical analysis. *International Journal of Services. Economics and Management*, *8*(1/2), 109–131.

Sidekerskienė, T., & Damaševičius, R. (2023, April). Out-of-the-box learning: Digital escape rooms as a metaphor for breaking down barriers in stem education *Sustainability (Basel)*, *15*(9), 7393. doi:10.3390u15097393

Sikveland, R. O., Solem, M. S., & Skovholt, K. (2021). How teachers use prosody to guide students towards an adequate answer. *Linguistics and Education*, *61*, 100886. doi:10.1016/j.linged.2020.100886

Singh, A. P., & Dangmei, J. (2016). Understanding the generation Z: The Future Workforce. *South -. Asian Journal of Multidisciplinary Studies*, *3*(3), 1–5.

Singh, M., James, P. S., Paul, H., & Bolar, K. (2022). Impact of cognitive-behavioral motivation on student engagement. *Heliyon*, *8*(7), e09843. doi:10.1016/j.heliyon.2022.e09843 PMID:35815149

Sirkiä, T. (2018). Jsvee & Kelmu: Creating and tailoring program animations for computing education. *Software: Evolution and Process, 30*(2), e1924. https://onlinelibrary.wiley.com/doi/10.1002/smr.1924

Skills, T. P. for 21st C. (2009). *Framework for 21st Century Learning*.

Somerkoski, B., Tarkkanen, K., Oliva, D., Lehto, A., & Luimula, M. (2022). Pedagogic solutions and results in designing a mobile game for fire safety teaching. In *Proceeding of the 6th GamiFIN conference*, online, pp. 44-53.

Sotomayor, S. (2021). Long-term benefits of field trip participation: Young tourism management professionals share their stories. *Journal of Hospitality, Leisure, Sport and Tourism Education*, *29*, 100285. https://doi.org/https://doi.org/10.1016/j.jhlste.2020.100285. doi:10.1016/j.jhlste.2020.100285

Spector, J. M., Ifenthaler, D., Sampson, D. G., & Yang, L. (Eds.). (2021). *Educational scenarios: From dreams to action*. Springer.

Spitzer, K. L., & Brinkley-Etzkorn, K. E. (2016). Designing authentic educational experiences in online courses through scenario-based learning. *Online Learning : the Official Journal of the Online Learning Consortium*, *20*(3), 98–114.

Stacey, E., & Gerbic, P. 2009. Effective Blended Learning Practices: Evidence-Based Perspectives in ICT-Facilitated Education, https://services.igi-global.com/resolvedoi/resolve.aspx?doi=10.4018/978-1-60566-296-1. IGI Global.

Stasko, J., Domingue, J., Brown, M. H., & Price, B. A. (Eds.). (1998). *Software visualization*. The MIT Press.

State vs No of Institutes, 2018-19. (2019). Retrieved May 20, 2019, from https://www.facilities.aicte-india.org/dashboard/pages/angulardashboard.php#!/graphs

Stehle, S. M., & Peters-burton, E. E. (2019). Developing student 21 st Century skills in selected exemplary inclusive STEM high schools. *International Journal of STEM Education*, *6*(39), 1–15. doi:10.118640594-019-0192-1

Steinmayr, R., Weidinger, A. F., Schwinger, M., & Spinath, B. (2019). The Importance of Students' Motivation for Their Academic Achievement – Replicating and Extending Previous Findings. *Frontiers in Psychology*, *10*, 10. doi:10.3389/fpsyg.2019.01730 PMID:31417459

Stern, L., & Naish, L. (2002). Visual representations for recursive algorithms. In *Proceedings of the 33th SIGCSE technical symposium on computer science education, SIGCSE'02*, pp. 196-200. https://doi.org/10.1145/563340.563414

Stiggins, R. J. (2010). *An introduction to student-involved assessment FOR learning*. Pearson.

Stohlmann, M. S. (2020). Escape room math: Luna's lines. Mathematics Teacher: Learning and Teaching PK-12, 113(5), 383-389.

Struthers, C. W., Perry, R. P., & Menec, V. H. (2000). An examination of the relationships among academic stress, coping motivation, and performance in college. *Research in Higher Education*, *41*(5), 581–592. doi:10.1023/A:1007094931292

Subramaniam, K. (2006). Creating a microteaching evaluation form: The needed evaluation criteria. *Education*, *126*(4), 666–677.

Subramony, D. P. (2003). Dale's Cone revisited: Critically examining the misapplication of a nebulous theory to guide practice. *Educational Technology*, *7-8*(25-30).

Suharwoto, G. (2006).*Secondary mathematics preservice teachers' development of technology pedagogical content knowledge in subject-specific, technology- integrated teacher preparation program* [Unpublished doctoral dissertation]. Oregon State University, Oregon.

Sunagawa, M., Shikii, S., Nakai, W., Mochizuki, M., Kusukame, K., & Kitajima, H. (2020). Comprehensive Drowsiness Level Detection Model Combining Multimodal Information. *IEEE Sensors Journal*, *20*(7), 3709–3717. doi:10.1109/JSEN.2019.2960158

Sundsbø, K. (2018). Open Access Escape Room. figshare (2018): https://figshare. com/projects/ Open Access Escape Room/56915 (accessed January 24, 2019).

Sun, Z., Anbarasan, M., & Praveen Kumar, D. (2021). Design of online intelligent English teaching platform based on artificial intelligence techniques. *Computational Intelligence*, *37*(3), 1166–1180. doi:10.1111/coin.12351

Sutherland, L.-A., & Marchand, F. (2021). On-farm demonstration: Enabling peer-to-peer learning. (). Taylor \& Francis.]. *Journal of Agricultural Education and Extension*, *27*(5), 573–590. doi: 10.1080/1389224X.2021.1959716

Swacha, J., Queiros, R., & Paiva, J. C. (2023). Gatugu: Six perspectives of evaluation of gamified systems. *Information (Basel)*, *14*(2), 136. doi:10.3390/info14020136

Sweller, J., van Merriënboer, J. J., & Paas, F. (2019). Cognitive architecture and instructional design: 20 years later. *Educational Psychology Review*, *31*(2), 261–292. doi:10.100710648-019-09465-5

Taatila, V. (2017). Paradigm Shift in Higher Education? On The Horizon, 25(2), pp. 103-108. https://doi.org. doi:10.1108/OTH-06-2016-0030

Taatila, V., & Raij, K. (2012). Philosophical Review of Pragmatism as a Basis for Learning by Developing Pedagogy. *Educational Philosophy and Theory*, *44*(8), 831–844. doi:10.1111/j.1469-5812.2011.00758.x

Tang, Y. M., Lau, Y., & Chau, K. Y. (2022). Towards a sustainable online peer learning model based on student's perspectives. *Education and Information Technologies*, *27*(9), 12449–12468. doi:10.100710639-022-11136-y PMID:35668899

Taraldsen, L. H., Haara, F. O., Lysne, M. S., Jensen, P. R., & Jenssen, E. S. (2022). A review on use of escape rooms in education – touching the void. *Education Inquiry*, *13*(2), 169–184. doi: 10.1080/20004508.2020.1860284

Teague, F. A., Rogers, D. W., & Tipling, R. N. (1994). *Technology and media*. Kendall / Hunt.

Tercanli, H., Martina, R., Ferreira Dias, M., Wakkee, I., Reuter, J., Amorim, M., Madaleno, M., Magueta, D., Vieira, E., & Veloso, C. (2021). Educational escape rooms in practice: research, experiences, and recommendations.

Terrasi, B., Badoux, L., Abou Arab, O., Huette, P., Bar, S., Leviel, F., Amsallem, C., Ammirati, C., Dupont, H., & Lorne, E. (2020). Escape game training to improve non-technical team skills in the operating room. *Medical Teacher*, *42*(4), 482–482. doi:10.1080/0142159X.2019.1638505 PMID:31304836

Thai, V. V., Balasubramanyam, L., Yeoh, K. K. L., & Norsofiana, S. (2013). Revisiting the seafarer shortage problem: The case of Singapore. *Maritime Policy & Management*, *40*(1), 1–25. doi:1 0.1080/03088839.2012.744480

The Rectors' Conference of Finnish Universities of Applied Sciences ARENE (2018). Towards the World's Best Higher Education System. The structural development working group report. https://www.arene.fi/julkaisut/raportit/rake-selvitys/

Thomas, G. E. (2023). *Micro-teaching with video-reflection in education* [Unpublished doctoral dissertation]. Indiana State University.

Ting, C., & Shukor, N. A. (2022). Effects of Peer Learning on Pupils' Learning Performance and Creativity in English Writing Skills using Digital Storytelling. *Sains Humanika, 14*(3–2), 105–115.

Tok, T. N. (2007). Methods and techniques for effective teaching. In A. Doğanay (Ed.), *Teaching principles and methods* (pp. 161–214). Pegem A Press.

tom Dieck, M. C., Cranmer, E., Prim, A., & Bamford, D. (2023). Can augmented reality (ar) applica-tions enhance students' experiences? gratifications, engagement and learning styles. *Information Technology & People*. Advance online publication. doi:10.1108/ITP-10-2021-0823

Tondeur, J., Braak, J., Sang, G., Voogt, J., Fisser, F., & Ottenbreit-Leftwich, A. (2012). Preparing preservice teachers to integrate technology in education: A synthesis of qualitative evidence. *Computers & Education*, *59*(1), 134–144. doi:10.1016/j.compedu.2011.10.009

Topali, P., & Mikropoulos, T. A. (2019). Digital learning objects for teaching computer programming in primary students. Technology and Innovation in Learning, Teaching and Education: First International Conference, TECH-EDU 2018, Thessaloniki, Greece, June 20–22, 2018, Revised Selected Papers 1, Unal, E., & Cakir, H. (2021). The effect of technology-supported collaborative problem solving method on students' achievement and engagement. *Education and Information Technologies*, *26*(4), 4127–4150.

Topol, E. (2019). High-performance medicine: The convergence of human and artificial intelligence. *Nature Medicine*, *25*(1), 44–56. https://doi.org/https://doi.org/10.1038/s41591-018-0300-7. doi:10.103841591-018-0300-7 PMID:30617339

Topping, K. J. (2005). Trends in Peer Learning. *Educational Psychology*, *25*(6), 631–645. doi:10.1080/01443410500345172

Turku, U. A. S. (2021). FIT Turku Competence Center (Futuristic Interactive Technologies. https://www.tuas.fi/en/services/products/fit-turku-competence-center/

Turku, U. A. S. (2022a). The minutes of the meeting of the board of Turku University of Applied Sciences March 17th, 2022. https://www.turkuamk.fi/media/filer_public/f4/6c/f46c94de-7481-4d9d-98e3-9cadc0385bef/turun_amk_oy_hallitus_1732022_poytakirja.pdf

Turku, U. A. S. (2022b). The minutes of the meeting of the board of Turku University of Applied Sciences, December 12, 2022. https://www.turkuamk.fi/media/filer_public/44/e0/44e02fb3-249f-499c-987e-2b0d5ea7e0b5/turun_amk_oy_hallitus_12122022_poytakirja.pdf

Turku, U. A. S. (2023). Turku UAS - impact across the world of work. https://www.tuas.fi/en/about-us/operations-and-organization/values-and-strategy/

TurkuU. A. S. (n.d.). https://www.tuas.fi/en/about-us/tuas/

Uçar, M. U., & Özdemir, E. (2022). Recognizing Students and Detecting Student Engagement with Real-Time Image Processing. *Electronics (Basel)*, *11*(9), 1500. doi:10.3390/electronics11091500

Upadhayay, L., & Vrat, P. (2016a). An ANP Based Selective Assembly Approach Incorporating Taguchi's Quality Loss Function to Improve Quality of Placements in Technical Institutions Introduction. *The TQM Journal*, *28*(1), 112–131. doi:10.1108/TQM-06-2014-0054

Upadhayay, L., & Vrat, P. (2016b). Analysis of impact of industry-academia interaction on quality of technical education: A system dynamics approach. *Computers & Industrial Engineering*, *101*, 313–324. doi:10.1016/j.cie.2016.09.022

Upadhayay, L., & Vrat, P. (2017). Policy boomerang in technical education: A system dynamics perspective. *Journal of Advances in Management Research*, *14*(2), 143–161. doi:10.1108/JAMR-08-2016-0065

Upadhyay, S. K. (2017). Microteaching, an efficient technique for learning effective teaching. *International Research Journal of Multidisciplinary Studies*, *3*(1), 252–270.

Uriarte-Portillo, A., Iba'nez, M. B., Zatarain-Cabada, ˜. R., & Barron´-Estrada, M. L. (2023). Comparison of using an augmented reality learning tool at home and in a classroom regarding motivation and learning outcomes. *Multimodal Technologies and Interaction*, *7*(3), 23. doi:10.3390/mti7030023

Valdes, B., Mckay, M., & Sanko, J. S. (2021). The Impact of an Escape Room Simulation to Improve Nursing Teamwork, Leadership and Communication Skills: A Pilot Project. *Simulation & Gaming*, *52*(1), 54–61. doi:10.1177/1046878120972738

Valencia-Arias, A., Chalela-Naffah, S., & Bermúdez-Hernández, J. (2019). A proposed model of e-learning tools acceptance among university students in developing countries. *Education and Information Technologies*, *24*(2), 1057–1071. doi:10.100710639-018-9815-2

van der Meijden, H., & Veenman, M. V. (2018). *Designing scenario-based learning: A practical guide for teachers.* Routledge.

van Dinther, M., Dochy, F., & Segers, M. (2011). Factors affecting students' self-efficacy in higher education. *Educational Research Review*, *6*(2), 95–108. https://doi.org/https://doi.org/10.1016/j.edurev.2010.10.003. doi:10.1016/j.edurev.2010.10.003

Van Goolen, R., Evers, H., & Lammens, C. (2014). International Innovation Labs: An Innovation Meeting Ground between SMEs and Business Schools. *Procedia Economics and Finance*, *12*, 184–190. doi:10.1016/S2212-5671(14)00334-7

van Laar, E., van Deursen, A. J. A. M., van Dijk, J. A. G. M., & de Haan, J. (2017). The relation between 21st-century skills and digital skills: A systematic literature review. *Computers in Human Behavior*, *72*, 577–588. https://doi.org/https://doi.org/10.1016/j.chb.2017.03.010. doi:10.1016/j.chb.2017.03.010

Vanbecelaere, S., Van den Berghe, K., Cornillie, F., Sasanguie, D., Reynvoet, B., & Depaepe, F. (2020). The effectiveness of adaptive versus non-adaptive learning with digital educational games. *Journal of Computer Assisted Learning*, *36*(4), 502–513. doi:10.1111/jcal.12416

Vani, V. V. (2016). Enhancing Students' Speaking Skills through Peer Team Teaching: A Student Centered Approach. *Journal on English Language Teaching*, *6*(4), 19–26.

Vanneste, P., Oramas, M. J., Verelst, T., Tuytelaars, T., Raes, A., Depaepe, F., & Van den Noortgate, W. (2021). Computer Vision and Human Behaviour, Emotion and Cognition Detection: A Use Case on Student Engagement. *Mathematics*, *9*(3), 287. doi:10.3390/math9030287

VARK. (2021). *A Guide to Learning Styles.* Retrieved from https://vark-learn.com/introduction-to-vark/

Vasconcelos, S., & Melo, C. (2023). A Learning Journey Towards Sustainable Tourism Education – Mapping an Interdisciplinary Project. In L. G. Chova, A. L. Martînez & J. Lees (Eds.) *INTED2023 Proceedings*, (pp. 3582-3586). 10.21125/inted.2023.0967

Vasconcelos, S., Melo, A., Melo, C., Liberato, D., & Lopes, M. C. (2022). Soft Skills in Action: Developing Tourism Students Skills Through Interdisciplinarity. In J. V. Carvalho, P, Liberato & A. Peña (Eds), Advances in Tourism, Technology and Systems. Smart Innovation, Systems and Technologies, 284 (2), (pp. 203-213). Springer. doi:10.1007/978-981-16-9701-2_17

Vasconcelos, S., Melo, C., Melo, A., & Liberato, D. (2022). Interdisciplinarity in Action: Developing Students' Soft Skills Through Project-Based Learning and Field Work. In L. G. Chova, A. L. Martínez & I. C. Torres (Eds.), *INTED2022 Proceedings* (pp.4852–4859). IATED Academy. 10.21125/inted.2022.1267

Vasconcelos, S., Melo, A., Melo, C., & Mouta, C. (2022). Fostering Student Agency in Tourism Education: Examples from the Tourism and Hospitality Field. In L. G. Chova, A. L. Martînez, & J. Lees (Eds.), *Edulearn22 Proceedings* (pp. 6457–6461). IATED Academy., doi:10.21125/edulearn.2022.1526

Vasconcelos, S., & Melo, C. (2022). Transforming Tourism Education: An Interdisciplinary Approach to Sustainable Tourism Management. In L. C. Carvalho, N. Teixeira, & P. Pardal (Eds.), *Interdisciplinary and Practical Approaches to Managerial Education and Training* (pp. 100–119). IGI Global., doi:10.4018/978-1-7998-8239-8.ch006

Velázquez Iturbide, J. Á., Hernán-Losada, I., & Pérez-Carrasco, A. (2016). A «multiple executions» technique of visualization. In *Proceedings of the 21st annual conference on innovation and technology in computer science education, ITiCSE'16*, pp. 59-64. https://doi.org/10.1145/2899415.2899451

Velázquez Iturbide, J. Á., & Ivanov-Andreev, R. (2022) Recursion-based visualizations of search algorithms in state-spaces. In *Proceedings of the 2022 international symposium on computers in education, SIIE'22*. https://doi.org/10.1109/SIIE56031.2022.9982362

Velázquez-Iturbide, J. Á., & Debdi, O. (2011). Experimentation with optimization problems in algorithm courses. In IEEE international conference on computer as a tool, EUROCON'11, 4 pp. https://doi.org/ doi:10.1109/EUROCON.2011.5929294

Velázquez-Iturbide, J. Á. (2000). Recursion in gradual steps (is recursion really that difficult?). In *Proceedings of the 31st SIGCSE technical symposium on computer science education, SIGCSE'00*, pp. 310-314. https://doi.org/10.1145/330908.331876

Velázquez-Iturbide, J. Á. (2021). A unified framework to experiment with algorithm optimality and efficiency. *Computer Applications in Engineering Education*, 29(6), 1793–1810. doi:10.1002/cae.22423

Velázquez-Iturbide, J. Á., Debdi, O., Esteban-Sánchez, N., & Pizarro, C. (2013). GreedEx: A visualization tool for experimentation and discovery learning of greedy algorithms. *IEEE Transactions on Learning Technologies*, 6(2), 130–143. doi:10.1109/TLT.2013.8

Velázquez-Iturbide, J. Á., & Pérez-Carrasco, A. (2010). InfoVis interaction techniques in animation of recursive programs. *Algorithms*, 3(1), 76–91. doi:10.3390/a3010076

Velázquez-Iturbide, J. Á., & Pérez-Carrasco, A. (2016). Systematic development of dynamic programming algorithms assisted by interactive visualization. In *Proceedings of the 21st Annual Conference on Innovation and Technology in Computer Science Education, ITiCSE'16*, pp. 71-76. https://doi.org/10.1145/2899415.2899450

Velázquez-Iturbide, J. Á., Pérez-Carrasco, A., & Urquiza-Fuentes, J. (2008). SRec: An animation system of recursion for algorithm courses. In *Proceedings of the 13th annual conference on innovation and technology in computer science education, ITiCSE'08*, pp. 225-229. https://doi.org/10.1145/1384271.1384332

Velázquez-Iturbide, J. Á., Pérez-Carrasco, A., & Urquiza-Fuentes, J. (2009). A design of automatic visualizations for divide-and-conquer algorithms. *Electronic Notes in Theoretical Computer Science*, *224*, 159–167. doi:10.1016/j.entcs.2008.12.060

Veldkamp, A., van de Grint, L., Knippels, M.-C. P., & van Joolingen, W. R. (2020). Escape education: A systematic review on escape rooms in education. *Educational Research Review*, *31*, 100364. doi:10.1016/j.edurev.2020.100364

Veloso Gomes, P., Donga, J., & Sá, V. J. (2021). Software requirements definition processes in gamification development for Immersive environments. In R. A. P. de Queirós & A. J. Marques (Eds.), *Handbook of Research on Solving Modern Healthcare Challenges With Gamification* (pp. 68–78). IGI Global., doi:10.4018/978-1-7998-7472-0.ch005

Verdict (2022) Leading game companies in the metaverse theme. https://www.verdict.co.uk/top-ranked-gaming-companies-in-metaverse/

Vergne, M. J., Smith, J. D., & Bowen, R. S. (2020). Escape the (remote) classroom: An online escape room for remote learning. *Journal of Chemical Education*, *97*(9), 2845–2848. doi:10.1021/acs.jchemed.0c00449

Vesely, A., & ... (2011). Theory and methodology of best practice research: A critical review of the current state. *Central European Journal of Public Policy*, *5*(02), 98–117.

Vestal, M. E., Matthias, A. D., & Thompson, C. E. (2021). Engaging Students with Patient Safety in an Online Escape Room. *The Journal of Nursing Education*, *60*(8), 466–469. https://doi.org/doi:10.3928/01484834-20210722-10. doi:10.3928/01484834-20210722-10 PMID:34346812

Viswanadhan, K. G. (2009). Quality indicators of engineering education programmes: A multi-criteria analysis from India. *International Journal of Industrial and Systems Engineering*, *4*(3), 270–282. doi:10.1504/IJISE.2009.023542

Viswanadhan, K. G., Rao, N. J., & Mukhopadhyay, C. (2005). Impact of privatization on engineering education. *Journal of Services Research*, (special), 109–129.

Vygotsky, L. (1962). *Thought and Language* (E. Hanfmann & G. Vakar, Eds.). MIT Press. doi:10.1037/11193-000

Walker, A., & White, G. (2013). *Technology Enhanced Language Learning: connecting theory and practice-Oxford Handbooks for Language Teachers*. Oxford University Press.

Warmelink, H., Mayer, I., Weber, J., Heijligers, B., Haggis, M., Peters, E., & Louwerse, M. (2017). AMELIO: Evaluating the team-building potential of a mixed reality escape room game. Extended abstracts publication of the annual symposium on computer-human interaction in play, Westera, W. (2015). Games are motivating, aren't they? Disputing the arguments for digital game-based learning. *International Journal of Serious Games*, *2*(2). Advance online publication. doi:10.17083/ijsg.v2i2.58

Watson, J. (2008). *Blended Learning: The Convergence of Online and Face-to-Face Education. Promising Practices in Online Learning*. North American Council for Online Learning.

Weintrop, D. (2019). Block-based programming in computer science education. *Communications of the ACM*, *62*(8), 22–25. doi:10.1145/3341221

Wiggins, G. P. (1989). A true test: Toward more authentic and equitable assessment. *Phi Delta Kappan*, *70*(9), 703–713.

wiki-Learning_styles. (2023). https://en.wikipedia.org/wiki/Learning_styles

Wilby, K. J., & Kremer, L. J. (2020). Development of a cancer-themed escape room learning activity for undergraduate pharmacy students. *International Journal of Pharmacy Practice*, *28*(5), 541–543. doi:10.1111/ijpp.12622 PMID:32307797

Wilder, M., & Shuttleworth, P. (2005). Cell Inquiry: A 5e Learning Cycle Lesson. *Science Activities*, *41*(4), 37–43. doi:10.3200/SATS.41.4.37-43

Wiley, D. A. (2000). Connecting learning objects to instructional design theory: A definition, a metaphor, and a taxonomy. *The instructional use of learning objects, 2830*(435), 1-35.

Willey, K., & Gardner, A. P. (2010). Collaborative peer learning to change learning culture and develop the skills for lifelong professional practice. *Annual Conference of Australasian Association for Engineering Education*.

Wogu, I. A. P., Misra, S., Assibong, P. A., Olu-Owolabi, E. F., Maskeliūnas, R., & Damasevicius, R. (2019). Artificial intelligence, smart classrooms and online education in the 21st century: Implications for human development. *Journal of Cases on Information Technology*, *21*(3), 66–79. doi:10.4018/JCIT.2019070105

Wong, A., & Wong, C.-K. S. (2009). Factors Affecting Students' Learning and Satisfaction on Tourism and Hospitality Course-Related Field Trips. Journal of Hospitality \& Tourism Education, 21(1), 25–35. doi:10.1080/10963758.2009.10696934

Wurdinger, S., & Qureshi, M. (2015). Enhancing College Students' Life Skills through Project Based Learning. *Innovative Higher Education*, *40*(3), 279–286. doi:10.100710755-014-9314-3

Xavier, A. R. C., & Leite, C. (2019). Mapeamento da Formação Pedagógica de docentes universitários nas Universidades Públicas Portuguesas. *Revista Lusófona de Educação*, *45*(45), 109–123. doi:10.24140/issn.1645-7250.rle45.08

Xie, H., Chu, H.-C., Hwang, G.-J., & Wang, C.-C. (2019). Trends and development in technology-enhanced adaptive/personalized learning: A systematic review of journal publications from 2007 to 2017. *Computers & Education*, *140*, 103599. doi:10.1016/j.compedu.2019.103599

Xie, P. F. (2004). Tourism field trip: Students' view of Experiential Learning. *Tourism Review International*, *8*(2), 101–111. doi:10.3727/1544272042782219

XR4All (2022). Definition – What is XR? XR4All Horizon, 2020. https://xr4all.eu/xr/

Yang, L., & Gottlieb, M. (2023). Gamification Mobile Applications: A Literature Review of Empirical Studies. In *International Conference on Interactive Collaborative Learning* (pp. 933-946). Springer.

Yang, Y. T. C., Gamble, J. H., Hung, Y. W., & Lin, T. Y. (2014). An online adaptive learning environment for critical-thinking-infused E nglish literacy instruction. *British Journal of Educational Technology*, *45*(4), 723–747. doi:10.1111/bjet.12080

Yıldırım, A., & Şimşek, H. (2013). *Qualitative research methods in the social sciences* (9th ed.). Seçkin Press.

Yıldırım, B., & Akkuş, A. (2020). Developing a scale to assess teachers' perceptions towards using web 2.0 tools in lectures (TPUWL scale). *Participatory Educational Research*, *7*(3), 124–138. doi:10.17275/per.20.38.7.3

Yiu, M., & Law, R. (2012). A Review of Hospitality Internship: Different Perspectives of Students, Employers, and Educators. Journal of Teaching in Travel \& Tourism, 12(4), 377–402. doi:10. 1080/15313220.2012.729459

Yustika, G. P., & Iswati, S. (2020). Digital literacy in formal online education: A short review. *Dinamika Pendidikan*, *15*(1), 66–76. doi:10.15294/dp.v15i1.23779

Zajacova, A., Lynch, S. M., & Espenshade, T. J. (2005). Self-Efficacy, stress and academic success in college. *Research in Higher Education*, *46*(6), 677–706. doi:10.100711162-004-4139-z

Zannin, M., Lima, N., & Pinto, C. (2021). Use of Hands-on and Remote Lab with an Inquiry-Based Approach to Learn Statistics in Engineering. In *Ninth International Conference on Technological Ecosystems for Enhancing Multiculturality (TEEM'21)* (pp. 565-569). 10.1145/3486011.3486513

Zhang, X. C., Lee, H., Rodriguez, C., Rudner, J., Chan, T. M., & Papanagnou, D. (2018). Trapped as a Group, Escape as a Team: Applying Gamification to Incorporate Team-building Skills Through an 'Escape Room' Experience. *Cureus*, *10*(3), e2256. doi:10.7759/cureus.2256 PMID:29725559

Zhang, Z., Hansen, C. T., & Andersen, M. A. E. (2016). Teaching Power Electronics With a Design-Oriented, Project-Based Learning Method at the Technical University of Denmark. *IEEE Transactions on Education*, *59*(1), 32–38. doi:10.1109/TE.2015.2426674

Zheng, M., Bender, D., & Lyon, C. (2021). Online learning during COVID-19 produced equivalent or better student course performance as compared with pre-pandemic: Empirical evidence from a school-wide comparative study. *BMC Medical Education*, *21*(1), 1–11. doi:10.118612909-021-02909-z PMID:34530828

Zhou, F., Duh, H. B.-L., & Billinghurst, M. (2008) Trends in augmented reality tracking, interaction and display: A review of ten years of ISMAR. In *Proceedings of the 7th IEEE/ACM International Symposium on Mixed and Augmented Reality*, Cambridge, UK, 15–18 September 2008, pp. 193–202.

Compilation of References

Zlckazov, K., Voroshilova, M., Pirozhkova, I., & Lapenok, M. V. (2018). Eye Tracking Technology for Assessment of Electronic Hybrid Text Perception by Students. In V. L. Uskov, R. J. Howlett, & L. C. Jain (Eds.), *Smart Education and E-Learning 2017, Smart Innovation, Systems and Technologies* (pp. 245–252). Springer International Publishing., doi:10.1007/978-3-319-59451-4_24

Zou, B., Wang, D., & Xing, M. (2016). Collaborative tasks in wiki-based environment in EFL learning. *Computer Assisted Language Learning*, 29(5), 1001–1018. doi:10.1080/09588221.2015.1121878

Zou, D., & Xie, H. (2019). Flipping an English writing class with technology-enhanced just-in-time teaching and peer instruction. *Interactive Learning Environments*, 27(8), 1127–1142. doi:10.1080/10494820.2018.1495654

Zwoliński, G., Kamińska, D., Laska-Leśniewicz, A., Haamer, R. E., Vairinhos, M., Raposo, R., Urem, F., & Reisinho, P. (2022). Extended Reality in Education and Training: Case Studies in Management Education. *Electronics (Basel)*, 11(3), 336. doi:10.3390/electronics_1030336

About the Contributors

Ricardo Queirós holds a PhD on Computer Science and is an assistant professor of Computer Science at the Media Arts and Design School of the Polytechnic Institute of Porto. He is also a researcher in the field of e-learning interoperability and programming languages learning at the Center for Research in Advanced Computing Systems (CRACS) research group of INESC TEC Porto. He is also the author of 10 books regarding mobile and Web development and has almost 200 scientific publications focused on computer science education.

Mário Cruz is an Associate Professor in Foreign Language Teaching (English and Spanish), at the School of Education of the Polytechnic of Porto, where he teaches Spanish as a Foreign Language, Hispano-American Literatures and Cultures, English Teaching in Primary Education, Didactic Resources in Teaching English and supervises the pedagogical practice of future teachers. He is also an integrated researcher at inED - Center for Research and Innovation in Education at the School of Education of the Polytechnic of Porto and a collaborator at CIDTFF at the University of Aveiro. Being professionalized in recruitment groups 120 - English, 220 - Portuguese and English, 330 - English, 340 - German, 350 - Spanish and 910 - Special Education, he has worked as a teacher in public schools of basic and secondary education, since the school year of 2001-2002 until the school year 2013-2014. He also collaborated at the Paula Frassinetti School of Education (from 2003 to 2012) where he taught English Language, English Language Didactics, Information and Communication Technologies in Education, Information and Communication Technologies in Inclusive Education Contexts, Educational Technologies in English Teaching, Deep Issues of Differentiated Intervention, among other curricular units. He holds a PhD in Didactics and Professional Development from the University of Aveiro, a PhD in Linguistic Studies from the University of Vigo and a MA in Language Didactics (University of Aveiro), Teaching English and Spanish in Basic Education (Polytechnic of Porto - Escola Superior de Educação) and Teaching English and Spanish at the 3rd of Basic Education and Secondary Education (University of Aveiro). His main doctoral theses and dissertations and MA's reports focus on: critical hyper-pedagogy, the intercultural and multilingual approach, the use of technologies in the teaching-learning process and linguistic and cultural varieties. He is currently coordinator of the thematic line "Teacher Training" at inED, where he directs the research projects: "CLIL 4 U - implementation, monitoring and evaluation of bilingual teaching projects", "PEPPA 6/7 - Primary English Practice Program for Ages 6/7", "Schoolers and Scholars (SnS): Role-Playing Games (RPG) in the teaching and learning process at Primary Education" and "VarLang - Linguistic and cultural varieties in the teaching of foreign languages".

Carla Pinto is a Coordinating Professor in the School of Engineering, Polytechnic of Porto, Portugal. She has a PhD degree in the scientific area of Mathematics, since January 2004. Her main research topic is epidemiology, in particular Mathematical Epidemiology. She is interested in mathematical challenges and their role in providing advice on public health policies. Dr. Pinto is trained in Nonlinear Dynamics, Bifurcation Theory. Previous research included the analysis of Central Pattern Generators for Animal and Robot Locomotion, coupled cell networks, neuron-like equations (Hodgkin-Huxley equations, Fitz-Hugh Nagumo, Morris-Lecar).

Daniela Mascarenhas is an assistant teacher at the Porto School of Education linked to the training of early childhood educators and teachers from the 1st and 2nd Basic Education Cycle. She has published several articles and she is a researcher in several projects, allocated to the CeiED and INED research centers. Participating as a trainer in several ongoing training actions for teachers and educators in Portugal and Sao Tome and Principe. Post-Doctorate in Educational Sciences, in the specialty of Pedagogical Supervision, by the University of Minho (2019). PhD in Education and Didactics of Mathematics by the Faculty of Education Sciences of the University of Granada (2011). She obtained the Diploma of Advanced Studies in Education and Didactics of Mathematics by the Faculty of Education Sciences of the University of Granada (2010). Graduated in Mathematics from the University of Minho (2003).

* * *

Fatma Alkan is works as associate professor in Hacettepe University Faculty of Education, Chemistry Teaching Program. She has published many articles in national and international peer-reviewed journals. She works as a field editor in peer-reviewed journals.

Prasanna Chavare was a working professional in merchant navy and had research orientation towards marine education system in India.

Luis Coelho is an adjunct professor at the Engineering School of Polytechnic Institute of Porto. He is a PhD in Telecommunications and Signal Processing since 2012, and a MsC in Electronics Engineering, since 2005. As a researcher he has published several scientific articles in conferences and journals. He actively collaborates with the scientific community as participant, reviewer, organizer of scientific conferences or as journal editor. His main research interests are on image and signal processing, human-machine interaction and management, all topics with a special focus on the healthcare area.

João Donga has a degree in Computing and Systems Engineering, a Title of Specialist in Media and Audiovisual Production is a member of Multimedia Department at School of Media Arts and Design, Polytechnic of Porto, a member of LabRP, Psychosocial Rehabilitation Laboratory affiliated with the School of Health of the Polytechnic of Porto and the Faculty of Psychology and Education Science of the University of Porto and member of Elearning department of Polytechnic of Porto. Research interests centre on multimedia, virtual worlds, neurofeedback and e-learning. At present is Pedagogic Council President at School of Media Arts and Design.

Paulo Veloso Gomes is MSc in Information Management and has an Advanced Studies Diploma in Social and Medical Sciences and Scientific Documentation. Researcher in Psychosocial Rehabilitation Laboratory affiliated with the School of Health of the Polytechnic of Porto and the Faculty of Psychology and Education Science of the University of Porto. Experienced Professor in the School of Health of the Polytechnic of Porto, with a demonstrated history of working in the higher education industry. Strong education professional skilled in Computer Science, Health Communication, Health Literacy, Virtual and Augmented Reality, Web Creation Contents, Knowledge Management, Information Management, Information Systems and Digital Media Art.

Timo Haavisto works as a Senior Advisor and Technical Lead in Futuristic Interactive Technologies research group for Turku University of Applied Sciences. In addition to planning, designing and leading the development of various projects´ systems and integrations, his research focuses are on the use of neural networks in learning analytics and metaverse platform customization in massive multiuser education context, as well as remote operations, autonomous systems, haptics, eye-tracking, and biosensors.

Marjo Joshi works as Head of Pedagogical Development at Turku University of Applied Sciences, Finland. She develops pedagogical approaches for onsite, hybrid and online learning contexts at organisational level. She has extensive teaching experience at local and international level. Currently she is managing a project that aims to develop national online degree programme networks. Her current research interests include the design of student-centered education, pedagogical solutions, and professional development of teachers.

Carla Melo graduated in Management and Planning in Tourism, Master in Information Management, Specialist in Tourism and PhD student in Tourism at the Tilburg School of Social and Behavioral Sciences, Tilburg University, Netherlands. She is currently an Adjunct Guest Professor at the School of Hospitality and Tourism of the Polytechnic of Porto. Her priority areas of research are transformative tourism experiences, creative tourism, yoga tourism, gastronomic tourism, and tourism education.

Fatma Merve Mustafaoğlu works as doctor in Hacettepe University Faculty of Education, Chemistry Teaching Program. She has published many articles in national and international peer-reviewed journals.

Sara Reis is an MSc in Clinical Process Optimization. PhD in Bioethics / Biomedical Engineering. Polytechnic Higher Education Teacher with the category of Prof. Adjunct. Interest in the area of Biomedical Engineering, namely in the areas of Innovation and Health Management.

Vítor Sá holds a Masters in Computer Science and a PhD in Information Systems and Technologies. Its main activity has been teaching in higher education, currently teaching at the Universidade Católica Portuguesa. He lived for four years in Germany as a Guest Researcher at the Institute for Computer Graphics (Fraunhofer IGD) in Darmstadt. He has provided consultancy and training to several companies, through the PMO Projects company. Vítor Sá is a Chartered Member of the Portuguese Association of Engineering, a member of the Project Management Institute, member of the Portuguese Association of Information Systems, and holds a Certificate of Pedagogical Aptitude issued by the Portuguese Institute of Employment and Vocational Training. He has participated and published in several international scientific events, having also published several book chapters. Vítor Sá develops its research activity in the ALGORITMI Centre (University of Minho), in the Intelligent Data Systems group. He is a lecturer in the Master's degree in Digital Communication, having been a member of the Advisory Board for the application of Braga to UNESCO Creative City in the category of Media Arts.

Emine Sendurur received her PhD in Computer Education and Instructional Technology from Middle East Technical University, Turkey, in 2012. In 2005, she was hired as a research assistant in the same department. After completing her PhD, she worked as an instructor in Computer Programming department. She recently works as an instructor in Computer Education and Instructional Technologies department at Ondokuz Mayıs University, Turkey. She teaches courses including instructional design, computer science, learning theories, Internet based programming and human-computer interaction. Her main research interests consist of user experience, informal learning, social networking sites, cognitive load theory, instructional message design, and eye-tracking methodology.

Polat Sendurur received his bachelor degree in Computer Education and Instructional Technology from Middle East Technical University, Turkey, in 2004, and then he was hired as computer science teacher by Turkish Ministry of Education. In 2006, he started to his PhD education and was hired as a research assistant in Computer Education and Instructional Technology from Middle East Technical University. He recently works as an associate proffessor in Computer Education and Instructional Technologies department at Ondokuz Mayıs University, Turkey. He teaches courses including teaching methods, fundamentals of distance education, qualitative research methods in instructional technologies, and introduction to programing. His main research interests consist of technology integration, cognitive tools, computational thinking, and computer science education.

Tatjana Sidekerskienė obtained a Bachelor of Science degree in Mathematics from the Faculty of Fundamental Sciences at Kaunas University of Technology (KTU) in Kaunas, Lithuania, in 2003. She went on to complete her Master of Science studies in 2006. She is presently employed as a Lecturer at the Department of Applied Mathematics at KTU, where she teaches mathematics courses. Her primary research interest was in the field of time series analysis. Currently, her research is focused on STEAM education. Tatjana Sidekerskienė has achieved notable success, having won the internal competition twice for her contributions to enhancing the quality of education and promoting innovative teaching practices at the Kaunas University of Technology.

Geraldo Soares de Castro lives and works in Porto, Portugal. PhD in Drawing and its Techniques of Expression, by Facultad de Bellas Artes de San Carlos de la Universitat Politècnica de València, España, 2013, with Diploma in Advanced Studies and University Specialist Title, 2009 by the same Faculty. Master in Design and Multimedia Production, by the Facultat de Belles Arts de la Universitat de Barcelona, España, 2006. Graduated in Communication Design branch, Escola Superior de Artes & Design - Matosinhos, Portugal, 1999. She dedicates herself to research in the scientific activity area of Design and Technology of New Media Arts and in the specialization field of Interactive Art, Sound and Image, Electronic and Digital Art.

Anugamini Srivastava is Assistant Professor in HRM at Symbiosis Institute of Business Management Pune, Symbiosis International (Deemed) University. She is Guest Editor for the upcoming special issue of European Journal of Training and Development, (Emerald, UK). She has book chapters and several research papers to indexed, abstracted and ABDC ranked journals of international repute to her credit. She is Recognized reviewer of Elsevier Journals and has reviewed articles for international journals. Her research interests are Human resource practices, Training, leadership, and other relevant topics of organisational behaviour.

Vesa Taatila works as the rector and president of Turku University of Applied Sciences, a member of the national research and innovation council in Finland and as an adjunct professor of innovation pedagogy in the University of Turku. Previously he has worked in executive and expert positions in both academia and multinational business sector. His main area of interest is creation of world-class practical excellence and putting new innovations into action, either through continuous development in existing organizations or by establishing start-up companies.

Sandra Vasconcelos is an Assistant Professor at the School of Hospitality and Tourism, Polytechnic Institute of Porto. She holds a PhD in Multimedia in Education and is an integrated member of the Research Centre "Didactics and Technology in Education of Trainers". In addition to teaching Technical English and Intercultural Communication to graduate students, she has been involved in research projects within the scope of tourism education, e-learning, b-learning, English for Specific Purposes (ESP), informal learning, interdisciplinary practices and the use of digital technology in education and is currently part of ATLAS' (Association for Tourism and Leisure Education) SIG on Tourism Education, which aims to provide a platform to research and address transversal challenges in tourism education and training. She is also her School's representative at the Polytechnic of Porto's Centre for Pedagogical Innovation and advisor for Distance Education, having an active role in the development and implementation of teacher training workshops that promote innovative methodologies and pedagogies.

Index

Milton Keynes UK
Ingram Content Group UK Ltd.
UKHW031051020923
427894UK00010B/284